Space Law and Policy

Series Editor
Maria A. Pozza, Gravity Lawyers, Christchurch, New Zealand

Space activities in the Asia-Pacific, specifically in New Zealand and Australia is rising dramatically. Over the past year, both nations have seen growth in not only local and national economy, technological developments and innovative design, the world's view of these two-nations as hubs for space activities has also grown. This reputation will continue to grow and it is inevitable that both nations will see a marked increase in space activities as well as space related activities.

Whilst this presents much opportunity for both New Zealand and Australia, there is also critical scope for failure to acknowledge the detriment that can result from moving pace too fast and failing to learn lessons along the way. Space law and policy is now at its most critical time for development. With any regulatory matrix, policy informs law and law informs risk management and identification. However, space presents newer challenges in that the weight associated to international law, foreign relations and geo-security – is now a fundamental part of the framework which will inform our space law and policy at a domestic level.

The Asia-Pacific, and specifically Australia and New Zealand, will need to start learning fast lessons on the importance of these international dimensions that will impact their respective domestic activities pertaining to space activities and space related activities.

This series aims to offer a unique perspective and guidance to a range of stakeholders that is published by experts in the fields of space. Its aim is to appeal to:

- the academic and scholarly community on the quintessential framework of the Asia-Pacific (with a specific focus on New Zealand and Australia);
- provide practical assessments and guidance that will appeal to space professionals, policy makers and legislative drafters; and
- become an internationally recognised series that informs, educates and promotes change through thought leadership.

Maria A. Pozza
Editor

Ascending to Space

Critical Perspectives from New Zealand and other Nations

Springer

Editor
Dr. Maria A. Pozza
Gravity Lawyers
Hornby, New Zealand

ISSN 2662-9054 ISSN 2662-9062 (electronic)
Space Law and Policy
ISBN 978-981-97-0713-3 ISBN 978-981-97-0714-0 (eBook)
https://doi.org/10.1007/978-981-97-0714-0

This Springer imprint is published by the registered company Springer Nature Singapore Pte Ltd.
The registered company address is: 152 Beach Road, #21-01/04 Gateway East, Singapore 189721, Singapore

Paper in this product is recyclable.

Otago Foreign Policy School, Opening Address[1]

01 July 2022
Hon Nanaia Mahuta, Minister for New Zealand Foreign Policy

Manawa maiea te pūtanga o Matariki
Manawa maiea te ariki o te rangi
Manawa maiea te mātahi o te tau!

Introduction

I'm pleased to join you for my second address at the 56th Annual Otago Foreign Policy School.

The topic for this year is Space.

Given that we are in the phase of Matariki it's only fitting that we call on ngā tātai arorangi – the wisdom of the universe and space – to discuss how Aotearoa New Zealand might consider its inclusion in our foreign policy and our approach to international engagement.

Space policy is growing in importance globally. There are more states, more actors, more interests, more opportunities, and more risks in this area than at any time previously. And most of them require in fact obligate a commitment to a global response – much like climate change, responding to a global pandemic and indeed the pursuit of peace and stability.

[1] Mahuta, N, Hon. "Otago Foreign Policy School, Opening Address". 01 July 2022. Otago Foreign Policy School, opening address | Beehive.govt.nz

Indigenous Wisdom as A Star Path

Before I turn to the consideration of space foreign policy, I want to propose that we have much to learn from indigenous peoples around the world. This applies also to the formation of space policy.

Polynesian ancestors traversed the Pacific Ocean in the quest to seek out new lands, an abundance of resources, and a place to call home.

So when the great migration of my tūpuna arrived to these shores, they already had an advanced knowledge base of the universe, the natural environment, navigation and survival. Much of that understanding was forged through decades of observation of star patterns, the flight path and migration of birds, ocean currents and tidal sequences, of winds, currents and flotsam.

But critical to that navigation were the stars and where and when they appear on the horizon. With neither modern instruments nor printed maps, Polynesian navigators could memorise and chart accurate journeys of thousands of miles to reach tiny island destinations. They assessed the existence of these distant and larger southerly islands and navigated the stars and signs to find them.

When here, akin to many peoples who live close to nature, they depended for survival on the cycles and patterns of the seasons. For some 600 years, Māori were guided by moon and stars in their cycles of land preparation, planting and harvest and in the timing of hunting and fishing.

By using the maramataka the lunar calendar, knowledge was passed down and survival guaranteed. The depth of this knowledge was held by tohunga often in whare wānanga and passed on with much care, growing in depth and local content over time.

I'm sure there are similarities with European navigational techniques and knowledge systems.

Our challenge is to draw on the wisdom of both.

Given that whakapapa, maybe it is no surprise that space remains a bold and innovative part of our national endeavour.

In 2017, New Zealand joined just a handful of countries that are launch nations, through the vision and work of Rocket Lab which, like those earlier ventures, saw not limits but only possibility. In order for that possibility to be transformative for our nation, it needs to reflect the wisdom of indigenous insight to create intergenerational advantage and stewardship or kaitiakitanga.

Space a Final Frontier or a New Horizon?

People may be forgiven for wondering why space is all of a sudden such a big foreign policy issue. Why did the Prime Minister spend time discussing space with the President and Vice President of the United States during her visit last month? Why, indeed, has this year's Otago Foreign Policy School turned its gaze to space policy?

One reason is that space services are now ubiquitous and important. In 2022, space infrastructure and data touch on almost all aspects of modern life. Precise position, navigation, and timing data is critical to our economy, underpinning financial transactions, efficient supply chains and services relying on global navigation satellite systems – from airliners, to property titles, to pizza delivery. Remote sensing data supports weather forecasting, climate monitoring and cutting-edge agricultural systems, and enables sovereign states to safeguard national security and national interests.

A second reason is that space is not subject to national appropriation. Space cannot be exclusively owned, and while a growing number and variety of actors are present in space and many more are using space-dependent services, no-one can regulate it alone. Like the oceans, the climate or the earth's biodiversity, we have no option but to work collectively to agree and define the rules that govern this common domain and vital resource.

Thirdly, space carries risks and is at risk. As with all commons, the potential for abuse of the commons is ever present. Space is not empty, but increasingly congested and contested. Unilateral actions have the potential to do unintended, rapid and lasting damage. And space also carries the risk that it is used in ways that threaten the security of states and people. Space is of strategic importance. In the old manuscripts of my tribe, there is a reference that space has the properties of water: "he wai katoa". In that regard, perhaps the international legal framework is akin to the way we think about international waters and the rules and norms expressed in UNCLOS.

Matariki, Tautoru, Tawera Guide Our Approach

In the traditional knowledge of my ancestors, there are recitations that speak of a certain time that will pass and it engenders peace, prosperity and wellbeing. More precisely, the star patterns that demarcate this time in the lunar calendar is the placement of Matariki (Pleiades), Tautoru (Orion's belt) and Tāwera (Venus).

First, Matariki (Pleiades) denotes the beginning of the Maori New Year, a time to recognise those that have been lost, celebrate that which we have and seed intention for the time ahead.

Space Is for All Humankind

Space is for all humankind, and therefore, we must think about its sustainable wellbeing.

The Outer Space Treaty, adopted more than half a century ago, recognised that outer space was the province of all humankind and should therefore be used for the benefit of all countries, irrespective of their state of development. This provided a clear, purposeful and overarching legal principle to guide the development and use of space. It was relevant in 1967 and remains even more relevant now. As a country, we firmly endorse this principle and support its ongoing application. Drawing on indigenous concepts and the evolution of legal frameworks to truly capture the essence of stewardship or kaitiakitanga of space, Aotearoa New Zealand could introduce a similar concept to space as we have done for example for the absolute protection of the Whanganui River and recognising space as a 'living entity'. Treating space like an ancestor with rules and norms to guide decision-making and behaviours would certainly invoke a different mentality for nation states around the world.

Second, Tāwera (Venus). My understanding is that is a fixed point in the night sky and the brightest planet that can be seen during the time of Matariki. Space must be kept peaceful, and we should reject the potential of militarising it. The Outer Space Treaty provides an enduring framework for addressing some of these issues but is insufficient for managing space in the twenty-first century. As a small country, Aotearoa New Zealand has always sought to establish, maintain and protect rules-based systems. It is no different for space. This protective principle relates closely to our positions on global environment issues and on non-proliferation, disarmament and arms control. We must be precautionary when there are serious risks at stake. The principle of peace and stability must be an abiding factor to ensure multilateral commitment towards space.

Thirdly, Tautoru (Orions Belt) is a star constellation that can be seen from the northern and southern hemispheres. In this regard, space holds opportunities from which New Zealand, alongside other nation states seek to benefit. New Zealand's rapidly developing space industry provides us with significant economic opportunities, including researchers and high-paying, highly skilled jobs up and down the value chain. Our industry has strengthened existing relationships and provided the catalyst for new ones. But all this has to be balanced against our obligations to ensure we, both as a launch state and as a nation dependent on space data, work with others to keep space a peaceful domain and used in a sustainable way. In many instances, we have seen the benefits of collaborative research – protein innovation, in the Antarctic, to create a vaccine for a global pandemic, the innovation of artificial intelligence and the list goes on. By integrating western science and traditional knowledge, there is further potential for dynamic innovation in space.

Engagement on space policy needs to be broad and inclusive. To that end, the Minister for Economic and Regional Development recently announced a public consultation on space policy to be conducted later this year. As a government, we are keen to hear from a wide range of voices. In announcing this consultation, we have specifically noted the need to recognise Māori interests in space, as we are a relatively new entrant into the space matters. Our policy machinery had to move at speed to put in place the legal, regulatory and policy settings that ensure New Zealanders can take the economic opportunities this exciting sector provides in a manner consistent with our values.

There is room for continued improvement, but the thinking and engagement with Māori must be deliberate and reflect te Tiriti o Waitangi.

As an example, last year, my colleague, Minister Woods, announced Project Tāwhaki, a joint venture between the government and Ngai Tahu to develop the site at Kaitōrete spit. The purpose of this is to protect the taonga and habitats of this unique location, while drawing on its suitability as a site for aerospace development. This project acknowledges Kaitōrete as a significant ongoing cultural landscape for Ngai Tahu. It is right that mana whenua for this land have a role in the development and protection of this area, the industry and the supporting policy.

Matariki Ahunga Nui: A time of Shared Prosperity

At last year's school, I outlined how Aotearoa New Zealand's unique identity and values inform and advance our foreign policy. This is true in space also.

Some might see space policy as somehow futuristic, requiring a new framework. I am clear that our longstanding values of Kaitiakitanga, kotahitanga and mahi tahi are fundamental to how we should think about space. These principles require that, even as we pursue our interests, we think carefully about our relationship with space, with others, with the world and with the future.

Space is a domain where we can ensure our collective activities benefit our commitment to humanity and our ongoing survival. This is a value that Aotearoa New Zealand holds – but one rightly enshrined as a legal requirement in the Outer Space Treaty.

Perhaps most important is kaitiakitanga or guardianship. This is fundamental to a tirohanga Māori and indigenous view. We are not owners of space, but stewards for its future, for the benefit of future generations. With use comes deep responsibilities. The space environment, particularly the low earth orbit, is a finite resource that must be protected for the future.

These values all require that a long-term intergenerational view drives today's decisions. Space is a taonga; it is precious. Kaitiakitanga seeks to allow use while safeguarding this environment from degradation. Much like other shared resources, the sooner we can put in place regimes to manage its sustainability, the better.

Aotearoa as a Responsible Launch Nation

Of course, a key context and contributor to Aotearoa New Zealand's emerging space foreign policy is our status as a launch nation and the opportunities, issues and interests that come with that status.

We want to ensure the domestic and international conditions that allow a modern, innovative, inclusive and growing domestic industry to develop in a responsible and peaceful manner.

Rocket Lab's success has proven to be the catalyst for the development of a vibrant space sector in Aotearoa New Zealand. A 2019 report by Deloitte estimated the sector contributed $1.69 billion to our economy. This includes a range of firms in the value chain supporting hundreds of highly skilled jobs. The world-class research and development being carried out by New Zealand companies, and research institutions also holds much promise for coming years.

New Zealand's Outer Space and High-altitude Activities Act is a world-leading regime for regulating space activities. It provides a predictable regulatory environment for industry while protecting our national interests, adhering to our international obligations and leading the international conversation on sustainability.

The Act allows the responsible minister, my colleague Minister Nash as the minister for Economic and Regional Development, to decline a payload approval if it is not considered in the national interest. In 2019, Cabinet agreed on four principles to guide the minister's decision making on what is in the national interest. These include sustainability, safety, responsibility and alignment with New Zealand's values, policies, interests and laws.

Consistent with this, Cabinet also approved four categories of payloads that are not in the national interest. These include:

- Payloads that contribute to nuclear weapons programmes of capabilities
- Payloads with the intended end use of harming, interfering with, or destroying other spacecraft, or space systems on Earth
- Payloads with the intended end use of supporting or enabling specific defence, security, or intelligence operations that are contrary to government policy
- Payloads where the intended end use is likely to cause serious or irreversible harm to the environment

When we passed the OSHAA Act in 2017, parliament understood that this was a fast-moving and constantly innovating industry; it built in a review mechanism following three years of operation. That review has just been completed, and the findings tabled in parliament. Over the coming months, officials will report to ministers on the outcomes of the review, including whether any further amendments to the Act are required.

In the future review, I would hope that further consideration be given to the approach set out in this speech to enable greater congruence with the values and knowledge systems of indigenous peoples and a responsible approach towards opportunities in space innovation.

Ko Te Kawa O Runga: Responsible Behaviours

The nature and unique challenges of space call for the deployment of the broad range of tools available to us. Conflict or accidents in space are a particular concern, with potential for major consequences. The destruction of space craft and equipment which causes debris, creates a greater risk of collisions, and the potential for catastrophic problems.

And of course, there is the prospect of conflict in space potentially provoking conflict on Earth.

Because space is largely unregulated by rules and norms to govern behaviour, this can cause uncertainty and mistrust, and elevate room for misperception and misunderstanding. It is a small step from there to perceptions of threat, rising tension and miscalculation.

As an international community, we need to find and agree ways to facilitate beneficial space operations while guarding against the misperception of malign intent.

We support the UK-led responsible behaviours initiative at the United Nations. We participated in the first session of the open-ended working group on responsible behaviours in outer space in Geneva in May. This work recognises that, while the world may not currently be in a position to rule out certain capabilities, we should be able to come to agreement on how the behaviour of operators can reduce the perception of threat.

Beyond the kinetic threats in space, this work also recognises non-kinetic threats that also need to be addressed – for example, cyber-attacks on space infrastructure, jamming of signals and directed energy attacks designed to impair sensors on satellites.

We are only at the beginning of that process, but we are optimistic that this approach can lead to a pragmatic and constructive outcome. Aotearoa New Zealand sees this as a first step. It will take time and will require ongoing attention to ensure the rules remain fit for purpose. Eventually, this may mean the negotiation of a comprehensive legally binding treaty.

Risks of conflict in space are not hypothetical. Recent years have seen a number of direct-ascent anti-satellite missile tests – missiles launched from Earth to intercept satellites in orbit.

Not only do such tests create debris clouds and risk to space infrastructure, they also raise tensions on Earth and increase potential for the misperceptions I have discussed.

Russia's destructive anti-satellite missile test carried out in November last year created 1,500 pieces of trackable debris, which resulted in astronauts aboard the International Space Station being advised to take shelter in their docked capsules in case debris collided with the ISS itself.

Our Government has been very clear these tests are irresponsible. For that reason, we welcome the United States' declaration in April this year that it will not conduct destructive direct-ascent anti-satellite missile tests and its call on all countries with the capability to make the same commitment.

Today, I'm pleased to announce that Aotearoa New Zealand will join this declaration and make the same commitment. We will not conduct destructive direct-ascent anti-satellite missile testing. We do not have that capability, and neither are we looking to develop it.

But our commitment is a further expression of our multilateral commitment towards establishment of rules and norms for te tātai arorangi.

Ko Rona, Ko Artemis Ko Tātou Katoa!

Another significant recent development has been the Artemis Accords. Now I understand that Artemis is a goddess of the moon and also of hunting. Our story of Rona being entrapped by the moon seems an appropriate connection. Rona now represents the dark and light phases of the moon – guiding tides and appropriate times for fishing, hunting, planting and gathering food.

Back to Artemis who represents the hunter and gatherer of food.

In 2020, the United States invited New Zealand as one of a small group of countries to collaborate on the development of a set of principles to guide the next phase in space exploration. These principles became known as the Artemis Accords, which New Zealand signed in June 2021.

Signing the Artemis Accords was a strong signal that Aotearoa New Zealand is committed to ensuring the next phase of space exploration is conducted in a safe, sustainable and transparent manner and in full compliance with international law.

One key aspect of the Artemis Accords concerns the utilisation of space resources. Existing international law provides some high-level rules which apply to space resource utilisation – including that any such activity must be for the benefit and in the interests of all countries. But there are some significant gaps especially regarding long-term sustainable management of space resources and the space environment. I have already outlined the unique perspective that Aotearoa New Zealand can bring to that conversation in particular integrating indigenous perspectives in space policy.

The Artemis Accords are another step towards achieving that objective. There are 19 members, from a diverse range of countries. In recent months, we have welcomed Colombia, Bahrain and Singapore as the newest members. Our next step is to take the principles enshrined in the Accords, with the support of the growing membership, and seek to turn these plurilateral principles into a multilateral instrument.

Conclusion

In closing, I will return to where I began. Our contribution to the development of space policy can draw on indigenous values and concepts that can broaden the way we think about shared interests, mutual obligations, intergenerational stewardship and what is often referred to as the concept of "the commons".

Space remains a bold and innovative part of our national endeavour. As we engage in space matters, we must remind ourselves that it's also a part of our legacy and identity.

You will have noted, from the perspective I have conveyed, that an approach to space policy is not so different to other areas of our foreign policy. Our modus operandi is to work with others, large and small, multilateral, plurilateral or bilateral –

where we share values and a purpose and where we see genuine potential to make gains.

In an era of strategic competition, space has acquired a heightened level of importance and presents new risks. That's why we must develop rules to safeguard a common good in this domain. Our contribution must reflect the values I have mentioned, advance our interests and build on our ability to work collaboratively, inclusively and innovatively with others. There is an urgent need to modernise the multilateral rules architecture and that will be a priority.

And as we bring new thinking through the innovation of companies like Rocket Lab, we must also seek to advance innovative thinking on legislative approaches. We are not new to innovative management of common resources on Earth, whether that be the sustainable management of fisheries, the preservation of threatened species or the creation of legal personality in the natural domain, evident in Te Awa Tupua.

Finally, let me draw on the wisdom of voyagers, navigators and great adventurers when they said:

"Ko te pae tawhiti whāia kia tata,
Ko te pae tata whakamaua kia tīna!"
"Seek out distant horizons, and cherish those you attain"

We want to see space used for the benefit of all humankind; we want to see it protected, peaceful and sustainable; and we want to continue to draw on its benefits, alongside others – but not at the risk of te tātai arorangi – or Space itself.

Thank you.

Acknowledgements

As more nations ascent to space, writing a book on critical issues is not an easy task and certainly one that cannot be undertaken alone. It is with pleasure that I thank the Otago Foreign Policy School Committee for allowing me to direct and lead the 56th Otago Foreign Policy School that focuses on outer space. The collective wisdom and support from the members of the school have been truly invaluable. The school also received generous funding support from the following funders:

- Delegation of the European Union to New Zealand
- Konrad Adenauer Stiftung , Canberra, Australia
- Ministry of Foreign Affairs and Trade, New Zealand
- University of Otago, Vice-Chancellor`s Fund, New Zealand
- University of Otago, Division of Humanities, New Zealand

My heartfelt thanks to all of the funders for their continued and generous support to the school.

I must also give a very special thanks to Austin Gee for tirelessly providing proofreading chapters and always being incredibly supportive in putting this book together. Equally, my heartfelt thanks to: Dr. Ricky J. Lee for always being available to discuss the many aspects of legal issues in outer space; Val Sim and Hon Nania Mahuta for their continuing contributions to New Zealand's ongoing space framework; Professor Dale Stephens for his wisdom and insights into the changing nature of space activities; William Achauer from Springer for being a wonderful colleague and checking through my various queries; and Emeritus Professor John Hearnshaw for his ongoing support and guidance in my many space-based projects and endeavours.

Finally, my heartfelt thanks to the authors for their wonderful contributions to the book. Their continued specialised work in their respective fields of expertise in the space sector will continue to shape the future of how we ascend to space.

Maria A. Pozza

Contents

Chapter 1
Introduction and Overview

Maria A. Pozza

Now, and perhaps more than ever, space has become an important area of focus for many Nation States, especially New Zealand. Space exploration and utilisation is growing from both a military and a commercial perspective, with interest heightening in the ways in which space can be utilised to assist Nation States in these respective endeavours.

At the time of writing, New Zealand implemented a new strategic national space policy focus that aligns its values and objectives posture with regard to space development (New Zealand Space Agency, 2023). Importantly, New Zealand's National Space Policy focuses on its international obligations with a view towards encompassing the best approaches to stewardship, innovation, responsibility, partnership and sustainability (New Zealand Space Agency, 2023). As a new spacefaring Nation State, New Zealand's posture is one which embraces an inclusive space sector that promotes innovation and enterprise (Pozza & Dennerley, 2022). From a foreign policy perspective, partnership with other spacefaring nations and activities that are undertaken in conformance with international obligations are important elements that this book focuses on.

This book derives from the themes and discussions at the 56th Otago Foreign Policy School held in Dunedin in July 2022 (University of Otago, 2022), where experts from around the world spoke on the importance of space from a range of foreign policy perspectives. The School, which I was privileged to be invited to direct and lead by the Otago Foreign Policy School Committee, aimed to provide a multidisciplinary view of the current elements that touch space. New Zealand's Minister for Foreign Affairs, Honourable Nanaia Mahuta, provided one of the opening addresses, in which she noted the rise in space-related activities in Aotearoa New Zealand and the opportunities that the domain promises. The foreign minister's

M. A. Pozza (✉)
Gravity Lawyers, Christchurch, New Zealand
e-mail: Maria.pozza@gravitylawyers.co.nz

M. A. Pozza (ed.), *Ascending to Space*, Space Law and Policy,
https://doi.org/10.1007/978-981-97-0714-0_1

opening speech is included in this book as a segue into perspectives on foreign policy from the New Zealand posture. The need to ensure international cooperation, an element of focus in the foreign minister's speech, reminds us that international cooperation is a fundamental, cornerstone principle of the Treaty on Principles Governing the Activities of States in the Exploration and Use of Outer Space, including the Moon and Other Celestial Bodies – the Outer Space Treaty (UN Office for Outer Space Affairs, 1967). The minister rightly noted that the importance of space is growing, especially when we think about the increase in the number of space actors as well as the vast opportunities presented to us by the space domain. However, like anything that presents opportunities, we must be attuned to the challenges that come with it.

There are indeed many important elements that require consideration in the space field, and the 56th Foreign Policy School focused on four key themes: international law and regulations that govern outer space activities, specifically those activities that are increasing in the current era; thereafter, focus was devoted to the scientific and educational considerations in the advancement of technology in outer space and how New Zealand has responded to the increase in collaborative efforts to better understand our universe. In this respect, several case studies were presented that focused on their impacts on New Zealand from a critical perspective, including light pollution and space weather. With the increase in scientific collaboration, consideration of the context in which the growth occurs needs to be assessed, and in this way, the School considered defence and commercial postures resulting from the increased utilisation of space, specifically looking at this from the legal and policy dimensions. However, it is not just New Zealand that has had to reflect on and review its national and foreign policy postures but also other Nations, and in this vein, perspectives from other Nation States that have focused on new technologies adopted for space activities were considered at the School.

The Structure of the Chapters

To note that international space law is a complex domain is perhaps an understatement. Space as a realm is open to all yet belongs to no one, is an area that is influenced by international law and relations, and one in which we are seeing increasing activity.

Setting the scene for the realm of space necessarily required this book to take a holistic overview of the international issues currently under consideration. With five major multilateral treaties focusing on space, the foundation of the international law pertaining to outer space is laid out in Chap. 2 by Professor Małgorzata Polkowska of the Law and Administration Faculty of the War Studies University, Warsaw. This chapter aims to set the scene by providing a comprehensive overview of the space law treaties. Next, growing issues at the international level within the space domain are considered. Is the international law still applicable, or do we need to see changes as a result of the increase in commercial space activities such as space tourism? Such issues are considered by Dr Ricky J. Lee of Jesus College, Cambridge, the United Kingdom, in Chap. 3, which considers the emergency assistance and rescue obligations of spacefarers when conducting activities in space.

To assist with our understanding of the ways in which international law applies to these new and emerging trends in space, we next turn to the measures adopted by Nation States' space agencies to provide international governance in their quest for further space exploration. This is certainly a growing area, with more Nations implementing programmes for human exploration. Yet, the question of how we govern these areas has seen much consideration among nations at the international level, with the formation of the Artemis Accords. To help us better understand the Accords as they apply at the international level, in Chap. 4, Dr E. Prema, of the School of Law at the Vellore Institute of Technology in Chennai, and her co-authors explain both its benefits and challenges within the international framework.

To continue with the theme of governance, in Chap. 5, Heloise Vertadier considers the growing risk of safety zones on the lunar surface as more space actors aim to reach the Moon. Issues of national and international security then naturally follow when we think about the space domain, and in Chap. 6, Professor Dale Stephens, University of Adelaide Law School and Editor/Chair of the Woomera Manual Project Governance Board, helps us better understand military postures in the face of growing space activities. He focuses on the changing nature of military activities in space alongside its growing commercial utilisation.

To illustrate the complex nature of the vertical integration of international space law and policy into Nation States' domestic framework, we consider several Nations' experiences thus far. From a local New Zealand perspective, Val Sim from the Ministry of Business, Innovation & Employment considers New Zealand's Space Act in Chap. 7. This is followed by K. R. Sridhara Murthi and V. Gopalakrishnan on the transformation of India's space programme in Chap. 8. At the time of writing, India has successfully launched the Chandrayaan-3 and successfully landed the Vikram lander on the Moon. The increase in space exploration, especially when thinking about the Moon, has led Nations to once again consider their own space policy by questioning whether it continues to be fit for purpose, and looking at this question from the UK perspective is Dr Fionagh Thomson of Durham University in Chap. 9.

In this vein, when thinking about critical issues in space and looking at the importance of collaboration, New Zealand's growing space industry has seen much in the way of contributions by the science sector. Or put another way, one must also look at how current space activities have evolved in the current era, and considering this from the perspective of an international or governmental regime alone is no longer the only way to consider these issues; we must look at the multidisciplinary partnerships that involve the postures and views from the sciences. Further explanation of key scientific collaboration is provided in Chap. 10, by Professor Jörg Frauendiener, Chair of Applied Mathematics at Otago University, with his PhD student Salvo Vultaggio, who explains the multidisciplinary global project – laser interferometer space antenna (LISA) from the angle of New Zealand's involvement.

Carrying through the theme of international scientific collaboration is Professor Craig Rodger, Department of Physics at the University of Otago who along with his co-authors in Chap. 11 explores the importance of space weather to New Zealand's domestic infrastructure. The importance of space and its effects on our infrastructure is the contention that we must also necessarily consider the impacts of increasing space activities in our observation and study of space. John Hearnshaw, Emeritus Professor of Astronomy at the University of Canterbury, in Chap. 12 looks at light pollution caused by the increase in space activities and what this means for our continued observation and study of the night sky.

Finally, the book closes with a view of the changing nature of New Zealand's growing space sector from a technological and scientific perspective by Dr Nicholas Rattenbury of the Department of Physics at the University of Auckland.

Bibliography

New Zealand Space Agency and Ministry of Business, Innovation & Employment. (2023, May). National Space Policy May 2023. www.mbie.govt.nz/dmsdocument/26656-national-space-policy

Pozza, M., & Dennerley, J. (2022). Risk management in outer space activities: An Australian and New Zealand perspective. In M. Pozza et al. (Eds.), *Risk management through New Zealand's and Australia's space legislative frameworks* (Space law and policy series). Springer.

United Nations Office for Outer Space Affairs. (1967). Treaty on principles governing the activities of states in the exploration and use of outer space, including the moon and other celestial bodies (outer space treaty). *Resolution 2222*(XXI), 1966. www.unoosa.org/pdf/gares/ARES_21_2222E.pdf

University of Otago. (2022). *56th Otago Foreign Policy School.* Ascending into space: New Zealand's role as a space-faring nation 1–3 July 2022. www.otago.ac.nz/foreign-policy-school/2022/otago825661.html

Chapter 2
International Space Law: An Overview

Małgorzata Polkowska

Introduction

The five major space treaties,[1] created in the years 1967–1979, have been in force for several decades. Arguably, the first and most important treaty is the Outer Space Treaty,[2] adopted in 1967, which outlines the overarching principles concerned with space activities. However, all five of the major space treaties provide a number of important definitions and arrangements applicable to space-based activities ranging from launch, liability, governance, rescue of astronauts and assets, as well as international relations mechanisms that promote collaboration between States.

Outer space was recognised as the common good of humanity,[3] free access and peaceful use is the bedrock for space-based activities for all, as was freedom of research, and on the other hand, there was a prohibition on the stationing in space of

[1] Treaty on Principles Governing the Activities of States in the Exploration and Use of Outer Space, including the Moon and Other Celestial Bodies, 1967; Agreement on the Rescue of Astronauts, the Return of Astronauts and the Return of Objects Launched into Outer Space, 1968; Convention on International Liability for Damage Caused by Space Objects, 1972; Convention on Registration of Objects Launched into Outer Space, 1975; Agreement Governing the Activities of States on the Moon and Other Celestial Bodies, 1979; https://www.unoosa.org/oosa/en/ourwork/spacelaw/treaties/introouterspacetreaty.html

[2] Treaty on Principles Governing the Activities of States in the Exploration and Use of Outer Space, including the Moon and Other Celestial Bodies, 1967. https://www.unoosa.org/oosa/en/ourwork/spacelaw/treaties/introouterspacetreaty.html

[3] Art. 1 Treaty on Principles Governing the Activities of States in the Exploration and Use of Outer Space, including the Moon and Other Celestial Bodies, 1967. https://www.unoosa.org/oosa/en/ourwork/spacelaw/treaties/introouterspacetreaty.html

M. Polkowska (✉)
International and UE Department, Law and Administration Faculty, War Studies University, Warsaw, Poland
e-mail: m.polkowska@ron.mil.pl

M. A. Pozza (ed.), *Ascending to Space*, Space Law and Policy,
https://doi.org/10.1007/978-981-97-0714-0_2

weapons of mass destruction (WMD).[4] In recent years, there have been new problems which the international space treaties either did not take into account or were too general in their approach. Such issues include the pollution of space, the congestion of its lowest orbits, the lack of an international oversight body, and the growing need to create national space laws to update and fill the gaps left by international law. A number of economic initiatives, such as sourcing raw materials from celestial bodies, are blocked by international space law.[5]

One of the main contentious issues between States, however, is the question of the militarisation and security of space. For maintaining peaceful use of the cosmos stands, among others, the specialised organization, the UN Committee on the Peaceful Uses of Outer Space (COPUOS) with 102 members (when founded in 1958, it was only 18) and 49 organisations as observers was created.[6] A large part of this chapter is devoted to interpretations of the five space treaties, including the Moon Treaty. Due to the increased activity of States in space, the evolving observation mechanisms of outer space and the Earth through systems monitoring the safety of the occupants there, of which facilities play a much more important role than previously in the past was set up. Individual States have also created space situational awareness (SSA/SDA) programmes. The SSA system was created based on the US military programme called Space Domain Awareness (SDAs); the definitions and goals of SSA and SDA are similar, but the US system is more developed and covers more military fields (it covers additionally such areas as tactics, battlefield conditions, and cyberattacks). SDA is a new term substituting SSA, which existed earlier, and it is used mainly by the US Space Force. SDA is an improved and a more comprehensive SSA system.

SDA and SSA programmes (the latter currently covering also some military components) require, among others, frequent measurement of position of objects and provision of precise information about various kind of dangers in real time and in the future. Measurements can be performed from Earth or from Space with the use of optical sensors, radars, or in certain cases, a passive technology (radio frequency, RF).

The SSA programme has become a part of national Space strategies increasingly more often, but for the time being, it is impossible to include it in the international Space law.[7]

---

[4] Art. 4 Treaty on Principles Governing the Activities of States in the Exploration and Use of Outer Space, including the Moon and Other Celestial Bodies, 1967. https://www.unoosa.org/oosa/en/ourwork/spacelaw/treaties/introouterspacetreaty.html

[5] Open Letter to the Canadian Government Concerning Space Resources prepared by Outer Space Institute in 2020 which strongly urges the Government of Canada to reiterate its policy that outer space is a global commons and work through multilateral forums to seek a widely supported international agreement on how space resources should be recovered and used: https://www.outerspaceinstitute.ca/docs/Open_Letter_to_Cdn_FM_reUS_EO_on_Space_Mining.pdf

[6] https://www.unoosa.org/oosa/en/ourwork/copuos/members/evolution.html

[7] Polkowska, M. (2021). *Space Security and Safety: Law, Management, Policy* (p. 43). Warsaw: Instytut Wydawniczy EuroPrawo.

The field of space security is very important, and it often gives direction to international law through the creation of soft law, an example of which is the long-term stability of activities in space. Long-term sustainability (LTS)s in outer space was agreed by consensus at COPUOS in 2019.[8]

The general shape of international space law has not changed yet. However, the constantly emerging challenges set the directions for its future. It is arguable that space law needs to take stock of new space trends and be flexible enough to withstand the changes that the international community expects especially when regulating space activities. This does not necessarily entail normative instruments to create new conventions or international treaties – sometimes they take the form of soft law, such as guidelines, such as codes or recommendations, for example, the Inter-Agency Space Debris Coordination Committee (IADC)[9] or Space Traffic Management (STM).[10] Some representatives of the international community, however, still recognise that these activities are insufficient and ineffective.[11] It has been proposed, inter alia, that there needs to be the creation of a responsible international organisation that looks towards mitigating the effects of space debris by imposing positive obligations to remove debris from orbit with the possibility of a levy tax imposed on space actors that fail to do so. it.[12]

It is likely that space diplomacy and unified space management in space governance will see greater roles concerning space governance especially when we consider the rise of non-State actors from private organisations that are rapidly advancing into space. However, it is important to note that space activities increase via private non-State actors, or through States themselves, and international space law must be flexible in its application to continue to apply. As more space-based activities are conducted, there is a strong argument that the international space law regime must in turn also change or at the very least see States implement strong governing domestic space law to recognise their international legal obligations by providing oversight over space activities conducted from their jurisdictional territories.

[8]COPUOS. (2019). Report of the Committee on the Peaceful Uses of Outer Space. https://www.unoosa.org/res/oosadoc/data/documents/2019/a/a7420_0_html/V1906077.pdf/.

[9]https://www.iadc-home.org/

[10]Polkowska M., Space Traffic Management (STM) – Legal Aspects, Polish Political Science Yearbook, vol. 50 (2021), pp. 1–11; space traffic management (STM) is a new concept referring to space activities.

The highest priority is the safety and security of outer space and all conducted operations.

There is no definition of STM. There is an urgent need to regulate STM providing safety and security regulations at the international, regional, and national levels. Because there is no definition of STM, the regulator might use the example of existing regulations of the International Civil Aviation Organization on Air Traffic Management (ATM).

[11]Oltrogge, D.L. (2018). The "We" Approach to Space Traffic Management. arc.aiaa.org. https://doi.org/10.2514/6.2018-2668.

[12]Ailor W. Evolution of Space Traffic and Space Traffic Management. in K.U. Schrőgl (Ed.), Handbook on Space Security. Springer 2020.

This chapter considers the current international space law regime and considers the need for space law to begin evolving in order to meet the new challenges that arise from the increase of space activities and space actors.

The Outer Space Treaty, 1967

The Outer Space Treaty was largely based on the Declaration of Legal Principles Governing the Activities of States in the Exploration and Use of Outer Space, which had been adopted by the General Assembly in its resolution 1962 (XVIII) in 1963,[13] but added a few new provisions.[14] The Outer Space Treaty was adopted on 27 January 1967, signed simultaneously in Moscow, London, and Washington. Article I, sentence 2 of the Outer Space Treaty stipulates the freedom of outer space.[15] It affirms that outer space, including the Moon and other celestial bodies, is not subject to appropriation in any way and stresses that the exploration and use of outer space (terms not defined in the Outer Space Treaty) should serve the good of all mankind (the Common Heritage of Mankind, CHM).[16]

Outer space, including the Moon and other celestial bodies, is free for exploration and use by all States, without discrimination of any kind, on a principle of equality and in accordance with international law.[17] This freedom, defined by law (the principle of non-discrimination, equality, and compliance with international law), applies to both legal entities and international organisations. The Moon and other celestial bodies have been declared to be no man's property (*res nullius*) or common land (*terra communis*).[18]

The Outer Space Treaty does not define the exact boundary between airspace and outer space but does establish the basis of international space law. Defining the lower boundary of airspace would contribute to greater legal certainty, and as of yet, there is no formal demarcation line. Clear regulation of this issue will allow entities, including entrepreneurs, to State whether the activity they intend to undertake is a space activity or not. This is extremely important for legal certainty. Determining the boundary between air and space is also necessary when thinking about the development of the space tourism market and suborbital flights. The goal of the space

---

[13] UN General Assembly. (1962). Declaration of Legal Principles Governing the Activities of States in the Exploration and Use of Outer Space. https://www.unoosa.org/pdf/gares/ARES_18_1962E.pdf

[14] https://www.unoosa.org/oosa/en/ourwork/spacelaw/treaties/introouterspacetreaty.html

[15] https://www.unoosa.org/oosa/en/ourwork/spacelaw/treaties/status/index.html

[16] Kopal, V. (1995). Progressive development of space law and concept of Common Heritage of Mankind. In E. Pałyga (Ed.), *International Space Law: Miscellanea, liber amicorum honouring Andrzej Górbiel in his 65 Anniversary* (pp. 107–113). Warsaw: Koszalin.

[17] Baczynska-Wilkowska, M. (2018). Outer Space Treaty During Fourth Industrial Revolution. In A. Froehlich (Ed.), *A fresh view on the Outer Space Treaty* (p. 67). Cham: Springer.

[18] https://www.unoosa.org/pdf/gares/ARES_21_2222E.pdf

community to achieve such standards is as in aviation – to ensure safe and responsible transport and to allow entrepreneurs to invest in a new industry, space tourism.[19]

In the current application of the CHM concept, its five elements can be distinguished: it covers a specific region; it cannot be subject to national appropriation; all countries share the management of the region; the benefits derived from the exploitation of resources in the region must be shared among all; and the region must be used for peaceful purposes and preserved for future generations.[20]

Article I of the Outer Space Treaty provides that the exploration and use of outer space, including the Moon and other celestial bodies, shall be carried out for the benefit and in the interests of all countries, irrespective of their degree of economic or scientific development, and shall be the province of all mankind. Outer space, including the Moon and other celestial bodies, shall be free for exploration and use by all States without discrimination of any kind, on a basis of equality and in accordance with international law, and there shall be free access to all areas of celestial bodies. There shall be freedom of scientific investigation in outer space, including the Moon and other celestial bodies, and States shall facilitate and encourage international cooperation in such investigation.

Article II stipulates that neither the Moon nor other celestial bodies are subject to any appropriation (national, private, or otherwise) by States, either through the declaration of sovereignty, through use or occupation, or by 'any other means'. To be clear, this means that there is a prohibition of the appropriation of outer space, including the Moon and other celestial bodies.[21] It is important to note that Article II has been interpreted by experts and States differently, in the case of space mining practices and commercialisation of outer space (for example, the US Space Act, 2015).[22] In addition, there are several interpretations of the phrase 'by any other means'.[23] This is not explained in the Outer Space Treaty. Article VI of the Outer Space Treaty, 1967, prohibits any act of national appropriation supervised by a State, regardless of whether it is carried out directly by a State or a private entity. Hence, there is arguably a contradiction between Articles II (which concerns only States, no private entities) and VI. Therefore, and as a result of its application, it could be argued that Article II should be extended to private activities of national appropriation (as in activities carried out directly by the State itself). However, it should be

[19]Kłoda, M. T., Malinowska, K., Malinowski, B., Polkowska, M. (2011). Polish space law – challenges and trade-offs. *Przegląd Sejmowy, 3*(170), 102–108.

[20]Zhao, Y. (2004). An international space authority: A governance model for a space commercialization regime. *Journal of Space Law, 30*(2), 280.

[21]https://www.unoosa.org/pdf/gares/ARES_21_2222E.pdf p. 13.

[22]US Congress. (2015–16). H.R.2262 — 114th Congress (2015–2016). US Commercial Space Launch Competitiveness Act. https://www.congress.gov/bill/114th-congress/house-bill/2262

[23]https://www.unoosa.org/pdf/gares/ARES_21_2222E.pdf p. 13.

noted that Article II does not prohibit all forms of appropriation, only national ones.[24]

Under Article III of the Outer Space Treaty, State Parties to the treaty must conduct activities in the exploration and use of outer space (including the Moon and other celestial bodies) in accordance with international law (including the UN Charter), in the interests of maintaining international peace and security, and the development of cooperation and understanding among States.[25] Article IV stipulates that States undertake not to put into orbit around the Earth any objects carrying nuclear weapons or other weapons of mass destruction.[26] According to the second paragraph of this article, the Moon and other celestial bodies should be used exclusively for peaceful purposes. However the use of armed forces for scientific and peaceful purposes is not prohibited (for example, the anti-satellite or ASAT weapon systems which are designed to destroy enemy satellites, as well as ballistic missile defence (BMD) (BMD) system. There is no definition of the 'peaceful purposes'. Bearing in mind that the principle of self-defence is applicable in outer space as it is on Earth (Article 51 of UN Charter),[27] the use of outer space for defensive purposes could be argued to align with Article VI of the Outer Space Treaty. Article IV provides for the use of military personnel and military equipment and facilities necessary for peaceful exploration.[28]

According to Article V of the Outer Space Treaty, State Parties to the Outer Space Treaty consider astronauts as envoys of mankind in space and they shall render them all possible assistance in case of an accident, danger, or a forced landing on the territory of another State or on the high seas.[29] Astronauts, who make such a landing shall be safely and without delay returned to the State where their spacecraft is registered. While conducting activities in space and on celestial bodies, astronauts or cosmonauts of one State (a party to the Outer Space Treaty) will provide all possible assistance to astronauts of other State Parties to the Outer Space Treaty. The State must immediately inform the other States or the UN Secretary-General about any phenomena they discover in space, including the Moon and other celestial bodies, which may pose a danger to the life or health of astronauts.[30]

Article VI stipulates the scope of responsibility for activities in space. According to this provision, State Parties to the Outer Space Treaty bear responsibility internationally for their activities in outer space, including the Moon and other celestial bodies, whether conducted by governmental or non-governmental institutions, or by legal entities, as well as for ensuring that these activities comply with the provisions

[24] Fasan, E. (1987). Celestial bodies and the exploitative use of outer space. *Annals of Air and Space Law, 12*, 227–234.

[25] https://www.unoosa.org/pdf/gares/ARES_21_2222E.pdf p. 14.

[26] https://www.unoosa.org/pdf/gares/ARES_21_2222E.pdf p. 14.

[27] https://www.un.org/en/about-us/un-charter

[28] Hobe, S. (2019). *Space Law* (p. 77). Munich: Beck.

[29] https://www.unoosa.org/pdf/gares/ARES_21_2222E.pdf p. 14.

[30] https://www.unoosa.org/pdf/gares/ARES_21_2222E.pdf p. 14.

of the Outer Space Treaty.[31] Such activities require the authorisation and ongoing supervision by the State Party concerned. If activities in space are carried out by an international organisation, the responsibility for compliance with the Outer Space Treaty is borne by both the non-governmental entity and the State Parties to the Outer Space Treaty participating in such an organisation. Article VI is a compromise on the part of the State (the former USSR did not want to allow freedom of action in space to private entities, hence it agreed to a provision in the convention, according to which the state bears responsibility for such entities' international liability).[32]

A situation in which a non-governmental entity fails to fulfil the provisions of the Outer Space Treaty entails the automatic responsibility of the State over the activities undertaken by the non-governmental entity (and this necessarily extends to private space actors) conducting activities from the State. Both narrow and broad interpretations of Article VI are possible. Under the narrow interpretation, States grant themselves responsibility mainly to ensure that space activities comply with international law. Under the broad interpretation, the State will be responsible even for the private law of obligations of operating non-governmental entities if these were their own actions, for example, the non-payment of launching fees. National activities can be considered to be vicariously a State's own action, an action carried out by anyone within the territory of that State or with citizens of the State on board, outside its territorial or under its quasi-territorial jurisdiction, activities on board a ship of registration or performed by citizens, wherever they may be, if it is practical to subject them to effective jurisdiction.

Article VI further stipulates that the activities of non-governmental entities in space, including the Moon and other celestial bodies, will require authorisation (or permission) and permanent supervision by the relevant State. It is debatable whether the Outer Space Treaty establishes an obligation to prepare national legislation in each country to introduce its supervision and authorisation requirements. Article VI allows only States to be Parties to the convention, not international organisations, such as the European Union (although Article XIII contains a provision stipulating the affiliation of States with such organisations).[33] It follows from Article VI that non-governmental agencies may not do something that their States are prohibited from doing. The activities of the non-governmental agencies must therefore be consistent with international law.

According to Article VII of the Outer Space Treaty, the launching State is in fact responsible for the damage caused by a space object.[34] There is a need to amend and clarify some terms and definitions, such as 'astronauts', 'space debris', 'space object', and 'peaceful'. Creating clear definitions, such as for 'space object', would eliminate the interpretation problems when trying to understand these key

[31] https://www.unoosa.org/pdf/gares/ARES_21_2222E.pdf p. 14.

[32] Cheng, B. (1995). International Responsibility and liability for launch activities. *Annals of Space Law, 20*(6), 309.

[33] https://www.unoosa.org/pdf/gares/ARES_21_2222E.pdf p. 14.

[34] https://www.unoosa.org/pdf/gares/ARES_21_2222E.pdf p. 14.

terms at the granular level. The term 'launching State' has also caused a great deal of trouble. Originally, it meant simultaneously a launching State satellite (spacecraft and space vehicle) and placing something in space. This was due to the fact that the launching States both owned the satellite and was the means of launch (spaceport) from a spaceport (spaceport and launch site) on their territory.

According to Article VIII of the Outer Space Treaty, a State Party to the Outer Space Treaty in which an object launched into space is registered retains jurisdiction and control over that object and the crew on board it, when it is in space or on a celestial body.[35] Bin Cheng distinguished three types of jurisdiction that may apply to space law: The first deals with territorial jurisdiction (within the territorial boundaries of the State); the second quasi-territorial jurisdiction (for example, aboard aircraft and at sea); and the third personal jurisdiction (over persons or individuals and legal entities).[36] However, should a court hear a case concerning remote sensing then there would likely be great concern over territorial boundaries, data copyright, and environmental protection. In the case of unauthorised data, for example (as a result of remote sensing), and if there were an event of a conflict of laws, there is a presumption of territorial jurisdiction. These questions will only increase as more non-governmental entities join the realm of space.

Under Article VIII of the Outer Space Treaty, space objects launched into space, including objects that have landed on a celestial body or have been built in space, as well as their component parts, remain intact during their stay in space or on a celestial body, as well as after their return to Earth, are deemed to be owned by the launching State. These objects or their component parts, found outside the borders of the State Party in which they are registered, must be returned to that State Party.[37]

In accordance with Article IX of the Outer Space Treaty, in the exploration and use of outer space, including the Moon and other celestial bodies, the State Parties to the Outer Space Treaty must be guided by the principle of cooperation and mutual assistance and shall conduct all activities in outer space with due regard to the legitimate interests of all other State Parties to the Outer Space Treaty.[38] The States Parties are also obligated to conduct space studies and research in such a way as to avoid harmful pollution, as well as adverse changes in the terrestrial environment resulting from the introduction of extraterrestrial substances.[39]

In accordance with Article XI, there is a responsibility on State Parties to promote international cooperation in the peaceful exploration and use of outer space, the States conducting activities in outer space shall communicate to the UN

[35] https://www.unoosa.org/pdf/gares/ARES_21_2222E.pdf p. 14.

[36] Cheng B., From Air Law to Space Law, Current Legal Problems, Volume 13, Issue 1, 1 January 1960, Pages 228–254.

[37] https://www.unoosa.org/pdf/gares/ARES_21_2222E.pdf p. 14.

[38] https://www.unoosa.org/pdf/gares/ARES_21_2222E.pdf p. 14.

[39] Polkowska, M. (2021). *Eksploracja Kosmosu: Zagadnienia prawno-polityczne* (pp. 139–141). Warsaw: Instytut Wydawniczy EuroPrawo.

Secretary-General and to the public and the international scientific community information the nature, conduct, locations, and results of their activities.[40] This type of information sharing is problematic especially when one considers global security and international relations. How effectively this provision works in the context of security is questionable, and it is argued that States do have self-interest in such activities; it may be that not all activities, or findings for that matter, are always shared. This is an area where greater transparency and cooperation ought to be developed.

Similarly, all space stations, facilities, equipment, and vehicles on the Moon and on other celestial bodies are required to be accessible – on a reciprocal basis – to representatives of other State Parties to the Outer Space Treaty (Article XII). Accordingly, the provisions of the Outer Space Treaty apply to the activities of the States especially when undertaking space exploration and use of space, regardless of whether these activities are carried out by a single State Party to the Outer Space Treaty or jointly with other States, including activities within the framework of international organisations.[41] There is a strong basis here for better international cooperation, especially when we consider the growing interest by States to revisit the Moon and possibly Mars.

The Outer Space Treaty was considered a major political and legal achievement. At present, however, it requires some modifications, due to the major changes in space technology, and the rapid development of commercial exploitation, remote sensing, telecommunications and satellite broadcasting, as well as the increasing participation of private entrepreneurs in all aspects of space activities, including launching space objects. The Outer Space Treaty was created during a period of polarisation of politically and economically opposed systems and showed that the international community could find a peaceful solution to global problems. Its greatest virtue is the freedom of exploration and use of space by all States. It is also necessary to clarify some of the wording used in the text – there is some concern that private entities may dominate space since Article II prohibits only national appropriation.[42]

---

[40] https://www.unoosa.org/pdf/gares/ARES_21_2222E.pdf p. 14.

[41] Jakhu, R. S. (2006). Legal issues relating to the global public interest in outer space. *Journal of Space Law, 32*(1), 31–111.

[42] Cheng, B. (1998). The 1967 Outer Space Treaty: Thirtieth Anniversary. *Annals of Space Law, 23*(4/5), 156–165.

The Rescue Agreement, 1968[43]

According to Article 1 of the Rescue Agreement, any State that obtains information or determines that the crew of a spacecraft has suffered an accident or is in danger, or has made a forced or inadvertent landing in the territory under its jurisdiction, or in any other place not under the jurisdiction of any State, or on the high seas, then for all intents and purposes that State becomes a rescuing State. Under Article 1, there is an active obligation to the 'contracting State' or rescuing State to render assistance by immediately informing the launching State's authorities and the UN Secretary-General.[44] In the event that the assistance to the launching State could facilitate a speedy rescue or make a significant contribution to the effectiveness of the search and rescue operation, then the rescuing State must cooperate with that contracting State to effectively conduct the search and rescue operation.[45] Such assistance is amplified by Article 2 subject to the direction and control of the rescuing State (or as referred to under Article 2, the 'Contracting Party'), which will cooperate with the launching authority.[46] Further, Article 3 requires the rescuing State to safely return astronauts (or as Article 3 refers to them as 'representatives' discussed further below) to their launching authority.[47]

Article 4 stipulates that if, as a result of an accident, danger, or a forced or unintentional landing, the crew of a spacecraft lands in a territory under the jurisdiction of a contracting party or is found on the high seas or in any other place not under the jurisdiction of any State, it shall be safely and promptly handed over to representatives of the launching authorities.[48] Under Article 5 paragraph 1, any State that obtains information or determines that the space object or its components has returned to Earth at a location within its territory subject to its jurisdiction or on the high seas, or in any other place not under the jurisdiction of any State must notify the launching authorities and the UN Secretary-General.[49] Any State Party having jurisdiction over the territory where the space object or its components have been found shall undertake, at the request of the launching authorities and with their assistance (if requested), such measures they deem appropriate for the recovery of the object or its component parts (Article 5 paragraph 2)[50] According to Article

[43]United Nations (2002). Agreement on the Rescue of Astronauts, the Return of Astronauts and the Return of Objects Launched into Outer Space (p. 9). https://www.unoosa.org/pdf/publications/STSPACE11E.pdf

[44]Catalano Sgrosso, G. (1998). Legal status, rights and obligations of the crew in space. *Journal of Space Law, 26*(1–2), 163–186.

[45]https://www.unoosa.org/pdf/gares/ARES_22_2345E.pdf p. 6.

[46]https://www.unoosa.org/pdf/gares/ARES_22_2345E.pdf p. 6.

[47]https://www.unoosa.org/pdf/gares/ARES_22_2345E.pdf p. 6.

[48]https://www.unoosa.org/pdf/gares/ARES_22_2345E.pdf p. 6.

[49]https://www.unoosa.org/pdf/gares/ARES_22_2345E.pdf p. 6.

[50]https://www.unoosa.org/pdf/gares/ARES_22_2345E.pdf p. 6.

5 paragraph 3[51] at the request of the launching authorities, space-launched objects or their components found outside the territorial limits of these authorities will be returned to the representatives of the launching authorities, or kept at their disposal. A State which has reason to believe that a space object or its components found in territory under its jurisdiction, or recovered by it in any other place, is by its nature dangerous or harmful may notify the launching authority, which shall immediately take effective measures to eliminate the possible danger. Under Article 5 paragraph 5, expenses incurred in fulfilling obligations related to the recovery and return of the space object or its components shall be borne by the launching authorities.[52] However, from the wording of Article 5 of the Rescue Agreement, it is possible to conclude *a contrario*, according to which such non-refundable objects and their components may be appropriated by the State on whose territory they were found or which recovered them in a land area not subject to the sovereignty of any State. This is important when thinking about the necessary conditions for the admissibility of such appropriation not only because the prior notification of the finding of the space object or its components but also because the acquisition of reasonable assurance (among other things, by the passage of a reasonable period of time) that no State intends to demand their return.

By contrast, the Outer Space Treaty[53] uses the terms 'personnel' and 'crew of the of a space facility', in addition to the term 'astronaut'. The legal international space status of an astronaut is therefore now granted to all persons sent into extra-atmospheric space or celestial bodies, regardless of the intended purpose of their space journey and the nature of the activities performed there. Confirmation of the legitimacy of this interpretation of the term 'astronaut' is provided by the Liability Convention[54] – it speaks of 'persons on board a space object'.[55] This could be quite unambiguous, especially when one considered the interpretation is provided by Article 10 of the Moon Treaty[56] which considers that the persons sent into space are to be deemed as persons of the jurisdiction of the State of registration of the spacecraft. This occurs both when these persons are inside the spacecraft and when they leave it, when going into extra-atmospheric space, or while on the surface of a celestial body.[57] This principle stems from Article VIII of the Outer Space Treaty

---

[51] https://www.unoosa.org/pdf/gares/ARES_22_2345E.pdf p. 6.

[52] https://www.unoosa.org/pdf/gares/ARES_22_2345E.pdf p. 6.

[53] https://www.unoosa.org/oosa/en/ourwork/spacelaw/treaties/introouterspacetreaty.html

[54] United Nations. (2002). Convention on International Liability for Damage Caused by Space Objects (p. 13). https://www.unoosa.org/pdf/publications/STSPACE11E.pdf.United Nations. (2002). Convention on International Liability for Damage Caused by Space Objects (p. 13). https://www.unoosa.org/pdf/publications/STSPACE11E.pdf

[55] https://www.unoosa.org/pdf/publications/STSPACE11E.pdf Art. III.

[56] https://www.unoosa.org/pdf/gares/ARES_34_68E.pdf

[57] https://www.unoosa.org/pdf/gares/ARES_34_68E.pdf

and General Assembly Resolution 1962 (XVIII), which unambiguously place astronauts under the jurisdiction of the State of registration.[58]

The Liability Convention, 1972[59]

The body of international space law was expanded in 1972 with the Convention on International Liability for Damage Caused by Space Objects (analogous to the provisions of private Aviation law[60]). The Liability Convention uses the terms 'responsibility' and 'liability'. The term 'responsibility' is derived from the Latin *respondere* – English: to answer) and can simply mean 'authorship' of an action or mistake. The word 'liability' is associated with breaking the rules of law. 'Liability' expresses the aspect of responsibility in the case when the responsible person violates an obligation imposed on him and thereby causes harm to someone else. Although the Liability Convention contains numerous flaws, it could be argued that it represents a step forward from Articles VI and VII of the Outer Space Treaty, and its creation is an important step in the further development of legal provisions on space activities. This means that it might assist States in clearer interpretation of their responsibilities in using outer space and it might lead to better collaboration between them.

State responsibility can be direct or indirect. Direct responsibility concerns responsibility for one's own actions. It could be argued that since States act through their officials or agents, they are responsible for their actions as if they were its own. By contrast, it might be that indirect responsibility involves the protection of a State's citizens, as well as property within its own jurisdiction, especially territorial property. The responsibility of States can therefore be either voluntarily and assumed by them (assumed liability) or imposed by law (imposed liability). The responsibility of States for space activities is further confirmed by Article VI of the Outer Space Treaty and Article 14 of the Moon Treaty.

On the context of the above foundation, Article I of the Liability Convention defines the following terms: 'damage' – loss of life, injury, or other threat to health, or loss or damage to property or assets of States or natural or legal entities or property of international intergovernmental organisations; 'launching into space[61]' – this also includes intentional launching: 'launching' means a State which launches or procures the launching of a space object, or a State from whose territory or facilities a

[58] UN General Assembly. (1962). Declaration of Legal Principles Governing the Activities of States in the Exploration and Use of Outer Space. www.unoosa.org/pdf/gares/ARES_18_1962E.pdf

[59] United Nations. (2002). Convention on International Liability for Damage Caused by Space Objects (p. 13). https://www.unoosa.org/pdf/publications/STSPACE11E.pdf

[60] Convention on damage caused by foreign aircraft to Third Parties on the surface signed at Rome on 7 October 1952; https://www.mcgill.ca/iasl/files/iasl/rome1952.pdf

[61] https://www.unoosa.org/pdf/gares/ARES_26_2777E.pdf p. 25.

space object is launched; and 'space object' further includes components of the space object and the launching vehicle and its parts. Whilst Article 1 does provide a definition of 'damage', it does not include environmental damage; it speaks of direct damage, but there is no mention of indirect damage and consequential damage. As a result, this could cause confusion among States in the interpretation of the Liability Convention.

Importantly, when thinking about terminology, there is difficulty when interpreting the concept of 'harm' to possible harms of a moral nature. Accordingly, the launching State is absolutely obliged to pay compensation for damage that its space object causes on the Earth's surface, or to an aircraft in flight.[62] One could argue that this is implicitly an absolute liability obligation under Article II. Further, Article III stipulates that in the event of damage caused anywhere other than on the surface of the Earth (to a space object of the launching State or to persons and property on board such a space object) or by a space object of another launching State, the latter shall be liable only if the damage was caused by its fault or the fault of persons for whom it is responsible.[63] Article III of the Liability Convention provides that liability for damage caused in space by a space object will be determined on the basis of fault.[64]

The concept of fault, however, has different meanings in different legal systems. The provision is not entirely clear, as it does not specify the concept of 'another launching State' – rather, it should say 'launching State other than the first launching State'. In other words, Article III applies only if the damage caused is 'international' and not 'domestic' in nature. There is also ambiguity in interpretation regarding the concept of 'launching State' and the situation when a missile is launched from a platform drilling platform on the high seas – the definition of a launching State seems too broad here.

According to Article IV under the first paragraph, in the event of damage caused elsewhere than on the surface of the Earth to a space object of one launching State or to persons and property on board such a space object by a space object of another launching State, and damage caused in doing so to a third State or its natural or legal persons, the two first States shall be jointly and severally liable to that third State to the following extent: if the damage is caused to a third State on the ground or to an aircraft in flight, their liability to the third State shall be absolute; or if the damage was caused to a third country's space object or persons and property on board such space object anywhere other than on the surface of the Earth, their liability to the third State depends on the fault of the persons, each of whom is responsible.[65]

According to paragraph 2 of Article IV, in all cases of joint and several liabilities, the burden of compensation for damage shall be apportioned between the first two

---

[62] https://www.unoosa.org/pdf/gares/ARES_26_2777E.pdf p. 25 Art. II.

[63] https://www.unoosa.org/pdf/gares/ARES_26_2777E.pdf p. 25.

[64] Masson-Zwaan, T., Hofman, M. (2019). Introduction to Space Law (p. 26). Alphen aan den Rijn: Wolters Kluwer.

[65] https://www.unoosa.org/pdf/gares/ARES_26_2777E.pdf pp. 25–26.

States, according to the extent of their fault. If the extent of the fault of each of these States cannot be determined, the obligation to compensate shall be borne equally by both States.[66] Such apportionment is without prejudice to the right of the third State to claim full compensation due under the Liability Convention from any or all of the amounting States, which are liable jointly and severally. If, in accordance with paragraph 1 of Article V, two or more States launch a space object jointly, they are both jointly and severally liable for any damage caused. The launching State that has paid compensation for the damage shall have the right to make a claim for compensatory damages against the other participants in the joint launching.[67]

Participants in a joint launching may enter into agreements on the distribution of financial obligations among themselves, to the extent to which they are jointly and severally liable. Exemption from absolute liability is granted to the extent that the exporting State proves that the damage was caused in whole or in part due to gross negligence or an act or omission committed with the intent to cause damage on the part of the claimant State or the natural or legal persons it represents.[68] According to paragraph 2, the exemption is not available in cases where the damage resulted from activities carried out by the launching State, contrary to international law, in particular the UN Charter and with the Outer Space Treaty.

Article VI excludes State liability from absolute liability, provided that it arose from gross negligence or a wilful mistake on the part of the complaining State or its citizens. However, the Liability Convention does not provide a definition of the term 'gross negligence', which causes some difficulty when trying to interpret the extent of this provision especially when one thinks about the differing ways that each jurisdiction may treat this term. Some States are seeing an increase in their respective private sectors now wishing to access and provide services from, and as a result, this might lead to issues under Article VI. This highlights the importance that States implement national legislation which adequately translates the liability provision obligation to private operators. It is important to note that despite national legislation used as a mechanism for this, it does not exonerate States from their international legal responsibility under Article VI.

The provisions of Article VII of the Liability Convention do not apply to damage caused by a space object of the launching State to citizens of the launching State, or foreign nationals while they are participating in operations related to this space object from the moment of its launch, or at any stage thereafter up to its landing, or while being, at the invitation of the State launching the object, in the immediate vicinity of the planned launch or recovery zone of the object.[69] Article VII may also have application to space tourism activities. If, for example, a spaceship's passengers, who are nationals of the launching State, are not subject to the provisions of the Liability Convention, then if the damage occurred through the fault of the means of

[66] https://www.unoosa.org/pdf/gares/ARES_26_2777E.pdf p. 26.

[67] https://www.unoosa.org/pdf/gares/ARES_26_2777E.pdf p. 26.

[68] https://www.unoosa.org/pdf/gares/ARES_26_2777E.pdf p. 26 Art. VI.

[69] https://www.unoosa.org/pdf/gares/ARES_26_2777E.pdf p. 26.

transportation, they will not be able to make any claims. Assuming that a spacecraft flying into space is a space object, foreign citizens (who are passengers) are also not subject to the international protection afforded by the Liability Convention, and it is interesting to note that it may very well be that a tourist of a foreign nationality will therefore be unable to make a claim for the damage caused during space travel. Naturally, one might conclude that this will not promote the development of the space tourism industry. Perhaps liability should continue to remain with the non-governmental entities involved in launching objects or conducting other activities in space. A way forward towards the promotion of private launches and space activities might be to limit the liability of non-governmental agencies or private entities. The absolute and unlimited liability of the launching State under the Liability Convention could be replaced by a new convention or at least a new provision that allows more flexibility in this area. The international space law dealing with launches could be part of a new space transportation law applicable to private launches. Such a convention could be created based on aviation conventions dealing with damage caused by aircraft to Third Parties, namely the Rome Convention of 1952 and the Montreal Convention of 1978.[70] Liability to passengers could be based on a system similar to the Warsaw Convention of 1929[71] civil liability system, under which an air carrier has limited liability.

According to Article VIII under the first paragraph, the State that suffers damage or whose citizens or companies suffer damage may present to the launching State a claim for compensation.[72] Further, under the second paragraph of Article VIII, if the injured State does not present such a claim, another State may present one to the launching State with respect to damage caused on its territory to any natural or legal person. According to the third paragraph of Article VIII, if neither the launching State nor the State on whose territory the damage was caused presents a claim or notifies its intention to present a claim, another State may present a claim to the launching State for the damage suffered by its permanent residents. Under Article IX, a claim for compensation is usually presented to the launching State by diplomatic means.

There are numerous practical problems associated with Article VIII of the Liability Convention, for example, when selling a spacecraft. Questions arise about control, registration, and ownership. Under Article X (1), a claim for compensation could be presented to the owning State no later than 1 year from the date of the damage.[73] Accordingly, under Article XI, the presentation of a claim for

---

[70]Rome Convention. (1952). Convention on Damage Caused By Foreign Aircraft to Third Parties on the Surface. www.mcgill.ca/iasl/files/iasl/rome1952.pdf; Rome Convention. (1978). Protocol to amend the Convention on damage caused by foreign aircraft to Third Parties on the surface, signed at Rome on 7 October 1952, signed at Montreal, on 23 September 1978. https://www.mcgill.ca/iasl/files/iasl/rome1952.pdf

[71]Convention for the unification of certain rules relating to international carriage by air, signed at Warsaw on 12 October 1929, https://www.mcgill.ca/iasl/files/iasl/warsaw1929.pdf

[72]https://www.unoosa.org/pdf/gares/ARES_26_2777E.pdf p. 26.

[73]https://www.unoosa.org/pdf/gares/ARES_26_2777E.pdf p. 26.

compensation to the designating State does not require the prior exhaustion of all local means available to the State presenting the claim, or the natural or legal persons it represents. Nothing in the Liability Convention prevents a State, or a natural or legal person whom it may represent, from pursuing claims in the courts or administrative tribunals or in the offices of the exporting State.[74] Further, under Article XII, the compensation which the launching State is obliged to pay for the damage caused shall be determined in accordance with international law and in accordance with the principles of justice and equity in order to ensure such compensation for the damage as will restore the natural or legal entity, State, or international organisation on whose behalf the claim is made, the State that would have existed if the damage had not occurred.[75]

Unless the requesting State and the State obligated to provide compensation do not agree on a different method of compensation, then usually compensation is paid in the currency of the State making the demand or, at its request, in the currency of the State obligated to compensate for the damage, [76] Article XV under the Liability Convention establishes a dispute framework and stipulates that a Claim Commission will be established with the aim of deciding the matter.[77]

Accordingly, under Article XXI, if the damage caused by a space object poses a serious danger to human life or seriously affects the living conditions of the population or the functioning of vital centres, State Parties, especially the launching States, are required to undertake an examination of the possibility of providing appropriate and expeditious assistance to the affected State, if it so requests. However, nothing in the article affects the rights or obligations of the State Parties under the Liability Convention. Its provisions are without prejudice to other applicable international agreements. Nothing in the Liability Convention prevents States from entering into international agreements confirming, supplementing, or extending its provisions.[78]

The Liability Convention implements the general principles of liability derived from Articles VI and VII of the Outer Space Treaty. The Liability Convention applies only to the space activities of States and intergovernmental organisations, and not to space activities carried out by non-governmental entities, such as private companies, educational institutions, or non-governmental international organisations.[79] In this sense, the Liability Convention is more restrictive in its application than the Outer Space Treaty, Article VI of which imposes responsibility on States for all 'State activities' in space, even if such activities are carried out by either government agencies or non-governmental entities.

---

[74] https://www.unoosa.org/pdf/gares/ARES_26_2777E.pdf p. 26.

[75] https://www.unoosa.org/pdf/gares/ARES_26_2777E.pdf Art XII p. 26.

[76] https://www.unoosa.org/pdf/gares/ARES_26_2777E.pdf p. 26 Art. XIII.

[77] https://www.unoosa.org/pdf/gares/ARES_26_2777E.pdf pp. 26–27.

[78] https://www.unoosa.org/pdf/gares/ARES_26_2777E.pdf p. 27 Art. XXIII.

[79] https://www.unoosa.org/pdf/gares/ARES_26_2777E.pdf p. 25 Art III.

As an observation, it appears that the Liability Convention disregarded private activities in space during the time of drafting, which is understandable when one thinks of the Cold War context in which the international space law treaties were drafted. However, its greatest achievement was the inclusion of a third-party complaint system in the event of a dispute under international law into a time frame – after a certain amount of time, a final decision must be made, and the amount of compensation decided, even if it is only a recommendation, until the Parties agree that it should be binding.[80]

However, the Liability Convention's provisions lack clarity and precision. Like the Outer Space Treaty, the Liability Convention does not contain any instructions as to the definition of the term 'space object'. Also, the definitions of joint and several liabilities in Article V are unclear. In the event that a State is given the right to present a complaint on behalf of a permanent resident who is not a citizen, it is unclear when in fact this right can be exercised. Regulations are ineffective, and the liability procedures of the launching States fail to provide proper payments and compensation to victims of space accidents. It does not provide for a system of mandatory courts or any means by which a final and binding decision could be implemented; there is no guarantee that the complaining State will receive any compensation. The Liability Convention merely provides the complaining State with the prospect of obtaining reasonable compensation, which – possibly – would be finalised only if the responsible launching State acts in good faith, either through negotiations in resolving the dispute with the claimant State, through an agreement to refer the case to the Claims Commission, or by bringing public pressure to bear. The Liability Convention also does not deal with damages relating to the destruction of the environment. Similarly, there is no sanction mechanism.

Further, the existing liability regime contained in the Liability Convention regarding the prosecution of such activities is highly unsuitable for dealing with the problems caused by space debris.[81] It is controversial whether the Liability Convention covers damage caused in orbit by debris. Liability is not clearly attributed to the launching State because of the difficulty in identifying the damaged parts. It seems that in a situation in which multiple States are launching space objects, compensation should favour the victim. In such a situation, it is necessary to conclude that there needs to be more appropriate agreements in place that identify the relevant launching State and the amount of compensation. In the case of activities of private entities, there perhaps ought to be a guarantee of payment of damages to the victim. The amount of compensation that the launching State is able to pay amounting to a fine is not established in the Liability Convention, but instead in national law or in bilateral agreements. It is up to the State itself, depending on how high the limit of compensation has been set by the Parties, and this naturally leads to inconsistency in approach. The Liability Convention on damage caused by space

[80] https://www.unoosa.org/pdf/gares/ARES_26_2777E.pdf p. 25 Art. IV pp. 25–26.

[81] Stubbe, P. (2010, March). Common but differentiated responsibilities for space debris – New impetus for a legal appraisal of outer space pollution. *ESPI Perspectives, 31*, 2.

activities is arguably outdated due to increasing globalisation and the privatisation of the space industry. There is a need to amend the Liability Convention along the lines of the model of the liability convention in aviation and maritime law.[82]

The Registration Convention, 1975[83]

Article I of the Convention on Registration of Objects Launched into Outer Space (Registration Convention) provides the following definitions: 'launching State' – a State that lifts or causes a space object to be lifted, or a State from whose territory or facilities the space object is launched ('space object' also means the components of the space object and the launching vehicle and its parts) and 'registering State' – the launching State in whose register the space object is listed.[84]

According to Article II (1) of the Registration Convention, when a space object has been launched into orbit around the Earth or beyond, the launching State must register it by entering it in the appropriate register, which it will maintain.[85] Each launching State is also obligated to inform the UN Secretary-General regarding the establishment of such a registry. The Registration Convention does not specify when States must establish a space registry, nor the time at which the information should be provided (that is, whether before or after launch). Hence, States decide for themselves when to notify the Secretary-General.

It follows from Article II that there can be only one State of registration. In the case of several States jointly launching, it must be determined which of them will register the space object in its national registry.[86] States may agree as to the application of certain aspects of the legislation of a State that does not appear as the State of registration. Difficulties arise with regard to the transfer of satellites into orbit, mainly in the case of the sale of a satellite. The register, which is maintained by the UN Secretary-General, is public.[87] Pursuant to Article IV (1), each registrant state provides to the Secretary-General as soon as possible information regarding each space object included in its register. These are the name of the launching State or States, the relevant identification mark of the space object or its registration number, the date and territory or location of the launch, the main parameters of the

[82]Maniatis, D. (1997). The law governing liability for damage caused by space objects: from State responsibility to private liability. *Annals of Air and Space Law, 22*(1), 369–401.

[83]United Nations. (2002). Convention on Registration of Objects Launched into Outer Space (p. 22). www.unoosa.org/pdf/publications/STSPACE11E.pdf

[84]https://www.unoosa.org/pdf/gares/ARES_29_3235E.pdf p. 16.

[85]https://www.unoosa.org/pdf/gares/ARES_29_3235E.pdf p. 16.

[86]https://www.unoosa.org/pdf/gares/ARES_29_3235E.pdf p. 17.

[87]https://www.unoosa.org/pdf/gares/ARES_29_3235E.pdf Art. III par. 1 p. 17.

orbit (the period of circulation, inclination angle, apogee, and perigee), and the general purpose of the space object.[88]

Each registry State may, from time to time, transmit to the UN Secretary-General additional information regarding the space object entered in its register.[89] In the event that a state can identify the space object that caused damage, or when the object is dangerous, other State Parties, especially States that have facilities for observing and tracking space objects, should provide all assistance in identifying that object. The Registration Convention is not clear if under Article IV information must necessarily be transferred to national registries. The information contained in Article IV of the Registration Convention can serve as general recommendations for registry requirements at the national level.

In practice, many States fail to comply with the registration requirement in a timely manner, provide incomplete information required for registration, submit applications in different forms, or deliberately delay the adoption of the Registration Convention. For these reasons, the number of unregistered facilities is increasing, as is the number of collisions of objects. The Registration Convention rejects the thesis of the non-existence in the current *ius spatiale* of the concept of 'nationality' of space objects. Listing by a State of a spacecraft in its national register, as well as the transmission of the relevant data to the UN Secretary-General for entry in the international register maintained by it, constitutes a formal expression of a legal state characterised by the subjection of the vessel – regardless of its location – to the authority of that State. Registration establishes a bond between the state and the spacecraft. This bond has a dual purpose.

On the one hand, the Registration Convention provides the spacecraft with State protection; on the other hand, the interests of Third Parties are protected by the fact that the State is liable for the spacecraft registered with the state. The authority vested in the State over the object it has sent into extra-atmospheric space, as well as the authority over the persons in that object, could be deemed to qualify as a quasi-territorial competence.

Based on the Registration Convention, States have an active obligation to notify other States of the termination of a satellite that is still in orbit. All States concerned obviously need to know that this object is no longer active and has become space debris. This raises the problem of 'paper satellites', which have never been launched, but occupy a nominal orbital position on the International Telecommunication Union (ITU) list and require difficult coordination with other users of geostationary orbits. The possibility of applying the Registration Convention to nuclear-armed satellites still requires further research.

Some space agencies, such as NASA, maintain lists of active satellites.[90] In order to protect investors operating in the space market, a protocol to the Cape Town

[88] https://www.unoosa.org/pdf/gares/ARES_29_3235E.pdf p. 17.

[89] https://www.unoosa.org/pdf/gares/ARES_29_3235E.pdf p. 17

[90] https://www.nasa.gov/

Convention on International Safeguards for Mobile Equipment[91] has been created by the International Institute for the Unification of Private Law (UNIDROIT).[92] The protocol provides for the establishment of an international registry of space objects and their parts[93] (analogous to civilian aircraft) in order to facilitate the market for space objects. This legislation helps in the financing of the construction of spacecraft and their components, which, given the very high production costs, will be a tangible benefit for each party to the contract (the representatives of the industrial and financial sides).[94]

The Moon Treaty, 1979[95]

The provisions of the Moon Treaty applies to other celestial bodies within the solar system, excluding the Earth, unless there exist special legal norms with respect to any of these celestial bodies.[96]

According to paragraph 2 of Article 2 for the purposes of the Moon Treaty, any mention of the Moon will be considered also to refer to orbits around the Moon and other trajectories in the direction of or around the Moon. The Moon Treaty does not apply to extraterrestrial matter that reaches the Earth's surface by natural means.[97] All activities on the Moon, including its exploration and use, must be conducted in accordance with international law, in particular with the UN Charter, and taking into account the Declaration of Principles of International Law of 1970 (Article 2).[98] Importantly, Article 3 provides that the Moon shall be used by all State Parties exclusively for peaceful purposes and stipulates the prohibition to resort to any threat or use of force, or to perform a hostile act, on the Moon.[99] States are also prohibited to use the Moon for the purpose of committing such an act or applying such a threat

[91] Convention on international interests in mobile equipment (2001) https://www.unidroit.org/instruments/security-interests/cape-town-convention/

[92] https://www.unidroit.org/

[93] Protocol to the Convention on International interests in mobile equipment on matters specific to space assets (Berlin, 9 March 2012); https://www.unidroit.org/instruments/security-interests/space-protocol/ Art 12.

[94] UNIDROIT. (2012). Protocol to the Convention on International interests in mobile equipment on matters specific to space assets (Berlin, 9 March 2012). https://www.unidroit.org/instruments/security-interests/space-protocol/

[95] United Nations. (2002). Agreement Governing the Activities of States on the Moon and Other Celestial Bodies (p. 27). www.unoosa.org/pdf/publications/STSPACE11E.pdf

[96] https://www.unoosa.org/pdf/gares/ARES_34_68E.pdf p. 78.

[97] https://www.unoosa.org/pdf/gares/ARES_34_68E.pdf p. 78.

[98] United Nations General Assembly. (1970). Declaration on Principles of International Law concerning Friendly Relations and Co-operation among States, Resolution 2625 (XXV), annex. http://www.un-documents.net/a25r2625.htm

[99] https://www.unoosa.org/pdf/gares/ARES_34_68E.pdf p. 78.

to the Earth, the Moon, a spacecraft, or the personnel of that spacecraft or man-made space object. In addition to Article IX of the Outer Space Treaty, this provision exemplifies the importance of the obligation to protect the Moon's environment. Further, paragraph 3 of Article 3 includes a prohibition on States from placing in orbit around the Moon any object with nuclear weapons or other weapons of mass destruction.

It is important to note that under paragraph 4 of Article 3, States are not allowed to establish military bases, facilities, or fortifications on the Moon, or to conduct military manoeuvres; this provision is extremely important since more than 75% of satellites are used for military purposes and for all intents and purpose is a form of a sustainability mechanism on the Moon.

Article 4 specifically states that the exploration and use of the Moon shall be the domain of all mankind and shall be carried out for the general good and in the interest of all countries, regardless of their degree of economic or scientific development.[100] Accordingly, under paragraph 2 of Article 4, all activities concerning the exploration and use of the Moon fall under the State of which the State shall be guided by the principle of cooperation and mutual assistance. In accordance with Article 5, States are obliged to inform the UN Secretary-General as well as the international community about their scientific activities concerning the exploration and use of the Moon. Information regarding the date, objectives, locations, orbital parameters, and duration of each mission to the Moon need to be communicated as soon as possible after the start of the missions.[101] Information on the results of each mission, including scientific results, must be transmitted after the completion of the mission. Further, in accordance with paragraph 3 of Article 5, when carrying out activities, State Parties must promptly inform the UN Secretary-General, as well as the international community, of any phenomenon identified by them occurring in outer space, including the Moon, that may constitute a danger to human life and health, as well as inform them about any signs of organic life.[102]

Article 6 stipulates the freedom to conduct scientific research on the Moon and, importantly, applies to all State Parties, without discrimination, on a basis of equality and in accordance with international law. State Parties, in conducting scientific research and carrying out the provisions of the Moon Treaty, have the right to collect and take from the Moon samples of its minerals and other substances for scientific purposes.[103] Article 6 is further expanded to include that States Parties agree to the exchange of scientific personnel and other personnel during expeditions to the Moon or in facilities which are located on it. (paragraph 3). Article 6 is

[100] Boothby, W. (2016). Control in Weapons Law. In R. Bartels et al. (Eds), *Military Operations and the Notion of Control Under International Law, Liber Amicorum Terry D. Gill* (p. 370). Berlin: Springer.

[101] https://www.unoosa.org/pdf/gares/ARES_34_68E.pdf p. 78.

[102] https://www.unoosa.org/pdf/gares/ARES_34_68E.pdf p. 78.

[103] https://www.unoosa.org/pdf/gares/ARES_34_68E.pdf p. 78.

fundamental towards better international collaboration between State Parties because in essence, it promotes equality and the sharing of findings.[104]

According to paragraph 1 of Article 7, in exploring and using the Moon, the State Parties take measures to avoid disturbing the existing balance of its environment by causing harmful changes in it, endangering or polluting it by introducing foreign matter.[105] In accordance with paragraph 2, State Parties are obligated to inform the UN Secretary-General in advance, to the fullest extent possible, of their plans to place radioactive substances on the Moon and about the purposes of this activity. State Parties may notify other State Parties and the Secretary-General of sites on the Moon of special scientific interest in order to recognise them as protective scientific reserves.[106] This level of governance introduces transparency when States are engaged in the exploration of the Moon and is instrumental to serve better collaboration between State Parties.

Article 8 considers State Parties may conduct their activities in the exploration and use of the Moon on its surface or beneath it.[107] For this purpose, State Parties may land space objects on the Moon and send them from the Moon, place (and move) their personnel, as well as their vehicles, equipment, devices, space stations, and installations, anywhere on or below the surface of the Moon.[108] According to paragraph 3 of Article 8, the activities of the State Parties on the Moon should not interfere with the activities of other States on the Moon. When such interference may occur, the interested State Parties should undertake consultations according to Article 15 paragraphs 2 and 3.[109]

When considering Article 9, State Parties are able to establish stations on the Moon that may be either inhabited or uninhabited. The State Party that establishes a station must be careful to use only such area as is necessary for the needs of the station and must promptly inform the UN Secretary-General of the location of and purposes of the station.[110] Further, the stations must be established in such a way that they do not impede free access to all parts of the Moon by personnel, vehicles, and equipment of other State Parties conducting activities on the Moon.[111] The term "use" within Article 9 appears to refer to acts other than collecting and using in situ for scientific purposes and for industrial exploitation of the lunar soil. These may only be activities that prove necessary for the performance of the station's tasks under the jurisdictional and control powers vested in the State with respect to it. In this regard, the State may mark the boundaries of the area immediately adjacent to the area where the station is established on the Moon, within which other States

---

[104] https://www.unoosa.org/pdf/gares/ARES_34_68E.pdf p. 78.
[105] https://www.unoosa.org/pdf/gares/ARES_34_68E.pdf p. 78.
[106] https://www.unoosa.org/pdf/gares/ARES_34_68E.pdf p. 78.
[107] https://www.unoosa.org/pdf/gares/ARES_34_68E.pdf p. 78.
[108] https://www.unoosa.org/pdf/gares/ARES_34_68E.pdf p. 78.
[109] https://www.unoosa.org/pdf/gares/ARES_34_68E.pdf p. 79.
[110] https://www.unoosa.org/pdf/gares/ARES_34_68E.pdf p. 79.
[111] https://www.unoosa.org/pdf/gares/ARES_34_68E.pdf p. 79.

should not establish their space installations, so that it is not hindered or prevented from the activity already undertaken.

According to Article 10, State Parties need to take all possible measures to protect the lives and health of those on the Moon[112] is more detailed than in the Outer Space Treaty and add clarity to relevant concepts or the term 'astronaut' (Article 10 of the Moon Treaty uses the wording 'any person on the Moon'. This term under the Moon Agreement is also extended referring to the Rescue Agreement (which uses the term 'part of the personnel of a spacecraft'). People in distress should be protected by State Parties.[113]

When considering the Moon's natural resources, it is important to note that under Article 11, these constitute the common heritage of mankind.[114] The international regime is aimed at the orderly and safe exploitation of the Moon's natural resources, the rational management of these resources, and the equitable distribution among all State Parties to the benefits that these resources may offer, further, particular attention to the interests and needs of developing countries, as well as countries that have directly or indirectly contributed to the exploration of the Moon.[115] Similarly, the Moon must not be subject to appropriation by declaration of sovereignty, by exploitation or occupation, or by any other means.[116] Placing on the surface or beneath the surface of the Moon personnel or vehicles, equipment, devices, space stations, and installations, including structures associated with its surface or underground, will not create a property right with respect to the surface or underground of the Moon or any part thereof.[117] This is critical to the exploration of the Moon. If sovereign claims were to be recognised, then there is a strong argument that those States that could afford to reach the Moon could theoretically claim it. Such claims would likely cause an imbalance in global security, and so this provision becomes incredibly important from a global security and exploration perspective.

State Parties have the right to explore and use the Moon without any kind of discrimination of any kind, on the basis of equality, and in accordance with international law and the provisions of the Moon Treaty.[118] Accordingly, State Parties undertake to establish an international regime, including appropriate rules of conduct, to normalise the exploitation of the Moon's natural resources when such

[112] https://www.unoosa.org/pdf/gares/ARES_34_68E.pdf p. 79.

[113] https://www.unoosa.org/pdf/gares/ARES_34_68E.pdf p. 79.

[114] https://www.unoosa.org/pdf/gares/ARES_34_68E.pdf p. 79.

[115] Bini, A. (2008, October). The Moon Agreement: its effectiveness in the 21st Century. *ESPI Perspectives, 14*, 6.

[116] https://www.unoosa.org/pdf/gares/ARES_34_68E.pdf p. 79.

[117] Wasser, A., Jobes, D. (2008). Space settlements, property rights, and international law: Could a lunar settlement claim the lunar real estate it needs to survive? *Journal of Air Law and Commerce, 73*(1), 47–50, 59–61, 78.

[118] https://www.unoosa.org/pdf/gares/ARES_34_68E.pdf p. 79.

exploitation becomes possible.[119] In order to facilitate the international regime, State Parties are obligated to inform the UN Secretary-General as well as the international community, to the fullest and most practicable extent possible, of all natural resources they discover on the Moon.[120] The main objectives of the international regime concern the orderly and safe provision of the yield of the natural resources of the Moon, the rational management of these resources, development of the capacity to utilise these resources, and the equitable distribution among all State Parties of the benefits that these resources will bring, with particular attention to the interests and needs of developing states, as well as those states that directly or indirectly contributed to the exploration of the Moon.[121]

There is some contention with Article 11(7) (d) of the Moon Treaty, which provides for equal shares in the benefits of lunar exploitation. According to Article 12 (1), State Parties retain jurisdiction and control over their personnel, vehicles, equipment, facilities, stations, and installations on the Moon.[122] Therefore, those States bear international responsibility for their activities on the Moon, regardless of whether these activities are carried out by government institutions or non-governmental entities. Similarly, under Article 14(1), State Parties must further ensure that non-governmental entities under their jurisdiction undertake activities on the Moon only under the authority and permanent supervision of the relevant State Party.[123]

According to Article 15, Each State Party is also tasked with ascertaining whether the activities of other State Parties in the exploration and use of the Moon are in compliance with the provisions of the Moon Treaty. To this end, all vehicles, equipment, devices, stations, and space installations located on the Moon need to be accessible to other State Parties.[124] These States have an active obligation to notify, with reasonable notice in advance, the other States of any proposed visit in order to allow for appropriate consultations to be held and to take maximum precautions to ensure safety.[125]

In March 2008, several State Parties to the Moon Treaty (Austria, Belgium, the Philippines, the Netherlands, Chile, Mexico, and Pakistan) at the 47th session of COPUOS presented a 'joint statement on the benefits of joining an agreement' on the management of State activities on the Moon and other celestial bodies by State Parties to the agreement.[126] In their statement, the State Parties to the Moon Treaty

[119] https://www.unoosa.org/pdf/gares/ARES_34_68E.pdf p. 79.

[120] https://www.unoosa.org/pdf/gares/ARES_34_68E.pdf p. 79.

[121] https://www.unoosa.org/pdf/gares/ARES_34_68E.pdf p. 79.

[122] https://www.unoosa.org/pdf/gares/ARES_34_68E.pdf p. 79.

[123] https://www.unoosa.org/pdf/gares/ARES_34_68E.pdf p. 79.

[124] p. 79.

[125] https://www.unoosa.org/pdf/gares/ARES_34_68E.pdf p. 79

[126] A/AC.105/C.2/L.272 Joint statement on the benefits of adherence to the Agreement Governing the Activities of States on the Moon and Other Celestial Bodies by State Parties to the Agreement; https://digitallibrary.un.org/record/633417

presented the benefits of conducting broader activities in space.[127] The statement also asked whether the Moon Treaty is part of the UN's international space law and whether it has the same legal status as the other four space treaties, due to the very low ratification rate on the part of other States.[128] Clearly, a need exists to modernise the Moon Treaty.

This subject was discussed recently again due to the Artemis Accords[129] of 2020 and the new international mission to the Moon and Mars.[130] At the time of writing, the Artemis Accords had 24 State signatories. As an agreement between State's space agencies, the long-term potential benefits and challenges it presents for the future of space exploration are undetermined and will need to be considered on an ongoing basis.

Conclusions

The international space treaties (starting in 1967) regulate basic principles governing space, such as the prohibition of the appropriation of space, including the Moon and other celestial bodies, the recognition of outer space as the common heritage of humanity, the freedom of exploration and use of space, international responsibility of States for activities in outer space, or the supervision of States over these and similar activities. Space treaties were not ratified in large numbers. The largest number of States ratified the Outer Space Treaty (112 ratifications and 23 signatories).[131] Subsequent treaties obtained fewer and fewer ratifications and signatories: the Rescue Agreement gained 99 ratifications and 23 signatures; [132] the Liability Convention – 98 ratifications and 19 signatures; [133] while the Registration Convention received only 72 ratifications and 3 signatures.[134] The treaty-making process was interrupted in 1979 with the creation of the Moon Treaty, which received very little support (only 18 ratifications and 4 signatures).[135] Such a limited number of State Parties to the five space treaties prompts reflection and consideration of the best

[127] A/AC.105/C.2/L.272 Joint statement on the benefits of adherence to the Agreement Governing the Activities of States on the Moon and Other Celestial Bodies by State Parties to the Agreement; https://digitallibrary.un.org/record/633417, pp. 3–5.

[128] A/AC.105/C.2/L.272 Joint statement on the benefits of adherence to the Agreement Governing the Activities of States on the Moon and Other Celestial Bodies by State Parties to the Agreement; https://digitallibrary.un.org/record/633417, p. 5

[129] https://www.nasa.gov/specials/artemis-accords/img/Artemis-Accords-signed-13Oct2020.pdf

[130] Fino, I. (2021). Building a new legal model for settlement on Mars. In A. Froehlich (Ed.), *Assessing a Mars Agreement Including Human Settlements* (p. 75). Cham: Springer.

[131] https://www.unoosa.org/oosa/en/ourwork/spacelaw/treaties/status/index.html

[132] https://www.unoosa.org/oosa/en/ourwork/spacelaw/treaties/status/index.html

[133] https://www.unoosa.org/oosa/en/ourwork/spacelaw/treaties/status/index.html

[134] https://www.unoosa.org/oosa/en/ourwork/spacelaw/treaties/status/index.html

[135] https://www.unoosa.org/oosa/en/ourwork/spacelaw/treaties/status/index.html

way forward to modernise international space law especially when we consider the increase in space-based activities.

There is a need to revise the existing treaties so that they meet with greater State approval. In doing so, it is worth reflecting on the reasons why the space treaties have not met with wider acceptance. For example, many developing States do not have sufficient knowledge of new technologies in space and their possible benefits. Space-faring nations, on the other hand, are opposed to ratifying international treaties because it may be that they fear losing the economic benefits that they have already achieved. As indicated above, existing space conventions lack adequate provisions adapted to the current needs of space activities. This is due to the reluctance of more technologically advanced space-faring States, who have become accustomed to receiving the benefits derived from space activities. The way forward is problematic, either we do nothing and rely on natural mechanisms or take an active step towards the establishment of specific standards and an international regime, especially now with greater space activities underway.

Although the equality of States, regardless of status, is stated in the preamble to the UN Declaration of 1962[136] and the Outer Space Treaty speaks of the equal rights of States (regardless of their economic status), in practice there is no fair and proper international balance between developing and developed States. There is clearly a need to better inform and share knowledge with developing States about new technologies and services, in order to maintain this international balance.

Given the rapid development of space technologies and the incompatibility of the current international space law, it is possible to point to a list of issues relating to the possible revision and updating of existing international law. This is a task for COPUOS in cooperation with the International Civil Aviation Organization (ICAO) and the International Telecommunication Union (ITU).

Further complex problems that need to be regulated include the limits of State sovereignty, the role of the ITU in the allocation of radio spectrum and geostationary orbits, and the possibility of space exploration in the interest of all States (including developing ones). Regulation is required on issues related to the implementation of the CHM principle, relationship between the government and the private sector, commercialisation of activities in space, liability for pollution in space, insurance,[137] dispute resolution mechanism, registration of space objects, integration of national space law with international law, protection of intellectual property, arms control, protection of the space environment, creation of new international institutions (including a world space agency), terminology (terms such as 'space object',

[136] UN General Assembly. (1962). Declaration of Legal Principles Governing the Activities of States in the Exploration and Use of Outer Space. https://www.unoosa.org/pdf/gares/ARES_18_1962E.pdf

[137] Gaubert, C., Moysan, S. (2003). L'assurance spatiale. *Revue française de droit aérien et spatial, 3*, 249–263; Wells, C. (2005). Le contract d'assurance spatiale. In L. Ravillon (Ed.), Le droit des activités spatiales à l'aube du XXIe siècle: Actes du colloque des 10 et 11 Juin 2004, Dijon (p. 298). Paris: LexisNexis Litec.

'appropriate State', 'peaceful', 'benefits', 'launching authority', or 'outer space').[138]

The need to modernise existing space international law must be at the forefront of COPUOS attention. Since 1979, when the Moon Treaty was passed, no other space treaty has been agreed. It seems that 'hard law' based on the treaty and convention system has little chance of development. It is now clearly visible that the role played by 'soft law' and contractual agreements is growing such as the development and support of the Artemis Accords. It remains to be hoped that such mechanisms are enough to ensure security and equality in space (without exceptions) and sustainable access to it for all nations for peaceful purposes.[139] The lack of consistency within the existing regime of international space law not only provides economic incentives for space investors, but it also creates uncertainty as to property rights in relation to resources to be mined. On the other hand, a ban on appropriating outer space through sovereign claim is not recognised, and in this way, the international space law still has an important role to play.

There is growing importance on State national legislation implemented to regulate space activities in accordance with obligations under the international space law.[140] National law is generally easier to amend than international law.[141] However, the definitions and frameworks implemented by each State will lead to inconsistencies across States. International space law does not provide guidance on how States should implement their rules. In this way, it is vitally important that States establish a legal framework for space activities, including those carried out by private entities; national rules should contain standards for registration and licensing rules.[142]

It is important to note that national legislation can liberalise legislation to maximise the benefits of space exploration (including space mining),[143] especially when we consider the expansion of commercial activity in space, the need for robust national frameworks becomes self-evident.

---

[138] Grego, L. (2021). The Case for Space Arms Control. In M. de Zwart and S. Henderson (Eds), Commercial and Military Uses of Outer Space (p. 81). Singapore: Springer.

[139] Polkowska, M. (2019). Long Term Sustainability 9LTS) of Outer Space Activities vis a vis Space Awareness. *Teka Komisji Prawniczej PAN Oddział w Lublinie, 12*(2), 275–293.

[140] A. Froehlich, V. Seffinga, National Space legislation- a comparative and evaluative analysis, Springer 2018, p. 137.

[141] Hobe, S., Hettling, J. K. (2002). Challenges to space law in the 21st Century – Project 2001 plus, Proceeding of the forty fifth colloquium on the law of outer space, International Institute of Space Law of the International Astronautical Federation, 10–19 October 2002, Houston, Texas.

[142] von der Dunk, F. G. (2004). Implementing the United Nations Outer Space Treaties (pp. 139–144). Lincoln, Neb.: University of Nebraska; von der Dunk (2008) Implementing the United Nations outer space treaties: the case of the Netherlands [in:]Nationales Weltraumrecht - National space law: development in Europe, challenges for small countries / Brünner Ch.,Walter E. (ed.)

[143] Hobe, S. (2007). Adequacy of the current legal and regulatory framework relating to the extraction and appropriation of natural resources in outer space. *Annals of Air and Space Law, 32*, 115.

Bibliography

Articles, Monographies

Ailor, W. (2020). Evolution of space traffic and space traffic management. In K. U. Schrőgl (Ed.), *Handbook on space security*. Springer.

Baczynska-Wilkowska, M. (2018). Outer space treaty during fourth industrial revolution. In A. Froehlich (Ed.), *A fresh view on the outer space treaty* (p. 67). Springer.

Bini, A. (2008, October). The moon agreement: Its effectiveness in the 21st century. *ESPI Perspectives, 14*, 6.

Boothby, W. (2016). Control in weapons law. In R. Bartels et al. (Eds.), *Military operations and the notion of control under international law, Liber Amicorum Terry D. Gill* (p. 370). Springer.

Cheng, B. (1960, January). From air law to space law. *Current Legal Problems, 13*(1), 1.

Cheng, B. (1998). The 1967 outer space treaty: Thirtieth anniversary. *Annals of Space Law, 23*(4/5).

Fasan, E. (1987). Celestial bodies and the exploitative use of outer space. *Annals of Air and Space Law, 12*.

Fino, I. (2021). Building a new legal model for settlement on Mars. In A. Froehlich (Ed.), *Assessing a Mars agreement including human settlements* (p. 75). Springer.

Froehlich, A., & Seffinga, V. (2018). *National Space legislation- A comparative and evaluative analysis*. Springer.

Gaubert, C., & Moysan, S. (2003). L'assurance spatiale. *Revue française de droit aérien et spatial, 3*, 249–263.

Grego, L. (2021). The case for space arms control. In M. de Zwart & S. Henderson (Eds.), *Commercial and military uses of outer space* (p. 81). Springer.

Hobe, S. (2007). Adequacy of the current legal and regulatory framework relating to the extraction and appropriation of natural resources in outer space. *Annals of Air and Space Law, 32*, 115.

Hobe, S. (2019). *Space law* (p. 77). Beck.

Hobe, S., & Hettling, J. K. (2002). *Challenges to space law in the 21st Century – Project 2001 plus*. In: Proceeding of the forty fifth colloquium on the law of outer space, International Institute of Space Law of the International Astronautical Federation, 10–19 October 2002, Houston.

Jakhu, R. S. (2006). Legal issues relating to the global public interest in outer space. *Journal of Space Law, 32*(1).

Kłoda, M. T., Malinowska, K., Malinowski, B., & Polkowska, M. (2011). Polish space law – Challenges and trade-offs. *Przegląd Sejmowy, 3*(170).

Kopal, V. (1995). Progressive development of space law and concept of common heritage of mankind. In E. Pałyga (Ed.), *International space law: Miscellanea, liber amicorum honouring Andrzej Górbiel in his 65 anniversary* (pp. 107–113). Koszalin.

Maniatis, D. (1997). The law governing liability for damage caused by space objects: From state responsibility to private liability. *Annals of Air and Space Law, 22*(1), 369–401.

Masson-Zwaan, T., & Hofman, M. (2019). *Introduction to space law* (p. 26). Wolters Kluwer.

Oltrogge, D. L. (2018). *The "we" approach to space traffic management*. arc.aiaa.org. https://doi.org/10.2514/6.2018-2668

Polkowska, M. (2019). Long term sustainability 9LTS of outer space activities Vis a Vis space awareness. *Teka Komisji Prawniczej PAN Oddział w Lublinie, 12*(2).

Polkowska, M. (2021a). *Space security and safety: Law, management, policy* (p. 43). Instytut Wydawniczy EuroPrawo.

Polkowska, M. (2021b). Space traffic management (STM) – Legal aspects. In *Polish political science yearbook* (Vol. 50).

Polkowska, M. (2021c). *Eksploracja Kosmosu: Zagadnienia prawno-polityczneo* (pp. 139–141). Instytut Wydawniczy EuroPrawo.

Sgrosso, C. G. (1998). Legal status, rights and obligations of the crew in space. *Journal of Space Law, 26*(1–2).

Stubbe, P. (2010, March). Common but differentiated responsibilities for space debris – New impetus for a legal appraisal of outer space pollution. *ESPI Perspectives, 31*(2).

von der Dunk, F. G. (2004). *Implementing the United Nations outer space treaties* (pp. 139–144). University of Nebraska.

von der Dunk, F. G. (2008). Implementing the United Nations outer space treaties: The case of The Netherlands. In C. H. Brünner & E. Walter (Eds.), *Nationales Weltraumrecht – National space law: Development in Europe, challenges for small countries*.

Wasser, A., & Jobes, D. (2008). Space settlements, property rights, and international law: Could a lunar settlement claim the lunar real estate it needs to survive? *Journal of Air Law and Commerce, 73*(1).

Wells, C. (2005). Le contract d'assurance spatiale. In L. Ravillon (Ed.), *Le droit des activités spatiales à l'aube du XXIe siècle: Actes du colloque des 10 et 11 juin 2004, Dijon* (p. 298). LexisNexis Litec.

Zhao, Y. (2004). An international space authority: A governance model for a space commercialization regime. *Journal of Space Law, 30*(2), 280.

Documents

http://www.un-documents.net/a25r2625.htm
https://digitallibrary.un.org/record/633417
https://www.congress.gov/bill/114th-congress/house-bill/2262
https://www.iadc-home.org/
https://www.mcgill.ca/iasl/files/iasl/montreal1978.pdf
https://www.mcgill.ca/iasl/files/iasl/rome1952.pdf
https://www.mcgill.ca/iasl/files/iasl/warsaw1929.pdf
https://www.nasa.gov/
https://www.nasa.gov/specials/artemis-accords/img/Artemis-Accords-signed-13Oct2020.pdf
https://www.outerspaceinstitute.ca/docs/Open_Letter_to_Cdn_FM_reUS_EO_on_SpaceMining.pdf
https://www.un.org/en/about-us/un-charter
https://www.unidroit.org/
https://www.unidroit.org/instruments/security-interests/cape-town-convention/
https://www.unidroit.org/instruments/security-interests/space-protocol/
https://www.unoosa.org/oosa/en/ourwork/copuos/members/evolution.html
https://www.unoosa.org/oosa/en/ourwork/spacelaw/treaties/introouterspacetreaty.html
https://www.unoosa.org/oosa/en/ourwork/spacelaw/treaties/status/index.html
https://www.unoosa.org/pdf/gares/ARES_18_1962E.pdf
https://www.unoosa.org/pdf/gares/ARES_21_2222E.pdf
https://www.unoosa.org/pdf/gares/ARES_22_2345E.pdf
https://www.unoosa.org/pdf/gares/ARES_26_2777E.pdf
https://www.unoosa.org/pdf/gares/ARES_29_3235E.pdf
https://www.unoosa.org/pdf/gares/ARES_34_68E.pdf
https://www.unoosa.org/pdf/publications/STSPACE11E.pdf
https://www.unoosa.org/res/oosadoc/data/documents/2019/a/a7420_0_html/V1906077.pdf.

Chapter 3
Emergency Assistance and Rescue Obligations for Commercial and Private Spacefarers in the Context of the History, Present, and Future of Human Spaceflight

Ricky J. Lee

Introduction

The twentieth century saw significant advances in aerospace technology on 17 December 1903, the first powered flight of the *Kitty Hawk* by the Wright Brothers[1]; on 25 August 1919, the first regular scheduled international passenger air service, which was from London to Paris[2]; on 30 April 1940, the first regular trans-Tasman air service between Auckland and Sydney[3]; on 12 April 1961, the first launch of a person into outer space with Yuri Gagarin[4]; on 20 July 1969, the first footsteps on the Moon left by the Apollo 11 mission[5]; on 12 April 1981, the first of

[1] Combs, Harry. (1979). *Kill Devil Hill: Discovering The Secret of the Wright Brothers*. Englewood, Co.: TernStyle Press; Howard, Fred. (1988). *Orville and Wilbur: The Story of the Wright Brothers*. London: Hale; Culick, Fred E. C. (2001). Wright Brothers: First Aeronautical Engineers and Test Pilots. *AIAA Journal, 41*(6), 4.

[2] Street, Francesca. (2019, August 26). 100 years ago: The first scheduled international passenger flight departed. CNN. edition.cnn.com/travel/article/first-scheduled-international-passenger-flight/index.html

[3] Anon. (1940, April 30). First Flight: Tasman Service. *Auckland Star*, 9; Barton, Gerry, and Heath, Philip. (2015). *Coral Route: Tasman Empire Airways Ltd., Flying Boats, and the South Pacific*. Wellington: Steele Roberts.

[4] Walker, Stephen. (2021). *Beyond: The Astonishing Story of the First Human to Leave Our Planet and Journey into Space*. London: William Collins; Cole, Michael D. (1995). *Vostok 1: First Human in Space*. Springfield, N.J.: Enslow.

[5] Collins, Michael, and Aldrin, Edwin E. (1975). The Eagle Has Landed. In Edgar M. Cortright (Ed.), *Apollo Expeditions to the Moon* (pp. 203–224). Washington, D.C.: National Aeronautics and Space Administration; Chaikin, Andrew. (1994). *A Man on the Moon: The Triumphant Story of the Apollo Space Program*. New York: Penguin; Slayton, Donald K., and Cassult, Michael. (1994).

R. J. Lee (✉)
Jesus College, Cambridge, UK
e-mail: rl687@cam.ac.uk

M. A. Pozza (ed.), *Ascending to Space*, Space Law and Policy,
https://doi.org/10.1007/978-981-97-0714-0_3

the regular service of the US space shuttle fleet with the launch of *Columbia*[6]; and on 20 November 1998, the start of the construction of the International Space Station (ISS) with the launch of the *Zarya* control module.[7] By the end of 2022, over 600 people have crossed the 'Final Frontier' into outer space, and the vast majority of these 'spacefarers' are professionals trained and employed by their respective government space agencies to be spacefarers. However, the twenty-first century saw the dawn of private space tourism that began with the launch of Dennis Tito to the ISS on 28 April 2001 and culminated in the so-called 'billionaire space race' in July 2021, as commercial ventures raced to conduct regular space flights for 'amateur' private spacefarers and paying commercial passengers.[8]

On the other hand, the history and evolution of human space flight in the last six decades or so, though undeniably and groundbreakingly spectacular, have not been entirely without pain and loss. The Union of Soviet Socialist Republics (the 'Soviet Union' or 'USSR') suffered a number of accidents that led to loss of life, though these were not known publicly at the time[9]; the United States also had its share of human space disasters from the fire on board Apollo 1 on 27 January 1967[10] to the loss of the space shuttles *Challenger* on 28 January 1986 and *Columbia* on 1 February 2003 with all souls on board.[11] Unfortunately, the private sector is not

---

Deke! U.S. Manned Space: From Mercury to the Shuttle. New York: Forge; Harland, David. (1999). *Exploring the Moon: The Apollo Expeditions*. London: Springer.

[6] Sivolella, David. (2017). *The Space Shuttle Program: Technologies and Accomplishments*. New York: Springer–Praxis; Jenkins, Dennis R. (2016). *Space Shuttle: Developing an Icon—1972–2013*. Forest Lake, Minn.: Specialty Press; Slayton and Cassult, *Deke!*; see also Hendrickx, Bart, and Vis, Bert. (2007). *Energiya-Buran: The Soviet Space Shuttle*. New York: Springer–Praxis.

[7] Catchpole, John E. (2008). *The International Space Station: Building for the Future*. New York: Springer–Praxis; DeLucas, Lawrence J. (1996). International Space Station. *Acta Astronomica, 38*, 613; Cook, John. (2016). Challenges of Building the International Space Station. Paper presented at the AIAA Space Forum, 13–16 September 2016, in Long Beach, California, United States.

[8] Van Pelt, Michael. (2010). *Space Tourism: Adventures in Earth Orbit and Beyond*. New York: Copernicus; Fernholz, Tim. (2018). *Rocket Billionaires: Elon Musk, Jeff Bezos, and the New Space Race*. Boston, Mass.: Houghton Mifflin Harcourt; Davenport, Christian. (2018). *The Space Barons: Elon Musk, Jeff Bezos, and the Quest to Colonize the Cosmos*. New York: Public Affairs; Williams, Ollie A. (2021, December 21). Billionaire Space Race Turns into A Publicity Disaster. *Forbes*. www.forbes.com/sites/oliverwilliams1/2021/12/21/billionaire-space-race-turns-into-a-publicity-disaster

[9] Shayler, David. (2000). *Disasters and Accidents in Manned Spaceflight*. New York: Springer–Praxis; Siddiqi, Asif A. (2000). *Challenge to Apollo: The Soviet Union and the Space Race, 1945–1974*. Washington, D.C.: US Government Printing Office.

[10] Bergaust, Erik. (1968). *Murder on Pad 34*. New York: G. P. Putnam & Sons; Leopold, George. (2016). *Calculated Risk: The Supersonic Life and Times of Gus Grissom*. West Lafayette, Ind.: Purdue University Press.

[11] On the *Challenger* disaster, see Rogers, William P., et al. (1986). *Report of the Presidential Commission on the Space Shuttle Challenger Accident.* Washington, D.C.: National Aeronautics and Space Administration; McDonald, Allan J., and Hansen, James R. (2018). *Truth, Lies, and O-Rings: Inside the Space Shuttle Challenger Disaster*. Gainesville, Fla.: University Press of Florida; Boisjoly, Russell P., Curtis, Ellen Foster, and Mellican, Eugene. (1989). Roger Boisjoly and the Challenger Disaster: The Ethical Dimensions. *Journal of Business Ethics, 8*, 217; Vaughan,

immune from these tragedies, as an accident involving a test flight of Virgin Galactic's V.S.S. *Enterprise* on 31 October 2014 also led to loss of life.[12]

With continuing and new efforts by several countries towards establishing semi-permanent to permanent human facilities in orbit around the Earth, the surface of the Moon, and beyond, along with private ventures launching private and commercial spacefarers into outer space, this is perhaps the most appropriate time to consider the international legal obligations for emergency assistance and rescue in human space flight. For this purpose, one ought to review the history and the present state of human space flight, consider the terms used to describe or classify spacefarers, and analyse what implications, if any, they have on the applicable international legal obligations for emergency assistance and rescue of spacefarers in distress.

History of Human Space Flight

Governmental Programmes

Only the USSR (with the Russian Federation as its principal successor), the United States, and the People's Republic of China have launched their own nationals into space.[13] The USSR led the way on 12 April 1961 with the launch of the cosmonaut Yuri Gagarin into space on board Vostok 1.[14] This was followed soon after by the United States with the launch by its National Aeronautics and Space Administration (NASA) of the astronaut Alan B. Shepard, Jr. on board Freedom 7 on 5 May 1961.[15] Over four decades later, on 15 October 2003, China became only the third country to

---

Diane. (2016). *The Challenger Launch Decision: Risky Technology, Culture, and Deviance and N.A.S.A.* Chicago: University of Chicago Press. On the *Columbia* disaster, see Gehman, Harold, et al. (2003). *Report of Columbia Accident Investigation Board.* Washington, D.C.: National Aeronautics and Space Administration; Leinbach, Michael D., and Ward, Jonathan H. (2018). *Bringing Columbia Home: The Untold Story of a Lost Space Shuttle and Her Crew.* New York: Arcade Publishing; Stepaniak, Philip C., Lane, Helen W., and Davis, Jeffrey R. (2014). *Loss of Signal: Aeromedical Lessons Learned from STS-107 Columbia Space Shuttle Mishap.* Washington, D.C.: National Aeronautics and Space Administration.

[12] Chang, Kenneth, and Schwartz, John. (2014, November 1). Rocket Plane for Space Tourists Crashes in Desert, Killing a Pilot. *New York Times*, A1.

[13] As of 31 December 2022.

[14] Jenks, Andrew. (2012). Conquering Space: The Cult of Yuri Gagarin. In Mark Bassin and Catriona Kelly (Eds.), *Soviet and Post-Soviet Identities* (pp. 129–150). Cambridge: Cambridge University Press; Hall, Rex, and Shayler, David. (2001). *The Rocket Man: Vostok & Voskhod—The First Soviet Manned Spaceflights.* (Chichester: Praxis; Bizony, Piers. (2011). *Starman: The Truth Behind the Legend of Yuri Gagarin.* London: Bloomsbury; and Walker, *Beyond.*

[15] Hammack, Jerome B. (Ed.). (1961). *Postlaunch Report for Mercury-Redstone 3 (MR-3).* Washington, D.C.: National Aeronautics and Space Administration; Catchpole, John E. (2001). *Project Mercury: NASA's First Manned Space Programme.* New York: Springer–Praxis. Shepard was later promoted to rear admiral before his retirement in 1974.

send humans into space using its own spacecraft,[16] when the Chinese National Space Administration (CNSA) launched Shenzhou-5 with the taikonaut Yang Liwei on board.[17] Among the remaining spacefaring states, only India has declared an intention and initiated a programme to launch spacefarers into outer space using its own spacecraft.[18]

Of the 628 spacefarers who have ventured into outer space as of 1 December 2022:

- Four hundred ninety-two were professional spacefarers trained and employed by a country's government space agency and launched into space in the course of its space programmes.
- Fifty-one were professional spacefarers launched by, trained, and employed by a country's government space agency and launched into space by another country's government space agency as part of their joint space programmes, comprising:
  - Nine astronauts from the Canadian Space Agency (CSA)
  - Fifteen astronauts from the Japan Aerospace Exploration Agency (JAXA) and its predecessor agencies, including the National Space Development Agency of Japan (NASDA)
  - Three cosmonauts from the Kazakhstan National Space Agency (KazCosmos)
  - Twenty-four astronauts of the European Space Agency (ESA)
- Twenty were amateur spacefarers launched by a government space agency as part of one of its space programmes on what was intended to be their only space flight; 15 were amateurs launched by the Russian Federation's Roscosmos on a fee-paying basis.
- Fifty-one were launched by a commercial venture on a private mission, including one who was a professional astronaut.

While the status of the spacefarers in the first two categories is well known, it is those of the latter three categories that merit some further discussion.

---

[16] Mathieu, Charlotte. (2008). *Assessing Russia's Space Cooperation with China and India*. Vienna: European Space Policy Institute; Lukin, Artyom. (2021). The Russia-China Entente and its Future. *International Politics, 58*, 363; Schwartz, Paul N. (2021, June 21). The Changing Nature and Implications of Russian Military Transfers to China. Center for Strategic & International Studies. www.csis.org/analysis/changing-nature-and-implications-russian-military-transfers-china

[17] Translations by the author. See Goswami, Namata. (2018). China in Space: Ambitions and Possible Conflict. Strategic Studies Quarterly, 12, 74; Johnson-Freese, Joan. (2003). China's Manned Space Program: Sun Tzu or Apollo Redux? *Naval War College Review, 56*, 51; Uhalley, Stephen. (2016). China's 'Jade Rabbit' Rover on the Moon: A Wake-up Call: Chang'e 3 and Yutu on the Lunar Surface. *American Journal of Chinese Studies, 23*, 211; Yardley, Jim. (2003, October 15). China Sends a Man into Orbit, entering the U.S.–Russian Club. *New York Times*, A1.

[18] Rao, Mukund Kadursrinivas, Sridhara Murthi, K. R., and Prasad, M. Y. S. (2017). The Decision for Indian Human Spaceflight Programme—Political Perspectives, National Relevance, and Technological Challenges. Paper presented at the 68th International Astronautical Congress, 25–29 September 2017, in Adelaide, South Australia.

Amateur Spacefarers Launched into Space in the Course of a Government Space Programme

The Interkosmos Programme

In April 1967, the USSR introduced the Interkosmos (Интеркосмос) programme, which was to assist countries aligned with it to participate in human space flight missions. These countries were primarily those of the Warsaw Pact,[19] the Council for Mutual Economic Assistance (Comecon or CMEA),[20] others of the Second World or the Eastern Bloc,[21] and the (so-called) non-aligned countries that were friendly with the USSR at the time.[22] The first Interkosmos mission was Soyuz-28

[19]The Warsaw Pact, formally the Warsaw Treaty of Friendship, Cooperation, and Mutual Assistance, was created on 14 May 1955 and served as the European counterweight to the North Atlantic Treaty Organisation (NATO) until it was disbanded on 1 July 1991. Its member countries included Albania (until 1968), Bulgaria, Czechoslovakia, East Germany (until 1990), Hungary, Poland, Romania, and the USSR: see Warsaw Treaty of Friendship, Cooperation, and Mutual Assistance, opened for signature on 14 May 1955, 219 U.N.T.S. 3 (entered into force on 6 June 1955); Faringdon, Hugh. (1986). *Confrontation: The Strategic Geography of NATO and the Warsaw Pact*. London: Routledge; Umbach, Frank. (2005). *Das rote Bündnis: Entwicklung und Zerfall des Warschauer Paktes 1955 bis 1991*. Berlin: Christoph Links; Kramer, Mark N. (1985). Civil–Military Relations in the Warsaw Pact: The East European Component. *International Affairs, 61*, 45.

[20]The COMECON or CMEA was founded in 1949 as the socialist counterweight to the Marshall Plan and what later became the Organisation for Economic Cooperation and Development (OECD) and included Bulgaria, Cuba, Czechoslovakia, East Germany, Hungary, Mongolia, Poland, Romania, the USSR, and Vietnam: see Kaser, Michael. (1967). *Comecon: Integration Problems of the Planned Economies*. Oxford: Oxford University Press; Libbey, James. (2010). CoCom, Comecon, and the Economic Cold War. *Russian History, 37*, 133; Crump, Laurien, and Godard, Simon. (2018). Reassessing Communist International Organisations: A Comparative Analysis of COMECON and the Warsaw Pact in Relation to their Cold War Competitors. *Contemporary European History, 27*, 85; Lányl, Kamilla. (1993). The Collapse of the COMECON Market. *Russian & East European Finance and Trade, 29*, 68.

[21]Such as the Democratic Republic of Afghanistan (1978–92) and the Democratic People's Republic of Korea, among others: see Braithwaite, Rodric. (2011). *Afgantsy: The Russians in Afghanistan, 1979–1989*. Oxford: Oxford University Press; Szalontai, Balázs. (2005). *Kim Il Sung in the Khrushchev Era: Soviet–DPRK Relations and the Roots of North Korean Despotism, 1953–1964*. Stanford, Cal.: Stanford University Press; and generally Pearson, Raymond. (1998). *The Rise and Fall of the Soviet Empire*. London: Macmillan. It is important to note that, by this time, relations between China and the USSR had deteriorated to the extent that several skirmishes were fought in 1969 along their disputed borders: see Robinson, Thomas W. (1972). The Sino-Soviet Border Dispute: Background, Development, and the March 1969 Clashes. *American Political Science Review, 66*, 1175; Lüthi, Lorenz. (2012). Restoring Chaos to History: Sino-Soviet-American Relations, 1969. *The China Quarterly, 210*, 378; Yang, Kuisong. (2000). The Sino-Soviet Border Clash of 1969: From Zhenbao Island to Sino-American Rapprochement. *Cold War History, 1*, 21.

[22]Such as India and Syria: see Vojtech, Mastny. (2010). The Soviet Union's Partnership with India. *Cold War Studies, 12*, 50; Donaldson, Robert H. (1972). India: The Soviet Stake in Stability. *Asian Survey*, 12, 475; Gupta, Sisir. (1963). India and the Soviet Union. *Current History*, 44, 141; Ginat,

on 2 March 1978 that launched Vladimír Remek of Czechoslovakia (now Czechia and Slovakia) to the Salyut 6 space station, which made him the first spacefarer to go into outer space who was from neither the United States nor the USSR.[23] The fact that the mission's launch coincided with the 30th anniversary of the 1948 communist coup d'état in Czechoslovakia and that Remek was the son of a Czech mother and Slovak father maximised the propaganda value of the mission for both the USSR and the Communist regime in Czechoslovakia.[24] Between 1978 and 1988, cosmonauts from Afghanistan, Bulgaria, Cuba, East Germany,[25] Hungary, Mongolia, Poland, Romania, and Vietnam were launched into outer space under the Interkosmos programme.

In April 1979, during a brief period of détente in the Space Race that coincided with the Apollo–Soyuz Test Project (the first international space mission in history),[26] the USSR made an offer to France to send a French cosmonaut into space under the Interkosmos programme.[27] On 24 June 1982, Jean-Loup Chrétien, selected as the first French cosmonaut and '*spationaute*', was launched on the Soyuz T-6 mission to the Salyut 7 space station.[28] On 26 November 1988, he was launched for a second mission on board Soyuz TM-7 to visit the Mir space station, during which he made France the third country to have one of its nationals undertake a spacewalk.[29] Later, Chrétien was also selected as part of the NASA Astronaut Group 15 and flew on board the space shuttle on the STS-86 mission to revisit Mir on 25 September 1997, thus becoming the first and to date only person to be a cosmonaut, a *spationaute*, and an astronaut.[30] The USSR entered into similar arrangements under the Interkosmos programme with India for Rakesh Sharma and with Syria for Muhammed Ahmed Faris to be the first nationals of their respective countries to be launched into outer space.[31]

Rami. (2000). The Soviet Union and the Syrian Ba'th Regime: From Hesitation to Rapprochement. *Middle Eastern Studies, 36*, 150; Karsh, Efraim. (1991). *Soviet Policy towards Syria since 1970*. London: Palgrave Macmillan; Ramet, Pedro. (1986). The Soviet-Syrian Relationship. *Problems of Communism, 35*(5).

[23] Burgess, Colin, and Vis, Bert, (2015). *Interkosmos—The Eastern Bloc's Early Space Program*. New York: Springer–Praxis; Evans, Ben. *At Home in Space: The Late Seventies into the Eighties*. New York: Springer–Praxis.

[24] Evans, *At Home in Space*.

[25] The former Deutsche Demokratische Republik or German Democratic Republic (1949–90).

[26] Ezell, Edward C., and Ezell, Linda N. (1978). *The Partnership: A History of the Apollo-Soyuz Test Project*. Washington, D.C.: National Aeronautics and Space Administration; Slayton and Cassult, *Deke!*, 278–279; Battaglia, Debbora. (2012). Arresting Hospitality: The Case of the 'Handshake in Space'. *Journal of the Royal Anthropological Institute, 18*, S76.

[27] Sheehan, Michael. (2007). *The International Politics of Space* (pp. 59–61). London: Routledge.

[28] Chrétien, Jean-Loup, Baudry, Patrick, and Chabbert, Bernard. (1982). *Spatiale premier: The First French in Space*. Paris: Plon; Chrétien, Jean-Loup. (1993). *Sonata au clair de terre: Itinerary of a Frenchman in Space*. Paris: Denoël.

[29] Chrétien, *Sonata au clair de terre*.

[30] US National Aeronautics and Space Administration, S.T.S.-86. www.nasa.gov/mission_pages/shuttle/shuttlemissions/archives/sts-86.html

[31] Burgess and Vis, *Interkosmos*.

Space Flight Participants on US Shuttle Missions

As the US space shuttle fleet gained experience and some maturity through the early 1980s, NASA began to consider flying 'citizen passengers' into outer space. The Republican Senator Edwin Jacob 'Jake' Garn of Utah, who was then chair of the Senate Appropriations Committee that had oversight of the NASA budget, began to campaign publicly for a shuttle flight, and he was eventually flown on 12 April 1985 on board the space shuttle *Discovery* on the STS-51-D mission, ostensibly as a congressional observer and to study motion sickness.[32] Rather coincidentally, his space sickness was so extreme that the 'Garn scale' is now used to measure degrees of space sickness, with 1.0 being what Senator Garn suffered himself.[33] Garn was followed into space soon after by the Democratic Congressman Clarence William 'Bill' Nelson II of Florida, who was a payload specialist on board *Columbia* on the STS-61-C mission that was launched on 12 January 1986, the last shuttle launch before the *Challenger* disaster.[34]

On 27 August 1984, President Ronald Reagan announced the 'Teacher in Space Project' that would launch teachers into outer space on board the space shuttle, and S. Christa McAuliffe was selected, along with Barbara R. Morgan as her backup.[35] After McAuliffe perished along with the other members of the STS-51-L mission crew on board *Challenger* on 28 January 1986, when the orbiter exploded after lift-off, NASA cancelled the programme and from then launched only career professional astronauts into space.[36] Morgan retrained as a professional astronaut and on 8 August 2007 was launched into space on the STS-118 mission on board *Endeavour*,[37] having been on board a chase plane that followed *Columbia* on 1 February 2003 during its disintegration on re-entry.[38]

[32] Boffey, Philip M. (1984, November 9). A Space Inspection. *New York Times*, A29; Lamar, Jacob V., and Hannifan, Jerry. (1985, April 22). Jake Skywalker: A Senator boards the shuttle. *Time*.

[33] Thornton, William, and Bonato, Frederick. (2017). *The Human Body and Weightlessness* (p. 32). The Hague: Springer; Lyons, Richard D. (1985, May 5). One Thing NASA Can't Settle: Astronauts' Stomachs. *New York Times*, 4–26

[34] Nelson, Bill, and Buckingham, Jamie. (1988). *Mission: An American Congressman's Voyage to Space*. San Diego, Cal.: Harcourt Brace Jovanovich. Nelson later became a US Senator and became the fourteenth Administrator of NASA on 3 May 2021.

[35] Hohler, Robert T. (1986). *I Touch the Future: The Story of Christa McAuliffe*. New York: Random House.

[36] Rogers, *Report of the Presidential Commission on the Space Shuttle Challenger Accident*; McDonald and Hansen, *Truth, Lies, and O-Rings*.

[37] Dunn, Marcia. (2007, August 8). Shuttle Endeavour puts teacher in orbit. NBC News. www.nbcnews.com/id/wbna20178250

[38] Woodward, Tim. (2003, February 2). Disaster halts teacher's chance to fly—again. *Florida Today*, 10A.

Space Tourists and Commercial Missions by Roscosmos

In 1991, the Soviet Union collapsed and broke up, and its successor countries,[39] most notably the Russian Federation, had to make a difficult transition to a market economy with all sectors of their economies searching for revenue sources, especially those in Western currencies.[40] In response, Roscosmos sought to trade the one, and unique, service it could offer to the world—specifically, joyrides to the Mir space station and later to the ISS on board its Soyuz spacecraft—and space tourism was born.[41] No space tourist ever visited Mir as it was de-orbited on 23 March 2001, but not before the privately funded Soyuz TM-30 mission was launched on 4 April 2000 in an attempt to stabilise and repair it for future use as a commercially operated private space station, an effort that was ultimately unsuccessful.[42]

Dennis Tito, an American engineer and entrepreneur, became the first space tourist in history when he was taken to the ISS on board Soyuz TM-32 in April 2001, a privilege for which he paid a reported US$20 million.[43] Between 2001 and 2009, Roscosmos transported ten fare-paying spacefarers to the ISS, most of whom were private space tourists paying for their journey into outer space, while the

[39] The dissolution of the Soviet Union began with the secession of the Baltic states of Estonia, Latvia, and Lithuania in August 1990, followed by Armenia, Azerbaijan, Belarus, Georgia, Kazakhstan, Kyrgyzstan, Moldova, the Russian Federation, Tajikistan, Turkmenistan, Ukraine, and Uzbekistan: see Crawshaw, Steve. (1992). *Goodbye to the USSR: The Collapse of Soviet Power*. London: Bloomsbury; Beissinger, Mark R. (2009). Nationalism and the Collapse of Soviet Communism. *Contemporary European History, 18*, 331; Miller, Chris. (2016). *The Struggle to Save the Soviet Economy: Mikhail Gorbachev and the Collapse of the USSR*. Chapel Hill, N.C.: University of North Carolina Press.

[40] Islam, Shafiqul. (1993). Russia's Rough Road to Capitalism. *Foreign Affairs, 72*(2), 57; Brainerd, Elizabeth. (1998). Winners and Losers in Russia's Economic Transition. *American Economic Review, 88*, 1094; Power, Jeffrey K. (2011). *Power, Culture, and Economic Change in Russia: To the Undiscovered Country of Post-Socialism, 1988–2008*. London: Taylor & Francis; Stern, Nicholas. (1997). The Transition in Eastern Europe and the Former Soviet Union: Some Strategic Lessons from the Experience of 25 Countries over Six Years. In Salvatore Zecchini (Ed.), *Lessons from the Economic Transition: Central and Eastern Europe in the 1990s* (pp. 35–57). Dordrecht: Springer.

[41] Chang, Yi-Wei. (2015). The First Decade of Space Tourism. *Acta Astronomica, 108*, 79; Schwartz, John. (2008, October 10). Russia Leads Way in Space Tourism with Paid Trips into Orbit. *New York Times*; Taylor, Adam. (2021, July 20). How the collapse of the Soviet Union aided the birth of space tourism. *Washington Post*; Autio-Sarasmo, Sari. (2016). Technological Modernisation in the Soviet Union and Post-Soviet Russia: Practices and Continuities. *Europe–Asian Studies, 68*, 79. See also Minter, Adam. (2022, March 29). Russia Just Became the World's First Former Space Power. *Washington Post*.

[42] Harland, David. (2004). *The Story of Space Station* Mir. New York: Springer; Tyler, Patrick E. (2001, March 24). Russians Find Pride, and Regret, in Mir's Splashdown. *New York Times*, A-3; CNN. (2000, June 16). Future of Mir in doubt after cosmonauts return home. www.cnn.com/2000/TECH/space/06/16/mir.folo/index.html

[43] Wall, Mike. (2011, April 27). Wall, First Space Tourist: How a U.S. Millionaire Bought a Ticket to Orbit.', www.space.com/11492-space-tourism-pioneer-dennis-tito.html. The amount is equivalent to US$33.6 million in 2022 values.

remainder were launched into space under arrangements between their respective governments and Roscosmos. The latter category notably included Marcos Pontes of Brazil, who was trained at NASA as a mission specialist to fly to the ISS on board the space shuttle but switched to the Russian option when the Brazilian Government reached an agreement with Roscosmos after its discussions with NASA over the costs involved fell through.[44] Similarly, Yi So-yeon, Sheikh Muszaphar Shukor, and Hazza Al Mansouri were launched into outer space following bilateral agreements between Roscosmos and the Korean Astronaut Program of the Republic of Korea, the Malaysian National Space Agency (ANGKASA),[45] and the Mohammed bin Rashid Space Centre of the United Arab Emirates, respectively.[46]

Further, there are also those who flew on board the Soyuz to the ISS as 'corporate space tourists', in that their space flights were the result of work commitments under the auspices of a commercial arrangement between their employers and Roscosmos. This is distinct from the payload specialists employed by aerospace contractors and launched into space by NASA, in that these corporate space tourists do not perform any duties or functions related to the space programmes of NASA or their own governments.[47] On 2 December 1990, the Japanese journalist Akiyama Toyohiro was launched into space as part of the 40th-anniversary celebrations of the Tokyo Broadcasting System.[48] In October 2021, the Russian film director Klim Shipenko and actress Yulia Peresild spent 12 days on board the ISS filming scenes for a feature-length drama[49] while the Japanese online retail billionaire Yusaku Maezawa

[44]Rohter, Larry. (2006, April 8). Brazil's Man in Space: A Mere 'Hitchhiker' or a 'Hero'? *New York Times*, A-3; Young, Kelly. (2006, January 13). Brazilian astronaut to visit the space station. *New Scientist*. www.newscientist.com/article/dn8578-brazilian-astronaut-to-visit-the-space-station

[45]Since 2019, the Malaysian Space Agency (MYSA) following the merger of ANGKASA with the Malaysian Remote Sensing Agency.

[46]British Broadcasting Corporation. (2008, April 8). First S. Korean astronaut launches. News.bbc.co.uk/2/hi/asia-pacific/7335874.stm; Hammond, Andrew. (2007, October 1). Saudi prince says Islam proud of Malaysian spaceman. Reuters. www.reuters.com/article/reutersEdge/idUSL3034275220070930; Al Shurafa, Sara. (2019, September 26). UAE in space: What did Hazza Al Mansoori carry with him to space? *Gulf News*. gulfnews.com/uae/science/uae-in-space-what-did-hazzaa-almansoori-carry-with-him-to-space-1.1569476103518

[47]This includes Charles D. Walker who flew on STS-41-D, STS-51-D and STS-61-B for the McDonnell Aircraft Corporation; Robert J. Cenker who flew on STS-61-C for the RCA Corporation's Astro-Electronics Division (now part of Lockheed Martin); and Gregory B. Jarvis of the Hughes Aircraft Company who perished on board *Challenger* on STS-51-L.

[48]Otake, Tomoko. (2013, August 3). Toyohiro Akiyama: Cautionary tales from one not afraid to risk all. *Japan Times*. www.japantimes.co.jp/life/2013/08/03/people/toyohiro-akiyama-cautionary-tales-from-one-not-afraid-to-risk-all; Sanger, David E. (1990, December 8). A Japanese Innovation: The Space Antihero. *New York Times*, 1–1.

[49]Roulette, Joey. (2021, October 18). Russian Film Crew Wraps Shoot at Space Station and Returns to Earth. *New York Times*, A-10; Associated Press. (2021, October 17). In historic first, Russian film crew lands after shoot aboard ISS. NBC News. www.nbcnews.com/news/world/historic-first-russian-film-crew-lands-shoot-iss-rcna3148

brought along his assistant and videographer, Yozo Hirano, on his 12-day trip to the ISS in December 2021.[50]

Human Space Flight by Private Ventures

The Ansari X Prize

The X Prize, later called the Ansari X Prize, was established by Peter Diamandis in 1994 with a view to promoting the development by the private sector of a reusable crewed spacecraft, which followed the decision of NASA to carry only career professional astronauts on the space shuttle fleet after the *Challenger* disaster.[51] The prize, worth US$10 million, was to be awarded to the first privately built reusable spacecraft to carry a person into space and to do so again within 2 weeks.[52] More than a dozen entrants competed for the prize, which was ultimately won by Burt Rutan's Scaled Composites when its spacecraft, *SpaceShipOne*, launched into suborbital space on 29 September 2004 with Mike Melvill on board, followed less than a week later on 4 October 2004 with Brian Binnie in the pilot's seat.[53]

The success of *SpaceShipOne* led to the formation of The Spaceship Company in 2005, a joint venture between Scaled Composites and Virgin Galactic, which became the constructor of *SpaceShipTwo*, the suborbital passenger spacecraft designed and built for Virgin Galactic.[54] On 5 October 2012, The Spaceship Company became wholly owned by Virgin Galactic after it purchased Scaled Composites's 30 per cent shareholding following Northrop Grumman Corporation's

---

[50] Roulette, Joey. (2021, December 9). Japanese Mogul Reaches Space Station as Tourist. *New York Times*, A-10; Lies, Elaine. (2022, December 16). Going to space makes you 'obsessed with Earth', billionaire Yusaku Maezawa says. *Japan Times*. www.japantimes.co.jp/news/2022/01/07/national/yusaku-maezawa-spacex

[51] Dubbs, Chris, and Paat-Dahlstrom, Emeline. (2011). *Realising Tomorrow: The Path to Private Spaceflight* (pp. 167–191). Lincoln, Nebr.: University of Nebraska Press; Belfiore, Michael. (2007). *Rocketeers: How a Visionary Band of Business Leaders, Engineers, and Pilots Is Boldly Privatising Space*. New York: Smithsonian Books.

[52] Park, Ian. (2004, October 4). The X Prize. *New Yorker*, 52–63.

[53] Boyle, Alan. (2004, October, 3). SpaceShipOne wins $10 million X Prize. NBC News. www.nbcnews.com/id/wbna6167761; David, Leonard. (2004, October 4). SpaceShipOne Wins $10 Million Ansari X Prize in Historic 2nd Trip to Space. www.space.com/403-spaceshipone-wins-10-million-ansari-prize-historic-2nd-trip-space.html

[54] David, Leonard. (2005, July 27). Richard Branson and Burt Rutan Form Spacecraft Building Company. www.space.com/1356-richard-branson-burt-rutan-form-spacecraft-building-company.html; Hennigan, W. J. (2010, November 8). Spacecraft factory to break ground in Mojave. *Los Angeles Times*.

acquisition of Scaled Composites.[55] Together with Virgin Galactic, The Spaceship Company became Sir Richard Branson's vehicle for his participation in the billionaire space race, in which he and two other multi-billionaires, namely Jeff Bezos and Elon Musk (along with some existing multinational aerospace companies) competed to launch passengers into space commercially.

Commercial Crew Programme

Meanwhile, the end of the space shuttle programme with the return of *Atlantis* on its last mission on 21 July 2011 left NASA with the problem of needing to ferry astronauts to and from the ISS without a crewed vehicle of its own to do so.[56] The Commercial Crew Program was introduced by NASA at that time to contract with the private sector for spacecraft and launch services to ferry astronauts to and from the ISS, perhaps partly motivated by the capabilities demonstrated through the X Prize and the technical capabilities of existing NASA contractors.[57] The Space Exploration Technologies Corporation (SpaceX) and the Boeing Company's Defense, Space, and Security Division were ultimately selected to provide these services.[58] While Boeing is part of a long-standing multinational aerospace company with an established history of building launch vehicles and spacecraft,[59] SpaceX was founded on 14 March 2002 by Musk with stated ambitions not only in commercial human space flight to low Earth orbit but also for future human missions to the Moon and Mars.[60]

[55]Rhian, Jason. (2014, October 5). A Decade After *SpaceShipOne*'s Triumphant Flight—Commercial Flights Still a Ways Off. Spaceflight Insider. www.spaceflightinsider.com/missions/commercial/decade-later-spaceshipones-triumphant-flight-still-awaiting-first-flight-paying-customers

[56]Chow, Denise. (2011, April 14). NASA Faces Awkward, Unfortunate Spaceflight Gap. www.space.com/11387-nasa-future-human-spaceflight-hurdles-nss27.html; Wall, Mike. (2013, April 30). NASA to Pay $70 Million a Seat to Fly Astronauts on Russian Spacecraft. www.space.com/20897-nasa-russia-astronaut-launches-2017.html

[57]Garver, Lori. (2022). *Escaping Gravity: My Quest to Transform NASA and Launch a New Space Age*. New York: Diversion Books; Amos, Jonathan. (2010, September 30). US politicians cement a new philosophy for NASA. BBC. www.bbc.co.uk/blogs/thereporters/jonathanamos/2010/09/us-politicians-cement-a-new-ph.shtml; Faust, Jeff. (2010, July 26). Recasting the debate about commercial crew. Space Review. www.thespacereview.com/article/1671/1

[58]Foust, Jeff. (2014, September 19). NASA Commercial Crew Awards Leave Unanswered Questions. Space News. spacenews.com/41924nasa-commercial-crew-awards-leave-unanswered-questions; Berger, Eric. (2022, September 1). NASA will pay Boeing more than twice as much as SpaceX for crew seats. Ars Technica. arstechnica.com/science/2022/09/nasa-will-pay-boeing-more-than-twice-as-much-as-spacex-for-crew-seats

[59]Mann, Adam. (2021, October 25). The Boeing Company: From rockets to commercial crew. www.space.com/the-boeing-company

[60]Zubrin, Robert. (2019). *The Case for Space: How the Revolution in Spaceflight Opens up a Future of Limitless Possibility*. New York: Amherst.

SpaceX began providing services to NASA for passenger space flight in May 2020 using its Crew Dragon capsule, launched by its Falcon 9 rocket, that may seat up to seven people (though NASA would send no more than a crew of four on any specific launch).[61] The Crew Dragon is to be joined for service with NASA by the Boeing CST-100 Starliner sometime after April 2023. It is to be launched with the remaining Atlas V launchers and later with its replacement, the Vulcan Centaur,[62] both to be supplied by United Launch Alliance, itself a joint venture between Boeing and the Lockheed Martin Corporation to provide commercial and governmental launch services.[63]

During the development of the Commercial Crew Program, two other private entrants received funding from NASA for the development of commercial crewed spacecraft, but ultimately they were not selected as contractors to provide those services. One is the Dream Chaser, a human-rated spacecraft for a crew of up to seven that is to be developed by the Sierra Nevada Corporation, after its cargo version becomes operational for resupply services to the ISS and is to be launched using both the Vulcan Centaur and the Ariane 6 launcher at present under development by Arianespace S.A. with its first test launch scheduled for late 2023.[64] The other is the New Shepard launch and crew vehicle developed by Blue Origin, a company established by Bezos, the founder of Amazon.com.[65] These two companies, together with Boeing, announced on 25 October 2021 that they would develop

[61] Corbett, Tobias, and Barker, Nathan. (2020, November 15). With Resilience, NASA and SpaceX begin operational Commercial Crew flights. NASA Spaceflight. www.nasaspaceflight.com/2020/11/crew1-launch

[62] Shalal, Andrea, and Klotz, Irene. (2015, April 13). Vulcan rocket launch in 2019 may end US dependence on Russia. Reuters. www.reuters.com/article/lockheed-boeing-rockets/vulcan-rocket-launch-in-2019-may-end-u-s-dependence-on-russia-idUSL2N0XA2DE20150414; de Selding, Peter B. (2016, March 16). ULA intends to lower its costs, and raise its cool, to compete with SpaceX. Space News. spacenews.com/ula-intends-to-lower-its-costs-and-raise-its-cool-to-compete-with-spacex

[63] Mann, Adam. (2020, December 9). United Launch Alliance: Combing the forces of two aerospace giants. www.space.com/united-launch-alliance.html; Davenport, Christian. (2022, June 22). Disrupted by SpaceX, ULA was in 'serious trouble'. Now it's on the road back. *Washington Post.*

[64] Howell, Elizabeth. (2017, November 14). Dream Chaser: Sierra Nevada's Design for Spaceflight. www.space.com/19552-dream-chaser.html; Avery, Greg. (2022, December 8). Sierra Space exploring using Dream Chaser spacecraft for US military transport. *Denver Business Journal.* www.bizjournals.com/denver/news/2022/09/08/sierra-space-us-defense-pact-on-dream-chaser.html. See also Lee, Hae-Sung. (2022, May 30). Arianespace to rival SpaceX with competitive quality and price. *Korea Economic Daily.* www.kedglobal.com/us/aerospace-defense/newsView/ked202205300011; Amos, Jonathan. (2017, June 22). Full thrust on Europe's new Ariane 6 rocket. BBC. www.bbc.com/news/science-environment-40366736

[65] Fleishman, Glenn. (2018, September 19). Jeff Bezos Says Blue Origin Will Put People in Space in 2019. *Fortune.* fortune.com/2018/09/19/bezos-blue-origin-people-in-space-2019

and construct a commercial space station named Orbital Reef, to be operational by 2027, that would operate as a 'mixed-use business park' in low Earth orbit.[66]

The Billionaire Space Race

The incentivisation of the commercial space sector in the development of reusable passenger spacecraft has resulted in an undeclared contest between Blue Origin (Bezos), SpaceX (Musk), and Virgin Galactic (Branson) to be the first to launch private spacefarers into suborbital space.[67] This 'billionaire space race' culminated in successive launches by all three companies within just over 2 months of each other in 2021 to send their first private spacefarers into outer space.

On 11 July 2021, Virgin Galactic launched V.S.S. *Unity*, carrying six people, including Branson, to an altitude of 86 km (53.6 miles).[68] Some commentators, as well as Bezos, suggested that, as this altitude was below the von Kármán line,[69] the flight had not reached outer space, but it was enough for the purposes of the US Federal Aviation Administration (FAA) to award the passengers with the 'wings' of 'commercial astronauts'.[70] On 20 July 2021, Blue Origin launched the New Shepard on a fully automated flight with four passengers, including Bezos, to an altitude

[66] Manfredi, Lucas. (2022, August 26). NASA clears Blue Origin, Sierra Space's 'Orbital Reef' station for design phase. Fox Business. www.foxbusiness.com/technology/nasa-clears-blue-origin-sierra-space-orbital-reef-station-design-phase

[67] Downs, George. (2021, October 1). Who Will Win the Space Tourism Race? Virgin, Blue Origin, or SpaceX? *Wall Street Journal*. www.wsj.com/video/series/george-downs/who-will-win-the-space-tourism-race-virgin-blue-origin-or-spacex/50C78206-BD9A-48F4-B80A-51CB419F1022; Financial Times. Space, the final frontier of tycoon rivalry [editorial]. *Financial Times*. www.ft.com/content/532c41c9-0087-4fed-8168-078c8aed3f5a; Davenport, Christian. (2021, June 8). You are now free to move about the cosmos ... if you can afford it. *Washington Post*; and Fernholz, *Rocket Billionaires*.

[68] Gorman, Steve. (2021, July 12). Billionaire Branson soars to space abroad Virgin Galactic flight. Reuters. www.reuters.com/lifestyle/science/virgin-galactics-branson-ready-space-launch-aboard-rocket-plane-2021-07-11; Wattles, Jackie. (2021, July 12). Virgin Galactic founder Richard Branson successfully rockets into space. CNN. www.cnn.com/2021/07/11/tech/richard-branson-virgin-galactic-space-flight-scn/index.html

[69] The von Kármán line, named after the Hungarian astronautical engineer Theodore von Kármán, is the defined boundary between airspace and outer space, determined by the Fédération Aéronautique Internationale: Sanz Fernández de Córdoba, S. (2004, June 21). 100 km Altitude Boundary for Astronautics. FAI Astronautic Records Commission. www.fai.org/page/icare-boundary; Voosen, Paul. (2018, July 24). Outer space may have just gotten a bit closer. *Science*. www.science.org/content/article/outer-space-may-have-just-gotten-bit-closer

[70] Koren, Marina. (2021, July 19). Jeff Bezos is Ready to Cross a Cosmically Controversial Line. *The Atlantic*. www.theatlantic.com/science/archive/2021/07/jeff-bezos-blue-origin-branson/619476; Hur, Krystal. (2021, July 16). Jeff Bezos, Richard Branson, and Where Space Really Begins. *Wall Street Journal*; Fisher, Kristin. (2021, December 10). The US Gives Bezos, Branson, and Shatner their astronaut wings. CNN. www.cnn.com/2021/12/10/politics/astronaut-wings-bezos-branson-shatner/index.html

above the von Kármán line.[71] On 16 September 2021, SpaceX launched the Crew Dragon *Resilience* on the Inspiration4 mission that sent a fully private crew of four on the world's first private orbital passenger space flight, reaching an altitude of 585 km (364 miles).[72]The full list of private spacefarers launched into outer space by private ventures, including Blue Origin, SpaceX, and Virgin Galactic, as of 31 December 2022.

While many appear to appreciate the significance and the potential of the dawn of private human space flight as a commercial reality,[73] the billionaire space race has also exposed its participants to substantial criticism, for the money and resources expended[74]; for what is perceived as a vanity exercise by the über-rich[75]; and also for the carbon footprint left by space tourism in the absence of any tangible economic benefit.[76] What is undeniable, however, is the potential created by competitive commercial access to space for private individuals beyond career professionals and multimillionaires. This creates a corresponding need to consider the potential requirements for emergency assistance and rescue, both on Earth and in outer space. To explore these implications, an analysis of the definitional context and the obligations imposed by existing international law is required.

---

[71] Wall, Mike. (2021, July 20). Jeff Bezos launches into space on Blue Origin's first astronaut flight. www.space.com/jeff-bezos-blue-origin-first-astronaut-launch; Rincon, Paul. (2021, July 20). Jeff Bezos launches to space abroad New Shepard rocket ship. BBC. www.bbc.com/news/science-environment-57849364

[72] Kluger, Jeffrey. (2021, August 10). Four Civilian Astronauts. Three Days in Orbit. One Giant Leap. Meet the Inspiration4 Crew. *Time*. time.com/6083977/jared-isaacman-inspiration4-profile; Cameron, Doug. (2021, September 16). The SpaceX Inspiration4 Launch: What to Know About the Orbital Mission. *Wall Street Journal*.

[73] McArdle, Megan. (2021, July 13). The billionaire space race benefits the rest of us. Really. *Washington Post*; Vance, Ashlee. (2021, July 16). The Future of Space is Bigger Than Jeff Bezos, Richard Branson, or Elon Musk. Bloomberg. www.bloomberg.com/news/articles/2021-07-16/billionaire-space-race-between-bezos-branson-and-musk-is-just-the-beginning; Lynn, Matthew. (2021, July 12). Branson vs. Bezos: In praise of the billionaire space race. *The Spectator*.

[74] Anon. (2021, July 20). Billionaires in space wasting money and resources. *San Diego Union–Tribune*; Williams, Billionaire Space Race Turns Into A Publicity Disaster; Waddell, Laura. (2021, July 22). Space Race between billionaires like Jeff Bezos, Elon Musk, and Richard Branson is a grotesque display of wealth. *The Scotsman*.

[75] Hiltzik, Michael. (2021, July 6). The Bezos-Branson-Musk space race is a huge waste of money and scientifically useless. *Los Angeles Times*.

[76] Hirschfeld, Andy. (2021, July 28). What Is the Environmental Impact of the Billionaire Space Race? Experts Weigh In. *The Observer*; Kluger, Jeffrey. (2022, June 28). Billionaires Are Racing to Space—and the Climate Is Paying the Price. *Time*. time.com/6191846/billionaire-space-race-climate

Classifications of Spacefarers as Astronauts

Overview of the Controversy

Revisiting the categories of spacefarers adumbrated above, it has long been the case that the United States objected to amateur spacefarers being referred to as 'astronauts', considering it to be a title exclusive to career professionals. For instance, NASA classified Garn, Nelson, and McAuliffe as 'payload specialists', not 'astronauts', on their respective space shuttle flights, even though they each received substantial training with NASA beforehand. As McAuliffe said,

> I feel very fortunate to be on flight with this crew, but there's a lot of difference between a payload specialist or a space participant and an astronaut. I mean, they go through years of training, and I've had a glimpse of a lot of the things that they've done, but I do not understand an awful lot that goes on aboard the shuttle.[77]

When Tito, the world's first space tourist, arrived at NASA to join the astronauts and cosmonauts for training ahead of their mission to the ISS, he was refused admittance by the NASA astronauts, who refused to train with him.[78] As the then NASA Administrator Daniel S. Goldin testified on 2 May 2001 before the House of Representatives Science Committee's Subcommittee on Space and Astronautics,

> First, let me say that NASA, as it appears in the press, was against flying nonprofessional astronauts. That is not the case. We think there is a place for researchers, educators, artists, other people to go to space. But saying that, the real issue is the current situation has put an incredible stress on the men and women of NASA[.] I don't know how to measure it, but I could see it and I could feel it. They are dedicated to safety, and Mr. Tito does not realise the efforts of thousands of people in the United States and Russia that are working to protect his safety and the safety of everyone else taking extraordinary means. Now, I don't know the relationship he had in getting this contract, but I do know that the stress is real.[79]

The question of whether spacefarers may be considered 'astronauts' or otherwise may have some importance because, as discussed below, one of the relevant space law treaties refers to 'astronauts' without defining the term; another treaty refers to 'personnel of a spacecraft', again without defining the term; and a multitude of different terms are also used to classify different spacefarers under US domestic law. Accordingly, it is prudent to review the legal obligations concerning emergency

[77] A Major Malfunction. (2020, September 16). *Challenger: The Final Flight*. Directed by Daniel Junge and Steven Leckart. Limited series, episode 3. Netflix Inc.

[78] Harwood, William. (2001, March 20). NASA continues protesting space joyride of Dennis Tito. Spaceflight Now. spaceflightnow.com/news/n0103/20tito; Anon. (2001, April 19). Goldin Plans to Snub Koptev Conference over Tito Flight to ISS. Space Daily. www.spacedaily.com/reports/Goldin_Plans_To_Snub_Koptev_Conference_Over_Tito_Flight_To_ISS.html. See also Klerkx, Greg. (2004). *Lost in Space: The Fall of NASA and the Dream of a New Space Age*. New York: Random House.

[79] US House of Representatives. (2001, May 2). NASA Posture. Hearings before the Subcommittee on Space and Astronautics of the House Committee on Science. 107th Congress, 1st Session (pp. 67–68). (Testimony of Daniel S. Goldin).

assistance and rescue of private spacefarers in the context of these different classifications under both US law and international space law.

Government Spacefarers

One of the more contentious issues regarding the growth of private human space flight is the classification of such spacefarers as a matter of law and practice. The word 'astronaut' has its origin from the ancient Greek words ἄστρον (*astron*) and ναύτης (*nautes*), which literally means 'star sailor'.[80] It was first adopted by the NASA Space Task Group in 1958, and fittingly so, given the word 'aeronautics' in the name of NASA was already in use.[81] Since then, the United States has consistently used the term 'astronaut' to describe their career professional spacefarers. When the United States launches professional crew members for space agencies of other countries, particularly those of the CSA, ESA, or JAXA, they are also referred to as 'astronauts' by both NASA and the respective space agencies.[82]

Similarly, the Russian term космонавт (*cosmonaut*) is derived from the same Greek term but is based also on the Russian word космос (*kosmos*), which means 'space'. It is the term used as the equivalent of 'astronaut' by both the Soviet Union and its successor states, particularly Kazakhstan and the Russian Federation.[83] From 1967 to 1991, during the course of the Interkosmos programme, in all cases bar one they were the first of their nationality to be launched into space,[84] and almost

[80]Translation by the author.

[81]Dethloff, Henry C. (1993). *Suddenly Tomorrow Came: A History of the Johnson Space Centre* (pp. 23–24). Washington, D.C.: National Aeronautics and Space Administration.

[82]See, for example, European Space Agency. (n.d.). The European Astronaut Corps. www.esa.int/Science_Exploration/Human_and_Robotic_Exploration/Astronauts/The_European_astronaut_corps; Canadian Space Agency. (2021, April 6). Astronauts. www.asc-csa.gc.ca/eng/astronauts. See also Howell, Elizabeth. (2020, December 17). Canadian astronauts will start flying to the Moon in 2023 with NASA's Artemis missions. www.space.com/canadian-astronauts-artemis-moon-missions; Amos, Jonathan. (2021, June 23). Big numbers apply to be European astronauts. BBC. www.bbc.co.uk/news/science-environment-57530395; Hollinger, Peggy, and Cookson, Clive. (2022, June 14). Interview with E.S.A. astronaut Samantha Cristoforetti from space. *Financial Times*.

[83]Translation provided to the author by Daria Pavlova. See also Brzezinski, Mathew. (2007). *Red Moon Rising: Sputnik and the Hidden Rivalries that Ignited the Space Age* (p. 108). New York: Henry Holt & Co.; Burgess, Colin, and Hall, Rex. (2008). *The First Soviet Cosmonaut Team: Their Lives, Legacy, and Historical Impact*. New York: Springer; Banks, Peter M., and Ride, Sally K. (1989). Soviets in Space. *Scientific American, 260*, 32.

[84]Georgi Ivanov was the first Bulgarian to be launched into space, followed 9 years later by Aleksandr Aleksandrov: see Alexandrov, Svetoslav. Bulgarians still dream about space four decades after their first crewed mission. The Space Review. www.thespacereview.com/article/3638/1

invariably they were referred to as 'cosmonauts' at the time.[85] One exception was Chrétien, who participated in two Interkosmos missions as the first French national and first Western European to be launched into outer space, as he was trained by the Centre national d'études spatiales (National Space Centre or CNES) of France and was designated a '*spationaute*', the term derived from the Latin word *spatium*, meaning 'space', though the CNES and ESA now appear content to use the terms '*spationaute*' and '*astronaute*' interchangeably.[86] Since the dissolution of the USSR, space agencies or governments of various countries that paid Roscosmos to launch their first national into outer space, specifically those of the Republic of Korea, Malaysia, and the UAE, have referred to them interchangeably as 'astronauts' and 'cosmonauts'.

While Chinese career professional spacefarers launched by the CNSA have been referred to informally, particularly in the West, as 'taikonauts'—a term derived from the Chinese word '*tàikōng*' (太空), which means 'space'—the official term used by the People's Liberation Army Astronaut Corps is '*hángtiānyuán*' (航天员), which literally means 'sailor of heaven'.[87] In the beginning of the present century, following a bilateral agreement with the Russian Federation on the transfer of space technology, particularly in relation to the design and construction of the Soyuz spacecraft, China began to develop and build its own spacecraft for human space flight, culminating on 15 October 2003 in the launch of Shenzhou-5 with Yang on board.[88]

---

[85]This was the case even for states that were not part of the Eastern Bloc, e.g. Austria, France, Japan, and the United Kingdom. For instance, when Rakesh Sharma was awarded the Ashoka Chakra, the highest peacetime gallantry award in India, the citation referred to his selection as a 'cosmonaut': Ashoka Chakra Citation for Squadron Leader Rakesh Sharma. (1985, May 7). *Indian Gazette*, 57-Pres/85.

[86]Centre national d'études spatiales. (2010, January 27). Astronaute: l'espace à tout prix. jeunes. cnes.fr/fr/web/CNES-Jeunes-fr/8240-astronaute-la-vie-apres-l-espace.php (translated by Audrey Bailly for the author).

[87]Translated by the author. See China Global Television Network. (2022, June 28). Shenzhou-13 taikonaut welcomes cooperation in China's space station. news.cgtn.com/news/2022-06-28/Shenzhou-13-taikonaut-welcomes-cooperation-in-China-s-space-station-1bePAInwkpO/index.html; Deng Xiaoci and Fan Anqi. (2022, June 5). Shenzhou-14 spacecraft delivers three taikonauts to China Space Station to complete national space lab construction. *Global Times*. www.globaltimes.cn/page/202206/1267276.shtml

[88]Yuan, Jing-dong. (2010). Sino-Russian Defense Ties: The View from Beijing. In James Bellacqua (Ed.), *The Future of China–Russia Relations* (pp. 203–230). Lexington, Ky.: University Press of Kentucky; Oberg, James. (2003). China's Great Leap Upward. *Scientific American, 289*, 76.

Definitions in US Domestic Law

Some of the differentiation between 'astronauts' in the common understanding of the term and their private counterparts has a legal basis in the domestic law of the United States. Specifically, Title 51 of the US Code contains definitions of the various terms used to describe governmental spacefarers for the purposes of US domestic law, in particular the term 'astronaut' in a governmental context and a 'space flight participant' as the term has been used traditionally within the United States. The relevant definitions are as follows[89]:

> (2) 'crew' means any employee of a licensee or transferee, or of a contractor or subcontractor of a licensee or transferee, who perform activities in the course of that employment directly relating to the launch, re-entry, or other operation of or in a launch vehicle or re-entry vehicle that carries human beings . . .
> (4) 'government astronaut' means an individual who —
> (A) is designated by the National Aeronautics and Space Administration under section 20113(n);
> (B) is carried within a launch vehicle or re-entry vehicle in the course of his or her employment, which may include performance of activities directly relating to the launch, re-entry, or other operation of the launch vehicle or re-entry vehicle; and
> (C) is either —
> (i) an employee of the United States Government . . . or
> (ii) an international partner astronaut.
> (5) 'international partner astronaut' means an individual designated under Article 11 of the International Space Station Intergovernmental Agreement,[90] by a partner to that agreement other than the United States, as qualified to serve as an International Space Station crew member . . .
> (20) 'space flight participant' means an individual, who is not crew or a government astronaut, carried within a launch vehicle or re-entry vehicle.

From the above, it would appear that, for the purposes of US law, an individual who travel into space would be categorised as one of the following:

- 'government astronaut';
- 'crew', being a professional employee of a private contractor operating that private contractor's spacecraft, such as those licensed by NASA to ferry government astronauts into space and back; and
- 'space flight participants'.

---

[89] Title 51, US Code § 50902.

[90] Agreement among the Governments of Canada, Member States of the European Space Agency, Japan, Russian Federation, and the United States of America Concerning Cooperation on the Civil International Space Station, signed on 29 January 1998, UST 212 (entered into force on 27 March 2001). See Yakovenko, Alexander V. (1999). The Intergovernmental Agreement on the International Space Station. *Space Policy, 15*, 79; Nagel, Karl-Friedrich. (1998). Das neue Regierungsabkommen über die Internationale Raum Station [The new intergovernmental agreement on the ISS] (1998) *Zeitschrift für Luft- und Weltraumrecht, 47*, 143; Farand, André. (2000). Legal Environment for Exploitation of the International Space Station (ISS). In George Haskell and Michael J. Rycroft (Eds.), *International Space Station: The Next Space Marketplace* (pp. 141–153). Dordrecht: Springer.

The classification of 'crew' as distinct from 'government astronauts' arises from NASA's Commercial Crew Program, for which the designation 'crew' refers to professional staff engaged by contractors to operate their spacecraft to transport government astronauts to and from outer space. As for 'space flight participants', Steven Mirmina pointed out that they were considered by the US Congress at the time as 'spacefarers [and] primarily as adventure-seeking tourists[,] as opposed to professionally trained career astronauts', and that the Commercial Space Launch Competitiveness Act:

> requires that space flight participants waive claims against the Government. Moreover, the [Act] requires individuals to undertake space flight at their own physical and financial risk. Space flight participants are excluded from indemnification eligibility under the 2004 *Space Act* and are not entitled to the benefits of liability insurance coverage.[91]

Further complicating the myriad of definitional issues on the US domestic legal landscape is the classification of 'commercial astronauts' introduced by the FAA to recognise spacefarers launched into outer space on board private spacecraft on non-government missions, such as those launched by Blue Origin, SpaceX, and Virgin Galactic, presumably because not allowing them to be called 'astronauts' would affect public perceptions and expectations.[92] Although no legal or regulatory framework exists specifically as regards 'commercial astronauts', as a matter of stated policy, the FAA has recognised as 'commercial astronauts' private spacefarers who have flown more than 50 statute miles (80.5 km) above the surface of the Earth on an FAA-licensed mission.[93] The first to be recognised as such was Melvill, who was on board *SpaceShipOne* on 21 June 2004 as part of Scaled Composites's winning effort for the Ansari X-Prize.[94] Passengers on subsequent private and commercial launches, including in particular those of 2021 as part of the billionaire space race, have all been recognised by the FAA as commercial astronauts. As the United States remains to date the only country to have commercial entities engaged in launching private spacefarers into outer space, there are as yet no competing terms in the domestic laws and policies of other countries to the term 'commercial astronaut'.

---

[91] Ibid.

[92] See Title 14, Code of Federal Regulations, Part 460.

[93] Federal Aviation Administration. (2022, October 22). FAA Commercial Human Spaceflight Recognition. www.faa.gov/space/human_spaceflight/recognition

[94] Ibid. See also Anon. (2005, October 7). SpaceShipOne rockets to success. BBC. news.bbc.co.uk/1/hi/sci/tech/3712998.stm; and Belfiore, *Rocketeers*.

Legal and Policy Implications of the Classification of Private Spacefarers as 'Astronauts' or 'Cosmonauts'

Article V of the Outer Space Treaty

Of the five multilateral treaties negotiated and adopted under the auspices of the UN Committee on the Peaceful Uses of Outer Space (COPUOS), often referred to collectively as the 'United Nations Space Treaties', the Treaty on Principles Governing the Activities of States in the Exploration and Use of Outer Space, including the Moon and Other Celestial Bodies (the Outer Space Treaty) is the only one that contains the term 'astronaut' in one of its operative provisions.[95] Article V of the Outer Space Treaty states:

> States Parties to the Treaty shall regard astronauts as envoys of mankind in outer space and shall render to them all possible assistance in the event of accident, distress, or emergency landing on the territory of another State Party or on the high seas. When astronauts make such a landing, they shall be safely and promptly returned to the State of registry of their space vehicle.
>
> In carrying on activities in outer space and on celestial bodies, the astronauts of one State Party shall render all possible assistance to the astronauts of other States Parties.
>
> States Parties to the Treaty shall immediately inform the other States Parties to the Treaty or the Secretary-General of the United Nations of any phenomena they discover in outer space, including the moon and other celestial bodies, which could constitute a danger to the life or health of astronauts.

Article XVII of the Outer Space Treaty states that its Chinese, English, French, Russian, and Spanish texts are all equally authentic, and Article 33 of the Vienna Convention on the Law of Treaties provides for the same outcome.[96] In place of 'astronaut' in the English text of the Outer Space Treaty, the term 宇宙航行员 (meaning 'space sailor') is used in the Chinese text, *astronaute* in the French, космонавтов (cosmonaut) in the Russian, and *astronautas* in the Spanish. As with the English text, in none of the other language texts is the term given any definition. Consequently, what has been open for some debate is whether the obligations under Article V of the Outer Space Treaty extend only to 'astronauts'; i.e. the provisions

[95] Treaty on Principles Governing the Activities of States in the Exploration and Use of Outer Space, including the Moon and other Celestial Bodies, adopted on 19 December 1966 by UN General Assembly Resolution 2222 (XXI), opened for signature on 27 January 1967, 610 UNTS 205; TIAS 6347; 18 UST 2410; [1968] UKTS 10; [1967] ATS 24; [1967] CTS 19; [1968] NZTS 8; 6 ILM 386 (entered into force generally and for Australia on 10 October 1967 and for New Zealand on 31 May 1968).

[96] Vienna Convention on the Law of Treaties, opened for signature on 23 May 1979, 1155 UNTS 331; [1980] UKTS 57; [1974] ATS 2; [1980] CTS 37; [1971] NZTS 4; 15 SD 1; 8 ILM 679 (entered into force generally and for Australia and New Zealand on 27 January 1980). See Germer, Peter. (1970). Interpretation of Plurilingual Treaties: A Study of Article 33 of the Vienna Convention on the Law of Treaties. *Harvard International Law Journal, 11*, 400; Villiger, Mark E. (2008). *Commentary on the 1969 Vienna Convention on the Law of Treaties* (pp. 450–462). The Hague: Martinus Nijhoff.

may be considered not to afford any protection to other categories of spacefarers. However, the question must be considered in the context of the language of the Agreement on the Rescue of Astronauts, the Return of Astronauts, and the Return of Objects Launched into Outer Space (the Rescue Agreement) adopted by the UN General Assembly in 1968, the year following the adoption of the Outer Space Treaty.[97]

The Rescue Agreement

As early as 1959, when the COPUOS was established, the accidental re-entry and landing of crewed spacecraft was identified as a legal problem that necessitated priority treatment.[98] In March 1962, then Soviet Premier Nikita S. Khrushchev sent a letter to the then US President John F. Kennedy on this issue, urging for the conclusion of 'an international agreement providing for assistance in the search for and rescue of spaceships, sputniks and capsules that descend to the earth due to accident. Such an agreement seems even more necessary because the point in question here is the saving of the lives of cosmonauts.'[99]

After the exchange of several drafts and various proposals in the COPUOS (and its Legal Subcommittee) and the adoption of the Outer Space Treaty by the UN General Assembly in 1967, the Rescue Agreement expanded on some of the obligations under Article V of the Outer Space Treaty; the specific provisions of the Rescue Agreement concerning the rescue of and assistance to spacefarers are as follows:

> Article 2
>
> If, owing to accident, distress, emergency or unintended landing, the personnel of a spacecraft land in territory under the jurisdiction of a Contracting Party, it shall immediately take all possible steps to rescue them and render them all necessary assistance. It shall inform the launching authority and also the Secretary-General of the United Nations of the steps it is taking and of their progress. If assistance by the launching authority would help to effect a prompt rescue or would contribute substantially to the effectiveness of search and rescue operations, the launching authority shall co-operate with the Contracting Party with a view to the effective conduct of search and rescue operations. Such operations shall be subject to the direction and control of the Contracting Party, which shall act in close and continuing consultation with the launching authority.[100]

---

[97] Agreement on the Rescue of Astronauts, the Return of Astronauts, and the Return of Objects Launched into Outer Space, adopted on 19 December 1967 by General Assembly Resolution 2345 (XXII), opened for signature on 22 April 1968, 672 UNTS 119; TIAS 6599; 18 UST 2410; [1969] UKTS 56; [1986] ATS 8; [1975] CTS 6; [1969] NZTS 5; 169 SP 864; 7 ILM 151 (entered into force generally on 12 March 1968, for Australia on 18 March 1986, and for New Zealand on 8 July 1969).

[98] UN Doc. A/4141, 14 July 1959, Part III.

[99] Khrushchev, Nikita S. (1962, March 22). *New York Times*, 18.

[100] Rescue Agreement, Article 2.

Article 3

If information is received or it is discovered that the personnel of a spacecraft have alighted on the high seas or in any other place not under the jurisdiction of any State, those Contracting Parties which are in a position to do so shall, if necessary, extend assistance in search and rescue operations for such personnel to assure their speedy rescue. They shall inform the launching authority and the Secretary-General of the United Nations of the steps they are taking and of their progress.[101]

Article 4

If, owing to accident, distress, emergency or unintended landing, the personnel of a spacecraft land in territory under the jurisdiction of a Contracting Party or have been found on the high seas or in any other place not under the jurisdiction of any State, they shall be safely and promptly returned to representatives of the launching authority.[102]

Before considering the specific effects of the above provisions of the Rescue Agreement in conjunction with those under Article V of the Outer Space Treaty, it must be noted that these provisions do not use the term 'astronaut' but instead refer to 'personnel of a spacecraft'. Relevantly, Article 30 of the Vienna Convention of the Law of Treaties states:

2. When a treaty specifies that it is subject to, or that it is not to be considered as incompatible with, an earlier or later treaty, the provisions of that other treaty prevail.
3. When all the parties to the earlier treaty are parties also to the later treaty but the earlier treaty is not terminated or suspended in operation … the earlier treaty applies only to the extent that its provisions are compatible with those of the later treaty.
4. When the parties to the later treaty do not include all the parties to the earlier one:

(a) as between States Parties to both treaties the same rule applies as in paragraph 3;
(b) as between a State Party to both treaties and a State Party to only one of the treaties, the treaty to which both States are parties governs their mutual rights and obligations[.][103]

As of 1 December 2022, 112 countries are party to the Outer Space Treaty, and a further 23 have signed but not ratified it.[104] As for the Rescue Agreement, 99 countries are party to it and a further 23 have signed but not ratified it.[105] For the purposes of the present discussion, it is convenient (and appropriate) to consider those countries that have signed one of the treaties as being no different from those that have ratified it, particularly given Article 18 of the Vienna Convention on the Law of Treaties.[106] Accordingly, the countries of the world can thus be categorised as follows:

---

[101] Ibid., Article 3.

[102] Ibid., Article 4.

[103] Vienna Convention on the Law of Treaties, Article 30.

[104] UN Office of Outer Space Affairs. (2022, March 28). Status of International Agreements Relating to Activities in Outer Space as at 1 January 2022. UN Doc. A/AC.105/C.2/2022/CRP.10.

[105] Ibid.

[106] Article 18 of the Vienna Convention of the Law of Treaties requires a state to refrain from acts that would defeat the object and purpose of a treaty when it has signed but not ratified it unless it has made its intention clear not to become a party: see Gragl, Paul, and Fitzmaurice, Malgosia. (2019). The Legal Character of Article 18 of the Vienna Convention on the Law of Treaties. *International & Comparative Law Quarterly, 68*, 699; Villiger, *Commentary on the 1969 Vienna Convention on the Law of Treaties*, 242–254; Palchetti, Paolo. (2011). Article 18 of the 1969 Vienna Convention: A

1. the 112 countries that have obligations under both the Outer Space Treaty and the Rescue Agreement and, as such, there is no substantive difference between their obligations owed to 'astronauts' (under the Outer Space Treaty) and those owed to 'personnel of a spacecraft' (under the Rescue Agreement);
2. the ten countries that have obligations under the Rescue Agreement but not the OST and thus owe obligations to 'personnel of a spacecraft';[107]
3. the 23 countries that have obligations under the Outer Space Treaty but not the Rescue Agreement and thus owe obligations to 'astronauts'[108]; and,
4. the 62 or more countries that have no obligations under either the Outer Space Treaty or the Rescue Agreement, not being parties or signatories to either of them.

When the three operative provisions of the Rescue Agreement are analysed vis-à-vis the obligations imposed under Article V of the Outer Space Treaty, it is apparent that the only obligation owed to astronauts under the Treaty but not to the personnel of a spacecraft under the Rescue Agreement is the general obligation to render all possible assistance in outer space to astronauts in accident or distress. In other words, the obligations under the Rescue Agreement do not apply unless the personnel of the spacecraft have landed on Earth,[109] or otherwise have alighted from the spacecraft.[110] As Paul Dembling and Daniel Arons, both of the Office of General Counsel at NASA at the time, stated: 'Article 3 is limited to the situations in which astronauts have "alighted". It therefore does not cover a situation where an astronaut is in distress while travelling in outer space. However, assistance to astronauts while in outer space falls within the scope of the second paragraph of Article V of the Outer Space Treaty[.]'[111]

In sum, there are only two substantive effects of any differentiation between the scope of who may be regarded as an 'astronaut' or 'personnel of a spacecraft'. First, the ten countries that have signed the Rescue Agreement but have neither signed nor ratified the Outer Space Treaty may not owe emergency assistance and rescue obligations to anyone in outer space, but this is of negligible practical effect given

Vague and Ineffective Obligation or a Useful Means for Strengthening Legal Cooperation? In Enzo Cannizzaro (Ed.), *The Law of Treaties Beyond the Vienna Convention* (pp. 25–36). Oxford: Oxford University Press; Charme, Joni S. (1991). The Interim Obligation of Article 18 of the Vienna Convention on the Law of Treaties: Making Sense of an Enigma. *George Washington Journal of International Law and Economics, 25*, 71.

[107]These countries are Costa Rica, Croatia, Eswatini, Gabon, Georgia, the Maldives, Monaco, Montenegro, Senegal, and Serbia: UN Office of Outer Space Affairs, Status of International Agreements Relating to Activities in Outer Space as at 1 January 2022.

[108]These countries are Afghanistan, Algeria, Azerbaijan, Bahrain, Bangladesh, Benin, Burkina Faso, Burundi, the Central African Republic, Equatorial Guinea, Estonia, Ethiopia, Honduras, Kenya, Mali, Oman, Panama, Paraguay, Sri Lanka, Togo, Trinidad and Tobago, Uganda, and the Vatican City: U.N. Office of Outer Space Affairs, Status of International Agreements Relating to Activities in Outer Space as at 1 January 2022.

[109]Rescue Agreement, Articles 2 and 4.

[110]Ibid., Article 3.

[111]Dembling, Paul G., and Arons, Daniel M. (1968). The Treaty on Rescue and Return of Astronauts and Space Objects. *William & Mary Law Review, 9*(641), 649.

these ten countries do not have and are unlikely to be in any position to render any such assistance in the foreseeable future. Second, the 23 countries that have signed the Outer Space Treaty but have neither signed nor ratified the Rescue Agreement may not have emergency assistance, rescue, and return obligations to non-astronauts on Earth; however, as discussed below, the application of prevailing maritime law and aviation law obligations make this distinction somewhat irrelevant.

Emergency Assistance and Rescue of Spacefarers

Spacefarers Returned to Earth and Recovered on Land

Obligations Under Space Law

As set out above, there are four components to the obligations imposed under Article V of the Outer Space Treaty and Articles 2, 3, and 4 of the Rescue Agreement on countries regarding emergency assistance and the rescue of spacefarers on land. First, 'all possible assistance' must be provided to 'astronauts' or the 'personnel of a spacecraft' in the event of emergency, accident, or distress on land. Second, all possible assistance must be given to 'astronauts' and the 'personnel of a spacecraft' who have made an emergency landing. Third, rescued 'astronauts' and the 'personnel of a spacecraft' must be promptly returned to the State of registry of their spacecraft.[112] Fourth, a country that discovers any potential risk to the life and health of 'astronauts' must inform other countries or the UN Secretary-General.[113]

The obligations imposed under the Outer Space Treaty and the Rescue Agreement are supplemented by other international legal obligations under international aviation law.

Obligations Under International Civil Aviation Law

The 1944 Convention on International Civil Aviation (the Chicago Convention) has been the cornerstone of international aviation law for nearly eight decades.[114] Article 25 of the Chicago Convention provides that:

> Each contracting State undertakes to provide such measures of assistance to aircraft in distress in its territory as it may find practicable, and to permit, subject to control by its own authorities, the owners of the aircraft or authorities of the State in which the aircraft is

[112] On the issue of registration of spacecraft, see Article VIII of the OST.

[113] Presumably this obligation applies to both natural and human-made phenomena; in the case of human-made phenomena, there are additional obligations imposed under Article IX of the OST.

[114] Chicago Convention on International Civil Aviation, opened for signature on 7 December 1944, 15 UNTS 295; 148 BSP 38; [1953] UKTS 8; [1957] ATS 5; [1944] CTS 36; [1944] NZTS 7 (entered into force generally and for Australia and New Zealand on 4 April 1947).

> registered to provide such measures of assistance as may be necessitated by the circumstances. Each contracting State, when undertaking search for missing aircraft, will collaborate in coordinated measures which may be recommended from time to time pursuant to this Convention.

Annex 12 to the Chicago Convention contains the International Standards and Recommended Practices as regards search and rescue operations and procedures, and it is evident that the same indiscriminate approach applies to assistance and rescue in civil aviation.[115] Specifically, Paragraph 2.1.2 of Annex 12 states: 'In providing assistance to aircraft in distress and to survivors of aircraft accidents, Contracting States shall do so regardless of the nationality or status of such persons or of circumstances in which such persons are found'. Paragraph 5.5.1 of Annex 12 further states: 'Search and rescue operations shall continue, when practicable, until all survivors are delivered to a place of safety or until all reasonable hope of rescuing survivors has passed'.

It follows from the above that countries have a legal obligation under international civil aviation law to rescue anyone and everyone, including but not limited to crew, passengers, enemies, stowaways, and asylum seekers, regardless of nationality, classification, or status, who survive an accident. It would not be a difficult, legal, or logical extrapolation to consider the obligations under civil aviation law to extend to the emergency assistance and rescue of spacefarers who return to land, regardless of their legal status.

Spacefarers Returned to Earth and Recovered at Sea

Overview

Similar to the obligations relating to spacefarers to return on land, there are the same four components to the obligations imposed under Article V of the Outer Space Treaty and Articles 2, 3, and 4 of the Rescue Agreement on countries regarding emergency assistance and the rescue of spacefarers in the high seas. First, all possible assistance must be provided to 'astronauts' or the 'personnel of a spacecraft' in the event of emergency, accident, or distress on the high seas. Second, all possible assistance must be given to 'astronauts' and the 'personnel of a spacecraft' who have made an emergency landing on the high seas. Third, rescued 'astronauts' and the 'personnel of a spacecraft' must be promptly returned to the State of registry of their

[115] See Dempsey, Paul S. (2004). Compliance and Enforcement in International Law: Achieving Global Uniformity in Aviation Safety. *North Carolina Journal of International Law, 30*, 1; Spencer, Sinead. (2018). The Demand for a Single International Search and Rescue Agreement Template Flexible for Multi-Regional Use as Disseminated by the International Civil Aviation Organisation. *Perth International Law Journal, 3*, 115.

spacecraft. Fourth, a country that discovers any potential risk to the life and health of 'astronauts' must inform other countries or the UN Secretary-General.[116]

As for international maritime law, the duty to render assistance to persons in distress at sea has a long and consistent history in international law, in the context of both maritime safety and humanitarian considerations.[117] The relevant treaty provisions are found in multilateral treaties, some of which are administered by the International Maritime Organisation (IMO), specifically:

- the 1974 International Convention for the Safety of Life at Sea (the 'SOLAS Convention')[118];
- the 1979 International Convention on Maritime Search and Rescue (the 'SAR Convention'); and,[119]
- the 1982 United Nations Convention on the Law of the Sea ('UNCLOS').[120]

As can be seen in the analysis below, the assistance and rescue obligations in international maritime law do not distinguish between persons in danger based on whether they are crew or passengers, whether they are government employees or private individuals, or even stowaways, irregular migrants, or refugees at sea—and thus, by extension, regardless of whether they are astronauts, personnel of a spacecraft, or any kind of spacefarer.[121]

Obligations Under International Maritime Law on Countries

As a starting point, Article 98(1) of the UNCLOS states:

> (1) 'Every State shall require the master of a ship flying its flag, in so far as he can do so without serious danger to the ship, the crew, or the passengers:
>
> (a) to render assistance to any person found at sea in danger of being lost;
> (b) to proceed with all possible speed to the rescue of persons in distress, if informed of their need of assistance, in so far as such action may reasonably be expected of him;

[116] This obligation is not found in the Rescue Agreement.

[117] See, for example, Oxman, Bernard H. (1997). Human Rights and the United Nations Convention on the Law of the Sea. *Columbia Journal of Transnational Law, 36*(399), 414.

[118] International Convention for the Safety of Life at Sea, opened for signature on 11 January 1974, 1184 UNTS 278; [1980] UKTS 46; 32 UST 47; [1983] ATS 22; [1980] CTS 45; [1990] NZTS 19; 14 I.L.M. 959 (entered into force generally on 25 May 1980, for Australia on 17 November 1983, and for New Zealand on 23 May 1990).

[119] International Convention on Maritime Search and Rescue, opened for signature on 27 April 1979, 1405 UNTS 97; [1986] UKTS 59; [1986] ATS 29; [1985] CTS 27; [1985] NZTS 3 (entered into force generally and for Australia and New Zealand on 22 June 1985).

[120] United Nations Convention on the Law of the Sea, opened for signature on 10 December 1982, 1833 UNTS 3; [1994] ATS 31; [1996] NZTS 14; 21 ILM 1261 (entered into force generally and for Australia on 16 November 1994, and for New Zealand on 18 August 1996).

[121] See, for example, Tauman, Jessica E. (2002). Rescued at Sea, But Nowhere to Go: The Cloudy Legal Waters of the Tampa Crisis. *Pacific Rim Law & Policy Journal, 11*, 461.

(c) after a collision, to render assistance to the other ship, its crew, and its passengers and, where possible, to inform the other ship of the name of his own ship, its port of registry, and the nearest port at which it will call'.[122]

Similarly, Regulation 33 in Chapter V of the Annex to the SOLAS Convention states:

(1) The master of a ship at sea which is in a position to be able to provide assistance on receiving a signal from any source that persons are in distress at sea, is bound to proceed with all speed to their assistance, if possible informing them or the search and rescue service that the ship is doing so. If the ship receiving the distress alert is unable or, in the special circumstances of the case, considers it unreasonable or unnecessary to proceed to their assistance, the master must enter in the log-book the reason for failing to proceed to the assistance of the persons in distress, taking into account the recommendation of the [International Maritime] Organization, to inform the appropriate search and rescue service accordingly.
(2) The master of a ship in distress or the search and rescue service concerned, after consultation, so far as may be possible, with the masters of ships which answer the distress alert, has the right to requisition one or more of those ships as the master of the ship in distress or the search and rescue service considers best able to render assistance, and it shall be the duty of the master or masters of the ship or ships requisitioned to comply with the requisition by continuing to proceed with all speed to the assistance of persons in distress.
(3) Masters of ships shall be released from the obligation imposed by paragraph 1 on learning that their ships have not been requisitioned and that one or more other ships have been requisitioned and are complying with the requisition. This decision shall, if possible be communicated to the other requisitioned ships and to the search and rescue service.
(4) The master of a ship shall be released from the obligation imposed by paragraph 1 and, if his ship has been requisitioned, from the obligation imposed by paragraph 2 on being informed by the persons in distress or by the search and rescue service or by the master of another ship which has reached such persons that assistance is no longer necessary.[123]

Relevantly, the SAR Convention defines 'distress' as a 'situation wherein there is a reasonable certainty that a person, a vessel, or other craft is threatened by grave and imminent danger and requires immediate assistance', and 'rescue' as an 'operation to retrieve persons in distress, provide for their initial medical or other needs, and deliver them to a place of safety'.[124] However, even in the case of maritime law, the duties to assist and rescue at sea are not absolute; Article 98 of the UNCLOS necessitates the consideration of not endangering the rescuing vessel, its crew, or its passengers, while Regulation 33(1) of the SOLAS Convention excuses a vessel from such obligations if the assistance is considered unreasonable or unnecessary.[125]

It must be noted that the obligations under Article 98 of the UNCLOS and Regulation V-33 of the Annex to the SOLAS Convention are formulated to be as wide in scope as possible, and this is illustrated in a number of ways. First, the

[122] United Nations Convention on the Law of the Sea, Article 98.

[123] SOLAS Convention, Annex, Chapter V, Regulation 33.

[124] SAR Convention, Annex, Chapter 1, Article 1.3.

[125] Papanicolopulu, Irini. (2016). The Duty to Rescue at Sea, in Peacetime and in War: A General Overview. *International Review of the Red Cross, 98*(491), 497. See also Davies, Martin. (2003). Obligations and Implications for Ships Encountering Persons in Need of Assistance at Sea. *Pacific Rim Law & Policy Journal, 12*, 109.

obligations do not distinguish between different areas of waters, i.e. they are applicable regardless of whether they are in territorial waters, straits, exclusive economic zones, or the high seas. Second, the obligations apply regardless of the nature of the vessel in distress or the vessel being called upon to assist, whether they are government-owned or private, and regardless of whether they are civilian or military. Third, and most relevant to the present discussion, the obligations apply to any person at sea in danger of being lost, regardless of whether they are professional seafarers, crew, passengers, stowaways, asylum seekers, etc. The last point is emphasised by Article 2.1.10 of the Annex to the SAR Convention, which states: 'Parties shall ensure that assistance be provided to any person in distress at sea. They shall do so regardless of the nationality or status of such a person or the circumstances in which that person is found'.[126]

Obligations Imposed on Shipowners and Masters

Further, Article 11 of the Convention for the Unification of Certain Rules of Law Relating to Assistance and Salvage at Sea (the 'Brussels Salvage Convention') reinforces the obligations under international maritime law by stating:

> Article 11
>
> Every master is bound, so far as he can do so without serious danger to his vessel, her crew, and her passengers, to render assistance to everybody, even though an enemy, found at sea in danger of being lost.
>
> The owner of a vessel incurs no liability by reason of a contravention of the above provision.
>
> Article 12
>
> The High Contracting Parties, whose legislation does not forbid infringements of the preceding Article, bind themselves to take or to propose to their respective legislatures the measures necessary for the prevention of such infringements.
>
> The High Contracting Parties will communicate to each other as soon as possible the laws or regulations which have already been or may be hereafter promulgated in their States for giving effect to the above provision.[127]

While the obligations under the UNCLOS, the SAR Convention, and Article 12 of the Brussels Salvage Convention are imposed on the State, the obligations under the SOLAS Convention and Article 11 of the Brussels Salvage Convention are borne by the shipmasters and owners of vessels.[128] In most countries, such obligations are also codified into domestic law so as to be applicable to shipmasters in its

[126] SAR Convention, Annex, Chapter 1, Article 2.1.10.

[127] Convention for the Unification of Certain Rules of Law Relating to Assistance and Salvage at Sea, opened for signature on 29 September 1910, [1913] UKTS 4; USTS 579; 26 Hertslet 319; 103 SP 441; [1930] ATS 15; NZTS M1910/04 (entered into force generally on 1 March 1913, for Australia on 24 October 1930, and for New Zealand on 26 June 1913).

[128] Attard, Felicity G. (2020).*The Duty of the Shipmaster to Render Assistance at Sea under International Law*. The Hague: Brill. See also Papachristodoulou, Aphrodite. (2022). The Recognition of a Right to be Rescued at Sea in International Law. *Leiden Journal of International Law, 35*, 337.

territorial waters and on vessels under their flags.[129] As such, there is no doubt on the part of both the relevant countries or their shipmasters that they have an obligation under several international treaties and domestic laws to rescue anyone and everyone, including but not limited to crew, passengers, enemies, stowaways, and asylum seekers, regardless of nationality or status, who is at risk of being lost at sea.[130]

Spacefarers in Distress in Outer Space

Spacefarers in Outer Space or Alighted on Celestial Bodies

Without the spacefarers alighting the spacecraft, Article 3 of the Rescue Agreement has no application, and the only applicable provision is that of Article V of the Outer Space Treaty that limits its application to 'astronauts'. However, just as the term 'personnel of a spacecraft' in the Rescue Agreement cannot have a different scope or meaning depending on where such personnel are found, the same would apply to the term 'astronaut' in the Outer Space Treaty. If the legal obligations of countries to render assistance and rescue on Earth under the Outer Space Treaty extend to all spacefarers regardless of nationality, classification, status, or circumstance as 'astronauts', the same must be said for all spacefarers in space.

On the other hand, the practical difficulties as well as the risk posed to potential rescuers are reduced only negligibly, if at all, in circumstances where the spacefarers in distress remain on board their spacecraft. Accordingly, the prospect of a country or a private entity is in a position to render assistance or rescue to astronauts in outer space or on celestial bodies, in a practical manner and without jeopardising the safety of the rescuers, is so low as to render the distinction between 'astronaut' and 'personnel of a spacecraft' in this context to be moot.

Spacefarers Marooned in Outer Space or on Celestial Bodies

In the extremely limited and highly unlikely scenario of surviving spacefarers who have 'alighted' from their spacecraft but are wandering around on a celestial body or in outer space, countries have an obligation under Article 3 of the Rescue Agreement to render assistance and rescue to them as 'personnel of a spacecraft' to the extent that it is possible and necessary. Given limited time for life support and the practical difficulties involved in performing space-to-space or Earth-to-space search and rescue operations, it is difficult to envisage a scenario where a country or a private entity may be found to have contravened their obligations under the Rescue

[129] See, for example, Australia: *Navigation Act 1912* (Cth.), s. 265; Canada: *Canada Shipping Act 2001*, s. 131; New Zealand: *Maritime Transport Act 1994*, s. 32; United Kingdom: *Merchant Shipping Act 1995*, s. 93; and United States: Title 46, US Code § 2304.

[130] Tauman, Rescued at Sea, But Nowhere to Go.

Agreement in such circumstances.[131] In some ways, this is similar to the scenario often found in Antarctica or on the approaches to the peaks of the tallest mountains in the world, where practical difficulties as well as concerns over the risk posed to the potential rescuers make rescue operations unviable.

Observations and Conclusions

In recent years, with the rapid advances made in the privatisation and commercialisation of human space flight, a new age in which anyone and everyone may access outer space is fast becoming a reality. While much of the media and academic attention has been given to the appropriateness of billionaires expending millions of dollars competing to bring about private human space flight, many of the important legal and regulatory issues arising from increased private human access and presence in outer space remain unresolved.

The Outer Space Treaty and the Rescue Agreement have laid down some important principles regarding emergency assistance, distress, rescue, and return of spacefarers, but it has brought unnecessary and ultimately irrelevant attention to the question of whether private spacefarers ought to be classified as 'astronauts' as a matter of law. As discussed above, the existing treaties and IMO regulations of international maritime law and Annex 12 of the Chicago Convention can extend and apply to emergency assistance and rescue of spacefarers that return to the Earth. What remains to be determined is to plug the gap left by the Rescue Agreement as to what extent such assistance and rescue may be proffered or required in low Earth orbit or on the Moon, beyond the provision of communications facilities and networks as already provided for under resolutions made by the International Telecommunication Union.[132]

Current and future private human space flight will bring about a new age in a new world, bringing within it a significant number of uncertainties and obstacles to be overcome. The existence and applicability of legal principles relating to emergency assistance, distress, and the rescue and return of spacefarers ought not be one such uncertainty that humanity needs to overcome.

---

[131] See, for example, Cates, Grant. (2021). The In-space Rescue Capability Gap. *Journal of Space Safety Engineering, 8*, 202; Shayler, David J. (2009). *Space Rescue: Ensuring the Safety of Manned Spaceflight.* Berlin: Springer; David, Leonard. (2021, September 16). Humanity needs a space-rescue capability, report stresses. www.space.com/space-rescue-capability-needed-report

[132] International Telecommunication Union. Plenipotentiary Conference Resolution 136 (rev. Dubai, 2018), Plenipotentiary Conference Resolution 175 (rev. Dubai, 2018); World Telecommunication Development Conference Resolution 34 (rev. Buenos Aires, 2017), World Radiocommunication Conference Resolution 646 (rev. WRC-15) and World Radiocommunication Conference Resolution 647 (rev. WRC-15).

References

Title 51, US Code § 50902.

Al Shurafa, S. (2019, September 26). UAE in space: What did Hazza Al Mansoori carry with him to space? *Gulf News*. gulfnews.com/uae/science/uae-in-space-what-did-hazzaa-almansoori-carry-with-him-to-space-1.1569476103518

Alexandrov, S. Bulgarians still dream about space four decades after their first crewed mission. *The Space Review*. www.thespacereview.com/article/3638/1

Amos, J.. (2010, September 30). US politicians cement a new philosophy for NASA. *BBC*. www.bbc.co.uk/blogs/thereporters/jonathanamos/2010/09/us-politicians-cement-a-new-ph.shtml

Amos, J. (2017, June 22). Full thrust on Europe's new Ariane 6 rocket. *BBC*. www.bbc.com/news/science-environment-40366736

Amos, J. (2021, June 23). Big numbers apply to be European astronauts. *BBC*. www.bbc.co.uk/news/science-environment-57530395

Anon. (1940, April 30). First Flight: Tasman Service. *Auckland Star*, 9.

Anon. (2005, October 7). SpaceShipOne rockets to success. *BBC*. news.bbc.co.uk/1/hi/sci/tech/3712998.stm

Anon. (2021, July 20). Billionaires in space wasting money and resources. *San Diego Union–Tribune*.

Attard, F. G. (2020). *The duty of the shipmaster to render assistance at sea under international law*. Brill.

Autio-Sarasmo, S. (2016). Technological modernisation in the Soviet Union and post-soviet Russia: Practices and continuities. *Europe–Asian Studies, 68*, 79.

Avery, G. (2022, December 8). Sierra Space exploring using Dream Chaser spacecraft for US military transport. *Denver Business Journal*. www.bizjournals.com/denver/news/2022/09/08/sierra-space-us-defense-pact-on-dream-chaser.html

Banks, P. M., & Ride, S. K. (1989). Soviets in space. *Scientific American, 260*, 32.

Barton, G., & Heath, P. (2015). *Coral route: Tasman empire airways ltd., flying boats, and the South Pacific*. Steele Roberts.

Battaglia, D. (2012). Arresting hospitality: The case of the 'handshake in space'. *Journal of the Royal Anthropological Institute, 18*, S76.

Beissinger, M. R. (2009). Nationalism and the collapse of soviet communism. *Contemporary European History, 18*, 331.

Belfiore, M. (2007). *Rocketeers: How a visionary band of business leaders, engineers, and pilots is boldly Privatising space*. Smithsonian Books.

Bergaust, E. (1968). *Murder on Pad 34*. G. P. Putnam & Sons.

Berger, E. (2022, September 1). NASA will pay Boeing more than twice as much as SpaceX for crew seats. *Ars Technica*. arstechnica.com/science/2022/09/nasa-will-pay-boeing-more-than-twice-as-much-as-spacex-for-crew-seats

Bizony, P. (2011). *Starman: The truth behind the legend of Yuri Gagarin*. Bloomsbury.

Boffey, P. M. (1984, November 9). A space inspection. *New York Times*, A29.

Boisjoly, R. P., Curtis, E. F., & Mellican, E. (1989). Roger Boisjoly and the challenger disaster: The ethical dimensions. *Journal of Business Ethics, 8*, 217.

Boyle, A. (2004, October 3). SpaceShipOne wins $10 million X prize. *NBC News*. www.nbcnews.com/id/wbna6167761

Brainerd, E. (1998). Winners and losers in Russia's economic transition. *American Economic Review, 88*, 1094.

Braithwaite, R. (2011). *Afgantsy: The Russians in Afghanistan, 1979–1989*. Oxford University Press.

British Broadcasting Corporation. (2008, April 8). *First S. Korean astronaut launches*. https://news.bbc.co.uk/2/hi/asia-pacific/7335874.stm

Brzezinski, M. (2007). *Red moon rising: Sputnik and the hidden rivalries that ignited the space age* (p. 108). Henry Holt.

Burgess, C., & Hall, R. (2008). *The first soviet cosmonaut team: Their lives, legacy, and historical impact*. Springer.

Burgess, C., & Vis, B. (2015). *Interkosmos—The Eastern Bloc's early space program*. Springer.

Cameron, D. (2021, September 16). The SpaceX Inspiration4 launch: What to know about the orbital Mission. *Wall Street Journal*.

Canadian Space Agency. (2021, April 6). *Astronauts*. www.asc-csa.gc.ca/eng/astronauts

Catchpole, J. E. (2001). *Project mercury: NASA's first manned space Programme*. Springer.

Catchpole, J. E. (2008). *The international Space Station: Building for the future*. Springer.

Cates, G. (2021). The in-space rescue capability gap. *Journal of Space Safety Engineering, 8*, 202.

Centre national d'études spatiales. (2010, January 27). *Astronaute: l'espace à tout prix*. http://jeunes.cnes.fr/fr/web/CNES-Jeunes-fr/8240-astronaute-la-vie-apres-l-espace.php

Chaikin, A. (1994). *A man on the moon: The triumphant story of the Apollo space program*. Penguin.

Challenger: The Final Flight. Directed by Daniel Junge and Steven Leckart. Limited series, episode 3. Netflix Inc.

Chang, Y.-W. (2015). The first decade of space tourism. *Acta Astronomica, 108*, 79.

Chang, K., & Schwartz, J. (2014, November 1). Rocket plane for space tourists crashes in desert, killing a pilot. *New York Times*, A1.

Charme, J. S. (1991). The Interim Obligation of Article 18 of the Vienna Convention on the Law of Treaties: Making sense of an Enigma. *George Washington Journal of International Law and Economics, 25*, 71.

China Global Television Network. (2022, June 28). *Shenzhou-13 taikonaut welcomes cooperation in China's space station*. news.cgtn.com/news/2022-06-28/Shenzhou-13-taikonaut-welcomes-cooperation-in-China-s-space-station-1bePAInwkpO/index.html

Chow, D. (2011, April 14). NASA Faces Awkward, Unfortunate Spaceflight Gap. www.space.com/11387-nasa-future-human-spaceflight-hurdles-nss27.html

Chrétien, J.-L. (1993). *Sonata au clair de terre: Itinerary of a Frenchman in Space*. Denoël.

Chrétien, J.-L., Baudry, P., & Chabbert, B. (1982). *Spatiale premier: The First French in Space*. Plon.

Cole, M. D. (1995). *Vostok 1: First Human in Space*. Enslow.

Collins, M., & Aldrin, E. E. (1975). The Eagle has landed. In E. M. Cortright (Ed.), *Apollo expeditions to the Moon* (pp. 203–224). National Aeronautics and Space Administration.

Combs, H. (1979). *Kill devil hill: Discovering the secret of the wright brothers*. TernStyle Press.

Cook, J. (2016). *Challenges of Building the International Space Station*. Paper presented at the AIAA Space Forum, 13–16 September 2016, in Long Beach, California, United States.

Corbett, T., & Barker, N. (2020, November 15). *With Resilience, NASA and SpaceX begin operational Commercial Crew flights*. NASA Spaceflight. www.nasaspaceflight.com/2020/11/crew1-launch

Crawshaw, S. (1992). *Goodbye to the USSR: The Collapse of Soviet Power*. Bloomsbury.

Crump, L., & Godard, S. (2018). Reassessing communist international organisations: A comparative analysis of COMECON and the Warsaw Pact in relation to their Cold War competitors. *Contemporary European History, 27*, 85.

Culick, F. E. C. (2001). Wright Brothers: First Aeronautical Engineers and Test Pilots. *AIAA Journal, 41*(6), 4.

Davenport, C. (2018). *The Space Barons: Elon Musk, Jeff Bezos, and the Quest to Colonize the Cosmos*. Public Affairs.

Davenport, C. (2021, June 8). You are now free to move about the cosmos ... if you can afford it. *Washington Post*; and Fernholz, *Rocket Billionaires*.

Davenport, C. (2022, June 22). Disrupted by SpaceX, ULA was in 'serious trouble'. Now it's on the road back. *Washington Post*.

David, L. (2004, October 4). *SpaceShipOne Wins $ten Million Ansari X Prize in Historic second Trip to Space*. www.space.com/403-spaceshipone-wins-10-million-ansari-prize-historic-2nd-trip-space.html

David, L. (2005, July 27). *Richard Branson and Burt Rutan Form Spacecraft Building Company*. www.space.com/1356-richard-branson-burt-rutan-form-spacecraft-building-company.html

David, L. (2021, September 16). *Humanity needs a space-rescue capability, report stresses*. www.space.com/space-rescue-capability-needed-report

Davies, M. (2003). Obligations and implications for ships encountering persons in need of assistance at Sea. *Pacific Rim Law & Policy Journal, 12*, 109.

De Selding, P. B. (2016, March 16). ULA intends to lower its costs, and raise its cool, to compete with SpaceX. *Space News*. spacenews.com/ula-intends-to-lower-its-costs-and-raise-its-cool-to-compete-with-spacex

DeLucas, L. J. (1996). International space station. *Acta Astronomica, 38*, 613.

Dembling, P. G., & Arons, D. M. (1968). The treaty on rescue and return of astronauts and space objects. *William & Mary Law Review, 9*(641), 649.

Dempsey, P. S. (2004). Compliance and enforcement in international law: Achieving Global Uniformity in Aviation Safety. *North Carolina Journal of International Law, 30*, 1.

Deng Xiaoci, & Fan Anqi. (2022, June 5). Shenzhou-14 spacecraft delivers three taikonauts to China Space Station to complete national space lab construction. *Global Times*. www.globaltimes.cn/page/202206/1267276.shtml

Dethloff, H. C. (1993). *Suddenly tomorrow came: A History of the Johnson Space Centre* (pp. 23–24). National Aeronautics and Space Administration.

Donaldson, R. H. (1972). India: The Soviet Stake in Stability. *Asian Survey, 12*, 475.

Downs, G. (2021, October 1). Who will win the space tourism race? Virgin, Blue Origin, or SpaceX? *Wall Street Journal*. www.wsj.com/video/series/george-downs/who-will-win-the-space-tourism-race-virgin-blue-origin-or-spacex/50C78206-BD9A-48F4-B80A-51CB419F1022

Dubbs, C., & Paat-Dahlstrom, E. (2011). *Realising Tomorrow: The Path to Private Spaceflight* (pp. 167–191). University of Nebraska Press.

Dunn, M. (2007, August 8). Shuttle Endeavour puts teacher in orbit. *NBC News*. www.nbcnews.com/id/wbna20178250

European Space Agency. (n.d.). *The European Astronaut Corps*. www.esa.int/Science_Exploration/Human_and_Robotic_Exploration/Astronauts/The_European_astronaut_corps

Evans, B. *At Home in Space: The Late Seventies into the Eighties*. Springer.

Ezell, E. C., & Ezell, L. N. (1978). *The Partnership: A History of the Apollo-Soyuz Test Project*. National Aeronautics and Space Administration.

Farand, A. (2000). Legal Environment for Exploitation of the International Space Station (ISS). In G. Haskell & M. J. Rycroft (Eds.), *International space station: The next space marketplace* (pp. 141–153). Springer.

Faringdon, H. (1986). *Confrontation: The strategic geography of NATO and the Warsaw Pact*. Routledge.

Faust, J. (2010, July 26). Recasting the debate about commercial crew. *Space Review*. www.thespacereview.com/article/1671/1

Federal Aviation Administration. (2022, October 22). *FAA commercial human spaceflight recognition*. www.faa.gov/space/human_spaceflight/recognition

Fernholz, T. (2018). *Rocket Billionaires: Elon Musk, Jeff Bezos, and the New Space Race*. Houghton Mifflin Harcourt.

Financial Times. Space, the final frontier of tycoon rivalry [editorial]. *Financial Times*. www.ft.com/content/532c41c9-0087-4fed-8168-078c8aed3f5a

Fisher, K. (2021, December 10). The US Gives Bezos, Branson, and Shatner their astronaut wings. *CNN*. www.cnn.com/2021/12/10/politics/astronaut-wings-bezos-branson-shatner/index.html

Fleishman, G. (2018, September 19). Jeff Bezos Says Blue Origin Will Put People in Space in 2019. *Fortune*. fortune.com/2018/09/19/bezos-blue-origin-people-in-space-2019

Foust, J. (2014, September 19). NASA Commercial Crew Awards Leave Unanswered Questions. *Space News*. spacenews.com/41924nasa-commercial-crew-awards-leave-unanswered-questions

Garver, L. (2022). *Escaping Gravity: My Quest to Transform NASA and Launch a New Space Age*. Diversion Books.

Gehman, H., et al. (2003). *Report of Columbia Accident Investigation Board*. National Aeronautics and Space Administration.

Germer, P. (1970). Interpretation of Plurilingual Treaties: A Study of Article 33 of the Vienna Convention on the Law of Treaties. *Harvard International Law Journal, 11*, 400.

Ginat, R. (2000). The Soviet Union and the Syrian Ba'th Regime: From Hesitation to Rapprochement. *Middle Eastern Studies, 36*, 150.

Gorman, S. (2021 , July12). Billionaire Branson soars to space abroad Virgin Galactic flight. *Reuters*. www.reuters.com/lifestyle/science/virgin-galactics-branson-ready-space-launch-aboard-rocket-plane-2021-07-11

Goswami, N. (2018). China in Space: Ambitions and Possible Conflict. *Strategic Studies Quarterly, 12*, 74.

Government of India, Ashoka Chakra Citation for Squadron Leader Rakesh Sharma. (1985, May 7). *Indian Gazette*, 57-Pres/85.

Gragl, P., & Fitzmaurice, M. (2019). The Legal Character of Article 18 of the Vienna Convention on the Law of Treaties. *International & Comparative Law Quarterly, 68*, 699.

Gupta, S. (1963). India and the Soviet Union. *Current History, 44*, 141.

Hall, R., & Shayler, D. (2001). *The Rocket Man: Vostok & Voskhod—The First Soviet Manned Spaceflights*. Praxis.

Hammack, J. B. (Ed.). (1961). *Postlaunch Report for Mercury-Redstone 3 (MR-3)*. National Aeronautics and Space Administration.

Hammond, A. (2007 , October1). Saudi prince says Islam proud of Malaysian spaceman. *Reuters*. www.reuters.com/article/reutersEdge/idUSL3034275220070930

Harland, D. (1999). *Exploring the Moon: The Apollo expeditions*. Springer.

Harland, D. (2004). *The Story of Space Station Mir*. Springer.

Harwood, William. (2001, March 20). *NASA continues protesting space joyride of Dennis Tito*. Spaceflight Now. spaceflightnow.com/news/n0103/20tito; Anon. (2001, April 19). Goldin Plans to Snub Koptev Conference over Tito Flight to ISS. *Space Daily*. www.spacedaily.com/reports/Goldin_Plans_To_Snub_Koptev_Conference_Over_Tito_Flight_To_ISS.html

Hendrickx, B., & Vis, B. (2007). *Energiya-Buran: The Soviet Space Shuttle*. Springer.

Hennigan, W. J. (2010, November 8). Spacecraft factory to break ground in Mojave. *Los Angeles Times*.

Hiltzik, M. (2021, July 6). The Bezos-Branson-Musk space race is a huge waste of money and scientifically useless. *Los Angeles Times*.

Hirschfeld, A. (2021, July 28). What is the environmental impact of the billionaire space race? Experts weigh in. *The Observer*.

Hohler, R. T. (1986). *I touch the future: The story of Christa McAuliffe*. Random House.

Hollinger, P., & Cookson, C. (2022, June 14). Interview with E.S.A. astronaut Samantha Cristoforetti from space. *Financial Times*.

Howard, F. (1988). *Orville and Wilbur: The story of the Wright Brothers*. Hale.

Howell, E. (2017, November 14). *Dream Chaser: Sierra Nevada's design for Spaceflight*. www.space.com/19552-dream-chaser.html

Howell, E. (2020, December 17). *Canadian astronauts will start flying to the Moon in 2023 with NASA's Artemis missions*. www.space.com/canadian-astronauts-artemis-moon-missions

Hur, Krystal. (2021, July 16). Jeff Bezos, Richard Branson, and Where Space Really Begins. *Wall Street Journal*.

Islam, S. (1993). Russia's Rough Road to Capitalism. *Foreign Affairs, 72*(2), 57.

Jenkins, D. R. (2016). *Space Shuttle: Developing an Icon—1972–2013*. Specialty Press.

Jenks, A. (2012). Conquering space: The cult of Yuri Gagarin. In M. Bassin & C. Kelly (Eds.), *Soviet and Post-Soviet identities* (pp. 129–150). Cambridge University Press.

Johnson-Freese, J. (2003). China's Manned Space Program: Sun Tzu or Apollo Redux? *Naval War College Review, 56*, 51.

Karsh, E. (1991). *Soviet Policy towards Syria since 1970*. Palgrave Macmillan.
Kaser, M. (1967). *Comecon: Integration problems of the planned economies*. Oxford University Press.
Khrushchev, N. S. (1962, March 22). *New York Times*, 18.
Klerkx, G. (2004). *Lost in space: The fall of NASA and the dream of a new space age*. Random House.
Kluger, J. (2021, August 10). Four Civilian Astronauts. Three Days in Orbit. One Giant Leap. Meet the Inspiration4 Crew. *Time*. time.com/6083977/jared-isaacman-inspiration4-profile
Kluger, J. (2022, June 28). Billionaires are racing to space—and the climate is paying the price. *Time*. time.com/6191846/billionaire-space-race-climate
Koren, M. (2021, July 19). Jeff Bezos is ready to cross a cosmically controversial line. *The Atlantic*. www.theatlantic.com/science/archive/2021/07/jeff-bezos-blue-origin-branson/619476
Kramer, M. N. (1985). Civil–military relations in the Warsaw pact: The East European component. *International Affairs, 61*, 45.
Lamar, J. V., & Hannifan, J. (1985, April 22). Jake Skywalker: A Senator boards the shuttle. *Time*.
Lányl, K. (1993). The Collapse of the COMECON Market. *Russian & East European Finance and Trade, 29*, 68.
Lee, H.-S. (2022, May 30). Arianespace to rival SpaceX with competitive quality and price. *Korea Economic Daily*. www.kedglobal.com/us/aerospace-defense/newsView/ked202205300011
Leinbach, M. D., & Ward, J. H. (2018). *Bringing Columbia Home: The untold story of a lost space shuttle and her crew*. Arcade Publishing.
Leopold, G. (2016). *Calculated risk: The supersonic life and Times of Gus Grissom*. Purdue University Press.
Libbey, J. (2010). CoCom, Comecon, and the economic cold war. *Russian History, 37*, 133.
Lies, E. (2022, December 16). Going to space makes you 'obsessed with Earth', billionaire Yusaku Maezawa says. *Japan Times*. www.japantimes.co.jp/news/2022/01/07/national/yusaku-maezawa-spacex
Lukin, A. (2021). The Russia-China Entente and its future. *International Politics, 58*, 363.
Lüthi, L. (2012). Restoring Chaos to History: Sino-Soviet-American Relations, 1969. *The China Quarterly, 210*, 378.
Lynn, M. (2021, July 12). Branson vs. Bezos: In praise of the billionaire space race. *The Spectator*.
Lyons, R. D. (1985, May 5). One Thing NASA Can't Settle: Astronauts' Stomachs. *New York Times*, 4–26.
Manfredi, L. (2022, August 26). NASA clears Blue Origin, Sierra Space's 'Orbital Reef' station for design phase. *Fox Business*. www.foxbusiness.com/technology/nasa-clears-blue-origin-sierra-space-orbital-reef-station-design-phase
Mann, A. (2020, December 9). *United Launch Alliance: Combing the forces of two aerospace giants*. www.space.com/united-launch-alliance.html.
Mann, A. (2021, October 25). *The Boeing Company: From rockets to commercial crew*. www.space.com/the-boeing-company
Mathieu, C. (2008). *Assessing Russia's Space Cooperation with China and India*. European Space Policy Institute.
McArdle, M. (2021, July 13). The billionaire space race benefits the rest of us. Really. *Washington Post*.
McDonald, A. J., & Hansen, J. R. (2018). *Truth, Lies, and O-Rings: Inside the space shuttle challenger disaster*. University Press of Florida.
Miller, C. (2016). *The Struggle to Save the Soviet Economy: Mikhail Gorbachev and the Collapse of the USSR*. University of North Carolina Press.
Minter, A. (2022, March 29). Russia Just Became the World's First Former Space Power. *Washington Post*.
Nagel, K.-F. (1998). Das neue Regierungsabkommen über die Internationale Raum Station [The new intergovernmental agreement on the ISS] (1998). *Zeitschrift für Luft- und Weltraumrecht, 47*, 143.

Nelson, B., & Buckingham, J. (1988). *Mission: An American Congressman's voyage to space*. Harcourt Brace Jovanovich.

Oberg, J. (2003). China's great leap upward. *Scientific American, 289*, 76.

Otake, T. (2013, August 3). Toyohiro Akiyama: Cautionary tales from one not afraid to risk all. *Japan Times*. www.japantimes.co.jp/life/2013/08/03/people/toyohiro-akiyama-cautionary-tales-from-one-not-afraid-to-risk-all

Oxman, B. H. (1997). Human Rights and the United Nations Convention on the Law of the Sea. *Columbia Journal of Transnational Law, 36*(399), 414.

Palchetti, P. (2011). Article 18 of the 1969 Vienna Convention: A Vague and Ineffective Obligation or a Useful Means for Strengthening Legal Cooperation? In E. Cannizzaro (Ed.), *The law of treaties beyond the Vienna convention* (pp. 25–36). Oxford University Press.

Papachristodoulou, A. (2022). The Recognition of a Right to be Rescued at Sea in International Law. *Leiden Journal of International Law, 35*, 337.

Papanicolopulu, I. (2016). The Duty to Rescue at Sea, in Peacetime and in War: A General Overview. *International Review of the Red Cross, 98*(491), 497.

Park, I. (2004, October 4). The X Prize. *New Yorker*, 52–63.

Pearson, R. (1998). *The Rise and Fall of the Soviet Empire*. Macmillan.

Power, J. K. (2011). *Power, culture, and economic change in Russia: To the undiscovered country of post-socialism, 1988–2008*. Taylor & Francis.

Ramet, P. (1986). The Soviet-Syrian Relationship. *Problems of Communism, 35*(5).

Rao, M. K., Sridhara Murthi, K. R., & Prasad, M. Y. S. (2017). *The decision for Indian Human Spaceflight Programme—Political perspectives, national relevance, and technological challenges*. Paper presented at the 68th International Astronautical Congress, 25–29 September 2017, in Adelaide, South Australia.

Rhian, J. (2014, October 5). *A decade after SpaceShipOne's Triumphant Flight—Commercial flights still a ways off. spaceflight insider*. www.spaceflightinsider.com/missions/commercial/decade-later-spaceshipones-triumphant-flight-still-awaiting-first-flight-paying-customers

Rincon, P. (2021, July 20). Jeff Bezos launches to space abroad New Shepard rocket ship. *BBC*. www.bbc.com/news/science-environment-57849364

Robinson, T. W. (1972). The Sino-Soviet border dispute: Background, development, and the March 1969 Clashes. *American Political Science Review, 66*, 1175.

Rogers, W. P., et al. (1986). *Report of the presidential commission on the space shuttle challenger accident*. National Aeronautics and Space Administration.

Rohter, L. (2006, April 8). Brazil's man in space: A Mere 'Hitchhiker' or a 'Hero'? *New York Times*, A-3.

Roulette, J. (2021a, December 9). Japanese Mogul Reaches Space Station as Tourist. *New York Times*, A-10.

Roulette, J. (2021b, October 18). Russian Film Crew Wraps Shoot at Space Station and Returns to Earth. *New York Times*, A-10; Associated Press. (2021, October 17).

Sanger, D. E. (1990, December 8). A Japanese Innovation: The Space Antihero. *New York Times*, 1–1.

Sanz Fernández de Córdoba, S. (2004, June 21). *100 km Altitude Boundary for Astronautics*. FAI Astronautic Records Commission. www.fai.org/page/icare-boundary

Schwartz, John. (2008, October 10). Russia Leads Way in Space Tourism with Paid Trips into Orbit. *New York Times*.

Schwartz, P. N. (2021, June 21). *The changing nature and implications of Russian military transfers to China*. Center for Strategic & International Studies. www.csis.org/analysis/changing-nature-and-implications-russian-military-transfers-china

Shalal, A., & Klotz, I. (2015, April 13). Vulcan rocket launch in 2019 may end US dependence on Russia. *Reuters*. www.reuters.com/article/lockheed-boeing-rockets/vulcan-rocket-launch-in-2019-may-end-u-s-dependence-on-russia-idUSL2N0XA2DE20150414

Shayler, D. (2000). *Disasters and accidents in manned spaceflight*. Springer.

Shayler, D. J. (2009). *Space rescue: Ensuring the safety of manned spaceflight*. Springer.

Sheehan, M. (2007). *The international politics of space* (pp. 59–61). Routledge.
Siddiqi, A. A. (2000). *Challenge to Apollo: The Soviet Union and the Space Race, 1945–1974*. US Government Printing Office.
Sivolella, D. (2017). *The space shuttle program: Technologies and accomplishments*. Springer.
Slayton, D. K., & Cassult, M. (1994). *Deke! U.S. manned space: From Mercury to the shuttle*. Forge.
Spencer, S. (2018). The demand for a single international search and rescue agreement template flexible for multi-regional use as disseminated by the international civil aviation organisation. *Perth International Law Journal, 3*, 115.
Stepaniak, P. C., Lane, H. W., & Davis, J. R. (2014). *Loss of signal: Aeromedical lessons learned from STS-107 Columbia Space Shuttle Mishap*. National Aeronautics and Space Administration.
Stern, N. (1997). The transition in Eastern Europe and the Former Soviet Union: Some strategic lessons from the experience of 25 countries over six years. In S. Zecchini (Ed.), *Lessons from the economic transition: Central and Eastern Europe in the 1990s* (pp. 35–57). Springer.
Street, F. (2019, August 26). 100 years ago: The first scheduled international passenger flight departed. *CNN*. edition.cnn.com/travel/article/first-scheduled-international-passenger-flight/index.html
Szalontai, B. (2005). *Kim Il Sung in the Khrushchev Era: Soviet–DPRK relations and the roots of North Korean despotism, 1953–1964*. Stanford University Press.
Tauman, J. E. (2002). Rescued at sea, but nowhere to go: The cloudy legal waters of the Tampa crisis. *Pacific Rim Law & Policy Journal, 11*, 461.
Taylor, A. (2021, July 20). How the collapse of the Soviet Union aided the birth of space tourism. *Washington Post*.
Thornton, W., & Bonato, F. (2017). *The human body and weightlessness* (p. 32). Springer.
Tyler, P. E. (2001, March 24). Russians find pride, and regret, in Mir's splashdown. *New York Times*, A-3; CNN. (2000, June 16). Future of Mir in doubt after cosmonauts return home. www.cnn.com/2000/TECH/space/06/16/mir.folo/index.html
Uhalley, S. (2016). China's 'Jade Rabbit' Rover on the Moon: A Wake-up Call: Chang'e 3 and Yutu on the Lunar Surface. *American Journal of Chinese Studies, 23*, 211.
Umbach, F. (2005). *Das rote Bündnis: Entwicklung und Zerfall des Warschauer Paktes 1955 bis 1991*. Christoph Links.
US National Aeronautics and Space Administration, S.T.S.-86. www.nasa.gov/mission_pages/shuttle/shuttlemissions/archives/sts-86.html
Van Pelt, M. (2010). *Space tourism: Adventures in Earth orbit and beyond*. Copernicus.
Vance, A. (2021, July 16). *The future of space is bigger than Jeff Bezos, Richard Branson, or Elon Musk. Bloomberg*. www.bloomberg.com/news/articles/2021-07-16/billionaire-space-race-between-bezos-branson-and-musk-is-just-the-beginning
Vaughan, D. (2016). *The challenger launch decision: Risky technology, culture, and deviance and N.A.S.A*. University of Chicago Press.
Villiger, M. E. (2008). *Commentary on the 1969 Vienna convention on the Law of Treaties* (pp. 450–462). Martinus Nijhoff.
Vojtech, M. (2010). The Soviet Union's Partnership with India. *Cold War Studies, 12*, 50.
Voosen, P. (2018, July 24). Outer space may have just gotten a bit closer. *Science*. www.science.org/content/article/outer-space-may-have-just-gotten-bit-closer
Waddell, L. (2021, July 22). Space Race between billionaires like Jeff Bezos, Elon Musk, and Richard Branson is a grotesque display of wealth. *The Scotsman*.
Walker, S. (2021). *Beyond: The astonishing story of the first human to leave our planet and journey into space*. William Collins.
Wall, Mike. (2011, April 27). *Wall, First Space Tourist: How a U.S. Millionaire Bought a Ticket to Orbit*. www.space.com/11492-space-tourism-pioneer-dennis-tito.html
Wall, M. (2013, April 30). *NASA to Pay $70 Million a Seat to Fly Astronauts on Russian Spacecraft*. www.space.com/20897-nasa-russia-astronaut-launches-2017.html

Wall, M. (2021, July 20). *Jeff Bezos launches into space on Blue Origin's first astronaut flight*. www.space.com/jeff-bezos-blue-origin-first-astronaut-launch

Wattles, J. (2021, July 12). Virgin Galactic founder Richard Branson successfully rockets into space. *CNN*. www.cnn.com/2021/07/11/tech/richard-branson-virgin-galactic-space-flight-scn/index.html

Williams, O. A. (2021, December 21). Billionaire Space Race Turns Into A Publicity Disaster. *Forbes*. www.forbes.com/sites/oliverwilliams1/2021/12/21/billionaire-space-race-turns-into-a-publicity-disaster

Woodward, T. (2003, February 2). Disaster halts teacher's chance to fly—again. *Florida Today*, 10A.

Yakovenko, A. V. (1999). The intergovernmental agreement on the international space station. *Space Policy, 15*, 79.

Yang, K. (2000). The Sino-Soviet Border Clash of 1969: From Zhenbao Island to Sino-American Rapprochement. *Cold War History, 1*, 21.

Yardley, J. (2003, October 15). China Sends a Man into Orbit, entering the U.S.–Russian Club. *New York Times*, A1.

Young, K. (2006, January 13). Brazilian astronaut to visit the space station. *New Scientist*. www.newscientist.com/article/dn8578-brazilian-astronaut-to-visit-the-space-station

Yuan, J.-d. (2010). Sino-Russian Defense Ties: The View from Beijing. In J. Bellacqua (Ed.), *The future of China–Russia relations* (pp. 203–230). University Press of Kentucky.

Zubrin, R. (2019). *The case for space: How the revolution in spaceflight opens up a future of limitless possibility*. Amherst.

Chapter 4
The Artemis Accords: A New Phase in the Development of Outer Space Law

E. Prema, R. Vijaya Bharathi, and V. Shyam Sundar

Introduction

The United States (US) National Aeronautics and Space Administration (NASA) has drafted and successfully socialised the Artemis Accords with a number of other Nation States in a bid to ensure 'safe, responsible and transparent behaviour in space', including 'preserving and protecting the outer space environment to ensure a safe and sustainable future in space for all'.[1] At the time of launch in 2020 eight nation states signed the Accords,[2] with the aim to encourage bilateral and multilateral space cooperation between the Accords signatories, enhancing global understanding of the universe and enhancing global prosperity.[3] The Accords were signed by Australia, Canada, Italy, Japan, Luxembourg, the UAE, the United Kingdom, and the United States on 13 October 2020.[4] Importantly, the bold and multinational

[1]NASA. (n.d.). Artemis Accords. www.nasa.gov/specials/artemis-accords/index.html

[2]Strickland, A. (2020, October 14). *Eight States Sign NASA's Artemis Accords that Guide Cooperative Exploration of the Moon*. CNN. https://edition.cnn.com/2020/10/14/world/artemis-accords-States-sign-nasa-scn-trnd/index.html

[3]*Id.*

[4]NASA. (October 12). *International Partners Advance Cooperation with First Signings of Artemis Accords*. NASA Press release. https://www.nasa.gov/news-release/nasa-international-partners-advance-cooperation-with-first-signings-of-artemis-accords/#:~:text=International%20cooperation%20on%20Artemis%20is,mutual%20understanding%20and%20reducing%20misperceptions.

E. Prema (✉) · R. V. Bharathi
VIT School of Law, Vellore Institute of Technology, Chennai, Tamil Nadu, India
e-mail: prema.e@vit.ac.in

V. S. Sundar
Chennai Dr Ambedkar Government Law College, Pudupakkam, Tamil Nadu, India

M. A. Pozza (ed.), *Ascending to Space*, Space Law and Policy,
https://doi.org/10.1007/978-981-97-0714-0_4

vision for the future of space exploration has been postured as a key aspect of the Accords.[5] The Accords aim to promote lunar exploration, but they are also critical for enhancing global governance in general.

The signatories to the Accords agree to adhere to certain principles that will drive their civil space activities, such as sharing scientific information with the public,[6] mitigating space debris responsibly,[7] registering space objects,[8] and creating and implementing interoperability standards.[9] However, with increased activity on the Moon, there is a growing international battle over resource exploitation of the Moon that could be one potential source of conflict in the future. However, the Accords are only a codified understanding between the respective signatory Nation State space agencies and are not legally binding.[10] Further, the Accords address the rising problem of 'safety zones' where states are forbidden from interfering with each other's resource extraction operations.[11]

However, whilst these safety zone measures may be able to some extent ease tensions between States, they also run the risk of becoming the root of a new problem of actually creating the problem of 'safety zones' as an area of non-interference, which arguably is against the principle of non-appropriation and *res communis* and could be said to indirectly stop Nation States that are not signatories of the Accords, from accessing the Moon towards greater lunar exploration.

A plain reading of the Accords might look like it is compliant with the Outer Space Treaty (OST), 1967, but if we read the Accords holistically, we can see that it introduces concepts and principles which are not part of the OST. 'Hobe warns that the Artemis Accords are an attempt by the Americans to walk softly to legitimize their deviation from the Outer Space Treaty'.[12] Further, 'While describing the Artemis Accords as a political project, Von Der Dunk argues that the intention of the United States is to gather consensus around its interpretation of the OST regarding the exploitation of the Moon's resources'.[13] Perhaps there are grounds

[5]'Consequently, any discussion about being bold must also include understanding risk.' Keck Institute for Space Studies (KISS), 2022, Revolutionizing Access to the Mars Surface. Culbert, C.J., Ehlmann, B.L., Fraeman, A.A., editors. Final Workshop Report for the W.M. Keck Institute for Space Studies, Pasadena, CA. DOI: 10.7907/d1smmj77.

[6]Section 8 of The Artemis Accords, 2020.

[7]Section 12 of The Artemis Accords, 2020.

[8]Section 7 of The Artemis Accords, 2020.

[9]Section 5 of The Artemis Accords, 2020.

[10]Matthew, G. (2023). The Artemis Accords: International Cooperation in the Era of Space Exploration. *Harvard International Review*. https://hir.harvard.edu/the-artemis-accords/

[11]Cowing, K. (2020, May 17). *What Are The Artemis Accords And Why Do We Need Them?*. Spaceref. https://spaceref.com/science-and-exploration/what-are-the-artemis-accords-and-why-do-we-need-them/

[12]Deplano, R. (2021). The Artemis Accords: evolution or revolution in international space law?. *International & Comparative Law Quarterly*, 70 (3), 799–819. DOI: https://doi.org/10.1017/S0020589321000142

[13]Id.

for the Accords to implement a system in place to specify which Nation States acquire specific territories.

The Accords have spurred the interest of States such as Rwanda, which has entered space exploration,[14] and Nigeria, which has been involved in space activities for more than two decades. Nigeria and Rwanda are the first African States to become signatories of NASA's Artemis Accords, and so it is important to note that Rwanda signed the Artemis Accords because it is still a part of the least developed country (LDC) according to the 2021 triennial review of the United Nation's Department of Economic and Social Affairs Economic Analysis. Every State that has to date signed the Artemis Accords is a natural ally of the United States,[15] and it is important to consider that there is some concern by those States to expand their space sector and programme: the United Kingdom, Italy, and Canada are all hoping that the Artemis Program will boost their economies through the development of their space manufacturing industries[16], and Luxembourg enacted a law in 2017 that permits space mining.[17] In addition, the United Arab Emirates (UAE) and Australia, whose space agencies are relatively young, founded in 2014 and 2018, respectively, seek to strengthen their international ties and see Artemis as an opportunity to gain prominence.[18] Nevertheless, the two most notable countries, China and Russia, long-term space-faring States, are not signatories to the Artemis Accords. Among the space-faring States, Russia has lamented the impossibility of signing the Artemis Accords due to their being perceived as protecting the interests of the United States in pursuing the exploitation of the Moon's natural resources.[19] China has mostly remained silent due to NASA's legal inability to cooperate with Chinese agencies while disapproving of the US unilateral approach to regulating space activities.[20] This chapter considers that whilst the technological progress related to space exploration may relieve drastically fraught international relations and see greater

[14] Whittington, M R. (2022, December 25). *Why did Nigeria and Rwanda sign NASA's Artemis Accords?*. The Hill. https://thehill.com/opinion/international/3786847-why-did-nigeria-and-rwanda-sign-nasas-artemis-accords/

[15] Newman, C. (2020, October 19). *Artemis Accords: Why Many States Are Refusing to Sign Moon Exploration Agreement.* The Conversation. https://theconversation.com/artemis-accords-why-many-countries-are-refusing-to-sign-moon-exploration-agreement-148134

[16] *Id.*

[17] Luxembourg Space Agency. (2022, December 16). *Contribution of the Grand Duchy of Luxembourg on the Mandate and Purpose of the Working Group on Legal Aspects of Space Resource Activities.* https://www.unoosa.org/documents/pdf/copuos/lsc/space-resources/LSC2023/StatesResponses/Luxembourg_-_20221216_WG_SR_LU_Contribution.pdf. And see https://space-agency.public.lu/en/agency/legal-framework.html

[18] Matthew, G. (2023). The Artemis Accords: International Cooperation in the Era of Space Exploration. *Harvard International Review*. https://hir.harvard.edu/the-artemis-accords/

[19] Deplano, R. (2021). The Artemis Accords: evolution or revolution in international space law?. *International & Comparative Law Quarterly*, 70 (3), 799 819. DOI: https://doi.org/10.1017/S0020589321000142

[20] *Id.*

collaboration, there is some scepticism that the Accords may instead aggravate existing tensions.[21]

The Artemis Accords

The Artemis Accords (Accords) name-genesis is from the Greek goddess of the Moon[22] and is formulated to take US National Space Policy to the next level of space exploration in which the United States will work together with commercial and international partners to return to the Moon. The aim of the Accords is to advance the United States' interests in space and lead a new era of permanent human presence in space and on the Moon, Mars, and beyond through collaboration with other States.[23]

We understand that space activities are vital to our daily life existence in the sense that we utilise space assets on a daily basis such as global positioning system (GPS) or weather information.[24] Access to space activities is crucial to the international community.[25] Space activities are rapidly moving towards a new world of living and the ensuing new opportunities in multiple international sectors.[26] For instance, Telecommunications constitutes the largest, and most rapidly expanding, market in space products, and this growth area currently offers substantial financial opportunities to service providers, operators, and purveyors of infrastructure within both the already 'classical' area of mobile communications and the newer regime of information services.[27] The peaceful use of outer space should be carried out in line with international law pursuant to the principles in OST, with all States having equal and universal access to space. Space technology has helped with the development of

---

[21] World Economic Forum. (n.d.). *The Global Risks Report 2019*, 14th Edn. https://www3.weforum.org/docs/WEF_Global_Risks_Report_2019.pdf

[22] Lele, A. & Gopalakrishnan. V, (2020, October 24). *Artemis Accords: Utilateralization in Space*. Commentaries, Society for the Study of Peace and Conflict. https://sspconline.org/opinion-analysis/artemis-accords-unilateralization-space-sat-10242020

[23] The White House National Space Council. (2020, July 23). *A New Era for Deep Space Exploration and Development*. The National Space Strategy. https://csps.aerospace.org/sites/default/files/2021-08/NSpC%20New%20Era%20for%20Space%2023Jul20.pdf

[24] Pozza, M., "Space Law: An Overview"., VIT University Presentation (remote), 04 March 2022.

[25] United Nations General Assembly. (2022, October 26). *Fourth Committee Shifts Focus to Peaceful Uses of Outer Space with Speakers Emphasizing Need to Close Technological Gap*. Seventy-Seventh Session, 14th Meeting, General Assembly, UN Press Release. https://press.un.org/en/2022/gaspd760.doc.htm

[26] Raitt, D. et al. (2005, February). *The Impact of Space Activities upon Society*. The International Academy of Astronautics and European Space Agency. https://www.esa.int/esapub/br/br237/br237.pdf. And see, *NATO's Approach to Space*. North Atlantic Treaty Organization. https://www.nato.int/cps/en/natohq/topics_175419.htm

[27] International Space Exploration Coordination Group. (2013, September). *Benefits Stemming from Space Exploration*. International Space Exploration Coordination Group. https://www.nasa.gov/sites/default/files/files/Benefits-Stemming-from-Space-Exploration-2013-TAGGED.pdf

member states, which have benefitted from space technology such as broadcasting, environmental monitoring, and surveillance. Other useful applications continue to be discovered and put into practice, allowing for the successful achievement of the 'Space2030' Agenda and the Sustainable Development Goals.[28] At present, space activities are facing new challenges to the international community for that it requires careful development of regulation and global space governance that take into account current issues spanning from the incorporation of better sustainability of the space environment[29] as well as the promotion of safe and secure space operations for the development of economic aspects of the international community in preserving the benefits of space for future space operations.[30]

On a historical development point, space missions during Trump's presidency saw an increase in space-based activities both commercially and militarily with the establishment of the Space Force.[31] The Trump Administration developed the Artemis Program, mandating the Space Policy Directive 1 'reinvigorating America's Human Space Exploration Program' that tasked NASA with focusing on the mission to return humans to the Moon, followed by missions to Mars and beyond.[32] Further, in 2017, the US space policy appealed to NASA administrators to 'lead an innovative and sustainable program of exploration with commercial and international partners to enable human expansion across the solar system and to bring back to Earth new knowledge and opportunities'.[33] An expanded role for private aerospace companies, which also means that they produce hardware and potentially launch a lunar economy, was part of the Trump Administration's push towards the Moon. Companies such as SpaceX, Blue Origin, and Relativity Space are investing in the development and commercialization of new technologies such as reusable launch vehicles.[34] Elon Musk's SpaceX and Jeff Bezos' Blue Origin are among the 11 US businesses that received $45.5 million from NASA to create landers that can carry

---

[28] United Nations General Assembly. (2022, October 26). *Fourth Committee Shifts Focus to Peaceful Uses of Outer Space with Speakers Emphasizing Need to Close Technological Gap.* Seventy-Seventh Session, 14th Meeting, General Assembly, UN Press Release. https://press.un.org/en/2022/gaspd760.doc.htm

[29] Goguichvili, S. et al., (2020, October 1). *The Global Legal Landscape: Who Writes the Rules on the Final Frontier?* Wilson Center. https://www.wilsoncenter.org/article/global-legal-landscape-space-who-writes-rules-final-frontier

[30] *Id.*

[31] David. L. (2018, September 30). *Would Trump's "Space Force" Patrol the Moon.* Scientific American. https://www.scientificamerican.com/article/would-trumps-space-force-patrol-the-moon/

[32] Bukley, A P. (2020, October) *To The Moon and Beyond: Challenges and Opportunities for NASA's Artemis Program.* Space Agenda 2021, Center for Space Policy and Strategy. The Aerospace Corporation. P-4. https://csps.aerospace.org/sites/default/files/2021-08/Bukley_TheMoon_20201027.pdf

[33] *Id.*

[34] Coykendall, J. et al., (2023, March 22). *Riding the Exponential Growth in Space.* Deloitte Insights. https://www2.deloitte.com/us/en/insights/industry/aerospace-defense/future-of-space-economy.html/#endnote-13

men to the Moon's surface.[35] Further, SpaceX raised about US$2 billion in 2022 with an ambitious plan for 2023 which includes 87 rocket launches, a sustained moon exploration project, and expansion of Starlink Internet service. These private companies are also expanding to other segments, such as satellite-based services.[36]

The United States' policy of investing in the outer space sector has resulted in attracting private players. As a result, the Accords focused on futuristic policies which include opportunities for other states. Artemis Program,[37] heralding a new era for space exploration and utilization, and take one step closer to Mars.[38] As the lead agency for the Artemis Program, NASA has engaged in international partnerships to ensure a successful role of the Accords is adopted by it in order to achieve its aims, which principally look to establish a sustainable and robust presence on the Moon while preparing to conduct a historic human mission to Mars.[39] The Accords are a standard set of principles to govern outer space's civil exploration and use that to seek and implement a shared vision grounded in the 1967 OST[40]specifically in creating a safe and transparent environment that facilitates exploration, science and commercial activities for all humanity.[41] There are currently 23 signatories to the accords, representing every continent and a wide range of space interests and capabilities. Australia, Bahrain, Brazil, Canada, Colombia, France, Israel, Italy, Japan, the Republic of Korea, Luxembourg, Mexico, New Zealand, Nigeria, Poland, Romania, Rwanda, Saudi Arabia, Singapore, Ukraine, the UAE, the United Kingdom, and the United States have signed the Artemis Accords as an indication of their commitment to the peaceful, responsible and sustainable use of space.[42] These States

[35] Wall, M. (2019, May 17). *NASA Awards $45.5Million for Private Moon Lander Work on Project Artemis*. Space.com. https://www.space.com/nasa-private-moon-landers-funding-artemis.html. And see *Benzo's Blue Origin wins NASA contract to Build Astronaut Lunar Lander*. May 20, 2023, Economic Times. https://economictimes.indiatimes.com/tech/technology/bezos-blue-origin-wins-nasa-contract-to-build-astronaut-lunar-lander/articleshow/100364786.cms?from=mdr

[36] Coykendall, J. et al., (2023, March 22). *Riding the Exponential Growth in Space*. Deloitte Insights. https://www2.deloitte.com/us/en/insights/industry/aerospace-defense/future-of-space-economy.html/#endnote-13

[37] *The Artemis Program: Humanity's Return to the Moon*. Government of Canada Portal, 2023. https://www.asc-csa.gc.ca/eng/astronomy/moon-exploration/artemis-missions.asp

[38] Butterfield, S. (2023, May 25). *Artemis II to Continue NASA's Moon to Mars Goal*. Oelwein Daily Register. https://www.communitynewspapergroup.com/oelwein_daily_register/artemis-ii-to-continue-nasas-moon-to-mars-goal/article_d3f10a45-8490-5ed1-9ff0-824808680141.html . And see, Adam Mann, Ailsa Harvey, *NASA's Artemis Program: Everything You Need to Know*. December 12, 2022. https://www.space.com/artemis-program.html

[39] NASA. (2020, October 13). International Partners Advance Cooperation with First Signings of Artemis Accords. NASA Press Release. https://www.nasa.gov/press-release/nasa-international-partners-advance-cooperation-with-first-signings-of-artemis-accords

[40] NASA. *Principles for a Safe, Peaceful, and Prosperous Future*. The Artemis Accords. https://www.nasa.gov/specials/artemis-accords/index.html

[41] United States Embassy. (2020, October 20). Fact Sheet: Artemis Accords - United for Peaceful Exploration of Deep Space. https://br.usembassy.gov/fact-sheet-artemis-accords-united-for-peaceful-exploration-of-deep-space/

[42] *Id.*

are also leading the global dialogue on the future of space exploration.[43] For example, on 13 January 2023, the Framework Agreement for Cooperation in the Exploration and Use of Outer Space, including the Moon and Other Celestial Bodies, for Peaceful Purposes, 1979 (Moon Agreement), was finally signed by the United States and Japan after more than 10 years of negotiations. According to US Secretary of State, Antony Blinken, the future of space is collaboration, and this agreement would allow both States to 'go farther and learn even more together', he said during the signing ceremony at NASA Headquarters.[44] The Moon agreement additionally confirms Japan's support for the Artemis human spaceflight mission and also supports the Lunar Gateway project to build an orbiting lunar research station and assist future Mars missions.[45] Previously, at the 24th Asia Pacific Regional Space Agency Forum, leaders from several Asian States, such as Vietnam, Thailand, Malaysia, Indonesia, Japan, India, and South Korea, collaborated and considered that joining forces makes it easier to agree on a unified space policy and make future joint space explorations more probable.[46] NASA's spokesperson, Space lawyer Michael Gold, 'Even if some States are unable to contribute directly to lunar activities in the near future, their adherence to the Artemis Accords' guiding principles will increase the need for common international standards for space exploration and exploitation'.[47]

The Accords rely upon the following key principles:

(i) ***Peaceful purpose:*** The Accords recognise the importance of collaboration between States that bolsters space exploration and also strengthens international relations among States.[48] The intention that all activities be carried out for peaceful purposes in accordance with the principles of the OST forms the basis of the Artemis Accords.[49]

---

[43] US Department of State. (2022, December 15). *Nigeria and Rwanda: First African States Sign the Artemis Accords*. www.state.gov/nigeria-and-rwanda-first-african-States-sign-the-artemis-accords

[44] Japan, U. S. M. (2023, January 17). *US, Japan sign space collaboration agreement at NASA headquarters*. U.S. Embassy & Consulates in Japan. https://jp.usembassy.gov/us-japan-nasa-space-collaboration-agreement/

[45] Smith, Z. L. M (2023, February 2). *Going Farther Together: The U.S.-Japan Space Pact Is an Accelerator*. Center For Strategic & International Studies. https://www.csis.org/analysis/going-farther-together-us-japan-space-pact-accelerator

[46] Wood, J. (2018, October 25). *How States are Collaborating to Further Space Exploration*. SPECTRA. https://spectra.mhi.com/how-States-are-collaborating-to-further-space-exploration; also see Summary Report on the APRSAF-24 in Bengaluru India, January, 2018. https://sentinel-asia.org/meetings/SA3JPTM5/agenda/Day1/Session1/1.6_JAXA_APRSAF_Report.pdf

[47] Howell, E. (2022, August 25). Artemis Accords: Why the International Moon Exploration Framework Matters, space.com, https://www.space.com/artemis-accords-moon-space-exploration-importance

[48] Section 3 of the Artemis Accords, 2020.

[49] *Id.*

(ii) ***Transparency policy:*** The signatory States must consent to uphold the principle by publicly and transparently describing their policies and plans.[50]

(iii) ***Interoperability:*** System interoperability is essential for ensuring reliable and safe space exploration; as a result, the Artemis Accords mandate that signatory States make use of open international standards, create new standards when needed, and strive to the maximum extent possible to enable interoperability.[51]

(iv) ***Emergency assistance:*** Every responsible civil space programme must include the provision of emergency assistance to those in need.[52] The Agreement on the Rescue of Astronauts, the Agreement on the Rescue of Astronauts, the Return of Astronauts, and the Return of Objects Launched into Outer Space, 1968 ('Rescue of Astronauts Agreement'), is reaffirmed by the Artemis Accords. Additionally, as part of Artemis, NASA, the United States and its Signatory States agree to render assistance to the best of their ability to astronauts who are in need.[53]

(v) ***Registration of space objects:*** Registration of outer space objects is the foundation of establishing a secure and sustainable environment in which to carry out both public and private operations.[54] Coordination to prevent harmful interference cannot take place without proper registration of space assets. The Artemis Accords emphasize the need for registration and encourage any member who is not a signatory to the Convention on Registration of Objects Launched into Outer Space of 1974 (the 'Registration Convention') to do so as soon as possible.[55]

(vi) ***Sharing of scientific data:*** The timely, comprehensive, and open exchange of scientific data has always been a priority for NASA.[56] The Accords members agree to follow NASA's lead and make their scientific data available for public consumption.[57]

(vii) ***Protecting heritage:*** In space as on Earth, the Accords recognise that it is crucial to preserve historical sites and artifacts.[58] This Accord requires the signatories to conserve historic places and artefacts under the terms of the Artemis Accords.[59]

(viii) ***Space resources:*** This Accords specifies the promotion of safe and sustainable space travel and development as a pertinent element concerning the

---

[50] Section 4 of the Artemis Accords, 2020.

[51] Section 5 of the Artemis Accords, 2020.

[52] Section 6 of the Artemis Accords, 2020.

[53] *Id.*

[54] Section 7 of the Artemis Accords, 2020.

[55] *Id.*

[56] Section 8 of the Artemis Accords, 2020.

[57] *Id.*

[58] Section 9 of the Artemis Accords, 2020.

[59] *Id.*

extraction and use of resources sourced from the Moon, Mars, and asteroids.[60] The Artemis Accords reaffirm that the use and extraction of space resources can and will be carried out in accordance with the provisions of the OST, with a focus on sections 2, 6 and 11.[61]

(ix) ***Deconfliction activities:*** Another key principle of the OST, as recognised by the Accords, is the avoidance of harmful interference.[62] The Artemis Accords, in particular, require NASA and its partner agencies to inform the public of the location and broad nature of operations in order to determine the size and extent of 'Safety Zones'.[63] Section 9 of the OST and the principle of due regard will be strengthened, by notifying and coordinating partner States to respect such safety zones and preventing detrimental interference.

(x) ***Orbital debris and disposal of spacecraft:*** The Accords also emphasize the pollution and damage caused by recent space activities.[64] Both public and commercial activity in space depends on maintaining a secure and sustainable environment.[65] The decommissioning and disposal of spacecraft after the completion of their missions be provided for in a safe, timely, and effective manner by the United States and its partner governments.[66]

Issues with Artemis Accords

Artemis and the Other International Space Treaties

The common points of difference between the major space law treaties namely the Outer Space Treaty, 1967, the Rescue Agreement, 1968, the Liability Convention, 1972, the Registration Convention, 1975, the Moon Agreement, 1979, and the Artemis Accords, 2020, include the origin of the agreements, enforceability and implementation, multilateralism, purposes, and how the international community sees it. Firstly, the Committee on the Peaceful Uses of Outer Space (COPUOS) is the forum through which all the other agreements were formulated, but the Artemis Accords is the result of the US space initiative. The Accords were drafted by NASA and the US Department of State and the newly re-established National Space Council and had no relation with the COPUOS. Secondly, along the lines of enforceability, the space agreements are like any other international agreement and

[60] Section 10 of the Artemis Accords, 2020.

[61] *Id.*

[62] Section 11 of the Artemis Accords, 2020.

[63] *Id.*

[64] Section 12 of the Artemis Accords, 2020.

[65] *Id.*

[66] *Id.*

can be enforced as it is or through domestic laws after signing and ratification based on domestic practices.

But when it comes to the Accords, the nature of the Accords is a political commitment and not an international agreement, and the implementation of the Accords is done through incorporating the principles of the Accords in bilateral treaties between the signatories of the Accords. Thirdly, though the Artemis Accords emphasize on multilateral approach, it is not a result of a multilateral approach rather it is the result of the US interpretation of international space law.[67] Finally, the purpose for which the international space agreements and the Accords are made are different. A plain reading of the Accords and international space agreements may suggest just both the Accords and the Agreements have the same objective, but in actual fact, the purposes of the agreements are wider than the Accords because the Agreements deal with laying general rules of international law in matters of space and Accords is only in furtherance of the Artemis Program.

The Accords appear to be silent about the outer space liabilities of Nation States that are involved in the Artemis program. The point of similarity between the Rescue Agreement, 1968, and the Artemis Accords is that they both use the term ‘personnel’ in the context of rescue. However, the OST uses the term ‘astronaut’.[68] The former is wider in terms of application than the latter. The former is more inclusive and can include persons like astronauts as well as persons like space tourists.[69]

The Moon Agreement and the Artemis Accords

The Agreement Governing the Activities of States on the Moon and Other Celestial Bodies of 1979[70](also known as the ‘Moon Treaty’ or ‘Moon Agreement’) was signed by only four States, namely France, Guatemala, India, and Romania (Signed on 17 April 1980.)[71]; 18 other States are party to it.[72] The Moon Agreement states that the Moon should be used for peaceful purposes, for the benefit of the entire

[67] Tronchetti, F., and Liu, H. (2018). The Trump Administration and Outer Space: Promoting US Leadership or Heading Towards Isolation?. *Australian Journal of International Affairs,* 72 (5), 418–432.

[68] Article 5 of the Outer Space Treaty, 1967.

[69] Smith, W. A. (2021). Using the Artemis Accords to Build Customary International Law: A Vision for a U.S.- Centric Good Governance Regime in Outer Space. *Journal of Air Law and Commerce,* 86 (4), 661.

[70] United States Office for Outer Space Affairs. https://www.unoosa.org/oosa/en/ourwork/spacelaw/treaties/intromoon-agreement.html

[71] United States Treaty Collection. https://treaties.un.org/Pages/ViewDetails.aspx?src=IND&mtdsg_no=XXIV-2&chapter=24&clang=_en

[72] *Id.*

world community, and for the avoidance of international conflict over 'who owns the Moon'.[73]

Preamble and Article 2.1 of the UN Charter declare the equality of states regardless of their size, which is crucial for States to realize when thinking of utilizing outer space natural resources.[74] Further, the customary international law principle of *res communis omnium*, or the common heritage of humankind is applicable while it is the practice of states not to claim sovereignty over any fragment of outer space, accompanied by *opinion juris sive necessitatis*.[75] Article 11 of the Moon Agreement states that the concept of common heritage is constantly defined in the UN General Assembly's resolutions and the treaty systems,[76] in which it is applied to encompass four core elements: peaceful use; non-appropriation; an international regime to govern the management and conservation of resources for future generations; and an equitable sharing of benefits.

Australia: Moon Treaty or Artemis Accords?

Australia's case study is significant because it is the only country which is a part of both the Moon Agreement and the Artemis Accords. As discussed earlier, some of the provisions of the Artemis Accords reinstate the provisions of major outer space treaties like the Moon Treaty and Outer Space Treaty. The problem with the Accords is that it emphasizes certain principles that are not only part of the key outer space treaties but also incorporate principles that endorse a US interpretation of space law concepts that are not shared by all States.[77] Such principles include the establishment of heritage sites on the Moon's surface,[78] the right to extract and use celestial resources for commercial purposes,[79] and the right to establish safety zones.[80]

---

[73] McCarthy, N. (2019, July 19). *Infographic: The States That Signed The Moon Treaty*. Statista Infographics. www.statista.com/chart/18738/countries-that-are-signatories-or-parties-to-the-1979-moon-treaty

[74] Article 2.1 of the United Nations Charter, 1945.

[75] Arikoglu, E. (2022). The Concept of Common Heritage of Mankind and Legal Status of Outer Space in International Law. In B. E. Balin, V. N. Akun & S. Alis (Eds.), Proceedings for the First Symposium on Space Economy, Space Law and Space Sciences (pp. 109–116). https://doi.org/10.26650/PB/SS46PS01.2022.001.007

[76] Christol, C. Q. (1999). The 1979 Moon Agreement: Where is it Today?. *Journal of Space Law*, 27 (1), 1–35. https://airandspacelaw.olemiss.edu/pdfs/jsl-27-1.pdf

[77] Tronchetti, F & Liu, H. (2021). Australia's signing of the Artemis Accords: a positive development or a controversial choice?. *Australian Journal of International Affairs*, 75 (3), 243–251. DOI: 10.1080/10357718.2021.1893268

[78] Section 9 of the Artemis Accords, 2020.

[79] Section 10 of the Artemis Accords, 2020.

[80] Section 11 of the Artemis Accords, 2020. Also see, Tronchetti, F & Liu, H. (2021). Australia's signing of the Artemis Accords: a positive development or a controversial choice?. *Australian Journal of International Affairs*, 75 (3), 243–251. DOI: 10.1080/10357718.2021.1893268

There are certain philosophical inconsistencies between the Moon Agreements and the Accords in the way they approach multilateralism. The Moon Agreement, for example, adopts and incorporates multilateralism in governing the celestial activities and its management, but the Accords is not the result of multilateralism rather it is the single-handed efforts of the United States as part of its domestic regulatory mechanisms which reflect the American interests and the foreign policy approach of the Trump Administration.[81] The Moon Agreement adopts the common heritage approach; however, the principles of the Accords that govern the commercial use of resources and the involvement of private entities are in contrast with the Moon Agreement's common heritage principles because the Accords are commercially focused. Such principles relating to the use of celestial resources are a depiction of the US interpretation of the Outer Space Treaty.[82]

Another point of issue is that the Moon Agreement mandates the parties to negotiate a multilateral and international legal regime post the feasibility of economic exploitation of the celestial resources. Australia has not engaged in any of such negotiations and has become part of the Artemis Accords which is an initiative of the United States, a country that has rejected the Moon Agreement. This also raises certain scepticism with respect to the approach of Australia when it comes to resource utilization activities.[83]

Additionally, the Moon Agreement and the Artemis Accords clash in the area of environmental protection. Both agreements have prescribed certain principles relating to environmental protection, but the way they approach the issue is different. Where the Moon Agreement has adopted a wider approach to environmental concerns such as its consideration of the environmental impact of human activities on the celestial bodies' environment, an issue that has not been earlier considered by the other existing space treaties. Consequently, Article 7 of the Moon Agreement necessitates the members to avoid the interruption of the ecological equilibrium prevailing on the Moon, either by introducing adversative deviations to it or by causing detrimental pollution by introducing any extra-environmental matters.[84] The Accords adopts a narrower approach to environmental concerns. Its environmental concerns only extend to the extent of commercial activities like mitigation of orbital debris, disposal of spacecraft after the mission, etc.[85] Other areas of issues involve

---

[81] Tronchetti, F & Liu, H. (2018). The Trump Administration and Outer Space: Promoting US Leadership or Heading Towards Isolation?. *Australian Journal of International Affairs,* 72 (5), 418–432.

[82] Tronchetti, F. 2016. Title IV of the US Commercial Space Launch Competitiveness Act: A Legal and Political Assessment. *Air & Space Law,* 41 (2) 143–156. https://doi.org/10.54648/aila2016012

[83] Fountain, L. M. (2003). Creating Momentum in Space: Ending the Paralysis Produced by the Common Heritage of Mankind Doctrine. *Connecticut Law Review,* 35, 1753–1787.

[84] Tronchetti, F & Liu, H. (2021). Australia's signing of the Artemis Accords: a positive development or a controversial choice?. *Australian Journal of International Affairs,* 75 (3), 243–251. DOI: 10.1080/10357718.2021.1893268

[85] Dunk, V. D. Frans. (2007). The Moon Agreement and the Prospect of Commercial Exploitation of Lunar Resources. *Annals of Air & Space Law,* 32, 91–113.

the establishment of safety zones, use of space for peaceful purposes, and whether Australia has placed itself in a juxtaposition with the principle of '*pacta sunt servanda'* in the context of the Moon Agreement by becoming part of the Accords.[86]

The Accords and the Space-Faring States

Initially, the United States, specifically, during the time of President Donald Trump, demonstrated its interest in exploring and utilizing space resources. Consequently, the White House on 6 April 2020 announced a presidential Executive Order on 'Encouraging International Support for the Recovery and Use of Space Resources'.[87] The order pledges to continue nurturing the US private sector towards developing an 'innovative and sustainable program' that will 'lead the return of humans to the Moon for long-term exploration and utilization, followed by human missions to Mars and other destiStates'.[88] Further, the White House also stated that 'The order reaffirms U.S. support for the 1967 OST while continuing to reject the 1979 Moon Agreement, which only 17 of the 95 member states of the COPUOS have ratified in the past four decades'.[89] Further, 'The order further clarifies that the United States does not view outer space as a "global commons", and it reinforces the 2015 decision by Congress that Americans should have the right to engage in the commercial exploration, recovery, and use of resources in outer space'.[90]

While understanding the objective of the Accords, it is crucial to discuss the perspectives of other space-faring States, who are not party to the Accords yet. NASA, under the so-called Wolf Amendment in federal law, is restricted from bilateral cooperation with China. 'NASA, as an agency, will always follow the law, and law right now prohibits us from engaging China on bilateral activities'.[91] As Bridenstine stated that law could change, 'but at this point it's just not in the

---

[86]Tronchetti, F & Liu, H. (2021). Australia's signing of the Artemis Accords: a positive development or a controversial choice?. *Australian Journal of International Affairs,* 75 (3), 243–251. DOI: 10.1080/10357718.2021.1893268

[87]Executive Order on Encouraging International Support for the Recovery and Use of Space Resources, Issued on April 6, 2020. Donald J. Trump, The White House. https://trumpwhitehouse.archives.gov/presidential-actions/executive-order-encouraging-international-support-recovery-use-space-resources/

[88]*Id.*

[89]*Id.*

[90]Maday, M. (2020, April 8). *Trump Administration Issues Executive Order on Encouraging International Support for the Recovery and Use of Space Resources.* Space Watch Global. spacewatch.global/2020/04/trump-administration-issues-executive-order-on-encouraging-international-support-for-the-recovery-and-use-of-space-resources

[91]Foust, J. (2020, October 1). *Eight States Sign Artemis Accords.* SPACENEWS. https://spacenews.com/eight-countries-sign-artemis-accords/

cards'.[92] At present, States such as China exhibit their active participation in the exploration of space resources. For instance, in 2022, on 5 June, China launched the Shenzhou-14 spacecraft, which carried three taikonauts[93] on a six-month mission to its space station. During their stay in orbit, the crew witnessed two lab modules, the Tianzhou-5 cargo craft and Shenzhou-15 crewed spaceship, docking with the space station core module.[94]

At the time of writing, the China Aerospace Science and Technology Corporation is planning to establish an 'Earth–Moon Special Economic Zone' by 2050.[95] Further, China has realized the importance of space exploration seeing the potential for huge economic growth in furthering the study of reliable, low-cost aerospace transport systems between the Earth and the Moon.[96] Consequently, in 2019, i-Space – also known as Beijing Interstellar Glory Space Technology, launched a carrier rocket on its first successful orbital mission.[97] Specifically, the technology that China intends to deploy to power a lunar base, space-based solar power (SBSP), has already garnered investment.[98] SBSP will be deployed over time, with the first satellite going into low-earth orbit (LEO) by 2025 and the geostationary orbit (GEO)-based SBSP technology going into operation by 2050. Beijing also plans to examine the viability of 3D printing and lunar manufacturing by 2035, as well as launch a human lunar expedition by 2036, as further steps towards establishing an Earth–Moon economic zone.[99]

---

[92] *Id.*

[93] "The name used in the west for a Chinese astronaut. It comes from the Chinese word 'taikong' meaning space or cosmos. The official Chinese name is yuhangyuan, meaning 'travellers of the Universe'." Oxford Reference. https://www.oxfordreference.com/display/10.1093/oi/authority.20110803101916587;jsessionid=45F2502957689C6460CF7EE5E0A8E7B5

[94] Maoming, C. (2022, July 19). China's Consul General in Lagos, *China Proposes Cooperation in Outer Space*. Consulate-General of the People's Republic of China in Lagos. http://lagos.china-consulate.gov.cn/eng/zlszc/202207/t20220719_10723332.htm

[95] Anon. (2019, November 12). *China Proposes Establishing Moon-Based Special Economic Zone*. China Briefing. www.china-briefing.com/news/china-proposes-establishing-moon-based-special-economic-zone

[96] Kevin Pollpeter, et al. *China's Space Narrative- Examining the Portrayal of the US-China Space Relationship in Chinese Sources and Its Implications for The United States*. China Aerospace Studies Institute, 2020. https://www.airuniversity.af.edu/Portals/10/CASI/Conference2020/CASI%20Conference%20China%20Space%20Narrative.pdf

[97] Thomson Reuters. (2019, July 25). *Chinese Rocket Startup Puts Satellites into Orbit for First Time*. Thomson Reuters. https://www.reuters.com/article/us-china-space-idUSKCN1UK0KY

[98] Kevin Pollpeter, et al. *China's Space Narrative- Examining the Portrayal of the US-China Space Relationship in Chinese Sources and Its Implications for The United States*. China Aerospace Studies Institute, 2020. https://www.airuniversity.af.edu/Portals/10/CASI/Conference2020/CASI%20Conference%20China%20Space%20Narrative.pdf

[99] China Briefing. (2019, November 8). *China Proposes Establishing Moon-Based Special Economic Zone*. https://www.china-briefing.com/news/china-proposes-establishing-moon-based-special-economic-zone/#:~:text=China%20has%20already%20started%20investing,to%20be%20deployed%20by%202,050.

There are many States that have been involved for more than two decades in the development of the space sector; however, only a few States, such as Russia, the United States, China, India, and a few European states are very actively participating in the space race.[100] Many countries have dedicated agencies that are pioneering space technologies and are actively involved in space exploration such as NASA, USA, ROSCOSMOS (the Russian federal space agency), the Indian Space Research Organisation (ISRO), the European Space Agency (ESA), and the Japan Aerospace Exploration Agency (JAXA).[101]

Japan, for instance, has been involved in space exploration, having reliably built solar-powered satellites and made research investments since 1990.[102] In 2014, JAXA heralded a technology roadmap to establish an orbital solar power station (SPS) by 2030.[103] Likewise, India established its active participation in the space race, with successful missions that included Chandrayaan-1 in 2008 and Chandrayaan-2 in 2019.[104] Notably, India's plans to establish an Earth-orbiting space station by 2030 show its interest in space exploration.[105] Additionally, as a part of 'World Space Vision 2050', India believes that SPS technology is crucial to 'large-scale societal missions'.[106]

Artemis and Signatory States – Nigeria as an Example

The Nigerian National Space Research and Development Agency (NASRDA) under the supervision of the Federal Ministry of Science, Technology and Innovation was established in the year 1999.[107] The NASRDA was established with the objective to

---

[100] *The History of Space Exploration.* National Geography - Education. https://education.nationalgeographic.org/resource/history-space-exploration/

[101] States with Space Programs 2023, World Population Review. https://worldpopulationreview.com/country-rankings/countries-with-space-programs

[102] *History of the SSPS.* JAXA, Research and Development Directorate. https://www.kenkai.jaxa.jp/eng/research/ssps/ssps-ssps.html

[103] Vedda, James, & Jones, Karen. (2020, October 6). *Space-Based Solar Power: A Near-Term Investment Decision.* Aerospace Center for Space Policy and Strategy. csps.aerospace.org/papers/space-based-solar-power-near-term investment-decision

[104] Rajagopalan, R P. (2019, December). *India's Space Program International Competition and Evolution.* Center for Asian Studies. https://www.ifri.org/sites/default/files/atoms/files/rajeswari_pillai_rajagopalan_indias_space_program_2019.pdf

[105] *India Planning to Launch Own Space Station by 2030, ISRO Chief Says.* June 13, 2019, THE WIRE. https://thewire.in/space/isro-space-station-gaganyaan-chandrayaan-2

[106] A.P.J. Abdul Kalam, *World Space Vision 2050 and* India. Address During the Dedication of INSAT-4B Satellite to The Nation, Hassan, Bangalore, India. June 6, 2007, National Information Centre. http://abdulkalam.nic.in/sp080607-2.html

[107] Nigeria National Space Research and Development Agency (NASRDA). Office for Outer Space Affairs, UN-SPIDER Knowledge Portal. https://www.un-spider.org/nigeria-national-space-research-and-development-agency-nasrda

pursue the development and application of space and technology for the socio-economic benefit of Nigeria.[108] In 1961, NASA established its first satellite earth station – Tracking Station 5 – in Nigeria, which was established to monitor the Gemini and Apollo space missions[109] but was closed in 1963 even before the two missions were concluded, in 1966 and 1972, respectively.[110]

Nigeria launched its space ambitions in 1976 at the Economic Community of West African States (ECOWAS) meeting in Addis Ababa[111]; 23 years later, in 1999, Nigeria established the NASRDA with a broad objective to pursue the development and application of space science and technology for the socio-economic benefits of the nation.[112] After the establishment of NASRDA, the Nigeria government began to pursue formalized space projects such as satellite launches – it procured the first satellite launch, NigeriaSat-1, an Earth observation satellite that became part of the International Disaster Monitoring Constellation (DMC).[113] By establishing NASRDA, Nigeria unveiled a radical plan for its future plan such as manufacturing a Nigerian satellite and having a Nigerian astronaut.[114] Its mandate is to 'vigorously pursue the attainment of space capabilities as an essential tool for the socio-economic development and the enhancement of the quality of life of Nigerians'.[115] In 2000, a 25-year road map was set out in the National Space Policy, and its implementation was acknowledged in 2005.[116] The Defence Space Administration Act of 2016[117] was passed which regulated space activities. At the same time, Nigeria had companies such as Nigerian Communications Satellite and Geo Apps Plus, the former managing and operating Nigeria's communication satellites under the Ministry of Communications and Digital Economy, and the latter expected to manage the sale of satellite images acquired by Nigeria's earth observation satellites providing training in Geographic Information System and remote sensing for ministries, departments, and government agencies.

As a sign of progress in its interest in outer space activities, Nigeria in its National Space Policy includes important objectives such as defence, law enforcement, disaster prediction, earth observation, poverty alleviation, promotion of international

---

[108] *Id.*

[109] Goni, A. M. (2022, August 1). *How NASA Space Station in Kano Helped Put the First Man on the Moon*. Northpad Nigeria. https://northpad.ng/nasa-space-station-in-kano/

[110] Oneyibo, O. (2022, February 2). *After 23 years, Nigeria's space ambitions still look like a pipe dream*. Techpoint Africa. techpoint.africa/2022/01/27/nigerias-space-ambitions-pipe-dream.

[111] *Id.*

[112] *Id.*

[113] Tyler, W. (2020, June 24). *Challenges and Opportunities of Nigeria's Space Program*. AEROSPACE. https://aerospace.csis.org/challenges-and-opportunities-of-nigerias-space-policy/

[114] *Id.*

[115] Oneyibo, O. (2022, February 2). *After 23 years, Nigeria's space ambitions still look like a pipe dream*. Techpoint Africa. techpoint.africa/2022/01/27/nigerias-space-ambitions-pipe-dream.

[116] Isoun, T. Space Landings. Nature 456 (Suppl 1), 35 (2008). https://doi.org/10.1038/twas08.35a

[117] https://dsa.mil.ng/assets/download/Defence-Space-Administration-Establishment-Act-2016.pdf

cooperation, and establishment of research centres.[118] It is pertinent to note that the reason for understanding Nigeria's space development is that Nigeria and Rwanda became the first African States to sign the Artemis Accords.[119] By signing the Accords, Nigeria can access the scientific data and will not need to reinvent the wheel when they are ready to launch their satellite or engage in space travel. Further, Nigeria and Rwanda's accession to the Artemis Accords, has created a positive impact on Africa as a whole and address the gap between Africa and other regions in terms of space exploration and use.[120]

Rwanda and the Space Sector

With the key mission to develop Rwanda's space sector towards socio-economic development, utilizing space-based technologies and innovations, in 2020, the Rwanda Space Agency was established.[121] A new State in the space race, Rwanda in June 2022 signed a Memorandum of Understanding with the Global Satellite Operator's Association (GSOA) to explore the means of enhancing satellite communication services and fast-tracking Africa's digital inclusion plans.[122] Recently, in January 2023, Rwanda had discussions with Planet Labs, a US-based company that pioneers the revolutionizing of earth observation, on the cross-sectoral application of satellite imagery.[123]

---

[118] Oneyibo, O. (2022, February 2). After 23 years, Nigeria's space ambitions still look like a pipe dream. Techpoint Africa. techpoint.africa/2022/01/27/nigerias-space-ambitions-pipe-dream.

[119] U. S. Department of State. (2022, December 13). *Nigeria and Rwanda: First African States Sign the Artemis Accords.* Press Release. https://www.state.gov/nigeria-and-rwanda-first-african-States-sign-the-artemis-accords/#:~:text=At%20the%20first%20ever%20U.S.,to%20sign%20the%20Artemis%20Accords.

[120] Anne, U A. (2023, April 21). *Outer Space: Rwanda & Nigeria Sign An Accord For More Responsible Exploration- Why This Matters.* Down To Earth. https://www.downtoearth.org.in/blog/africa/outer-space-rwanda-nigeria-sign-an-accord-for-more-responsible-exploration-why-this-matters-88883#:~:text=Nigeria%20and%20Rwanda's%20accession%20to,data%20available%20to%20the%20public.

[121] Moyo, R. (2023, January 19). *Rwanda and Planet Labs Engage In Discussions Towards the Cross-sectoral Application of Satellite Imagery.* Space in Africa. africanews.space/rwanda-and-planet-labs-engage-in-discussions-towards-the-cross-sectoral-application-of-satellite-imagery.

[122] Iderawumi, M. (2022, June 6). *Rwandan Space Agency Signs MoU with the Global Satellite Operator's Association.* Space in Africa. africanews.space/rwandan-space-agency-signs-mou-with-the-global-satellite-operators-association

[123] Moyo, R. (2023, January 19). *Rwanda and Planet Labs Engage In Discussions Towards the Cross-sectoral Application of Satellite Imagery.* Space in Africa. africanews.space/rwanda-and-planet-labs-engage-in-discussions-towards-the-cross-sectoral-application-of-satellite-imagery

Non-signatory States to the Accords – Considerations

Interestingly, Russia and China (the China National Space Administration, CNSA) signed a Memorandum of Understanding on 9 March 2021 on establishing a permanent International Lunar Research Station (ILRS).[124]

The possibility of utilizing lunar resources (such as water ice, helium-3, and titanium), the potential to develop China's space capabilities, and the national prestige of China taking the lead in space research are the three key elements driving China's interest in the Moon.[125] For China to become a plausible space-faring nation, the Moon serves as a base and a reflection of its civilizational vibrancy, ideological dominance, and technical prowess.[126] Further, China has many exclusive space missions planned for the future, such as the Lunar South Pole Sample Return Mission in 2024, and a 100 kW SBSP demonstration at a LEO conference in 2025.[127] This shows clearly that the recent behaviour of states in establishing international cooperation, or of international partners in exploiting resources, is now being followed by the exploitation of lunar resources.

The Artemis Accords and India

If India participates in the Artemis Program by entering the Artemis Accords, the chances of it boosting its lunar exploration capacity will increase by means of cooperation and collaboration with other key players such as the United Kingdom, France, and Canada.[128] India can also benefit with regard to opportunities in financing lunar and other space exploration. The Artemis Program also increases the chances for India to secure access to crucial space technologies. Keeping in mind the recent entry of the private sector into space-related activities, the Artemis Program can facilitate trans-border trade opportunities for Indian private sector enterprises in space. It can enable the creation of a supply chain linking India with the other States which are participating and also enable technology transfer. Politically also the Artemis Accords are a viable option because of India's relationship

---

[124]Xiaodan, W. (2023). *The International Lunar Research Station: China's New Era of Space Cooperation and its new role in the Space Legal Order*. Space Policy. 65. DOI: https://doi.org/10.1016/j.spacepol.2022.101537

[125]Goswami, N. (2020, December). *Why is China Going to the Moon?* The Diplomat. https://thediplomat.com/2020/12/why-is-china-going-to-the-moon/

[126]Tiezzi, S. (2021, March 10). *China, Russia Agree to Cooperate on Permanent Moon Base*. The Diplomat. thediplomat.com/2021/03/china-russia-agree-to-cooperate-on-permanent-moon-base

[127]Goswami, N. (2020, December 18). *Why Is China Going to the Moon?* The Diplomat. thediplomat.com/2020/12/why-is-china-going-to-the-moon

[128]Ramanathan, A. (2022, September 26) *Takshashila Issue Brief-India & Artemis Programme: Next Step for Space Cooperation.* The Takshashila Institution. https://takshashila.org.in/research/india-amp-artemis-programme-next-step-for-space-cooperation

with the United States. On the other hand, the possibility of India becoming a party to the space deal between China and Russia is very limited. Though India is on good terms with Russia politically, the political and border conflicts between India and China make it impossible for India to join the space deal between China and Russia.

The development in outer space governance since the OST was signed has been meagre. The major space-faring States do not subscribe to the Moon Agreement of 1979, to which India is a party. The Accords are one of the recent legal instruments in matters of space and space-related activities which put forth guidelines relating to the use of space for peaceable purposes, interoperability, disclosure of scientific data, extraction and use of space resources, private rights in space, and managing of orbital debris. The current Indian legal system deals only with the dissemination of data and the regulation of the use of satellites. There is no legal framework dedicated to space-faring, lunar exploration, or the intellectual property rights relating to them. In spite of the criticisms mentioned above, the Accords will act as a basic framework in matters of lunar exploration and space governance. Being part of the Accords will enable India to gain a grip on determining the new legal framework for space governance in the coming years.

Criticisms

Though the Accords has a lot of positive elements as mentioned above, it also has faced severe criticisms from advocates of the *res communis* principle and from other States. Russia and China have even gone to the extent of referring to the Artemis Accords as an 'unconcealed attempt to create international space law that favours the United States' and 'the space version of the "Enclosure Movement"'.[129] The Accords could be argued to deviate from the spirit of 1967 OST which states that space exploration activities should be undertaken to benefit mankind as a whole, and not only to benefit a single country's growth.[130] Therefore, mining and other commercial activities in outer space continue to be a matter of uncertain legality, and these activities can potentially degrade the Moon's environment, leading to unfair competition among the countries, and can trigger international conflicts.[131]

The non-binding nature of the Accords and the lack of any dispute settlement mechanism under the Accords raise doubts relating to the enforceability and

[129] Giri, Chaitanya. (2020, May 12). *Artemis Accords propel India's space ambitions.* Gateway House. www.gatewayhouse.in/indias-artemis-moon.

[130] *Treaty on Principles Governing the Activities of States in the Exploration and Use of Outer Space, including the Moon and Other Celestial Bodies.* UNOOSA. https://takshashila.org.in/research/india-amp-artemis-programme-next-step-for-space-cooperation

[131] Tronchetti, F & Liu, H. (2021). Australia's signing of the Artemis Accords: a positive development or a controversial choice?. *Australian Journal of International Affairs,* 75 (3), 243–251. DOI: 10.1080/10357718.2021.1893268

settlement of disputes arising out of the agreement.[132] The Accords do not provide for any system for assessing liability for damage caused by lunar activities other than the mechanisms available under the 1967 OST.[133] There is also no mechanism for the mutual inspection of lunar facilities among the Artemis member states, which would build transparency and trust. The Accords are highly US centric, potentially resulting in undesirable effects for other countries, with China and Russia voicing some vehement opposition.[134]

Conclusion

The Artemis Accords would be very helpful for such States to achieve their goals and overcome the hurdles that hinder the progress of space-faring States. For instance, Scotland is one of the States whose space sector is developing rapidly, aiming to grow in value to £4 billion by 2030. Among the European countries, Scotland has expanded its space sector in satellite and rocket manufacturing, data, and groundbreaking research such as establishing a vertically launched spaceport. There are many space-faring States that drastically expand their space industry and Accords like Artemis would help international cooperation among the least-developed States and the developed States and contribute towards sustainable outer space exploration. It is laudable that NASA, through Artemis, aims to land the first woman and first person of colour on the Moon. Artemis's mission heralds a new era for space exploration and utilization, and India should become a part of it and excel in the space race.

International law can develop and evolve through practices so ingrained that states believe they have the status of law. The Artemis Accords will establish a generally accepted code of behaviour if more States agree upon them. The belief that the Accords constitute the applicable law for space mining, safety zones, and heritage protection will be strengthened as more States come to rely on them to regulate the conduct of space activities. The Artemis Accords may enhance existing international customary law, even if not international law.

The Artemis Accords have propelled many States to invest and become involved in the space sector, which is believed to benefit the economies of such States. Fictionally speaking, the space industry is a 'wonderland' or 'Asgardian treasury'.

[132] Gönczy, B. et al. (2023). The Artemis Accords. *International Legal Materials*, 1–11. doi:10.1017/ilm.2023.17.

[133] Deplano, R. (2021). The Artemis Accords: evolution or revolution in international space law?. *International & Comparative Law Quarterly*, 70 (3), 799–819. DOI: https://doi.org/10.1017/S0020589321000142

[134] *Id.*

There is currently no adequate and efficient international cooperation governing the usage of space resources by private players.[135] The 1967 OST is the most widely ratified space law. It affirms that States are not entitled to claim particular portions of the Moon or other space objects: 'National acquisition of outer space, including the Moon and other celestial bodies, by claim of sovereignty, by use or occupation, or by any other means, is not permitted'.

In conclusion, it can be understood that once the Artemis Accords were concluded, the space-faring States expedited their governance by establishing policies and legislative frameworks specifically for commercializing their space activities, such as extracting space resources. Under the Accords, the Artemis plan defines the legal justification for using space resources to assist the Artemis missions. The Accords are not a treaty, legally speaking, because they do not establish any agreements that are enforceable under international law. These are solely applicable to the United States and the other States intending to participate in the Artemis missions.

Bibliography

Anne, U A. (2023, April 21). *Outer space: Rwanda & Nigeria Sign an Accord for more responsible exploration- why this matters.* Down to Earth. https://www.downtoearth.org.in/blog/africa/outer-space-rwanda-nigeria-sign-an-accord-for-more-responsible-exploration-why-this-matters-88883#:~:text=Nigeria%20and%20Rwanda's%20accession%20to,data%20available%20to%20the%20public

Anon. (2019, November 12). China Proposes Establishing Moon-Based Special Economic Zone. *China Briefing.* www.china-briefing.com/news/china-proposes-establishing-moon-based-special-economic-zone

Bukley, A P. (2020, October) *To the moon and beyond: Challenges and opportunities for NASA's Artemis program.* Space agenda 2021, Center for Space Policy and Strategy. The Aerospace Corporation. P-4. https://csps.aerospace.org/sites/default/files/2021-08/Bukley_TheMoon_20201027.pdf

Butterfield, S. (2023, May 25). *Artemis II to continue NASA's moon to Mars goal.* Oelwein daily register. https://www.communitynewspapergroup.com/oelwein_daily_register/artemis-ii-to-continue-nasas-moon-to-mars-goal/article_d3f10a45-8490-5ed1-9ff0-824808680141.html and see, Adam Mann, Ailsa Harvey, *NASA's Artemis program: Everything you need to know.* December 12, 2022. https://www.space.com/artemis-program.html

China Briefing. (2019, November 8). *China proposes establishing moon-based special economic zone.* https://www.china-briefing.com/news/china-proposes-establishing-moon-based-special-economic-zone/#:~:text=China%20has%20already%20started%20investing,to%20be%20deployed%20by%202050

Christol, C. Q. (1999). The 1979 moon agreement: Where is it today? *Journal of Space Law, 27*(1), 1–35.

[135] Sophie, et al. (2021, October 1). *The Global Legal Landscape of Space: Who Writes the Rules on the Final Frontier?.* Wilson Center. https://www.wilsoncenter.org/article/global-legal-landscape-space-who-writes-rules-final-frontier

Cowing, K. (2020, May 17). What are the Artemis accords and why do we need them?. *Spaceref*. https://spaceref.com/science-and-exploration/what-are-the-artemis-accords-and-why-do-we-need-them/

Coykendall, J. et al. (2023, March 22). Riding the exponential growth in space. *Deloitte Insights*. https://www2.deloitte.com/us/en/insights/industry/aerospace-defense/future-of-space-economy.html/#endnote-13

David. L. (2018, September 30). Would Trump's "space force" patrol the moon. *Scientific American*. https://www.scientificamerican.com/article/would-trumps-space-force-patrol-the-moon/

Deplano, R. (2021). The Artemis accords: Evolution or revolution in international space law? *International & Comparative Law Quarterly, 70*(3), 799–819. https://doi.org/10.1017/S0020589321000142

Dunk, V. D., & Frans. (2007). The moon agreement and the prospect of commercial exploitation of lunar resources. *Annals of Air & Space Law, 32*, 91–113.

Fountain, L. M. (2003). Creating momentum in space: Ending the paralysis produced by the common heritage of mankind doctrine. *Connecticut Law Review, 35*, 1753–1787.

Foust, J. (2020, October 1). Eight States Sign Artemis Accords. *SPACENEWS*. https://spacenews.com/eight-countries-sign-artemis-accords/

Giri, C. (2020, May 12). Artemis accords propel India's space ambitions. *Gateway House*. www.gatewayhouse.in/indias-artemis-moon

Goguichvili, S. et al. (2020, October 1). *The global legal landscape: Who writes the rules on the final frontier?* Wilson Center. https://www.wilsoncenter.org/article/global-legal-landscape-space-who-writes-rules-final-frontier

Gönczy, B., et al. (2023). The Artemis accords. *International Legal Materials, 1–11*, 888. https://doi.org/10.1017/ilm.2023.17

Goni, A. M. (2022, August 1). *How NASA Space Station in Kano helped put the first man on the moon*. Northpad Nigeria. https://northpad.ng/nasa-space-station-in-kano/

Goswami, N. (2020, December 18). *Why is China going to the moon?* The diplomat. thediplomat.com/2020/12/why-is-china-going-to-the-moon

Howell, E. (2022, August 25). *Artemis Accords: Why the international moon exploration framework matters*, space.com, https://www.space.com/artemis-accords-moon-space-exploration-importance

Iderawumi, M. (2022, June 6). *Rwandan space agency signs MoU with the Global Satellite Operator's Association*. Space in Africa. africanews.space/rwandan-space-agency-signs-mou-with-the-global-satellite-operators-association

International Space Exploration Coordination Group. (2013, September). *Benefits stemming from space exploration*. International Space Exploration Coordination Group. https://www.nasa.gov/sites/default/files/files/Benefits-Stemming-from-Space-Exploration-2013-TAGGED.pdf

Japan, U. S. M. (2023, January 17). *US, Japan sign space collaboration agreement at NASA headquarters*. U.S. Embassy & Consulates in Japan. https://jp.usembassy.gov/us-japan-nasa-space-collaboration-agreement/

Kevin Pollpeter, et al. (2020). China's space narrative- examining the portrayal of the US-China space relationship in Chinese sources and its implications for the United States. China Aerospace Studies Institute. https://www.airuniversity.af.edu/Portals/10/CASI/Conference2020/CASI%20Conference%20China%20Space%20Narrative.pdf

Lele, A., & Gopalakrishnan, V. (2020, October 24). Artemis Accords*: Utilateralization in Space*. Commentaries, Society for the Study of Peace and Conflict. https://sspconline.org/opinion-analysis/artemis-accords-unilateralization-space-sat-10242020

Luxembourg Space Agency. (2022, December 16). Contribution of the Grand Duchy of Luxembourg on the Mandate and Purpose of the Working Group on Legal Aspects of Space Resource Activities. https://www.unoosa.org/documents/pdf/copuos/lsc/space-resources/LSC2023/StatesResponses/Luxembourg_-_20221216_WG_SR_LU_Contribution.pdf

Maday, M. (2020, April 8). *Trump administration issues executive order on encouraging international support for the recovery and use of space resources.* Space watch global. spacewatch.global/2020/04/trump-administration-issues-executive-order-on-encouraging-international-support-for-the-recovery-and-use-of-space-resources

Maoming, C. (2022, July 19). China's consul general in Lagos, *China Proposes Cooperation in Outer Space*. Consulate-General of the People's Republic of China in Lagos. http://lagos.china-consulate.gov.cn/eng/zlszc/202207/t20220719_10723332.htm

Matthew, G. (2023). The Artemis accords: International cooperation in the era of space exploration. *Harvard International Review*. https://hir.harvard.edu/the-artemis-accords/

McCarthy, N. (2019, July 19). Infographic*: The States That Signed The Moon Treaty.* Statista Infographics. www.statista.com/chart/18738/countries-that-are-signatories-or-parties-to-the-1979-moon-treaty

Moyo, R. (2023, January 19). Rwanda and planet labs engage in discussions towards the cross-sectoral application of satellite imagery. *Space in Africa*. africanews.space/rwanda-and-planet-labs-engage-in-discussions-towards-the-cross-sectoral-application-of-satellite-imagery

NASA. (2020a, October 12). *International partners advance cooperation with first signings of Artemis accords.* NASA Press release. https://www.nasa.gov/news-release/nasa-international-partners-advance-cooperation-with-first-signings-of-artemis-accords/#:~:text=International%20cooperation%20on%20Artemis%20is,mutual%20understanding%20and%20reducing%20misperceptions

NASA. (2020b, October 13). *International partners advance cooperation with first signings of Artemis accords.* NASA Press Release. https://www.nasa.gov/press-release/nasa-international-partners-advance-cooperation-with-first-signings-of-artemis-accords

NASA. *Principles for a Safe, Peaceful, and Prosperous Future.* The Artemis Accords. https://www.nasa.gov/specials/artemis-accords/index.html

NASA. (n.d.-a). *Artemis Accords*. www.nasa.gov/specials/artemis-accords/index.html

Newman, C. (2020, October 19). *Artemis Accords: Why many states are refusing to sign Moon exploration agreement.* The Conversation. https://theconversation.com/artemis-accords-why-many-countries-are-refusing-to-sign-moon-exploration-agreement-148134

Nigeria National Space Research and Development Agency (NASRDA). *Office for Outer Space Affairs, UN-SPIDER Knowledge Portal.* https://www.un-spider.org/nigeria-national-space-research-and-development-agency-nasrda

Oneyibo, O. (2022, February 2). *After 23 years, Nigeria's space ambitions still look like a pipe dream.* Techpoint Africa. techpoint.africa/2022/01/27/nigerias-space-ambitions-pipe-dream

Pozza, M. (2022). *Space Law: An overview*. VIT University Presentation (remote), 04 March 2022.

Raitt, D. et al. (2005, February). *The impact of space activities upon society.* The International Academy of Astronautics and European Space Agency. https://www.esa.int/esapub/br/br237/br237.pdf. And see, *NATO's approach to space*. North Atlantic Treaty Organization. https://www.nato.int/cps/en/natohq/topics_175419.htm

Rajagopalan, R. P. (2019, December). *India's space program international competition and evolution.* Center for Asian Studies. https://www.ifri.org/sites/default/files/atoms/files/rajeswari_pillai_rajagopalan_indias_space_program_2019.pdf

Ramanathan, A. (2022, September 26) *Takshashila issue Brief-India & Artemis Programme: Next step for space cooperation.* The Takshashila Institution. https://takshashila.org.in/research/india-amp-artemis-programme-next-step-for-space-cooperation

Smith, W. A. (2021). Using the Artemis accords to build customary international law: A vision for a U.S.- centric good governance regime in outer space. *Journal of Air Law and Commerce, 86*(4), 661.

Smith, Z. L. M. (2023, February 2). *Going farther together: The U.S.-Japan space pact is an accelerator*. Center For Strategic & International Studies. https://www.csis.org/analysis/going-farther-together-us-japan-space-pact-accelerator

Sophie, et al. (2021, October 1). *The global legal landscape of space: Who writes the rules on the final frontier?.* Wilson Center. https://www.wilsoncenter.org/article/global-legal-landscape-space-who-writes-rules-final-frontier

Strickland, A. (2020, October 14). Eight States Sign NASA's Artemis Accords that Guide Cooperative Exploration of the Moon. CNN. https://edition.cnn.com/2020/10/14/world/artemis-accords-States-sign-nasa-scn-trnd/index.html

The Artemis program: Humanity's return to the moon. Government of Canada Portal, 2023. https://www.asc-csa.gc.ca/eng/astronomy/moon-exploration/artemis-missions.asp

The White House National Space Council. (2020, July 23). *A New Era for Deep Space Exploration and Development.* The National Space Strategy. https://csps.aerospace.org/sites/default/files/2021-08/NSpC%20New%20Era%20for%20Space%2023Jul20.pdf

Thomson, R. (2019, July 25). *Chinese Rocket Startup Puts Satellites into Orbit for First Time.* Thomson Reuters. https://www.reuters.com/article/us-china-space-idUSKCN1UK0KY.

Tiezzi, S. (2021, March 10). *China, Russia agree to cooperate on permanent Moon Base.* The diplomat. thediplomat.com/2021/03/China-Russia-agree-to-cooperate-on-permanent-moon-base

Tronchetti, F. (2016). Title IV of the US commercial space launch competitiveness act: A legal and political assessment. *Air & Space Law, 41*(2), 143–156. https://doi.org/10.54648/aila2016012

Tronchetti, F., & Liu, H. (2018). The trump administration and outer space: Promoting US leadership or heading towards isolation? *Australian Journal of International Affairs, 72*(5), 418–432.

Tronchetti, F., & Liu, H. (2021). Australia's signing of the Artemis accords: A positive development or a controversial choice? *Australian Journal of International Affairs, 75*(3), 243–251. https://doi.org/10.1080/10357718.2021.1893268

Tyler, W. (2020, June 24). *Challenges and Opportunities of Nigeria's Space Program.* AEROSPACE. https://aerospace.csis.org/challenges-and-opportunities-of-nigerias-space-policy/

U. S. Department of State. (2022, December 13). *Nigeria and Rwanda: First African States Sign the Artemis Accords.* Press Release. https://www.state.gov/nigeria-and-rwanda-first-african-States-sign-the-artemis-accords/#:~:text=At%20the%20first%20ever%20U.S.,to%20sign%20the%20Artemis%20Accords

United Nations General Assembly. (2022, October 26). *Fourth committee shifts focus to peaceful uses of outer space with speakers emphasizing need to close technological gap.* Seventy-seventh session, 14th meeting, General Assembly, UN Press Release. https://press.un.org/en/2022/gaspd760.doc.htm

United States Embassy. (2020, October 20). *Fact Sheet: Artemis Accords- United for Peaceful Exploration of Deep Space.* https://br.usembassy.gov/fact-sheet-artemis-accords-united-for-peaceful-exploration-of-deep-space/

US Department of State. (2022, December 15). *Nigeria and Rwanda: First African States Sign the Artemis Accords.* www.state.gov/nigeria-and-rwanda-first-african-States-sign-the-artemis-accords

Vedda, J., & Jones, K. (2020, October 6). *Space-based solar power: A near-term investment decision.* Aerospace Center for Space Policy and Strategy. csps.aerospace.org/papers/space-based-solar-power-near-term-investment-decision

Wall, M. (2019, May 17). *NASA awards $45.5Million for private moon Lander work on project Artemis.* Space.com. https://www.space.com/nasa-private-moon-landers-funding-artemis.html. And see *Benzo's blue origin wins NASA contract to build astronaut lunar Lander.* May 20, 2023, economic times.

Whittington, M. R. (2022, December 25). Why did Nigeria and Rwanda sign NASA's Artemis accords? *The Hill.* https://thehill.com/opinion/international/3786847-why-did-nigeria-and-rwanda-sign-nasas-artemis-accords/

Wood, J. (2018, October 25). *How states are collaborating to further space exploration.* SPECTRA. https://spectra.mhi.com/how-States-are-collaborating-to-further-space-exploration also see, summary report on the APRSAF-24 in Bengaluru India, January, 2018. https://sentinel-asia.org/meetings/SA3JPTM5/agenda/Day1/Session1/1.6_JAXA_APRSAF_Report.pdf

World Economic Forum. (n.d.). *The Global Risks Report 2019*, 14th Edn. https://www3.weforum.org/docs/WEF_Global_Risks_Report_2019.pdf

Xiaodan, W. (2023). The international lunar Research Station: China's new era of space cooperation and its new role in the space legal order. *Space Policy, 65*, 101537. https://doi.org/10.1016/j.spacepol.2022.101537

Chapter 5
Deconfliction of Space Activities: Lunar Safety Zones

Heloise Vertadier

Introduction

International cooperation is going to be critical to establish a long-lasting presence on the Moon. The Artemis Program aims to open a new chapter in the history of lunar exploration. Named after Apollo's twin sister, the Program is led by the National Aeronautics and Space Administration (NASA) of the USA in collaboration with the European Space Agency (ESA), the Canadian Space Agency (CSA), the Japan Aerospace Exploration Agency (JAXA), and a few commercial partners. The aim of this Program is to build the necessary expertise in order to sustainably return to the Moon and lay the foundations for manned deep space exploration.[1] The Artemis Program also plans to bring the first woman and the first person of colour to the lunar surface in 2025.[2]

This chapter aims to present the Artemis Accords, which are part of the Artemis Program, and more specifically will focus on Section 11 of the Accords, which creates the principle of deconfliction of activities on the Moon with the introduction of safety zones. Although Section 11 is one of the most debated sections of the Artemis Accords, it must be noted that as of November 2022, the signatories to the Accords had not yet presented any implementation strategy of safety zones on the lunar surface. However, NASA published in November 2022 a Lunar Landing and Operations Policy Analysis, providing the Agency with recommendations

[1]NASA (2020). NASA's Lunar Exploration Program Overview. https://www.nasa.gov/sites/default/files/atoms/files/artemis_plan-20200921.pdf

[2]Gohd, C. (2021, November 10). NASA's Artemis astronauts won't land on the moon by 2024 deadline. *Space.com*. https://www.space.com/nasa-changes-artemis-moon-landing-goal-2024

H. Vertadier (✉)
Department of Politics, University of Otago, Dunedin, New Zealand
e-mail: verhe909@student.otago.ac.nz

M. A. Pozza (ed.), *Ascending to Space*, Space Law and Policy,
https://doi.org/10.1007/978-981-97-0714-0_5

regarding safety zone implementation.[3] These are non-binding recommendations; therefore, the following analysis is based on the assumption that they will be adopted and implemented in the course of the Program.

This chapter focuses on the question of safety zones, therefore the other principles listed above will not be analysed further.

The Artemis Accords

Rather than amending the Outer Space Treaty (OST)[4] or other international treaties, the United States used existing governance mechanisms, developed the principles of the Artemis Accords and broadened the scope of the lawfulness of space activities. The Accords are a set of bilateral agreements with the space agencies of other countries who want to join the Artemis Program. Made public on 15 May 2020, the Artemis Accords formalise concepts identified by NASA as essential to oversee the exploration of the Moon and resource utilisation there, as well as future expeditions to Mars.[5] Despite some scepticism,[6] the Accords are considered a turning point in global space governance.[7]

The Artemis Accords aim to incorporate existing principles found in the Outer Space Treaty in order to 'establish a common vision via a practical set of principles, guidelines, and best practices to enhance the governance of the civil exploration and use of outer space with the intention of advancing the Artemis Program'.[8] NASA suggests that the Artemis Accords will allow for the transparent and safe exploration

[3] Swiney, G. and Hernandez, A. (2022). *Lunar Landing and Operations Policy Analysis*. https://www.nasa.gov/sites/default/files/atoms/files/lunar_landing_and_operations_policy_analysis_final_report_24oct2022_tagged_0.pdf

[4] Treaty on Principles Governing the Activities of States in the Exploration and Use of Outer Space, including the Moon and other Celestial Bodies, adopted on 19 December 1966 by UN General Assembly Resolution 2222 (XXI), opened for signature on 27 January 1967, 610 UNTS 205; TIAS 6347; 18 UST 2410; [1968] UKTS 10; [1967] ATS 24; [1967] CTS 19; [1968] NZTS 8; 6 ILM 386 (entered into force generally and for Australia on 10 October 1967 and for New Zealand on 31 May 1968).

[5] Fidler, D. P. (2020). The Artemis Accords and the Next Generation of Outer Space Governance. Council on Foreign Relations. https://www.cfr.org/blog/artemis-accords-and-next-generation-outer-space-governance

[6] Wang, G. (2020) 'NASA's Artemis Accords: the path to a united space law or a divided one?', *The Space Review*, 24 August. Available at: https://www.thespacereview.com/article/4009/1

[7] Deplano, R. (2021) 'The Artemis Accords: Evolution or Revolution in International Space Law?', *International and Comparative Law Quarterly*, 70(3), pp. 799–819. doi: 10.1017/S0020589321000142.

[8] NASA (2020). The Artemis Accords – Principles for a Safe, Peaceful, and Prosperous Future. https://www.nasa.gov/specials/artemis-accords/index.html.

of the Moon, scientific research and commercial activities in space for the benefit of all humanity.[9]

The main principles of the Artemis Accords are:

- Ensuring that missions serve peaceful purposes.
- Requiring transparency in plans and policies.
- Advocating for the interoperability of space systems.
- Providing emergency assistance in space, thus reaffirming the obligations of the Rescue Agreement[10].
- Promoting the registration of space objects and encouraging partners to ratify the Registration Convention[11].
- Requiring the publication of scientific data.
- Protecting historical sites and artefacts on the Moon.
- Allowing the extraction and use of space resources, thus reaffirming the principles of the US *Commercial Space Launch Competitiveness Act* of 2015.
- Deconflicting activities through transparency and the creation of safety zones.
- Committing the signatories to respect the UN guidelines on space debris mitigation.[12]

Safety zones are introduced in Section 11, paragraph 7, of the Artemis Accords as:

> In order to implement their obligations under the Outer Space Treaty, the Signatories intend to provide notification of their activities and commit to coordinating with any relevant actor to avoid harmful interference. The area wherein this notification and coordination will be implemented to avoid harmful interference is referred to as a 'safety zone'. A safety zone should be the area in which nominal operations of a relevant activity or an anomalous event could reasonably cause harmful interference. The Signatories intend to observe the following principles related to safety zones:
>
> (a) The size and scope of the safety zone, as well as the notice and coordination, should reflect the nature of the operations being conducted and the environment that such operations are conducted in.
> (b) The size and scope of the safety zone should be determined in a reasonable manner leveraging commonly accepted scientific and engineering principles.
> (c) The nature and existence of safety zones is expected to change over time reflecting the status of the relevant operation. If the nature of an operation changes, the operating Signatory should alter the size and scope of the corresponding safety zone as

[9] Fidler, The Artemis Accords.

[10] Agreement on the Rescue of Astronauts, the Return of Astronauts, and the Return of Objects Launched into Outer Space, adopted on 19 December 1967 by General Assembly Resolution 2345 (XXII), opened for signature on 22 April 1968, 672 UNTS 119; TIAS 6599; 18 UST 2410; [1969] UKTS 56; [1986] ATS 8; [1975] CTS 6; [1969] NZTS 5; 169 SP 864; 7 ILM 151 (entered into force generally on 12 March 1968, for Australia on 18 March 1986, and for New Zealand on 8 July 1969).

[11] Convention on Registration of Objects Launched into Outer Space, adopted on 12 November 1974 by General Assembly Resolution 3235 (XXIX), opened for signature on 14 January 1975, 1023 UNTS 15; TIAS 8480; [1978] UKTS 70; [1986] ATS 5; [1976] CTS 36 (entered into force generally and for Australia on 11 March 1986 and for New Zealand on 23 January 2018).

[12] NASA, The Artemis Accords.

appropriate. Safety zones will ultimately be temporary, ending when the relevant operation ceases.

(d) The Signatories should promptly notify each other as well as the Secretary-General of the United Nations of the establishment, alteration, or end of any safety zone, consistent with Article XI of the Outer Space Treaty.[13]

This provision is the main reason why concerns and scepticism were triggered after the Artemis Accords were announced in May 2020.[14] However, by October 2020, the Artemis Accords had been signed by eight countries: Australia, Canada, Italy, Japan, Luxembourg, the United Arab Emirates, the United Kingdom, and the United States. Subsequent signatories include Bahrain, Brazil, Colombia, Israel, Mexico, New Zealand, Nigeria, Poland, Romania, Rwanda, Saudi Arabia, Singapore, South Korea, and Ukraine.[15] Significantly, on 7 June 2022, France became the twentieth country to sign the Artemis Accords. France is an important player in the European and international space industry and contributes the most to the European Space Agency's budget alongside Germany.[16] Further, France is the only European country, apart from Russia, to have a launching pad with the Guiana Space Center, also known as the European Spaceport.[17] The Spaceport allows launches of the Ariane 5 rockets, the Soyuz rocket, and Vega rockets.[18] Therefore, it was vital to have France on board with the United States for their Artemis missions and other ambitions on the Moon according to Gabriel Swiney.[19] Further, Mike Gold, Executive Vice President for Civil and External Affairs at Redwire and former NASA official who led the development of the Artemis Accords, said that[20]:

> Today's signature is not just a victory for America and France, our nation's first international ally, but represents a dramatic step forward for norms of behaviour generally ... France joining the already robust Artemis Accords family of nations shows that there is a strong desire globally to honour and implement the principles of the Outer Space Treaty and other international agreements.[21]

[13] Ibid.

[14] McKeown, B., Dempster, A. G. and Saydam, S. (2022) 'Artemis Accords: Are Safety Zones Practical for Long Term Commercial Lunar Resource Utilisation?', *Space Policy*. Elsevier Ltd. doi: 10.1016/j.spacepol.2022.101504.

[15] Ibid.

[16] 'ESA Budget 2022' (2022). European Space Agency. Available at: https://www.esa.int/ESA_Multimedia/Images/2022/01/ESA_budget_2022

[17] French Guiana is a French department located overseas. https://www.esa.int/Enabling_Support/Space_Transportation/Europe_s_Spaceport/Europe_s_Spaceport2

[18] *The Spaceport* (2023). Available at: https://www.arianespace.com/spaceport-facility/

[19] Grush, L. (2022) 'Why France signing NASA's lunar exploration pact is the most important signature yet', *The Verge*, 10 June. Available at: https://www.theverge.com/2022/6/10/23159558/nasa-artemis-accords-france-signing-moon-exploration-significance.

[20] Foust, J. (2022, June 8). France joins Artemis Accords. *Space News*. spacenews.com/france-joins-artemis-accords

[21] Foust, J. (2022, June 8). France joins Artemis Accords. *Space News*. spacenews.com/france-joins-artemis-accords

As the future implementation of safety zones will be clarified by NASA and the Artemis Accords signatories, it is expected that the norms of behaviour on the lunar surface will be clarified, and other actors convinced by the goals of the Accords. However, despite the concerns and debates surrounding this principle, safety zones are not a new idea in international law.

Safety Zone Precedents in International Law

There are numerous precedents established in maritime and aviation law regarding the management of specific areas as part of international zones. Their governance models could be used as examples of the implementation of safety zones as described by the Artemis Accords. Examples include air defence identification zones, as well as exclusive economic zones and safety zones in maritime law.

Air and Defence Identification Zones

Air and Defence Identification Zones (ADIZ) are an example of how the concept of safety zones was introduced in international aviation law. ADIZs are a designated area of airspace where civil aircrafts are expected to abide by special identification and reporting requirements in the interests of national security, and references to them are found in Annex 15 of the Chicago Convention on International Civil Aviation of 1944.[22] The civil air traffic services are supplemented by these identification and reporting methods. The United States created the first ADIZ in 1950, and currently, comparable zones have been formed in almost 20 different countries.[23]

Although there is no existing treaty provision of international law that specifically allows for the creation of ADIZs, there are some indications to suggest that they are permitted as a matter of customary international law. The references made to them in Annex 15 of the Chicago Convention, which would require civilian aircraft of any and all nationality to have regard to the special regulations or requirements imposed by individual ADIZs, only lend support to this.[24]

[22] Chicago Convention on International Civil Aviation, opened for signature on 7 December 1944, 15 UTS 295; 148 BSP 38; [1953] UKTS 8; [1957] ATS 5; [1944] CTS 36 (entered into force generally on 4 April 1947 and for New Zealand on 6 April 1947).

[23] Office of the Staff Judge Advocate (2021). Air Defense Identification Zones. *International Law Studies, 97.*

[24] See also Abeyratne, R. (2011). In search of theoretical justification for air defence identification zones. Journal of Transportation Security, 89; and Bakhtiar, H. S., Djanur, N. A., Ashri, M., and Hendrapati, M. (2016). Air Defence Identification Zone (ADIZ) in International Law Perspective. *Journal of Law, Policy, and Globalisation*, 56, 16.

Exclusive Economic Zones and Safety Zones

The rights of a coastal State over its exclusive economic zone (EEZ) are defined by Article 56 1. (a) of the United Nations Convention on the Law of the Sea (UNCLOS), which stipulates that:

> 1. In the exclusive economic zone, the coastal State has:
>
> (a) sovereign rights for the purpose of exploring and exploiting, conserving and managing the natural resources, whether living or non-living, of the waters superjacent to the seabed and of the seabed and its subsoil, and with regard to other activities for the economic exploitation and exploration of the zone, such as the production of energy from the water, currents and winds[.][25]

The UNCLOS also identified four categories of areas that coastal states can have some degree of control over. These regions are the following, listed in order of the degree of control recognised as belonging to coastal states:

- The territorial sea: any state has the right to determine this territory up to 12 nautical miles from baselines established in accordance with the convention (Article 3).
- The contiguous zone: its limit may not exceed 24 nautical miles from the baseline (Article 33).
- The EEZ: a new development in international law, which cannot extend beyond 200 nautical miles from the baseline (Article 56).
- The continental shelf: set at 200 nautical miles from the coastal baseline (Article 76).[26]

In addition to these four zones, the high seas can be identified as a fifth area which cannot be subjected to any national sovereignty. Article 89 of the UNCLOS clearly codified the historic principle of *mare liberum*, or freedom of the high seas, by stating that: 'No State may validly purport to subject any part of the high seas to its sovereignty'.[27]

A coastal state has sovereign rights over its EEZ for the purposes of the exploration, exploitation and conservation of maritime resources, whether biological or non-living. These exclusive rights were established as a result of the Cold Wars, a 1950s–1970s international dispute between Iceland and the United Kingdom that occurred before UNCLOS was adopted in 1982. The disagreement started because Iceland wanted to forbid foreign trawlers from fishing in the waters within 3–12 miles of the Icelandic coast. When the United Kingdom eventually acknowledged the legitimacy of the Icelandic claims, the conflict was finally declared to be

[25] United Nations Convention on the Law of the Sea (1982). https://www.un.org/depts/los/convention_agreements/texts/unclos/unclos_e.pdf

[26] Ibid.

[27] Ibid.

over in 1976.[28] This event enabled the establishment of a more precise framework determining territorial claims over the sea surrounding a coastal state, and currently 32 percent of the oceans' surface area is made up of EEZs.[29]

Additionally, States are permitted to impose safety zones, which are implemented as exclusion zones, with a maximum radius of 500 metres around artificial islands or installations under Article 60 of UNCLOS. These safety zones are restricted to approved vessels only; all other vessels are not permitted entry.[30]

By supporting a structured and organised international system, UNCLOS helped put an end to the anarchic appropriation of international waters by States. However, it is crucial to highlight that the principle of *mare liberum* remains in effect outside the EEZ and safety zones, notwithstanding the development of a certain level of national appropriation of an international territory.

These two examples of how safety zones are already present in international law could help shape the implementation of safety zones on the Moon and ease the concerns of some actors regarding an unlawful appropriation of strategic zones on the lunar surface.

The Difficult Definition of Safety Zones as Presented in the Artemis Accords

Questions regarding the legality of and compliance with the Artemis Accords, and safety zones as presented in Section 11, with the OST, particularly Article II defining the non-national appropriation principle, have been raised and concerns have been expressed regarding the definition and implementation of such zones. These will be explored in the following sections.

The Difficult Definition of Safety Zones on the Moon

The Hague International Space Resources Governance Working Group (The Hague Working Group) initially discussed the concept of safety zones in space in 2016. The principle was presented by private organisations and technical experts and representatives. The Hague Working Group, founded by The Hague Institute for Global Justice in 2014, is regarded as the main international body working on the legal

[28] Anand, R. P. (1976). The 'Cod War' Between the UK and Iceland. *India Quarterly, 32*(2), 215–220.

[29] Ardus, Dennis A., and Champ, Michael A. (Eds). (2012). Ocean Resources: Volume I: Assessment and Utilisation. Dordrecht: Springer Netherlands.

[30] UN Convention on the Law of the Sea (1982).

challenges associated with space mining.[31] The Hague Working Group's goal is to 'identify and formulate building blocks for the governance of space resource activities as a basis for negotiations on an international agreement or non-legally binding instruments'[32] and to 'provide recommendations on the implementation strategy' and to be a 'forum for negotiations' of such legally binding or non-binding agreements.[33] It is composed of 25 members and a large number of observers. In November 2019, the Hague Working Group adopted the Building Blocks for the Development of an International Framework on Space Resource Activities,[34] which contains the Building Block 11.3 that introduced the Working Group's definition of safety zones. It stipulates that:

> Taking into account the principle of non-appropriation under Article II OST, the international framework should permit States and international organisations responsible for space resource activities to establish a safety zone, or other area-based safety measure, around an area identified for a space resource activity as necessary to assure safety and to avoid any harmful interference with that space resource activity. Such safety measure shall not impede the free access, in accordance with international law, to any area of outer space by personnel, vehicles and equipment of another operator. In accordance with the area-based safety measure, a State or international organization may restrict access for a limited period of time, provided that timely public notice has been given setting out the reasons for such restriction.[35]

Further, Building Block 11.4 provides that 'The international framework should provide that appropriate international consultations are undertaken in case of possible overlap of safety zones or conflicts involving the freedom of access recognized by international law'.[36]

Surprisingly, neither the Hague Working Group Building Blocks[37] nor the Artemis Accords[38] provide a precise definition of what a safety zone on the Moon is. Instead, they outline the role of a safety zone, how a space actor may use it, and provide guidelines for communication and coordination requirements between

[31] Sundahl, M. J. and Davis, C. (2017). The Hague Working Group on Space Resources: Creating the Legal Building Blocks for a New Industry. *Law Faculty Articles and Essays*. Cleveland State University. engagedscholarship.csuohio.edu/cgi/viewcontent.cgi?article = 2055&context = fac_articles.

[32] International Institute of Air and Space Law (2022). The Hague International Space Resources Governance Working Group. https://www.universiteitleiden.nl/en/law/institute-of-public-law/institute-of-air-space-law/the-hague-space-resources-governance-working-group

[33] Ibid.

[34] The Hague International Space Resources Governance Working Group (2019). *Building Blocks for the Development of an International Framework on Space Resource Activities*. https://www.universiteitleiden.nl/binaries/content/assets/rechtsgeleerdheid/instituut-voor-publiekrecht/lucht%2D%2Den-ruimterecht/space-resources/bb-thissrwg%2D%2Dcover.pdf

[35] Ibid.

[36] Ibid.

[37] Ibid.

[38] NASA, The Artemis Accords.

partners.[39] This lack of specificity in the description of safety zones is directly linked to their evolutive nature, which makes a one-size-fits-all definition challenging, if not impossible, to find.

However, notwithstanding the ambiguity of international treaties and documents regarding what constitutes a safety zone, several authors have attempted to describe them. According to Alex Gilbert in Safety Zones for Lunar Activities under the Artemis Accords, there are four recurring descriptions of safety zones: (1) safety zones are similar to keep-out zones in order to protect security and economic interests of a party; (2) they are operational and safety areas around certain activities; (3) they are 'notice-and-deconfliction' zones which prevent conflicts; (4) they provide a registry of activities.[40] Gilbert offers his own definition of a safety zone, which he describes as 'a safety zone is one method to meet state obligations under the Outer Space Treaty that defines a geographic, temporal, and/or other delimited circumstances under which a mission operator believes their operational safety requires third parties to commence consultations to avoid harmful interference and related risks'.[41] This definition is interesting as it encompasses the notions of both The Hague Working Group's and the Artemis Accords' descriptions. The emphasis is placed on the importance of international collaboration and the adherence to established international treaties. The definition centres around the concept that safety zones in space should be firmly based on the Outer Space Treaty, particularly Article IX, which prohibits harmful interference. This aligns with the reasoning behind the Artemis Accords.

Further, the author adds that these zones can have multiple dimensions:

- 'One-dimensional. The safety zone is delimited solely by a space object or an astronaut'.
- 'Two-dimensional. A safety zone is a line constituting a space object trajectory or a pathway between an astronaut and their spacecraft'.
- 'Three-dimensional. A three-dimensional area around a space object'.
- 'Four-dimensional. A four-dimensional area around a space object bound for an area that varies in time'.[42]

This definition offers an alternative perspective on safety zones and challenges the contested area-based definition of safety zones. In fact, this description appears to be one of the best thought-out and most precise yet, considering the imprecision of national and international texts. Gilbert suggests a definition that puts an emphasis on international co-operation and compliance with existing international treaties, and

[39] Mallowan, L., Rapp, L., & Topka, M. (2021). *Reinventing Treaty Compliant "Safety Zones" in the Context of Space Sustainability.*

[40] Gilbert, A. Q. (2023) 'Implementing safety zones for lunar activities under the Artemis Accords', *Journal of Space Safety Engineering*. doi: https://doi.org/10.1016/j.jsse.2022.12.007

[41] Ibid.

[42] Ibid.

offers a complete overview of how safety zones could impact not only territorial resources but multiple other dimensions as well.

Nevertheless, uncertainty will persist until a broadly accepted agreement establishing the definition and implementation regime of safety zones is ratified by a significant number of actors. Additionally, the ambiguities of these zones as presented in the Artemis Accords can be expected to have geopolitical ramifications in the near future.

The Ambiguities of the Artemis Accords' Safety Zones

To support the establishment and implementation of safety zones, the Artemis Accords make reference to Article IX of the Outer Space Treaty. For reference, the main focus of this Article is avoiding harmful interference; it proclaims that:

> if a State Party to the Treaty has reason to believe that an activity or experiment planned by it or its nationals in outer space, including the Moon and other celestial bodies, would cause potentially harmful interference with activities of other States Parties in the peaceful exploration and use of outer space, including the Moon and other celestial bodies, it shall undertake appropriate international consultation before proceeding with any such activity or experiment.[43]

Article IX does not suggest a duty to avoid harmful interference, rather a state's obligation is to convene an international consultation whenever a risk of harmful interference arises. As a result, Guoyu Wang argues that it might be invalid to use the provisions of Article IX of the Outer Space Treaty to support the creation of safety zones, as suggested by the Artemis Accords.[44]

In light of this argument, the concern naturally turns to the previously described balance between the rights and interests of space actors creating a safety zone on the lunar surface. The Artemis Accords recognise a right to commercial space mining in Section 10, which provides that 'The Signatories affirm that the extraction of space resources does not inherently constitute national appropriation under Article II of the Outer Space Treaty, and that contracts and other legal instruments relating to space resources should be consistent with that Treaty'.[45] Put in conjunction with safety zones may make it more difficult to distinguish between the freedom to use outer space and the non-appropriation principle. Through the acknowledgement of the right to use lunar resources for commercial purposes and the creation of safety zones,

[43] United Nations Office for Outer Space Affairs (19 December 1966). *Resolution Adopted by the General Assembly 2222(XI). Treaty on Principles Governing the Activities of States in the Exploration and Use of Outer Space, including the Moon and Other Celestial Bodies.* https://www.unoosa.org/pdf/gares/ARES_21_2222E.pdf

[44] Wang, G. (2020, August 24). NASA's Artemis Accords: the path to a united space law or a divided one? *The Space Review.* https://www.thespacereview.com/article/4009/1

[45] NASA. The Artemis Accords.

the Accords have the potential to generate "spheres of influence of a State"[46] on the Moon, as per Guoyu Wang. Such a situation may have geopolitical consequences on Earth and could result in conflict among various stakeholders.

Ultimately, under the terms of the Artemis Accords, and without a clear and adopted implementation mechanism, it might be difficult and challenging to distinguish between excluding other space actors from an established safety zone to prevent interference and seizing control over that zone. The provisions of the Artemis Accords are not specific or inclusive enough to effectively avoid harmful interference and prevent the creation of spheres of influence when mining activities start on the Moon. By using bilateral agreements rather than international organisations such as the UN Committee on the Peaceful Uses of Outer Space, the Artemis Accords present one interpretation of international space law and exclude de facto major space powers such as Russia and China from the discussions.[47]

Implementation of the Safety Zones: Concluding Remarks

It has to be noted however that the aforementioned interpretations are only theoretical since no implementation mechanism has been published by the signatories of the Artemis Accords. It will be interesting to see how the signatories decide to implement such safety zones and how the decision will be agreed between them. The following sections will focus on the different implementation mechanisms that exist and on the recommendations published by NASA in September 2022.

Practicalities of Implementing Safety Zones

The main debate surrounding the implementation of safety zones relates to whether they will only be a notification zone which would be free to access upon notification by the implementing space actor, or an exclusion or keep-out zone, which would prevent any actor from accessing it.

On that note, in *Lunar Landing and Operations Policy Analysis*, NASA recommends that 'the most critical element of safety zones is what they are not: they are not exclusion zones'.[48] The report adds that other actors are not compelled to keep out of safety zones, but they must give the zone's creator advance notice and seek consultation in order to lessen interference. Further, the report recommends that, following the principle of Article XI of the Outer Space Treaty, the Artemis Accords' signatories must notify each other as well as the UN Secretary-General whenever they

[46] Wang. NASA's Artemis Accords.

[47] Ibid.

[48] Swiney and Hernandez. *Lunar Landing and Operations Policy Analysis*.

create, alter or terminate any safety zone. The emphasis is clearly on promoting transparency and communication between signatories so that others can respect the established safety zones and prevent or mitigate any interference that might occur when entering that zone.[49]

Interestingly, the report also mentions non-signatories of the Artemis Accords and argues that although they have not agreed to respect safety zones as described in the Accords, by publicly announcing safety zones around signatories' operations, non-signatories open themselves to the notice and consultation requirements under Article XI of the Outer Space Treaty. Therefore, the signatories 'put the international community on notice', as written by Swiney and Hernandez put it, and the responsibility to respect the non-interference principle falls on the non-signatory party. Further, the authors also recommend that NASA and the US Government respect safety zones or similar zones established by non-signatories too, in order to 'mitigate criticism of safety zones'.[50]

Although the authors of *Lunar Landing and Operations Policy Analysis* temper the imposition of putting the responsibility of respecting signatories' safety zones onto non-signatories by recommending NASA and the US Government respect those of others,[51] this interpretation could lead to conflict over safety zones if two actors decide to create a zone on the same spot, for instance. The report also makes no mention of other signatories, and only recommends NASA respect the zones of non-signatories, which prompts the question of whether the implementation of safety zones will lead to harmonisation amongst the signatories, or if the United States will impose their own interpretation on the other signatories without consultations.

Regarding the intricacies of the technical implementation of safety zones, questions arise including the size of safety zones, whether their establishment and creation would be agreed on prior missions, who would be allowed to establish these zones and what would the registration process look like, for instance.[52] The NASA report does not answer these questions with precision and remains relatively broad. However, Swiney and Hernandez argue that another way to avoid international criticism of safety zones would be to minimise their size and number, to terminate them at the end of missions and to provide reasonable scientific and technical justifications for their design. This could help mitigate geopolitical repercussions.[53] Regarding the question of registration, the report only recommends that US Government regulators should include safety zone measures in their licensing requirements.[54] No mention is being made of international registration measures.

[49] Ibid.

[50] Ibid.

[51] Ibid.

[52] McKeown, B., Dempster, A. G., and Saydam, S. (2022). Artemis Accords: Are Safety Zones Practical for Long Term Commercial Lunar Resource Utilisation? *Space Policy, 62*, 101,504.

[53] Swiney and Hernandez, *Lunar Landing and Operations Policy Analysis*.

[54] Ibid.

Finally, a brief mention is made of the distinction between safety zones and heritage protection. Safety zones do not seem to be the right tool to protect cultural heritage on the Moon because of their temporary nature, and other policy tools will have to be created in order to protect them in the long run.[55]

Implementing safety zones is still a very broad concept and it will be interesting to see if the United States creates a space for the Artemis Accords' signatories to discuss their implementation and whether it will be done in a harmonised manner among the signatories. Another question remains regarding the respect for safety zones by non-signatories of the Artemis Accords and the potential for conflict that could arise if two parties make a similar claim. Currently, no conflict resolution mechanism exists to deal with such questions, but it will need to be considered, especially for high-risk zones such as the South Pole of the Moon, for instance.

Proposal: Aligning Technological and Geopolitical Needs

If the Artemis Accords, as they stand today, end up setting a precedent and gain international momentum regarding safety zones and subsequently resource utilisation and commercialisation, and no modification is made to their interpretation and the implementation of their principles, commercial actors might wonder if the Artemis Accords are going to be sufficiently legally sustainable for them to invest billions in developing resource extraction and utilisation mechanisms. Currently, the Artemis Accords are creating a lot of debate and raising several questions without providing much certainty regarding the implementation of their principles. While these bilateral agreements are still rather new, the space industry is moving at a rapid pace, with missions going to the Moon as soon as the end of 2022 to extract and analyse lunar resources.

A one-size-fits-all proposal is most probably not the solution to the implementation of safety zones in a sustainable manner compliant with international law. But whether safety zones are implemented as recommended in the aforementioned report, or in a different way, there is a need to answer questions about the safety of operations issues posed by proximity operations.

Safety zones are a clever way to create a framework around lunar activities, and examples in international law have shown that such zones can be effectively enforced and created for the benefit of all parties. But there are still many uncertainties regarding their implementation and the respect accorded to established safety zones by non-signatories, which could eventually hinder the development of lunar activities. Therefore, one solution as of now would be to open the discussion regarding the implementation of safety zones to space agencies, private actors, scholars, and signatories as well as non-signatories of the Artemis Accords in order to find the most balanced and sustainable way to implement them. Creating

[55] Ibid.

a safe environment for lunar activities to develop sustainably will be critical if missions like the Artemis Program are to be successful in the long run. It also would create a positive precedent of international cooperation and coordination regarding a heavily debated issue, and eventually create norms of behaviour which would focus on finding a balance among all the different stakeholders on the Moon.

Bibliography

Abeyratne, R. (2012). In search of theoretical justification for air defence identification zones. *Journal of Transportation Security, 5*, 87–94.

Agreement on the Rescue of Astronauts, the Return of Astronauts, and the Return of Objects Launched into Outer Space, adopted on 19 December 1967 by General Assembly Resolution 2345 (XXII), opened for signature on 22 April 1968, 672 UNTS 119; TIAS 6599; 18 UST 2410; [1969] UKTS 56; [1986] ATS 8; [1975] CTS 6; [1969] NZTS 5; 169 SP 864; 7 ILM 151 (entered into force generally on 12 March 1968, for Australia on 18 March 1986, and for New Zealand on 8 July 1969).

Anand, R. P. (1976). The 'cod war' between the UK and Iceland. *India Quarterly, 32*(2), 215–220.

Ardus, D. A., & Champ, M. A. (Eds.). (2012). *Ocean resources: Volume I: Assessment and utilisation*. Springer Netherlands.

Bakhtiar, H. S., Djanur, N. A., Ashri, M., & Hendrapati, M. (2016). Air defence identification zone (ADIZ) in international law perspective. *Journal of Law, Policy, and Globalisation, 56*, 16.

Chicago Convention on International Civil Aviation, opened for signature on 7 December 1944, 15 UTS 295; 148 BSP 38; [1953] UKTS 8; [1957] ATS 5; [1944] CTS 36 (entered into force generally on 4 April 1947 and for New Zealand on 6 April 1947).

Convention on Registration of Objects Launched into Outer Space, adopted on 12 November 1974 by General Assembly Resolution 3235 (XXIX), opened for signature on 14 January 1975, 1023 UNTS 15; TIAS 8480; [1978] UKTS 70; [1986] ATS 5; [1976] CTS 36 (entered into force generally and for Australia on 11 March 1986 and for New Zealand on 23 January 2018).

Deplano, R. (2021). The Artemis Accords: Evolution or revolution in international space law? *International and Comparative Law Quarterly, 70*(3), 799–819. https://doi.org/10.1017/S0020589321000142

ESA Budget 2022. (2022). *European space agency*. Available at: https://www.esa.int/ESA_Multimedia/Images/2022/01/ESA_budget_2022.

Fidler, D. P. (2020). The Artemis Accords and the next generation of outer space governance. *Council on Foreign Relations*. www.cfr.org/blog/artemis-accords-and-next-generation-outer-space-governance.

Foust, J. (2022, June 8). France joins Artemis Accords. *Space News*. spacenews.com/france-joins-artemis-accords.

French Guiana is a French Department Located Overseas. (n.d.). https://www.esa.int/Enabling_Support/Space_Transportation/Europe_s_Spaceport/Europe_s_Spaceport2.

Gilbert, A. Q. (2023). Implementing safety zones for lunar activities under the Artemis Accords. *Journal of Space Safety Engineering*. https://doi.org/10.1016/j.jsse.2022.12.007

Gohd, C. (2021, November 10). NASA's Artemis astronauts won't land on the moon by 2024 deadline. *Space.com*. www.space.com/nasa-changes-artemis-moon-landing-goal-2024.

Grush, L. (2022, June 10). Why France signing NASA's lunar exploration pact is the most important signature yet. *The Verge*. Available at: https://www.theverge.com/2022/6/10/23159558/nasa-artemis-accords-france-signing-moon-exploration-significance.

International Institute of Air and Space Law. (2022). The Hague international space resources governance working group. *Proceedings of the International Astronautical Congress, IAC*.

https://www.universiteitleiden.nl/en/law/institute-of-public-law/institute-of-air-space-law/the-hague-space-resources-governance-working-group

Mallowan, L., Rapp, L., & Topka, M. (2021). Reinventing treaty compliant "safety zones" in the context of space sustainability. *Journal of Space Safety Engineering, 8*(2), 155–166.

McKeown, B., Dempster, A. G., & Saydam, S. (2022). Artemis Accords: Are safety zones practical for long term commercial lunar resource utilisation? *Space Policy*. https://doi.org/10.1016/j.spacepol.2022.101504

NASA. (2020a). *NASA's lunar exploration program overview*. https://www.nasa.gov/wp-content/uploads/2020/12/artemis_plan-20200921.pdf.

NASA. (2020b). *The Artemis Accords – Principles for a safe, peaceful, and prosperous future*. https://www.nasa.gov/artemis-accords/.

Office of the Staff Judge Advocate. (2021). Air defense identification zones. *International Law Studies, 97*.

Sundahl, M. J., & Davis, C. (2017). The Hague working group on space resources: Creating the legal building blocks for a new industry. *Law faculty articles and essays*. Cleveland State University. http://engagedscholarship.csuohio.edu/cgi/viewcontent.cgi?article=2055&context=fac_articles.

Swiney, G., & Hernandez, A. (2022). *Lunar landing and operations policy analysis*. https://www.nasa.gov/sites/default/files/atoms/files/lunar_landing_and_operations_policy_analysis_final_report_24oct2022_tagged_0.pdf

The Hague International Space Resources Governance Working Group. (2019). *Building blocks for the development of an international framework on space resource activities*. https://www.universiteitleiden.nl/binaries/content/assets/rechtsgeleerdheid/instituut-voor-publiekrecht/lucht%2D%2Den-ruimterecht/space-resources/bb-thissrwg%2D%2Dcover.pdf

The Spaceport. (2023). Available at: https://www.arianespace.com/spaceport-facility/.

Treaty on Principles Governing the Activities of States in the Exploration and Use of Outer Space, including the Moon and other Celestial Bodies, adopted on 19 December 1966 by UN General Assembly Resolution 2222 (XXI), opened for signature on 27 January 1967, 610 UNTS 205; TIAS 6347; 18 UST 2410; [1968] UKTS 10; [1967] ATS 24; [1967] CTS 19; [1968] NZTS 8; 6 ILM 386 (entered into force generally and for Australia on 10 October 1967 and for New Zealand on 31 May 1968).

United Nations Convention on the Law of the Sea. (1982). https://www.un.org/depts/los/convention_agreements/texts/unclos/unclos_e.pdf

United Nations Office for Outer Space Affairs. (1966, December 19). Resolution Adopted by the General Assembly 2222(XI). Treaty on Principles Governing the Activities of States in the Exploration and Use of Outer Space, including the Moon and Other Celestial Bodies. https://www.unoosa.org/pdf/gares/ARES_21_2222E.pdf

Wang, G. (2020, August 24). NASA's Artemis Accords: The path to a united space law or a divided one? *The Space Review*. Available at: https://www.thespacereview.com/article/4009/1.

Chapter 6
Military Activities and Operations in Space: An Unfolding Legal Universe

Dale Stephens

Introduction

Military activity in space has been a constant ever since the dawn of the 'space age' with the launch of the first satellite into space Sputnik in 1957 by the Soviet Union, though it was initially restricted to a very few States with very advanced capabilities. Recently, however, the utility of space-based military assets and capabilities, in conjunction with the lowering of costs of entry to space, has led to greater military use of space and the recognition by many States that space itself has become a critical enabler. This has meant that space has progressively become a dedicated area of operations and that military doctrine concerning space use has developed accordingly. Such recognition and doctrinal focus has not generally been accompanied by a corresponding focus upon the law applicable to such military activities and operations.

There does exist a respectable body of treaty law that applies to space. Much of this law is, however, expressed in general and aspirational language. There is only one key provision in one generally subscribed treaty that directly regulates military activities in space, and that is Article IV of the 1967 Outer Space Treaty (OST).[1] This provision deals with one major weapon system and proscribes a limited number of activities on the Moon and other celestial bodies. Despite this measure of

[1] Noting that Article 3 of the poorly subscribed Moon Agreement largely repeats the prohibitions contained in Article IV of the OST, though adding an extra restriction of not undertaking 'any other hostile act or threat of hostile act on the moon', which term has not been definitively defined or applied through State practice. *Agreement governing the Activities of States on the Moon and Other Celestial Bodies* ('Moon Agreement'). Opened for signature 5 December 1979 (entered into force 11 July 1984). 1363 UNTS 3.

D. Stephens (✉)
University of Adelaide Law School, Adelaide, South Australia, Australia
e-mail: dale.stephens@adelaide.edu.au

M. A. Pozza (ed.), *Ascending to Space*, Space Law and Policy,
https://doi.org/10.1007/978-981-97-0714-0_6

limitation, another key provision of the OST, Article I, does apply all international law to space, including the law of State Responsibility, the UN Charter and all international humanitarian law (IHL), which affords a sound basis to assess and evaluate the general lawfulness of military activities and operations. This exercise is not without challenge. Although a number of provisions of existing treaty law seem to be eminently applicable to contribute to maintaining peace and stability in space, there has been limited State engagement on settling legal issues. This chapter will canvass the development of space as a recognised military operational area and will deal with three key legal issues to illustrate the types of challenges that need to be navigated in this field. Hence, the concepts of due regard, the use of force, and the law of neutrality will be examined to advance a view that they all have a particular capacity to inform responsible military behaviour in space. Moreover, effective legal engagement with these three topics is likely to contribute to the maintenance of peace and stability, or, in the case of neutrality, to ensure that the effects of armed conflict are limited to belligerent parties in the context of a space war.

Space: A Military Operational Area

Space has always been an arena of military attention. The German V2 rocket of the Second World War was the first human-made object to leave Earth's atmosphere,[2] and the race by the Allied powers to develop their own long-range missile weaponry became the stepping stone which led humanity into space.[3] The first human in space was of course a Soviet air force officer, Senior Lieutenant (eventually Colonel) Yuri Gagarin, and the majority of US astronauts to date have also been air force officers.[4]

Although States were initially reluctant to publicly recognise the potential military applications of space,[5] the advantages of possessing a military capability there

[2]Milazzo, M. P., Kestay, L. and Dundas, C. (2017). The Challenge for 2050: Cohesive Analysis of More Than One Hundred Years of Planetary Data. *Planetary Science Vision 2050 Workshop* (LPI Contribution No. 1989). www.hou.usra.edu/meetings/V2050/pdf/8070.pdf

[3]See for example Feigin, J. (2008). *The Office of Special Investigations: Striving for Accountability in the Aftermath of the Holocaust*, 331–338. Draft made available at Freedom of Information Act Library, United States Department of Justice. www.justice.gov/sites/default/files/criminal/legacy/2011/03/14/12-2008osu-accountability.pdf; Cameron, A. M. (1946). *Report on Operation 'Backfire'*, vol. I. *Scope and Organisation of the Operation*. London: War Office. library.si.edu/digital-library/book/report-operation-backfire (in particular page 27); Ramani, M. (2017, July 1). The German village that changed the war. *BBC Travel*. https://www.bbc.com/travel/article/20170629-the-german-village-that-changed-the-war

[4]Treat, J., Bennett, J. and Turner, C. (2020, November 6). How 'the right stuff' has changed. *National Geographic*. www.nationalgeographic.com/science/graphics/charting-how-nasa-astronaut-demographics-have-changed-over-time

[5]The first draft resolution submitted by the USSR to the United Nations proposed a blanket 'ban on the use of cosmic space for military purposes' (Union of Soviet Socialist Republics. (1958, November 7). *Draft Resolution*. UN Document A/C.1/L.219 – United Nations General Assembly),

were immediately apparent. This was particularly the case for reconnaissance. From 1960, the United States worked in earnest to develop space surveillance capabilities, and soon relied heavily on reconnaissance of this kind for assessment of foreign military capabilities[6] – although the USSR was outwardly opposed such use[7] there is little doubt that they were also launching surveillance satellites of their own at this time.[8]

A series of UN General Assembly resolutions and ongoing treaty negotiations in the early 1960s confirmed that there were no sovereign rights applicable to space itself.[9] As a result, traditional limitations concerning sovereignty which applied to airspace and territorial waters could be overcome through military use of the sovereignty-free realm of space. Ultimately, such reliable space-based reconnaissance had a positive effect in bolstering a parity of strategic confidence and therefore relative peace, with American President Jimmy Carter in 1978 calling surveillance satellites 'an important stabilizing factor in world affairs'.[10]

Over the past few decades, space assets have continued to provide critical reconnaissance and communications capabilities to military forces. This capability was universally recognised in the first Gulf War of 1991, which has been called by

---

while the United States' request to include outer space as an item on the General Assembly's agenda noted 'the potential uses of outer space for destructive purposes are only too apparent' (United States of America. (1958, September 2). *Request for the inclusion of an additional item in the agenda of the thirteenth session.* UN Document A/3902 – United Nations General Assembly). President Eisenhower's September 1960 address to the UN General Assembly called for it to be '"off limits" to military preparations', in the same way as Antarctica. The tension between the clear utility of space assets for military purposes and the concern about how far such use should be permissible (especially given the Cold War context) became a theme of the debates in the UN Committee on the Peaceful Uses of Outer Space for years leading up to the finalisation of the OST in 1967. A good example of this tension – and of the difference between public and private agendas – can be seen in the United States' formulation of their space policy, discussed on pages 6–7 of the National Reconnaissance Program Memorandum. (1969, 4 June) (pp. 2–5). National Reconnaissance Office digital archive. www.nro.gov/Portals/65/documents/foia/declass/Archive/NARP/1969%20NARPs/SC-2018-00033_C05111857.pdf

[6] National Reconnaissance Program Memorandum. (1969, 4 June), 2–5.

[7] Shreve, B. (2003, June 2). The US, the USSR and space exploration, 1957–1963. *International Journal on World Peace, 20*(2), 77.

[8] Richelson, J. T. (Ed.) (2015, February 4). *U.S. Intelligence and the Soviet Space Program: National Security Archive Electronic Briefing Book No. 501*. National Security Archive. nsarchive2.gwu.edu/NSAEBB/NSAEBB501

[9] United Nations General Assembly. (1961, December 20). *Resolution 1721 (XVI) – International co-operation in the peaceful uses of outer space.* UN Document A/RES/1721; United Nations General Assembly. (1963, December 13). *Resolution 1962 (XVIII) – Declaration of Legal Principles Governing the Activities of States in the Exploration and Use of Outer Space*. UN Document A/RES/1962.

[10] See Carter, J. (1978, October 1). *Remarks at the Congressional Space Medal of Honor Awards Ceremony*. Kennedy Space Center, Florida. From Weekly Compilation of Presidential Documents. (1978, October 9), 1684. National Security Archives. nsarchive2.gwu.edu/NSAEBB/NSAEBB231/doc32.pdf

some the 'first space war'.[11] This war has that distinction not because hostilities were conducted in space itself, but rather that the air, land and sea operations were heavily dependent upon space assets – in particular, global positioning system (GPS) satellites.[12] In more recent times, the capacity for States such as the United States to conduct global operations has depended heavily upon space assets. GPS satellites have also come to play an essential role in targeting since the advent of GPS-guided Joint Direct Attack Munitions in the 1990s.[13] Such satellites also provide the very basis for the conduct of global uncrewed aerial vehicle (UAV) operations. Such UAV systems may well be prioritised in future defence acquisition decision-making processes, thus further enhancing the relevance of space in the military context.

In 2019, NATO formally recognised the relevance of space by declaring outer space to be a formal theatre of operations.[14] The New Zealand[15] and Australian[16] governments similarly have recognised space as one of the five operational theatres alongside the land, sea, air and cyberspace environments. This growing recognition of the key relevance of space has been accompanied by developing space operations doctrine[17] by many nations and has seen the appearance of space operations as a distinct chapter within publications such as the US Department of Defense Law of War Manual (Chap. XIV).[18] From a doctrinal perspective, it is clear that space is transitioning from a supporting to a supported military operational environment.

---

[11] Anson, P. and Cummings, D. (1991). The First Space War: The Contribution of Satellites to the Gulf War. *RUSI Journal, 136*(4), 45–53.

[12] Lambakis, S. (1995, Summer). Space Control in Desert Storm and Beyond. *Orbis*, *39*(3), 419.

[13] Tirpak, J. A. (2003, November). The Next Generation. *Air Force Magazine*, 45.

[14] North Atlantic Treaty Organization. (2019, December 4). *London Declaration – Issued by the Heads of State and Government Participating in the meeting of the North Atlantic Council in London 3–4 December 2019* (press release). www.nato.int/cps/en/natohq/official_texts_171584.htm

[15] New Zealand Government, Ministry of Defence. (2018). *Strategic Defence Policy Statement*, 7. www.defence.govt.nz/assets/Uploads/8958486b29/Strategic-Defence-Policy-Statement-2018.pdf

[16] Australian Government Department of Defence. (2020, September 21). *Defence Annual Report 2019–20*, 96. www.defence.gov.au/about/information-disclosures/annual-reports

[17] See US Space Force. (2020, June). *Spacepower: Doctrine for Space Forces*. Space Capstone Publication. www.spaceforce.mil/Portals/1/Space%20Capstone%20Publication_10%20Aug%202020.pdf; US Joint Chiefs of Staff. (2018, April 10). *Joint Publication 3–14 – Space Operations*. (Revised edition as at 26 October 2020). US Department of Defense. www.jcs.mil/Portals/36/Documents/Doctrine/pubs/jp3_14ch1.pdf; UK Ministry of Defence, Development, Concepts and Doctrine Centre. (2022, September). *Joint Doctrine Publication 0–40 – UK Space Power*. assets.publishing.service.gov.uk/government/uploads/system/uploads/attachment_data/file/1101450/20220831-JDP_0_40_UK_Space_Power_web.pdf; French Ministry for the Armed Forces. (2019). *Space Defence Strategy: Report of the 'Space' working group*. Délégation à l'information et à la communication de la Défense; general discussion of doctrine and policy positions on a state-by-state basis in Weeden, B. and Samson, V. (Eds). (2022, April). *Global Counterspace Capabilities* (Report). Secure World Foundation. swfound.org/media/207350/swf_global_counterspace_capabilities_2022_rev2.pdf.

[18] US Department of Defense, Office of General Counsel. (2015, June 12). *Department of Defense Law of War Manual*. (Revised edition as at December 2016), 942. dod.defense.gov/Portals/1/

With this increase in recognised capability in space comes a correlative recognition of the vulnerabilities of space and the space environment with respect to national security. The United States has declared that while the use of outer space must be for peaceful purposes, it is 'preparing for the reality that space must be defended from those who will seek to undermine our goals in space'.[19] Similarly, the People's Republic of China has recognised that space is a military domain since 2015 and is actively embarking upon a programme to develop its anti-satellite launch capabilities, as well as shaping its doctrinal focus upon space with express recognition of the need to 'strengthen comprehensive space technology applications supporting and serving national defense and state security, economic and social development, and the deployment of strategic power around the globe'.[20] Tellingly in this regard, an international report has observed that Chinese commentators take the view that 'the center of gravity in military operations has transitioned from the sea to the air and is now transitioning to space'.[21] Russia too is developing its counter-space capabilities, the same report observing that it is paying special attention to its co-orbital anti-satellite capability.[22]

The Australian Government recognised in its 2020 *Defence Strategic Update* that space was a critical area of development for the Australian Defence Force's 'warfighting effectiveness, situational awareness and the delivery of real-time communications and information',[23] and it was investing approximately seven billion Australian dollars in developing a sovereign space capability.[24] With respect to the policy and legal national security environment of space, the *Update* observed that the 'rules, norms and institutions that help maintain peace and security and guide global cooperation are under strain' and that the 'thresholds for activities that could trigger a military response are unclear in space and cyberspace as they lack the more clearly defined boundaries of national borders and geography'.[25] Similarly, in recognising emerging threats to national security, New Zealand has identified the critical place of space in its 2021 *Defence Assessment*, noting that 'we ... anticipate increasing risks to New Zealand's physical, electronic and space-based international connections' and in 'terms of New Zealand's interests in the defence and security of

---

Documents/pubs/DoD%20Law%20of%20War%20Manual%20-%20June%202015%20Updated%20Dec%202016.pdf?ver=2016-12-13-172036-190

[19] US Space Force. *Spacepower: Doctrine for Space Forces*. 17.

[20] Stokes, M., Alvarado, G. Weinstein, E., and Easton, I. (2020, March 30). *China's Space and Counterspace Capabilities and Activities* (Research Report), 9. US–China Economic and Security Review Commission, citing a Chinese policy document.

[21] Weeden & Samson. *Global Counterspace Capabilities*.

[22] Ibid.

[23] Australian Government Department of Defence. (2020, July). *2020 Defence Strategic Update*, 38. www.defence.gov.au/about/strategic-planning/2020-defence-strategic-update

[24] Ibid., p. 39.

[25] Ibid., p. 12.

the Indo-Pacific, we consider the most significant conflict risks include ... conflicts in and through space and cyber-space'.[26]

Given this escalating recognition of the criticality of space for national security purposes, it is necessary to better understand the role of law in regulating the field and its capacity to promote stability. As will be advanced below, while the apparent exuberance for developing space capability is likely to continue, space is not a 'Wild West', and well-established treaty law provisions restrain and condition military activity. However, despite this fact, it is equally acknowledged that there are many grey areas of law that await responsible State behaviour to better inform the capacity in the existing law to ensure continued peaceful human activity in space.

Space Law and Military Activities

While cyberspace and outer space are two newly recognised military operational environments (cyberspace having been recognised by NATO as such in July 2016), there is a significant distinction between the two in the context of legal prescription. Unlike cyberspace, there is a comprehensive regime of treaty law that applies to space that provides the foundation for regulating, directly or indirectly, military activities and operations. Moreover, leading space-faring States such as the United States, China, Russia and India are all parties to the primary treaty, namely the OST. In sum, there exist five principal treaties that regulate human activity in space:

1. 1967 Outer Space Treaty[27]
2. 1968 Rescue Agreement[28]
3. 1972 Liability Convention[29]
4. 1975 Registration Convention[30]

[26] New Zealand Ministry of Defence. (2021). *He Moana Pukepuke e Ekengia e Te Waka: A Rough Sea Can Still be Navigated: Defence Assessment 2021*, 21, 25. www.defence.govt.nz/assets/publication/file/Defence-Assessment-2021.pdf

[27] *Treaty on Principles Governing the Activities of States in the Exploration and Use of Outer Space, Including the Moon and Other Celestial Bodies*. Opened for signature 27 January 1967 (entered into force 10 October 1967). 610 UNTS 205. https://www.unoosa.org/pdf/publications/STSPACE11E.pdf

[28] *Agreement on the Rescue of Astronauts, the Return of Astronauts and the Return of Objects Launched into Outer Space*. Opened for signature 22 April 1968 (entered into force 3 December 1968). 672 UNTS 119. https://www.unoosa.org/pdf/publications/STSPACE11E.pdf

[29] *Convention on the International Liability for Damage Caused by Space Objects*. Opened for signature 29 March 1972 (entered into force 1 September 1972) 961 UNTS 187. https://www.unoosa.org/pdf/publications/STSPACE11E.pdf

[30] *Convention on Registration of Objects Launched into Outer Space*. Opened for signature 14 January 1975 (entered into force 15 September 1976). 1023 UNTS 15. https://www.unoosa.org/pdf/publications/STSPACE11E.pdf

5. 1979 Moon Treaty[31]

However, despite the wide scope of treaty law that applies to military activities and operations in space, there is only one substantive provision of one generally subscribed treaty that deals directly with such activities, and that is Article IV of the OST.

(a) *Military Prohibitions and Their Limits*

Article IV of the OST contains two principal paragraphs. The first paragraph provides that 'States Parties to the Treaty undertake not to place in orbit around the Earth any objects carrying nuclear weapons or any other kinds of weapons of mass destruction, install such weapons on celestial bodies, or station such weapons in outer space in any other manner'.[32]

The second paragraph provides that:

> The Moon and other celestial bodies shall be used by all States Parties to the Treaty exclusively for peaceful purposes. The establishment of military bases, installations and fortifications, the testing of any type of weapons and the conduct of military manoeuvres on celestial bodies shall be forbidden. The use of military personnel for scientific research or for any other peaceful purposes shall not be prohibited. The use of any equipment or facility necessary for peaceful exploration of the Moon and other celestial bodies shall also not be prohibited.[33]

The OST is not a general disarmament treaty for space. It is clear that Article IV, paragraph 1 does prohibit weapons of mass destruction in full orbit around the earth, their stationing in space or installation on the surface of celestial bodies. However, this Article does not, even by its literal terms, prohibit weapons of mass destruction in partial orbit,[34] nor does it prohibit weapons that are not weapons of mass destruction in full or partial orbit, their installation on the Moon or their stationing in outer space. As the US Law of War Manual notes, 'Article IV of the OST does not establish any prohibitions with respect to weapons that are not weapons of mass destruction (*e.g.*, anti-satellite laser weapons or other conventional weapons)'.[35]

Article IV, paragraph 2 does provide that the Moon and other celestial bodies shall be used 'exclusively for peaceful purposes'. However, despite the similarity in wording between the OST and the 1959 Antarctic Treaty, there is no general prohibition on military activities in space as there is in the Antarctic. Rather, specific

---

[31] *Agreement governing the Activities of States on the Moon and Other Celestial Bodies*. Opened for signature 5 December 1979 (entered into force 11 July 1984). 1363 UNTS 3. https://www.unoosa.org/pdf/publications/STSPACE11E.pdf

[32] *Treaty on Principles Governing the Activities of States in the Exploration and Use of Outer Space, Including the Moon and Other Celestial Bodies*. Opened for signature 27 January 1967 (entered into force 10 October 1967). 610 UNTS 205. https://www.unoosa.org/pdf/publications/STSPACE11E.pdf. Art IV.

[33] Ibid.

[34] US Department of Defense. *Department of Defense Law of War Manual*, 942.

[35] Ibid., 943.

military activities enumerated in this paragraph are prohibited; however, the terms of the prohibition are not given specific definition, thereby creating a level of uncertainty. Of course, resort can be made to the customary rules of international legal interpretation that underpin Article 31 of the 1969 Vienna Convention on the Law of Treaties (VCLT) to interpret these terms.[36] In this regard, meaning must be given to what is a 'military base, installation and fortification'. At the same time, the paragraph makes clear that military personnel are permitted on the Moon (and other celestial bodies), and that providing security or even participating in a peacekeeping operation would, prima facie, likely not be prohibited under Article IV (paragraph 2). On this basis, a facility or habitat which military personnel may occupy when undertaking these tasks would not likely be designated as a 'base', thus leaving open the question of how broad or narrow the terms 'base', 'installation' and 'fortification' can be. Similarly, weapons testing is prohibited, but not weapons themselves (other than weapons of mass destruction), and while 'military manoeuvres' are specifically prohibited, other military activities are not. Of course, there is a general requirement that military activities must be directed towards peaceful purposes, noting that the term 'peaceful purposes' in the context of the OST has been interpreted to mean non-aggressive[37] consistent with general international law that applies by virtue of Article III.

The specificity of wording used in Article IV has given rise to efforts by China and Russia to ban particular weapons and to address particular capabilities in space.[38] Such efforts have not progressed very far because of multiple objections made by States regarding weapons systems not covered in these proposals but easily directed towards space (i.e. land-based ASAT weapons), issues of verification and, finally, questions about expanding definitions of the use of force under the UN Charter.[39] While greater specificity is always a welcome addition to any interpretative exercise, it is equally clear that the nuances and capabilities of military space

[36] *Vienna Convention on the Law of Treaties*. Opened for signature 23 May 1969 (entered into force 27 January 1980). 1155 UNTS 331. Art 31. https://legal.un.org/ilc/texts/instruments/english/conventions/1_1_1969.pdf

[37] See for example US Department of Defense, *Department of Defense Law of War Manual*, 942. and Canada. (1986, July 16). *Terminology Relevant to Arms Control and Outer Space* (Working Paper), 8–16. Conference on Disarmament. UN Document CD/716 & CD/OS/WP.15, as well as the extensive state practice evidencing non-aggressive military use such as reconnaissance satellites.

[38] Ministry of Foreign Affairs of the People's Republic of China. (2008, February 2). *China and Russia jointly submitted the draft Treaty on PPWT to the Conference on Disarmament*. Department of Arms Control — News. www.fmprc.gov.cn/mfa_eng/wjb_663304/zzjg_663340/jks_665232/jkxw_665234/200802/t20080212_599177.html; Ministry of Foreign Affairs of the People's Republic of China. (2014, June 16). *Treaty on the Prevention of the Placement of Weapons in Outer Space, the Threat or Use of Force against Outer Space Objects (Draft)*. www.fmprc.gov.cn/mfa_eng/wjb_663304/zzjg_663340/jks_665232/kjfywj_665252/201406/t20140616_599726.html

[39] Wood, R. A. (2019, 14 August). The threats posed by Russia and China to security of the outer space environment (statement to Conference on Disarmament Plenary Meeting). U.S. Mission to International Organizations in Geneva. geneva.usmission.gov/2019/08/14/statement-by-ambassador-wood-the-threats-posed-by-russia-and-china-to-security-of-the-outer-space-environment

activities and capabilities are not so easily susceptible to such broad definition and regulation. This is often because of concerns about lingering ambiguity, as well as under- and over-inclusiveness.

Although Article IV does offer some definitive prohibitions, it also leaves open many other possibilities. Some possibilities for military activities and operations in space are consistent with ensuring proper security and the maintenance of peace, others less so. Despite the existence of just one provision in the OST dealing directly with military activities in space, there are several other provisions of general wording that apply to military activities. In addition, Article III of the OST applies all international law to space, and it is through this mechanism that legal and practical opportunities and challenges need to be navigated. Three key legal concepts will be discussed below that apply to military activities and operations in space, either directly under a provision of the OST or indirectly, through Article III's extension of other international law to the space environment. Such an analysis serves to illustrate the way legal reasoning and operational activity may support a more durable basis for responsible military activity in space.

Preserving Stability and Peace in Space

The space law treaty regime contains many ambiguities of wording and construction. While stand-alone treaties in their own right, it is possible to view the 1968 Rescue Agreement, the 1972 Liability Convention and the 1975 Registration Convention as effectively 'protocols' to the OST that provide greater specificity to terms and concepts already contained in that original treaty.[40] While subsequent treaties and protocols are always useful instruments to provide greater clarity, international law also allows for subsequent State practice to inform treaty meaning (VCLT, Article 31(3)(b)). It is in this context that the International Law Commission (ILC) has undertaken a multi-year study on how such practice may be manifested and how it can inform treaty meaning.[41] In the context of space, especially regarding States' growing military capacity and reliance on space assets, such a mechanism can provide a useful means for identifying the 'true' meaning of ambiguous terms. In identifying relevant State practice, the ILC has directed that attention be given to 'official statements concerning the treaty's meaning, protests against

[40]The United Nations Office for Outer Space Affairs indicates in each case these conventions 'elaborate on' selected articles of the OST – see United Nations Office for Outer Space Affairs. (n.d.). *Agreement on the Rescue of Astronauts, the Return of Astronauts and the Return of Objects Launched into Outer Space*. www.unoosa.org/oosa/en/ourwork/spacelaw/treaties/introrescueagreement.html

[41]International Law Commission (2022, June 9). *Analytical Guide to the Work of the International Law Commission – Subsequent agreements and subsequent practice in relation to interpretation of treaties*. legal.un.org/ilc/guide/1_11.shtml

non-performance, or tacit consent to statements or acts by other parties'.[42] Such State practice is relevant as a primary means of interpretation under Article 31(3)(b) where it is part of a pattern of actions which establish agreement between the parties as to the treaty's meaning, but, according to the ILC, is still useful as a potential supplementary means of interpretation under Article 32, even where it does not establish such agreement.[43] Issues such as silence and acquiescence also have a significant role to play, but of course are not without their necessary ambiguity.[44]

Against this background, it is through iterative actions and reactions of States that a more durable understanding of treaty terms and acceptable practice can be identified. Given the many ambiguous and undefined terms contained within the space treaty regime, a focus on identifying State behaviour and conditioning the acceptability of actions in space can have a more enduring impact upon establishing stability than can endless grand technical proposals to define terms and focus on particular weapon systems.[45]

Military actions (and reactions) in the increasingly congested context of space activities and operations have started to test ambiguous and potentially uncertain treaty terms. Such activity has the capacity to generate greater agreement as to boundaries and thresholds that in turn can prevent strategic miscalculation. Conversely, this activity also has the potential to create an element of distrust among, and unpredictable reactions, by States – hence the need to ensure greater legal clarity.

(a) *The Woomera Manual on the International Law of Military Space Activities and Operations*

The role of international military operational law manuals in shaping normative behaviour has been the subject of considerable academic attention as to their purpose and impact.[46] The frequency of their publication, their citation and invocation by States and international tribunals or bodies, and their multiple published editions, all speak to their value, acceptance and impact. Key manuals of this type include the

---

[42] International Law Commission. (2013, March 19). *First Report on subsequent agreements and subsequent practice in relation to the interpretation of treaties, by Mr. Georg Nolte, Special Rapporteur* (p. 74). UN Document A/CN.4/660. legal.un.org/ilc/documentation/english/a_cn4_660.pdf

[43] Ibid., 73.

[44] International Law Commission. (2014, March 26). *Second Report on subsequent agreements and subsequent practice in relation to the interpretation of treaties, by Mr. Georg Nolte, Special Rapporteur* (pp. 129–131). UN Document A/CN.4/671. legal.un.org/ilc/documentation/english/a_cn4_671.pdf

[45] Smith Adamopoulos, N. (2021, April). U.S. Advocates for Binding Rules on Behaviour in Space. *Arms Control Association*. www.armscontrol.org/act/2021-04/news/us-advocates-binding-rules-behavior-space

[46] Crawford, E. (2022, February 3). Non-Binding Norms in the Law of Armed Conflict. *Articles of War*. lieber.westpoint.edu/non-binding-norms-law-of-armed-conflict; Stephens, D. (2021). Manuals and Courts: International Humanitarian Law, Informal Law-Making and Normativity. In Krieger, H. (Ed.) *Law-Making and Legitimacy in International Humanitarian Law* (pp. 253–75). Cheltenham and Northampton, Mass.: Edward Elgar.

San Remo Manual on the law of naval warfare,[47] the *HPCR Manual on International Law Applicable to Air and Missile Warfare*[48] and the *Tallinn Manual 2.0 on the International Law Applicable to Cyber Operations.*[49] Added to this genre is the forthcoming *Woomera Manual on the International Law of Military Space Activities and Operations.*[50]

Commenced in 2018, the Woomera Manual aims to articulate and clarify extant law applicable to military activities and operations associated with the space domain. This relates to the law applicable in peacetime, in periods of tension and crisis (when States and non-State actors may consider using force) and in the event of outright hostilities. The Woomera Manual process involves four key Universities that are spearheading the project (the University of Adelaide, the University of Nebraska–Lincoln, the University of Exeter and the University of New South Wales Canberra). The participants comprised more than 25 legal and technical experts and observers. In June 2022, the Dutch Government hosted a State consultation process in The Hague to assess the then draft content of the manual, issuing invitations globally to other States. Twenty-four countries, as well as the International Committee of the Red Cross, attended the State consultation process held in The Hague in June 2022 and provided valuable commentary on the draft.

The Woomera Manual process has revealed much about State approaches to military activities and operations in space, as well as identifying the methodological preferences of States in locating and articulating law applicable to military space activities. Drawing upon this experience, three key issues will be discussed below that relate closely to military activities in space, namely the obligation of due regard, the issue of use of force and the issue of neutrality in a time of armed conflict. These topics provide useful case studies where focus upon rules of behaviour by States might be further developed to provide greater certainty, predictability and safety for military activities and operations in space.

(b) *Due Regard*

The principle of due regard is well accepted within international law. It operates to ensure that States, particularly in areas beyond national territorial jurisdiction, exercise their rights with appropriate regard to the rights of other States in the relevant context.[51] It sets no prescriptive formula but instead acts to promote a sense of judicious balancing of rights and obligations between States. It is a concept

[47] Doswald-Beck, L. (Ed). (1995). *San Remo Manual on International Law Applicable to Armed Conflicts at Sea*. Cambridge: Cambridge University Press.

[48] Harvard University Program on Humanitarian Policy and Conflict Research. (2013). *HPCR Manual on International Law Applicable to Air and Missile Warfare*. Cambridge: Cambridge University Press.

[49] Schmitt, M. N. (Ed). (2017). *Tallinn Manual 2.0 on the International Law Applicable to Cyber Operations*. Cambridge: Cambridge University Press.

[50] University of Adelaide. (2018). *The Woomera Manual*. law.adelaide.edu.au/woomera.

[51] *Chagos Marine Protected Area Arbitration (Mauritius v. United Kingdom) (Award).* (2015, 18 March). 2011–03 (p. 202) (ITLOS).

that has featured heavily in international maritime law and the UN *Convention on the Law of the Sea* in particular (being mentioned 22 times in that instrument, including for example in Articles 27, 39, 56, 58, 60, 66, 79 and 87, among others).[52]

Due regard finds expression in Article IX of the OST. Its presence is ambiguous in part because it seems tied to another obligation, namely that which imposes duties upon States regarding avoiding harmful interference in the use of (and experiments in) space by other States. Despite this, the views of some States who specifically addressed this issue at the Woomera Manual State consultation process supported the conclusion that the obligation of due regard in space was an independent and stand-alone one. This has also been reflected by several recent State submissions to the UN Office for Disarmament Affairs Open-Ended Working Group on reducing space threats through norms, rules and principles of responsible behaviour.[53]

The principle of due regard was not controversial during the negotiation of the OST. The only real point of note during that process was that the concept of giving 'due regard' (as contained in Article IX) was viewed as a softening of an initial suggestion that States be required to conduct consultations prior to undertaking any activity that might invoke its application.[54] Hence it was a duty of conduct, not result, that applied to the State in its planning and execution of activities. Despite its presence in Article IX, State practice in space has been very sparse with respect to this principle.

The Government of the Philippines submitted a paper specifically on the duty of 'due regard' in space to the May 2022 session of the above-mentioned UN Open-Ended Working Group.[55] This is a rare and helpful example of a State giving its express view as to what the obligation of due regard entails in the context of space. This paper considers the concept of 'due regard' in tandem with that of 'potentially harmful interference', and makes particular reference to consultation requirements. It draws an overt parallel between the obligations of due regard in the space and maritime contexts, and effectively supports the extension to space of the Permanent Court of Arbitration's general understanding of due regard in the law of the sea

---

[52] *United Nations Convention on the Law of the Sea*. Opened for signature 10 December 1982 (entered into force 16 November 1994). 1833 UNTS 3. https://www.un.org/depts/los/convention_agreements/texts/unclos/unclos_e.pdf

[53] Republic of the Philippines. (2022, May 6). The Duty of "due regard" as a foundational principle of responsible behaviour in space (para. 3). UN Document A/AC.294/2022.WP. (Advance Unedited working paper); United Kingdom. (2022). UK working paper for the UN open ended working group on reducing space threats through norms, rules and principles of responsible behaviour (para. 17). UN Document A/AC.294/2022.WP.9; New Zealand Ministry of Foreign Affairs and Trade. (2021). Norms, Rules and Principles of Responsible Behaviours in Space. Submission to the United Nations Office for Disarmament Affairs Open-Ended Working Group on reducing space threats through norms, rules and principles of responsible behaviours – May 2021 (p. 3).

[54] Legal Sub-Committee, United Nations Committee on the Peaceful Uses of Outer Space. (1963, May 1). Provisional summary record of the twenty-fourth meeting (p. 11). UN Document A/AC.105/C.2/SR.24.

[55] Republic of the Philippines. The Duty of "due regard" as a foundational principle of responsible behaviour in space.

context—in essence finding that the actions required by a State to show due regard in space would depend on 'the nature of the rights and duties involved, their importance, the extent of the anticipated impairment, the nature and importance of the activities contemplated, and the availability of alternative approaches' (para. 11.1). The paper expresses the view that, similarly to the law of the sea, the demonstration of due regard in outer space requires 'a conscious balancing of rights and interests' (para. 11.2) and, consistently with general international law obligations, an ongoing duty of 'due diligence' upon a State's own activities (para. 11.3). The Philippines considers that while the content of the obligation of due regard 'does not constitute a blanket limit on state conduct, it also does not permit states to merely note other states' rights and still do as they wish' (para. 11.1).

It is notable that in the (non-legally binding) *Artemis Accords* of 2020, there is also reference to due regard in Section 11, which is directed towards 'Deconfliction of Space Activities'. While the content of due regard is not articulated in Section 11, concepts such as 'safety zones' and recognition of activities that 'pose a safety hazard' are.[56]

While it is unlikely that the duty of due regard at present compels a State to engage in prior consultations with other States before undertaking any activity in space, States would be likely to discharge their obligation of due regard when undertaking such consultations. Article IX of the OST also mandates consultation of this nature when the activity is expected to cause 'potentially harmful interference'.

The Philippine paper also identifies a close relationship between the obligations of due diligence and due regard. Such a relationship has resonance within space treaty law, given the impact of Article VI of the OST, which attributes the behaviour of nationals in space more readily to the State than what exists under general rules of State Responsibility. Hence, the need for States to ensure that proper control and oversight is exercised over their nationals when undertaking 'national activities' in space.

There is significant scope for State practice to develop with respect to the concrete application of due regard to military space operations. One possible example of this effort to bring substance to the principle is the recent unilateral declaration by the United States not to engage in anti-satellite (ASAT) testing using kinetic means.[57] Several States in recent years have undertaken such ASAT testing by targeting their

[56]National Aeronautics and Space Administration. (2020, October 13). *The Artemis Accords: Principles for Cooperation in the Civil Exploration and Use of the Moon, Mars, Comets and Asteroids for Peaceful Purposes*. www.nasa.gov/specials/artemis-accords/img/Artemis-Accords-signed-13Oct2020.pdf

[57]The White House. (2022, April 18). Fact Sheet: Vice President Harris Advances National Security Norms in Space. *Briefing Room*. www.whitehouse.gov/briefing-room/statements-releases/2022/04/18/fact-sheet-vice-president-harris-advances-national-security-norms-in-space

own satellites.[58] Each test has resulted in the creation of significant debris, causing potential interference with the space activities of other States. Such a consequence has, not surprisingly, provoked international criticism of such activity, though notably no State has declared the testing to be unlawful, nor has any State expressly and unequivocally complained that Article IX consultations were not undertaken prior to such testing. While the unilateral declaration made by the United States was not expressly made under the principle of due regard, it is clearly arguable that such responsible behaviour (which as of April 2023, had already been joined by New Zealand, Australia, Canada, Germany, Japan, The Netherlands, Austria plus six other countries)[59] conforms to such an obligation.

Another area where the due regard principle can be given concrete application is in the conduct of military-to-military talks. Such talks occur principally in the air and sea contexts between senior military officers of opposing nations to ensure that intentions are not misinterpreted and to allow for the safe conduct of military activity in peacetime.[60] At present there is no standing forum where senior military leaders of potentially opposing space forces meet to discuss similar space-based activities. In initiating such a forum, leading space countries (whether large, medium or small) would not only ensure that potential misinterpretation and conflict would be avoided, but also allow for the development of a dialogue that could give greater tangible meaning to the due regard principle in practice.

(c) *Use of Force*

As highlighted above, Article III of the OST applies all international law to space, including specifically the UN Charter. The Charter includes a prohibition on the use of force and the threat of the use of force (Article 2(4)). In space, discerning intention can be difficult, especially in the context of ascertaining whether a particular action is a precursor to the use of force or an armed attack. There exist no national boundaries per se, no concept of the legal nationality of a satellite[61] and no set prohibition on how close the orbits of satellites may be to each other. In addition, there is

[58] Secure World Foundation. (2022, May). *Anti-Satellite Weapons: Threatening the Sustainability of Space Activities* (infographic). swfound.org/media/207392/swf-asat-testing-infographic-may2022.pdf

[59] Smith, M. (2023, April 9), 'Three More Countries Join Pledge Against Destructive ASAT tests', *SpaceNews*. https://spacepolicyonline.com/news/three-more-countries-join-pledge-against-destructive-asat-tests/

[60] Wong, C. (2021, December 30). Chinese, US militaries resume maritime safety talks after last year's no-show. *South China Morning Post*. www.scmp.com/news/china/diplomacy/article/3161614/chinese-us-militaries-resume-maritime-safety-talks-after-last; Ali, I. (2021, August 28). Pentagon holds talks with Chinese military for first time under Biden, official says. *Reuters*. www.reuters.com/world/exclusive-pentagon-holds-talks-with-chinese-military-first-time-under-biden-2021-08-28

[61] There is no equivalent provision to Article 91 of the 1982 Law of the Sea Convention which establishes vessel nationality based on the 'flag State', or Article 17 of the 1944 Convention on International Civil Aviation which establishes aircraft nationality based on registration.

considerable sensitivity in relation to any action that occurs in the vicinity of the early warning satellites of states that possess nuclear weapons.[62]

In the context of maritime operations within the terrestrial environment, guidance in regard to similar concerns about safety and construing intention (i.e. whether an approach could be a precursor to an 'armed attack') is provided by the 1972 Convention on the International Regulations for Preventing Collisions at Sea. Provisions within such a treaty set out requirements to assess and avoid potential collisions, and for ensuring who gives way to whom in such a context (Part B). In space there is no such set of equivalent rules. While States (in particular the United States) have developed Space Situational Awareness data sharing programmes, this is merely an information exchange process.[63]

In recent years, Russia has undertaken experiments in manoeuvring its satellites in close proximity with those of other nations which have caused considerable disquiet. The Luch and Cosmos 2543 incidents are illustrative of how such actions can be reckless and potentially can unwittingly trigger forceful responses. The Luch satellite was launched in 2014 and occupied 19 different positions in the Geostationary belt between 2014 and 2019, closing within a few kilometres of neighbouring satellites.[64] In 2015, Intelsat, the operator of two satellites that were the subject of such close proximity operations, sought to raise concerns with Russia, but without success.[65] In 2017, Russia engaged in a manoeuvre which brought its Luch satellite into proximity with a French military communications satellite. In response, the French defence minister condemned the action, stating that 'trying to listen to your neighbours is not only unfriendly, it's an act of espionage'.[66] While the legal foundation of such a claim is contestable in space, where there is no territorial sovereignty, it nonetheless highlights the potential for misunderstanding that can result in an escalation of the use of force that could be avoided.

In December 2019, 2 weeks after its launch, the Russian satellite Cosmos 2543 deployed a 'sub-satellite' (Cosmos 2542). This sub-satellite then appeared to actively manoeuvre into a synchronised orbit with USA-245 (a 'classified imaging

[62]Wilson, H. (2017, December 2). Panel Discussion with Heather Wilson, U.S. Secretary of the Air Force (remarks). Reagan National Defense Forum. www.c-span.org/video/?438064-2/national-security-space-strategy

[63]U.S. Space Command. (2022, April 7). USSPACECOM and Sweden sign a Space Situational Awareness sharing agreement. *U.S. Space Command*. www.spacecom.mil/Newsroom/News/Article-Display/Article/2992854/usspacecom-and-sweden-sign-a-space-situational-awareness-sharing-agreement

[64]Roberts, T. G. (2022, September 1). Unusual Behaviour in GEO: Luch (Olymp-K). *Aerospace Security*. aerospace.csis.org/data/unusual-behavior-in-geo-olymp-k

[65]Gruss, M. (2015, October 9). Russian Satellite Maneuvers, Silence Worry Intelsat. *SpaceNews*. spacenews.com/russian-satellite-maneuvers-silence-worry-intelsat

[66]Chrisafis, A. (2018, September 8). 'Act of Espionage': France accuses Russia of trying to spy on satellite data. *The Guardian*. www.theguardian.com/world/2018/sep/07/france-accuses-russia-spying-satellite-communications-espionage

satellite' of the US National Reconnaissance Office).[67] The Commander of US Space Command claimed in February 2020 that this was an intentional and uninvited act, and stated that 'there need[ed] to be a discussion on norms of behavior and on responsible behavior in space'.[68] Cosmos 2543 later released a further object. The United States has stated that this was inconsistent with Russia's stated purpose for the satellite, and that they believe this was an on-orbit anti-satellite weapons test.[69]

It is in this fraught area, where intentions are opaque and can easily be misconstrued, that an agreed code of conduct setting out conditions and acceptable norms of behaviour could be constructively developed. The maritime environment offers a useful precedent in this regard. The Western Naval Pacific Symposium a decade ago developed a Code for Unplanned Encounters at Sea (CUES) between armed forces that sets out a series of safety and communication procedures to ensure that intentions are not misconstrued. While voluntary and non-binding, CUES has clear normative impact and can, through iterative compliance, constitute subsequent state practice for interpretative purposes under Article 31(3)(b) of the VCLT. CUES deals with topics such as safe distances, manoeuvring instructions and assurance measures for naval ships and military aircraft. With regard to this latter issue, CUES provides an outline of activities that might be avoided to ensure no misinterpretation occurs (section 2.8). Hence, there should be no simulation of attacks by aiming weapons or undertaking acts recognised as preparatory to use of force (2.8(a)); no discharging of weapons in the direction of other ships or aircraft (2.8(b)); no illumination of navigation bridges (2.8(c)); no laser marking in a manner that may cause harm to people or equipment (2.8(d)); and no aerobatics in the vicinity of ships encountered (2.8(e)). Such specificity of focus has an obvious application in the space context where there are yet to be any settled norms of behaviour between military forces, especially in relation to encounters between military space objects in close proximity to each other. While the UN Conference on Disarmament is the likely mechanism whereby such measures could be advanced, it has an unfortunate track record of being in 'prolonged paralysis'.[70] Accordingly, direct military-to-military talks between senior representatives of the world's major space forces or elements would be likely to serve as a more effective means by which such operational agreements and understanding could be advanced.

---

[67] Erwin, S. (2020, February 10). Raymond calls out Russia for "threatening behavior" in outer space. *SpaceNews*. spacenews.com/raymond-calls-out-russia-for-threatening-behavior-in-outer-space

[68] Ibid.

[69] U.S. Space Command Public Affairs Office. (2020, July 23). Russia conducts space-based anti-satellite weapons test. *U.S. Space Command*. www.spacecom.mil/Newsroom/News/Article-Display/Article/2285098/russia-conducts-space-based-anti-satellite-weapons-test

[70] Meyer, P. (2021, August 3). Does the Conference of Disarmament Have a Future? *Journal for Peace and Nuclear Disarmament, 4*(2), 287–294.

(d) *Neutrality*

The law of neutrality applies during an armed conflict to ensure that those countries that are not belligerents remain largely unaffected by that conflict. The law of neutrality seeks to protect neutral States from the effects of an armed conflict by preserving their peacetime legal rights, especially with respect to other neutral States. Traditionally, the law of neutrality, as reflected in treaty law (Hague Convention (V)), was based upon the territory of the State and the flag status of its ships and aircraft (known as the 'domain-based' view). However, as a result of Article II of the OST, there can be no national acquisition of space or a celestial body, hence no national territory in space. Similarly, as discussed above, there is no concept of a flag State of a satellite. Accordingly, there is an academic view that, given the absence of such central foundations, the law of neutrality cannot generally apply to space.[71] Such a view taken to its logical extreme would mean that any third-party rights that States may have in space under the space treaty regime, or under general principles of international law, would necessarily be subject to principles of military necessity under the law of armed conflict, given its *lex specialis* nature.[72]

An alternative view is that the law of neutrality is not so dependent upon territory and flag State nationality, and is instead predicated upon the conduct of third-party States (the 'conduct-based approach'). Such a perspective is primarily based upon the behaviour of States in avoiding the violation of neutrality rules that advantage a particular belligerent. The basic authority for this position draws upon the underlying principles of customary international law, which apply the principles of neutrality during any international armed conflict, no matter what the circumstances are.[73] Such customary international law is informed by basic principles that underpin this body of law, such as third-party States remaining impartial, abstaining from activities that advantage a particular belligerent and undertaking actions to end or prevent belligerent actions that violate neutrality.[74]

There has (thankfully) been no State practice in the context of armed conflict in space itself to necessitate drawing upon a definitive determination on the resolution of the issue of neutrality law. To date, only the Danish *Military Manual* references neutrality in space, stating that the

---

[71] Heintschel von Heinegg, W. (2017, December 20). Neutrality and Outer Space. *International Law Studies*, *93*(1), 526–547.

[72] United Nations International Law Commission. (2011). *Draft articles on the effects of armed conflicts on treaties, with commentaries* (p. 110). legal.un.org/ilc/texts/instruments/english/commentaries/1_10_2011.pdf

[73] Dinstein, Y. and Dahl, A. W. (2020). *Oslo Manual on Select Topics of the Law of Armed Conflict* (p. 15). Cham: Springer; Stephens, M. (2022). The Application and Implications of the Law of Neutrality to Armed Conflict in Outer Space. Adelaide University Research Unit on Military Law and Ethics Research Report.

[74] See, generally, Oppenheim, L. (1912). *International Law: A Treatise*, vol. 2: *War and Neutrality* (p. 379). (2nd ed.) London: Longmans, Green & Co.

> classic neutrality rules provide that neutral infrastructure … must not be made the object of attack regardless of whether the infrastructure is privately owned or State-owned. Nor is it permissible to attack, State-owned infrastructure of neutral States, even if the infrastructure is located in outer space, in international airspace, or on the high seas.[75]

Despite the lack of significant State practice in this context, the International Court of Justice has been sweeping in its statement concerning the law of neutrality in its *Legality of the Threat or Use of Nuclear Weapons (Advisory Opinion)*, observing that 'international law leaves no doubt that the principle of neutrality, whatever the content, is applicable … to all international armed conflict'.[76] Similarly, the International Committee of the Red Cross has expressly stated that 'Military operations in, or in relation to, outer space do not occur in a legal vacuum but are constrained by existing international law, notably the UN Charter, the Outer Space Treaty, I[nternational] H[umanitarian] L[aw] and the law of neutrality'.[77]

During the course of the *Woomera Manual* State consultation process in The Hague, the issue of neutrality in space did not result in the articulation of a strong view, one way or the other, as to how to approach the conundrum of a domain-based or conduct-based perspective. The issue awaits a concrete application and a case-by-case assessment. While the technical requirements of territoriality do not support a clear foundation for the law of neutrality in the space environment, there has been no statement by any State that the law of neutrality does not apply to armed conflict occurring in space. Moreover, the statements that have been made by international bodies have been to positively assert the application of the law of neutrality in all contexts. It would be an unusual outcome if States not party to an armed conflict extending to space itself were not to rely upon the law of neutrality to assert protection from the effects of such a conflict. Ironically, the purpose of Article II of the OST in its non-recognition of national acquisition of space and celestial bodies is to avoid the very territorial competition that has led to conflict on earth.[78] While the realist political views held by some States might advance such a legal position to ensure greater military freedom in space, this should, and no doubt will, be resisted by other States, which rightfully seek to contain the effects of armed conflict. It is at present an unresolved theoretical issue as to how the law of neutrality might apply in

---

[75] Knudsen, J. R. (Ed.). (2020). *Military Manual on International Law Relevant to Danish Armed Forces in International Operations* (p. 60). Copenhagen: Danish Ministry of Defence and Defence Command Denmark.

[76] *Legality of the Threat or Use of Nuclear Weapons (Advisory Opinion)* (p. 261, para. 89). (1996, July 8). 1996 ICJ 2.

[77] International Committee of the Red Cross. (2022, May 3). Constraints under International Law on Military Operations in, or in relation to, outer space during armed conflicts (working paper). Submitted to United Nations open-ended working group on reducing space threats through norms, rules and principles of responsible behaviours – 2022 (p. 6). www.icrc.org/en/document/constraints-under-international-law-military-space-operations

[78] Legal Sub-Committee, United Nations Committee on the Peaceful Uses of Outer Space. (1966, October 20). Summary record of the fifty-seventh meeting (p. 4). UN Document A/AC.105/C.2/SR.57.

the context of armed conflict in space, though it will surely be resolved in favour of such law applying once tested in the practical context of such a conflict.

(e) *The Woomera Manual and Its Impact Upon Foreign Policy*

As is the case with all works of this type,[79] the Woomera Manual has no inherent legal authority. Rather, the Manual's relevance comes from its contribution to accurately identifying and re-stating the law. When States are determining their positions with respect to their military activities in space, they should be confident that each rule and every line of commentary within the Manual has been parsed carefully through years of research, debate, and editorial attention.

A goal of the Woomera Manual is to provide an accurate articulation of the law as it applies to military activities and operations in space. As the 2020 *Australian Defence Strategic Update* noted, 'rules, norms and institutions that help maintain peace and security and guide global cooperation are under strain'[80] and, further, the legal thresholds relating to military actions and reactions are unclear.[81] Hence, referring to a reference such as the Woomera Manual should better assist States determine where these thresholds exist and where the residual uncertainties may lie. As locating and recording State practice was a key methodological focus of the work, it necessarily follows that there are sometimes gaps and ambiguity in the conclusions reached in the Manual. Despite this, several States at The Hague State consultation process specifically stated that they were comfortable with such ambiguity. This enables a present opportunity for States to fully consider their positions with respect to these ambiguities with respect to future foreign policy decisions and shaping of the law.

At the same time, the Manual does provide certainty in areas where State practice has allowed a more confident statement of the law. For example, critical thresholds in the Use of Force spectrum as they apply to space have been identified based upon existing State practice; their inclusion in the Manual should contribute towards avoiding strategic miscalculation. Hence, the Manual should serve as a useful reference point for States to engage in dialogue to confirm or further refine their understanding of the applicable law and to bridge conceptual gaps.

[79] For example: Doswald-Beck, L. (ed). *San Remo Manual on International Law Applicable to Armed Conflicts at Sea*. (1995) Cambridge: Cambridge University Press. Harvard University Program on Humanitarian Policy and Conflict Research. (2013). *The HPCR Manual on International Law Applicable to Air and Missile Warfare*. Cambridge: Cambridge University Press. Schmitt, M. N. (ed). (2017) *Tallinn Manual 2.0 on the International Law applicable to Cyber Warfare* Cambridge: Cambridge University Press.

[80] Australian Government Department of Defence. (2020). *2020 Defence Strategic Update* (p. 12, para. 1.6). Australia: Commonwealth of Australia.

[81] Ibid.

Conclusion

The acceptance of the operational utility of space has seen military doctrine and planning develop quickly in the past few years. While the development of tactics, techniques and procedures for the conduct of military operations within space, including even in the context of possible armed conflict, has escalated, there has not been a corresponding focus on the articulation of legal controls and restraints. The OST regime does contain many general and aspirational provisions that necessarily lack specificity, however it is generally still 'fit for purpose'. International law provides methodological tools for ensuring that critical details and applications of legal restraint can be realised, through techniques such as the concept of subsequent State practice, as envisioned in the VCLT.

As States develop and expand their military capabilities in space, there is a correlative need to apply imagination and care in understanding not just how the laws of physics can apply to such systems, but also how human-made law applies to novel contexts. Focusing less on the specific technical legal meanings of terms in favour of identifying responsible behaviours that conform to legal prescriptions would seem a likely optimal approach. Concepts such as due regard, use of force and neutrality have been highlighted in this chapter as deserving of special attention, but they are just three legal concepts among many that are deserving of renewed focus in the contemporary environment. While space offers a very useful venue for ensuring effective national security goals are met, it is also an environment where human ingenuity and capability for the peaceful use and exploration of space should be fostered. If humanity is to be an interplanetary species, then it must transcend the perils of distrust and cynical behaviour, which can lead to conflict. The law has a major role to play in conditioning that behaviour, and the time to meaningfully understand the challenges and meet them is now.

Bibliography

Ali, I. (2021, August 28). Pentagon holds talks with Chinese military for first time under Biden, official says. *Reuters*. www.reuters.com/world/exclusive-pentagon-holds-talks-with-chinese-military-first-time-under-biden-2021-08-28

Anson, P., & Cummings, D. (1991). The first space war: The contribution of satellites to the Gulf war. *RUSI Journal, 136*(4), 45–53.

Australian Government Department of Defence. (2020a, July). *2020 Defence Strategic Update*, 38. www.defence.gov.au/about/strategic-planning/2020-defence-strategic-update

Australian Government Department of Defence. (2020b, September 21). *Defence Annual Report 2019–20*, 96. www.defence.gov.au/about/information-disclosures/annual-reports

Cameron, A. M. (1946). *Report on operation 'backfire', vol. I. Scope and organisation of the operation*. War Office. library.si.edu/digital-library/book/report-operation-backfire.

Carter, J. (1978, October 1). *Remarks at the Congressional space medal of honor awards ceremony*. Kennedy Space Center, Florida. From Weekly Compilation of Presidential Documents. (1978, October 9), 1684. National Security Archives. nsarchive2.gwu.edu/NSAEBB/NSAEBB231/doc32.pdf

Chrisafis, A. (2018, September 8). 'Act of Espionage': France accuses Russia of trying to spy on satellite data. *The Guardian*. www.theguardian.com/world/2018/sep/07/france-accuses-russia-spying-satellite-communications-espionage

Crawford, E. (2022, February 3). Non-binding norms in the law of armed conflict. *Articles of War*. lieber.westpoint.edu/non-binding-norms-law-of-armed-conflict

Dinstein, Y., & Dahl, A. W. (2020). *Oslo manual on select topics of the law of armed conflict*. Springer.

Doswald-Beck, L. (Ed.). (1995). *San remo manual on international law applicable to armed conflicts at sea*. Cambridge University Press.

Erwin, S. (2020, February 10). Raymond calls out Russia for "threatening behavior" in outer space. *SpaceNews*. spacenews.com/raymond-calls-out-russia-for-threatening-behavior-in-outer-space

Feigin, J. (2008). *The office of special investigations: Striving for accountability in the aftermath of the holocaust*. Draft made available at Freedom of Information Act Library, United States Department of Justice. www.justice.gov/sites/default/files/criminal/legacy/2011/03/14/12-2008osu-accountability.pdf

Gruss, M. (2015, October 9). Russian satellite maneuvers, silence worry intelsat. *SpaceNews*. spacenews.com/russian-satellite-maneuvers-silence-worry-intelsat

Harvard University Program on Humanitarian Policy and Conflict Research. (2013). *HPCR manual on international law applicable to air and missile warfare*. Cambridge University Press.

Heintschel von Heinegg, W. (2017, December 20). Neutrality and outer space. *International Law Studies, 93*(1), 526–547.

International Committee of the Red Cross. (2022, May 3). *Constraints under International Law on Military Operations in, or in relation to, outer space during armed conflicts* (working paper). Submitted to United Nations open-ended working group on reducing space threats through norms, rules and principles of responsible behaviours – 2022. www.icrc.org/en/document/constraints-under-international-law-military-space-operations

International Court of Justice. (1996, July 8). *Legality of the threat or use of nuclear weapons (advisory opinion)* 1996 ICJ 2.

International Law Commission. (2013, March 19). *First report on subsequent agreements and subsequent practice in relation to the interpretation of treaties, by Mr. Georg Nolte, Special Rapporteur*. UN Document A/CN.4/660. legal.un.org/ilc/documentation/english/a_cn4_660.pdf

International Law Commission. (2014, March 26). *Second report on subsequent agreements and subsequent practice in relation to the interpretation of treaties, by Mr. Georg Nolte, Special Rapporteur*. UN Document A/CN.4/671. legal.un.org/ilc/documentation/english/a_cn4_671.pdf

International Law Commission. (2022, June 9). *Analytical guide to the work of the International Law Commission – Subsequent agreements and subsequent practice in relation to interpretation of treaties*. legal.un.org/ilc/guide/1_11.shtml

Knudsen, J. R. (Ed.). (2020). *Military manual on international law relevant to danish armed forces in international operations*. Danish Ministry of Defence and Defence Command Denmark.

Lambakis, S. (1995, Summer). Space control in desert storm and beyond. *Orbis, 39*(3), 419.

Meyer, P. (2021, August 3). Does the conference of disarmament have a future? *Journal for Peace and Nuclear Disarmament, 4*(2), 287–294.

Milazzo, M. P., Kestay, L., & Dundas, C. (2017). *The challenge for 2050: Cohesive analysis of more than one hundred years of planetary data*. In Planetary science vision 2050 workshop (LPI contribution no. 1989). www.hou.usra.edu/meetings/V2050/pdf/8070.pdf

Ministry of Foreign Affairs of the People's Republic of China. (2008, February 2). *China and Russia jointly submitted the draft Treaty on PPWT to the Conference on Disarmament*. Department of Arms Control – News. www.fmprc.gov.cn/mfa_eng/wjb_663304/zzjg_663340/jks_665232/jkxw_665234/200802/t20080212_599177.html

Ministry of Foreign Affairs of the People's Republic of China. (2014, June 16). *Treaty on the prevention of the placement of weapons in outer space, the threat or use of force against outer space objects* (Draft). www.fmprc.gov.cn/mfa_eng/wjb_663304/zzjg_663340/jks_665232/kjfywj_665252/201406/t20140616_599726.html

New Zealand Ministry of Defence. (2018). *Strategic defence policy statement*, 7. www.defence.govt.nz/assets/Uploads/8958486b29/Strategic-Defence-Policy-Statement-2018.pdf

New Zealand Ministry of Defence. (2021). *He Moana Pukepuke e Ekengia e Te Waka: A rough sea can still be navigated: Defence assessment 2021*. www.defence.govt.nz/assets/publication/file/Defence-Assessment-2021.pdf

New Zealand Ministry of Foreign Affairs and Trade. (2021). *Norms, rules and principles of responsible behaviours in space*. Submission to the United Nations Office for Disarmament Affairs Open-Ended Working Group on reducing space threats through norms, rules and principles of responsible behaviours – May 2021.

North Atlantic Treaty Organization. (2019, December 4). *London Declaration – Issued by the heads of state and government participating in the meeting of the North Atlantic Council in London 3–4 December 2019* (Press release). www.nato.int/cps/en/natohq/official_texts_171584.htm

Oppenheim, L. (1912). *International law: A treatise* (War and neutrality) (Vol. 2, 2nd ed., p. 379). Longmans, Green.

Ramani, M. (2017, July 1). The German village that changed the war. *BBC Travel*. https://www.bbc.com/travel/article/20170629-the-german-village-that-changed-the-war

Republic of the Philippines. (2022, May 6). *The Duty of "due regard" as a foundational principle of responsible behaviour in space (para. 3)*. UN Document A/AC.294/2022.WP. (Advance Unedited working paper).

Republic of the Philippines. *The Duty of "due regard" as a foundational principle of responsible behaviour in space*.

Richelson, J. T. (Ed.) (2015, February 4). *U.S. Intelligence and the Soviet Space Program: National security archive electronic briefing book no. 501*. National Security Archive. nsarchive2.gwu.edu/NSAEBB/NSAEBB501

Roberts, T. G. (2022, September 1). Unusual Behaviour in GEO: Luch (Olymp-K). *Aerospace Security*. aerospace.csis.org/data/unusual-behavior-in-geo-olymp-k

Schmitt, M. N. (Ed.). (2017). *Tallinn manual 2.0 on the international law applicable to cyber operations*. Cambridge University Press.

Secure World Foundation. (2022, May). *Anti-satellite weapons: Threatening the sustainability of space activities* (infographic). swfound.org/media/207392/swf-asat-testing-infographic-may2022.pdf

Shreve, B. (2003, June 2). The US, the USSR and space exploration, 1957–1963. *International Journal on World Peace, 20*(2), 77.

Smith, M. (2023, April 9). Three more countries join pledge against destructive ASAT tests. *Space News*. https://spacepolicyonline.com/news/three-more-countries-join-pledge-against-destructive-asat-tests

Smith Adamopoulos, N. (2021, April). *U.S. Advocates for binding rules on behaviour in space*. Arms Control Association. www.armscontrol.org/act/2021-04/news/us-advocates-binding-rules-behavior-space

Stephens, D. (2021). Manuals and courts: International humanitarian law, informal law-making and normativity. In H. Krieger (Ed.), *Law-making and legitimacy in international humanitarian law* (pp. 253–275). Edward Elgar.

Stephens, M. (2022). *The application and implications of the law of neutrality to armed conflict in outer space*. Adelaide University Research Unit on Military Law and Ethics Research Report.

Stokes, M., Alvarado, G. Weinstein, E., & Easton, I. (2020, March 30). *China's space and counterspace capabilities and activities* (Research report), 9. US–China Economic and Security Review Commission, citing a Chinese policy document.

Tirpak, J. A. (2003, November). The next generation. *Air Force Magazine*, p. 45.

Treat, J., Bennett, J., & Turner, C. (2020, November 6). How 'the right stuff' has changed. *National Geographic*. www.nationalgeographic.com/science/graphics/charting-how-nasa-astronaut-demographics-have-changed-over-time

Union of Soviet Socialist Republics. (1958, November 7). *Draft Resolution. UN Document A/C.1/L.219 – United Nations General Assembly.*

United Kingdom. (2022). *UK working paper for the UN open ended working group on reducing space threats through norms, rules and principles of responsible behaviour* (para. 17). UN Document A/AC.294/2022.WP.9.

United Kingdom Ministry of Defence, Development, Concepts and Doctrine Centre. (2022, September). *Joint Doctrine Publication 0–40 – UK Space Power.* assets.publishing.service.gov.uk/government/uploads/system/uploads/attachment_data/file/1101450/20220831-JDP_0_40_UK_Space_Power_web.pdf

United Nations. (1967). *Treaty on principles governing the activities of states in the exploration and use of outer space, including the moon and other celestial bodies.* Opened for signature 27 January 1967 (entered into force 10 October 1967). 610 UNTS 205. https://www.unoosa.org/pdf/publications/STSPACE11E.pdf

United Nations. (1968a). *Agreement on the rescue of astronauts, the return of astronauts and the return of objects launched into outer space.* Opened for signature 22 April 1968 (entered into force 3 December 1968). 672 UNTS 119. https://www.unoosa.org/pdf/publications/STSPACE11E.pdf

United Nations. (1968b). *Return of objects launched into outer space.* Opened for signature 22 April 1968 (entered into force 3 December 1968). 672 UNTS 119. https://www.unoosa.org/pdf/publications/STSPACE11E.pdf

United Nations. (1972). *Convention on the international liability for damage caused by space objects.* Opened for signature 29 March 1972 (entered into force 1 September 1972) 961 UNTS 187. https://www.unoosa.org/pdf/publications/STSPACE11E.pdf

United Nations. (1975). *Convention on registration of objects launched into outer space.* Opened for signature 14 January 1975 (entered into force 15 September 1976). 1023 UNTS 15. https://www.unoosa.org/pdf/publications/STSPACE11E.pdf.

United Nations. (1979). *Agreement governing the activities of states on the moon and other celestial bodies.* Opened for signature 5 December 1979 (entered into force 11 July 1984). 1363 UNTS 3. https://www.unoosa.org/pdf/publications/STSPACE11E.pdf

United Nations. (1980). *Vienna convention on the law of treaties.* Opened for signature 23 May 1969 (entered into force 27 January 1980). 1155 UNTS 331. Art 31. https://legal.un.org/ilc/texts/instruments/english/conventions/1_1_1969.pdf

United Nations. (1982). *United Nations convention on the law of the sea.* Opened for signature 10 December 1982 (entered into force 16 November 1994). 1833 UNTS 3. https://www.un.org/depts/los/convention_agreements/texts/unclos/unclos_e.pdf

United Nations Committee on the Peaceful Uses of Outer Space, Legal Sub-Committee. (1963, May 1). *Provisional summary record of the twenty-fourth meeting.* UN Document A/AC.105/C.2/SR.24.

United Nations Committee on the Peaceful Uses of Outer Space, Legal Sub-Committee. (1966, October 20). *Summary record of the fifty-seventh meeting* (p. 4). UN Document A/AC.105/C.2/SR.57.

United Nations, Conference on Disarmament. (1975). UN Document CD/716 & CD/OS/WP.15.

United Nations General Assembly. (1961, December 20). *Resolution 1721 (XVI) — International co-operation in the peaceful uses of outer space.* UN Document A/RES/1721.

United Nations General Assembly. (1963, December 13). *Resolution 1962 (XVIII) – Declaration of legal principles governing the activities of states in the exploration and use of outer space.* UN Document A/RES/1962.

United Nations International Law Commission. (2011). *Draft articles on the effects of armed conflicts on treaties, with commentaries* (p. 110). legal.un.org/ilc/texts/instruments/english/commentaries/1_10_2011.pdf

United Nations Office for Outer Space Affairs. (n.d.). *Agreement on the rescue of astronauts, the return of astronauts and the return of objects launched into outer space*. www.unoosa.org/oosa/en/ourwork/spacelaw/treaties/introrescueagreement.html
United States Department of Defense, Department of Defense Law of War Manual, 942 and Canada. (1986, July 16). *Terminology relevant to arms control and outer space* (Working paper).
United States Department of Defense, Office of General Counsel. (2015, June 12). *Department of Defense Law of War Manual* (Revised edition as at December 2016), 942. dod.defense.gov/Portals/1/Documents/pubs/DoD%20Law%20of%20War%20Manual%20-%20June%202015%20Updated%20Dec%202016.pdf?ver=2016-12-13-172036-190
United States National Aeronautics and Space Administration. (2020, October 13). *The Artemis Accords: Principles for cooperation in the civil exploration and use of the moon, mars, comets and asteroids for peaceful purposes*. www.nasa.gov/specials/artemis-accords/img/Artemis-Accords-signed-13Oct2020.pdf
United States National Reconnaissance Program Memorandum. (1969, June 4). *National Reconnaissance Office digital archive*. www.nro.gov/Portals/65/documents/foia/declass/Archive/NARP/1969%20NARPs/SC-2018-00033_C05111857.pdf
United States of America. (1958, September 2). *Request for the inclusion of an additional item in the agenda of the thirteenth session*. UN Document A/3902 – United Nations General Assembly.
United States Space Command. (2022, April 7). *usspacecom and Sweden sign a Space Situational Awareness sharing agreement*. U.S. Space Command. www.spacecom.mil/Newsroom/News/Article-Display/Article/2992854/usspacecom-and-sweden-sign-a-space-situational-awareness-sharing-agreement
United States Space Command Public Affairs Office. (2020, July 23). *Russia conducts space-based anti-satellite weapons test*. U.S. Space Command. www.spacecom.mil/Newsroom/News/Article-Display/Article/2285098/russia-conducts-space-based-anti-satellite-weapons-test.
United States Space Force. (2020, June). *Spacepower: Doctrine for space forces*. Space Capstone Publication. www.spaceforce.mil/Portals/1/Space%20Capstone%20Publication_10%20Aug%202020.pdf
University of Adelaide. (2018). *The Woomera Manual*. law.adelaide.edu.au/woomera. *Chagos Marine Protected Area Arbitration (Mauritius v. United Kingdom) (Award)*. (2015, 18 March). 2011–03 (ITLOS).
US Joint Chiefs of Staff. (2018, April 10). *Joint Publication 3–14 — Space Operations* (Revised edition as at 26 October 2020). US Department of Defense. www.jcs.mil/Portals/36/Documents/Doctrine/pubs/jp3_14ch1.pdf.
Weeden, B., & Samson, V. (Eds). (2022, April). *Global counterspace capabilities* (Report). Secure World Foundation. swfound.org/media/207350/swf_global_counterspace_capabilities_2022_rev2.pdf
White House. (2022, April 18). *Fact sheet: Vice President Harris advances national security norms in space*. Briefing Room. www.whitehouse.gov/briefing-room/statements-releases/2022/04/18/fact-sheet-vice-president-harris-advances-national-security-norms-in-space
Wilson, H. (2017, December 2). *Panel discussion with Heather Wilson, U.S. Secretary of the Air Force (remarks)*. Reagan National Defense Forum. www.c-span.org/video/?438064-2/national-security-space-strategy
Wong, C. (2021, December 30). Chinese, US militaries resume maritime safety talks after last year's no-show. *South China Morning Post*. www.scmp.com/news/china/diplomacy/article/3161614/chinese-us-militaries-resume-maritime-safety-talks-after-last
Wood, R. A. (2019, August 14). The threats posed by Russia and China to security of the outer space environment (statement to Conference on Disarmament Plenary Meeting). U.S. Mission to International Organizations in Geneva. geneva.usmission.gov/2019/08/14/statement-by-ambassador-wood-the-threats-posed-by-russia-and-china-to-security-of-the-outer-space-environment

Chapter 7
The New Zealand Outer Space and High-Altitude Activities Act 2017 and the Statutory Review: A Dance Between International and Domestic Law

Val Sim

Introduction

Since the Soviet Union successfully launched Sputnik 1, the first human-made space object, in October 1957, space-related technologies have continued to develop at a remarkable pace. The space environment is now very different from what it was in 1957 when the space treaties were being negotiated. Space has become a multi-billion-dollar global industry and is of huge strategic importance. Satellites enable the provision of critical everyday services and infrastructure, including banking, transportation, electricity, telecommunications, navigation and defence, to name but a few.

While for many years space was the domain of a small number of nation states and large corporations, advances in technology have enabled the production of smaller, cheaper, and more powerful satellites. Standardisation and mass production of small satellites have reduced barriers to entry to the space industry, with private players rather than State actors now playing an increasingly important role. The term 'new space' has been used to describe those activities that are now carried out by commercial rather than State actors.[1] Technological developments have also opened new activities that the treaty makers of half a century ago could never have envisaged.

Despite these changes, there is no appetite internationally to renegotiate the current international space treaties. As a result, a significant challenge when developing and implementing domestic law is how to interpret 50-year-old treaties in this vastly different space environment. This chapter briefly describes the interaction

[1] See for example Santamaría, Germán. (2021, July 22). What is New Space? Solar MEMS Technologies. https://www.solar-mems.com/what-is-new-space

V. Sim (✉)
Ministry of Business, Innovation and Employment, Wellington, New Zealand
e-mail: val.sim@mbie.govt.nz

M. A. Pozza (ed.), *Ascending to Space*, Space Law and Policy,
https://doi.org/10.1007/978-981-97-0714-0_7

between international and domestic space law (and discusses the findings of the recent review of the New Zealand Outer Space and High-altitude Activities Act 2017) to illustrate the challenges posed by rapidly changing technology.

The Space Treaties

The UN Committee on the Peaceful Uses of Outer Space (COPUOS) is one of the main fora for the development of international space law. COPUOS administers five space treaties. The cornerstone of modern space law is the Treaty on Principles Governing the Activities of States in the Exploration and Use of Outer Space, including the Moon and Other Celestial Bodies (the Outer Space Treaty), which entered into force in October 1967.[2] The principles of the Outer Space Treaty have been expanded upon in four later treaties: the Agreement on the Rescue of Astronauts, the Return of Astronauts and the Return of Objects Launched into Outer Space (the Rescue Agreement, 3 December 1968)[3]; the Convention on International Liability for Damage Caused by Space Objects (the Liability Convention, 29 March 1972)[4]; the Convention on Registration of Objects Launched into Outer Space (the Registration Convention, 15 September 1972)[5]; and the Agreement Governing the Activities of States on the Moon and Other Celestial Bodies (the Moon Agreement, 11 July 1984).[6]

These treaties are supported by non-binding declarations of legal principles and guidelines, including the recently adopted Guidelines for the Long-term Sustainability of Outer Space (June 2019) which were eventually adopted after more than

[2]UN Office for Outer Space Affairs. (1966). Treaty on Principles Governing the Activities of States in the Exploration and Use of Outer Space, including the Moon and Other Celestial Bodies. https://www.unoosa.org/oosa/en/ourwork/spacelaw/treaties/introouterspacetreaty.html

[3]UN Office for Outer Space Affairs. (1967). Agreement on the Rescue of Astronauts, the Return of Astronauts and the Return of Objects Launched into Outer Space. https://www.unoosa.org/oosa/en/ourwork/spacelaw/treaties/introrescueagreement.html

[4]UN Office for Outer Space Affairs. (1972). Convention on International Liability for Damage Caused by Space Objects. https://www.unoosa.org/oosa/en/ourwork/spacelaw/treaties/introliability-convention.html

[5]UN Office for Outer Space Affairs. (1976). Convention on Registration of Objects Launched into Outer Space. https://www.unoosa.org/oosa/en/ourwork/spacelaw/treaties/introregistration-convention.html

[6]UN Office for Outer Space Affairs. (1979). Agreement Governing the Activities of States on the Moon and Other Celestial Bodies. https://www.unoosa.org/oosa/en/ourwork/spacelaw/treaties/intromoon-agreement.html

8 years of negotiation.[7] New Zealand is a party to four of the five space treaties.[8] Like most other spacefaring nations, it is not a party to the Moon Agreement, which is much less widely subscribed to than the other space treaties. The Moon Agreement has only 18 parties.

The Outer Space Treaty

The Outer Space Treaty establishes the fundamental principles of space law (which almost certainly have the status of customary international law). Set against the backdrop of the Cold War and concerns about the proliferation of nuclear weapons,[9] the treaty contains preambular provisions recognising the common interest of all mankind in the progress of the exploration and use of outer space for peaceful purposes and emphasising the importance of international cooperation.[10] There were also concerns at the time about protecting the interests of non-spacefaring nations and protecting the space environment. The core principles established by the treaty (as described on the website of the UN Office of Outer Space Affairs)[11] include:

- The exploration and use of outer space shall be carried out for the benefit and in the interests of all countries and shall be the province of all mankind.
- Outer space shall be free for exploration and use by all States.
- Outer space is not subject to national appropriation by claim of sovereignty, by means of use or occupation, or by any other means.
- States shall not place nuclear weapons or other weapons of mass destruction in orbit or on celestial bodies or station them in outer space in any other manner.
- The Moon and other celestial bodies shall be used exclusively for peaceful purposes.
- Astronauts shall be regarded as the envoys of mankind.
- States shall be responsible for national space activities, whether carried out by governmental or non-governmental entities.

---

[7] UN Office for Outer Space Affairs. (2023). Long-term Sustainability of Outer Space Activities. https://www.unoosa.org/oosa/en/ourwork/topics/long-term-sustainability-of-outer-space-activities.html

[8] See New Zealand Ministry of Foreign Affairs & Trade. (2023). New Zealand Treaties Online. https://www.treaties.mfat.govt.nz/

[9] See, for example, Myers, Catherine. (2017, January 27). To Boldly Go Where No Treaty Had Gone Before. *Inside Science*. https://www.insidescience.org/news/boldly-go-where-no-treaty-had-gone

[10] These concerns are reflected in the 1962 Declaration of Legal Principles Governing the Activities of States in the Exploration and Use of Outer Space. https://www.unoosa.org/oosa/en/ourwork/spacelaw/principles/legal-principles.html

[11] UN Office for Outer Space Affairs. (1966). Treaty on Principles Governing the Activities of States in the Exploration and Use of Outer Space.

- States shall be liable for damage caused by their space objects.
- States shall avoid harmful contamination of space and celestial bodies.

As an overarching space treaty, the Outer Space Treaty is wide and varied covering a number of important elements arising from space-based activities. Accordingly, There are over 80 signatories to the Treaty and more than 110 state Parties to the Outer Space Treaty.[12]

Amongst other things, the Outer Space Treaty enshrines a principle of state responsibility for national space activities. The concept of State responsibility for national space activities is expanded upon in both the Liability Convention and the Registration Convention.

The Liability Convention 1972

Under the Liability Convention 1972 a launching State is absolutely liable for damage caused by its space objects on Earth (including to an aircraft in flight).[13] Once in space, the launching State is liable if the damage is due to its fault or the fault of someone for whom it is responsible.[14] The term 'launching State' is defined as the 'State which launches or procures the launch of a space object',[15] or 'whose territory or facility a space object is launched'.[16] The Liability Convention provides for circumstances where there are two or more launching States (as is inevitably the case with Rocket Lab launches from New Zealand, since it is a US company and most of its launches are procured by foreign satellite owners).[17] The Liability Convention also provides for the manner of making and settling liability claims. The primary mechanism is through diplomatic negotiations, although there is provision for the establishment of a multi-national Claims Commission if diplomatic efforts fail. The only known occasion when the Liability Convention has been invoked was by Canada through diplomatic channels after the re-entry and subsequent crash of the Soviet RORSAT Cosmos 954 on 24 January 1978 in north-west Canada. This led to a settlement for the costs of the clean-up and damages.[18]

---

[12] UN Office of Disarmament Affairs. (1967). Treaty on Principles Governing the Activities of States in the Exploration and Use of Outer Space, Including the Moon and Other Celestial Bodies. treaties.unoda.org/t/outer_space; UN Treaty Collection. (1967). Treaty on Principles Governing the Activities of States in the Exploration and Use of Outer Space, Including the Moon and Other Celestial Bodies. https://treaties.un.org/pages/showdetails.aspx?objid=0800000280128cbd.

[13] Article II.

[14] Article IV.

[15] UN Office for Outer Space Affairs. (1972). Convention on International Liability for Damage Caused by Space Objects, 25. https://www.unoosa.org/pdf/gares/ARES_26_2777E.pdf

[16] UN Office for Outer Space Affairs. (1972). Convention on International Liability for Damage Caused by Space Objects, p. 25. https://www.unoosa.org/pdf/gares/ARES_26_2777E.pdf

[17] Article V.

[18] Articles XIV and XV.

The Registration Convention 1976

Under the Registration Convention 1976,[19] States are required to maintain a national register of space objects, and launching States are required to provide information to the United Nations to maintain an international register of space objects.[20] Where there are two or more launching States, they are required to determine between them which is to be the State of registry.[21] This requires the States to reach an agreement as to which of the launching States will register the space object. In practice, almost all of Rocket Lab's launches have involved foreign satellite providers and the New Zealand Space Agency regularly engages with space agencies in other jurisdictions over questions of registration. Legally, the State of registry retains jurisdiction and control over a satellite, though not necessarily ownership.[22]

The Rescue Agreement 1967

The Rescue Agreement 1967[23] also builds upon an obligation in the Outer Space Treaty 1967 – in this case an obligation of return of astronauts in Articles 2 and 3.[24] The agreement builds upon this by imposing positive obligations to rescue astronauts, even outside a State's jurisdiction, if the State is in a position to do so and return them to the 'launching authority'. Further, Article 5 of the Rescue Agreement 1967 extends to the return of 'space objects' or 'component parts' that may have returned to Earth but landed in another State's territory.[25]

---

[19] UN Treaty Collection. (1976). Convention on Registration of Objects Launched into Outer Space, https://treaties.un.org/Pages/showDetails.aspx?objid%20=%2008000002800361b4

[20] Articles II, III and IV.

[21] Article II.2.

[22] Outer Space Treaty, Article VIII.

[23] UN Office for Outer Space Affairs. (1967). Agreement on the Rescue of Astronauts, the Return of Astronauts and the Return of Objects Launched into Outer Space. https://www.unoosa.org/pdf/gares/ARES_22_2345E.pdf

[24] UN Office for Outer Space Affairs. (1967). Agreement on the Rescue of Astronauts, the Return of Astronauts and the Return of Objects Launched into Outer Space, 6. https://www.unoosa.org/pdf/gares/ARES_22_2345E.pdf

[25] Ibid., 6–7. https://www.unoosa.org/pdf/gares/ARES_22_2345E.pdf

The Moon Agreement 1979

It is unnecessary to discuss the Moon Agreement 1979 in any depth since New Zealand is not a party (and with only 18 signatories[26] it is certainly not customary international law). However, it is worthy of note that the agreement was intended to establish a framework for regulating various space activities, including resource utilisation,[27] an issue that is now very topical and which is discussed further below.

Article 11 of the Agreement designates the moon and its natural resources as the common heritage of mankind and requires that States Parties establish an international regime to govern the exploitation of the natural resources of the moon when such exploitation becomes feasible.[28]

New Zealand's Participation in COPUOS

New Zealand became a member of COPUOS in 2016 shortly after Rocket Lab announced its intention to carry out frequent, low-cost launches from the country.[29] As one of a small number of states that has a launch service capability, and as a 'poster child for new space' activities, it has quickly established itself as an influential voice within COPUOS.

The work of COPUOS is undertaken by two subcommittees (the Scientific and Technical Subcommittee and the Legal Subcommittee) which meet annually with their work brought together at an annual plenary meeting. New Zealand participates actively in these meetings, advocating the development of additional rules, norms and standards where these are required to deal with emerging space issues and to fill gaps in the age-old treaties. New Zealand has a particular interest in ensuring the safe, sustainable and responsible use of space, and actively promotes these values.[30] New Zealand's contributions are also aligned with New Zealand's broader policy

[26] UN Office for Outer Space Affairs. (2023). Status of International Agreements relating to Activities in Outer Space. https://www.unoosa.org/oosa/en/ourwork/spacelaw/treaties/status/index.html

[27] UN Office for Outer Space Affairs. (1979). Agreement Governing the Activities of States on the Moon and Other Celestial Bodies, 77–80. https://www.unoosa.org/pdf/gares/ARES_34_68E.pdf

[28] Ibid., 79.

[29] UN Office for Outer Space Affairs. (2022). UN Committee on the Peaceful Uses of Outer Space: Membership Evolution. https://www.unoosa.org/oosa/en/ourwork/copuos/members/evolution.html

[30] New Zealand Ministry of Business, Innovation & Employment. New Zealand Ministry of Business, Innovation & Employment. (n.d.). Modelling sustainable space and Earth environments. https://www.mbie.govt.nz/science-and-technology/space/new-zealand-space-policy-review-consultation/modelling-sustainable-space-and-earth-environments

settings, including our interest in multilateralism.[31] However, COPUOS operates by consensus and progress is often slow. As a result, domestic law needs to be created in an environment where international law remains uncertain.

Domestic Space Law: The Outer Space and High-Altitude Activities Act 2017

When Rocket Lab first announced its launch intentions, New Zealand was a party to four of the five United Nations Space Treaties, but no steps had been taken to implement them. Legislation was urgently needed to address this and to manage the risks associated with Rocket Lab's activities. The Outer Space and High-altitude Activities Act (OSHAA) was enacted in July 2017 and came into force in December of that year.[32] While it was Rocket Lab's activities that provided the catalyst for the development of the Act, it regulates space activities generally and is not specific to Rocket Lab. The Act has several purposes, including facilitating the development of a space industry and providing for its secure and safe operation, implementing New Zealand's international obligations, managing liability, regulating high-altitude activities and preserving New Zealand's national security and national interests.[33]

The Act establishes a licensing regime to regulate the following activities:

- The launch of spacecraft: there are separate licensing types for entities that launch from New Zealand or that are New Zealand nationals that conduct launch activities overseas.[34] (The extraterritorial aspect is required to implement the obligations in the Outer Space Treaty that States take responsibility for national space activities, which is generally construed to mean both activities from its territory and activities carried out by its nationals.)
- Payload permits: these regulate operators that launch or procure the launch of satellites from New Zealand and the activities of New Zealanders who launch or procure the launch of satellites overseas.[35]
- Facility licences: these regulate those that operate facilities from which spacecraft are launched. While Rocket Lab owns and operates its own facility and could have been managed under a single licence, the act imposed separate licensing requirements to future-proof the regime.[36]

---

[31] New Zealand Ministry of Business, Innovation & Employment. (2023, May). National Space Policy. https://www.mbie.govt.nz/science-and-technology/space/national-space-policy

[32] New Zealand Parliamentary Counsel Office. (2017). New Zealand Legislation. Outer Space and High-altitude Activities Act 2017. https://www.legislation.govt.nz/act/public/2017/0029/latest/DLM6966275.html

[33] Section 3.

[34] Sections 7 and 23.

[35] Sections 15 and 31.

[36] Section 38.

- High-altitude activities: these are activities that take place above controlled airspace but do not involve the launch of spacecraft.[37] High-altitude licences are probably the most unique aspect of New Zealand's regime. These originated out of concerns about so-called 'near space activities' and the inability to manage them if they posed risks to national security or other national interest concerns. However, there is an increasing international interest in regulating suborbital activities, and New Zealand's regime already attracts significant international interest.

  In the case of each type of licence or permit (the tests differ slightly depending on the type of licence or permit), broadly speaking the Minister needs to be satisfied before granting a licence or permit that the activity is safe, is consistent with international obligations and, in the case of launch licences and payload permits, that orbital debris will be properly managed. Even if these threshold tests are met, the Minister can decline a licence or permit if he or she is not satisfied the operation of the permit is in the national interest. In considering the national interest for the purposes of subections (17(2), 25(2), 33(2) and 47(2)), the Minister may have regard to
- Economic or other benefits to New Zealand of the proposed operation.
- Any risks to national security, public safety, international relations, or other national interests.
- The extent to which the risks can be mitigated by licence or permit conditions.
- Any other matters that the Minister considers relevant.[38]
- The issue of whether New Zealand should grant permits to allow the launch of satellites procured by overseas military or security organisations or allow remote sensing satellites where overseas military or security agencies are end users of data is currently topical. Whatever view one takes of that, the legislation gives the Minister the ability to decline a permit if he or she is not satisfied that the activity is in the national interest. While the issue of where national interests lie can be difficult to assess and is ultimately a political judgement the legislative tools are there to support it.

When granting a licence or permit the Minister can impose bespoke conditions.[39] The ability to impose conditions is a useful regulatory tool because it ensures the requirements imposed on a licence or permit holder are commensurate with the risks of the activity that is being carried out and can manage unique risks not anticipated by regulation.

Two other aspects of New Zealand's space regime warrant mention. The first is the ability under section 51 of the Act of the Minister to recognise overseas licences, permits or authorisations as satisfying any one or more of the statutory prerequisites for a licence. This is an important tool to prevent unnecessary duplication in an activity that is likely to be regulated in more than one jurisdiction. For example,

[37] Section 45.

[38] Sections 9, 17, 40 and 47.

[39] Sections 26, 34, 41 and 48.

Rocket Lab, which as a US company is required to have a US licence. The Minister has recognised the US Federal Aviation Administration licence as satisfying the safety aspects of the launch licence requirements under OSHAA.[40] This is a win–win, as it avoids duplication and cost for Rocket Lab but also allows New Zealand to draw on US expertise in regulating the safety of launch vehicles which has been built up over decades and is maintained by a continuous flow of varied applicants. This an area of expertise that New Zealand does not currently have.

The second aspect is the broad-ranging regulation making powers. The rapid pace of technological change makes it hard for the law to keep up with the ever-changing nature of space activities. To future-proof the regime so far as possible, the Act's regulation-making powers provide some scope to deal with changes to technologies and markets. Regulations, which are made by the executive, can be put in place much more quickly than primary legislation, which is made by parliament. For example, the Act establishes regulation-making powers to prescribe things that are or are not, for the purposes of the act, a launch vehicle, space object or a high-altitude vehicle.[41] While powers of this kind that allow regulations to override a statute (often described as 'Henry VIII' clauses) are generally frowned upon, both the Legislation Advisory and Design Committee and subsequently the parliamentary Foreign Affairs, Defence and Trade Select Committee accepted that in areas such as this, where legislation struggles to keep up with rapid innovation, broad regulation-making powers are justified (albeit with safeguards, such as consultation requirements and a requirement for reasons to be given). The Act is supplemented by two sets of regulations.[42] Amongst other matters, these prescribe the information that is required to be provided with licence and permit applications and the requirements for an orbital debris mitigation plan.

---

[40] New Zealand Ministry of Business, Innovation & Employment. (2023, May 18). Permits and licences for space activities. https://www.mbie.govt.nz/science-and-technology/space/permits-and-licences-for-space-activities

[41] Section 88.

[42] New Zealand Parliamentary Counsel Office. (2017). New Zealand Legislation. Outer Space and High-altitude Activities (Definition of High-altitude Vehicle) Regulations 2017. https://www.legislation.govt.nz/act/public/2017/0029/latest/DLM6966275.html; Outer Space and High-altitude Activities (Licences and Permits) Regulations 2017. https://www.legislation.govt.nz/regulation/public/2017/0250/latest/DLM7364101.html.New Zealand Parliamentary Counsel Office. (2017). New Zealand Legislation. Outer Space and High-altitude Activities (Definition of High-altitude Vehicle) Regulations 2017. https://www.legislation.govt.nz/act/public/2017/0029/latest/DLM6966275.html; Outer Space and High-altitude Activities (Licences and Permits) Regulations 2017. https://www.legislation.govt.nz/regulation/public/2017/0250/latest/DLM7364101.html

The Statutory Review

Section 86 of the Act required the Minister to commence a review of the operation and effectiveness of the act as soon as reasonably practicable after the expiry of 3 years from its commencement. The review has now been completed, and the Minister's report on the review was tabled in parliament on 12 May 2022.[43] In carrying out the review on behalf of the Minister, the review team consulted domestic agencies involved in the licensing and permitting process, international regulatory agencies and industry stakeholders.[44] The consensus was that the Act operates very well and is achieving its objectives. The regime is well regarded internationally.[45] Nevertheless, the review made several recommendations for change.[46] Many of these were minor and technical. However, there were also some areas where more substantive recommendations were made. Many of these were the result of technological developments both within New Zealand and internationally.

The main issues identified in the three-year review involving the regulation of new and emerging technologies are discussed below.

The High-Altitude Vehicle Regime

Since the legislation was enacted, Rocket Lab has continued to innovate, including the development of a 'kick stage' for its launch vehicle to improve orbital deployment, the development of its photon satellite bus, and the carrying out of recovery missions aimed at making its rockets reusable.[47] It has been possible to accommodate these developments within the existing legislative framework.

The position is different with high-altitude technologies. At the time the legislation was developed, the high-altitude activities in contemplation were sounding rockets and high-altitude balloons, and the regime was designed on that basis. However, since then, increasingly sophisticated high-altitude activities are being developed in New Zealand. For example, a spaceplane is currently being developed by Dawn Aerospace, designed to conduct multiple suborbital flights per day,[48] while Kea Aerospace is developing a solar-powered, remotely piloted aircraft that will fly

[43] New Zealand Ministry of Business, Innovation & Employment. (2022). Statutory Review of the Outer Space and High-altitude Activities Act 2017. https://www.parliament.nz/resource/en-NZ/PAP_122789/69be1c790012398b63ffa1fa354494434db50ca0

[44] A list of submitters can be found at p. 12.

[45] Ibid., 14.

[46] A summary of the key findings and recommendations is set out in part two of the report.

[47] Rocket Lab. (2023). https://www.rocketlabusa.com/

[48] Dawn Aerospace. (2023). Introducing the Dawn Mk-II Aurora. https://www.dawnaerospace.com/spacelaunch

continuously in the stratosphere for months at a time to collect frequent high-resolution aerial images[49] – something that has traditionally been done by satellites. Potentially these newer technologies will enable travel to extremely high altitudes which could blur the boundaries between the space and high-altitude regimes.

The review identified several issues with the high-altitude regime that needed to be considered for possible legislative change. The first was the need to provide greater clarity to distinguish between the space and high-altitude regimes.[50] At the time the legislation was developed, there was a deliberate decision not to define the term 'space' or to prescribe the upper limit of 'high altitude' because there is no certainty in international law about where space begins or airspace ends.[51] There is no definition in the space treaties of the term 'outer space'.

The Chicago Convention of 1944,[52] which established the international civil aviation regime, is similarly silent on where airspace ends. This leaves considerable uncertainty about how to delimit space and airspace. Debate on how to delimit space and airspace has raged within COPUOS for almost 50 years, with differences of views on whether space needs to be defined and, if so, how. A spatial approach which sets an upper limit and a functional approach that defines whether a vehicle is a space object or an aircraft by reference to the function it performs are the predominant theories.[53] In New Zealand, the demarcation is dealt with through partial definition under s.4 of the Outer Space and High-Altitude Activities Act 2017 which defined it as 'an altitude above the higher of – (a) flight level 600; and (b) the highest upper limit of controlled airspace under the Civil Aviation Act 1990.'[54] By way of comparison, in Australia, the Space (Launches and Returns) Act 2018[55] adopted a spatial limit of 100 km above mean sea level in its definition of a space object, although its government has stressed that this is purely for the purpose of defining the scope of its regulation and does not mean it purports to define where space begins and ends. Denmark and the United Arab Emirates also have adopted spatial limits, the UAE adopting a lower limit than Australia or Denmark at 80 km above mean sea

---

[49] Kea Aerospace. (2023). https://www.keaaerospace.com/

[50] New Zealand Ministry of Business, Innovation & Employment. (2022). Statutory Review of the Outer Space and High-altitude Activities Act 2017, 19–21.

[51] However, Section 4 of the Act defines the lower limit of high altitude, which is the point at which a high-altitude licence is required. This is an altitude that is the higher of either flight level 600 or the highest upper limit of controlled airspace under the Civil Aviation Act 1990.

[52] International Civil Aviation Organization. (1944). Convention on International Civil Aviation. https://www.icao.int/publications/Documents/7300_cons.pdf (also known as Chicago Convention).

[53] A working group on the issue has been set up in the Legal Sub-committee. UN Office for Outer Space Affairs. (n.d.). Working Group on the Definition and Delimitation of Outer Space of the Legal Subcommittee. https://www.unoosa.org/oosa/en/ourwork/copuos/lsc/ddos/index.html, and the attached report sets out some of the differences in approach.

[54] Outer Space and High-altitude Activities (Definition of High-altitude Vehicle) Regulations 2017.

[55] Federal Register of Legislation, Australia. (2018). Space (Launches and Returns) Act 2018. https://www.legislation.gov.au/Details/C2021C00394

level.[56] The alternative approach canvassed in the report is to include a definition of 'launch activities' as those that go into Earth's orbit and beyond. The report favours this approach because the tests that apply under the act for a launch licence and a high-altitude licence are the same, except that a launch licence has an additional test relating to the management of orbital debris.[57] It therefore makes sense for the definitions to distinguish between those activities that create debris and those that do not. However, if this approach is adopted it will be necessary to consider how best to deal with vehicles that have a trajectory and altitude that means they cross the paths of objects that are in orbit, since they pose collision risks to space objects. To that extent, they can be seen as creating debris risks despite not going into orbit themselves.

The second question raised by the new high-altitude technologies is how to deal with high-altitude payloads. Under the current law, there are requirements for separate permits and licences for the satellites going into orbit and their launch vehicles. This is required by the space treaties.[58] However, there is no separate payload permitting regime for objects carried by high-altitude vehicles because the payload was seen as part and parcel of the high-altitude vehicle.

In a world where spaceplanes potentially carry out daily flights for multiple customers carrying out multiple activities, the review concludes that there will need to be separate licences for a high-altitude vehicle and the operations of its customers to manage national interest concerns. It recommends further work on whether this should be a licence for the payload, for example, equipment used in microgravity research, or a licence for the activity that is being carried out by the vehicle.

Managing Orbital Debris, Space Congestion and Protection of the Earth's Environment

The growing quantity of debris in space poses a danger to users of the orbital environment, such as spacecraft. It also increases the risk that humans or human-made structures could be impacted when objects re-enter Earth's atmosphere. Several international standards have been developed (and are updated from time to time) aimed at managing orbital debris and collision risks in space, including standards developed by the Inter-Agency Space Debris Coordination Committee

[56] Space Act 2016 (Denmark), Federal Law no 12 of 2019 on the Regulation of the Space Sector (UAE).

[57] New Zealand Ministry of Business, Innovation & Employment. (2022). Statutory Review of the Outer Space and High-altitude Activities Act 2017, 16.

[58] This follows from Article VI of the Outer Space Treaty that gives States Parties international responsibility for national activities in outer space and for assuring they are carried out in conformity with the provisions of the treaty.

(IACD), the US National Aeronautics and Space Administration (NASA), the European Space Agency (ESA) and the International Organization for Standardization (ISO).[59] The core features of these standards are similar and have been incorporated in New Zealand's Outer Space and High-altitude Activities (Licences and Permits) Regulations 2017 as requirements for an orbital debris mitigation plan that need to be met to secure a relevant licence or permit.[60]

In June 2019, the United Nations adopted the Guidelines for the Long-term Sustainability of Outer Space Activities of the Committee on the Peaceful Uses of Outer Space,[61] aimed at reducing risks to the long-term sustainability of the space environment. A working group has since been established to consider their implementation.[62] It will be possible to implement these guidelines using mechanisms under the existing law, such as conditions and regulations. In other words, conditions could be imposed on licences that reflect the recommendations in the guidelines or regulations could be made imposing requirements reflecting the recommendations in the guidelines. However, the review identified two areas where changes to the legislation might be required to enable the better management of orbital debris.

The first arises from the renewed interest in space exploration and was identified during the licensing of Rocket Lab's recent CAPSTONE mission. This was its first mission to lunar orbit, undertaken as part of the US Artemis programme.[63] If space exploration takes place beyond Earth's orbit, there is a potential for space debris that is non-Earth orbiting. This is particularly likely to arise in the context of the post-mission disposal of the launch vehicle, where this takes place beyond Earth's orbit. The current international standards do not currently address this issue. In the short term, the NZ Space Agency was able to manage this through a post-mission disposal policy and licence conditions, but in the longer term regulations may be required.

Related to this is the question of planetary protection. Article 9 of the Outer Space Treaty requires signatory States conducting exploration of outer space, the Moon and other celestial bodies to avoid their harmful contamination and adverse changes

---

[59] International Organization for Standardization. (2023). ISO 24113:2019. Space systems – Space debris mitigation requirements. https://www.iso.org/standard/72383.html; NASA. (n.d.). European Space Agency. (n.d.). Mitigating space debris generation. https://www.esa.int/Space_Safety/Space_Debris/Mitigating_space_debris_generation; Inter-Agency Space Debris Coordination Committee. (2020, March 1). IADC Space Debris Mitigation Guidelines. https://orbitaldebris.jsc.nasa.gov/library/iadc-space-debris-guidelines-revision-2.pdf

[60] New Zealand Parliamentary Counsel Office. (2017). New Zealand Legislation. Outer Space and High-altitude Activities (Licences and Permits) Regulations 2017. https://www.legislation.govt.nz/regulation/public/2017/0250/latest/DLM7364101.html

[61] UN Committee on the Peaceful Uses of Outer Space. (2018, June 27). Guidelines for the Long-term Sustainability of Outer Space Activities. https://www.unoosa.org/res/oosadoc/data/documents/2018/aac_1052018crp/aac_1052018crp_20_0_html/AC105_2018_CRP20E.pdf

[62] UN Committee on the Peaceful Uses of Outer Space. (2010). Terms of reference and methods of work of the Working Group on the Long-term Sustainability of Outer Space Activities of the Scientific and Technical Subcommittee: working paper submitted by the Chair of the Working Group. https://digitallibrary.un.org/record/693562?ln=en

[63] Rocket Lab. (n.d.). Capstone Mission. https://www.rocketlabusa.com/missions/lunar

in the environment of the Earth resulting from the introduction of extra-terrestrial matter and, where necessary, to adopt appropriate measures for this purpose. Currently, there are some international planetary protection guidelines aimed at protecting solar system bodies from contamination by Earth life and protecting Earth from possible life forms that may be returned from other solar system bodies. These include NASA's planetary protection policies and guidelines, developed by the Committee on Space Research (COSPAR).[64]

In anticipation of further space exploration missions taking place from New Zealand, the review of 2022 recommends that regulations be developed to manage space debris beyond Earth's orbit and implement requirements for planetary protection.[65] The second area where changes to New Zealand legislation might be required relates to technologies that are currently being developed for active debris removal and in the orbit servicing of satellites.[66] These technologies are seen as having huge potential for managing the problem of space debris, but they are very controversial because they are by their very nature multi-use. This gives rise to complex legal issues, including whether the consent of the owner of the debris is required, what the position is where there is no identifiable owner, and how the liability rules operate in the context of space debris and of on-orbit servicing, as well as the respective roles and responsibilities of the in-orbit servicing and client States.

The issue is not academic. These technologies are very imminent. Rocket Lab has announced it has secured a contract to launch a debris removal demonstration for the Japanese company Astroscale.[67] In anticipation, the NZ Space Agency has developed a policy for dealing with active debris removal missions.[68] The review noted, however, that more detailed regulations may also be required, to introduce more prescriptive requirements for active debris removal and in-orbit servicing in the future. Accordingly, it recommends the enactment of specific regulation-making powers to deal with these issues.[69]

[64] COSPAR. (n.d.). Planetary Protection Policy. https://cosparhq.cnes.fr/assets/uploads/2021/01/Research_Outreach_PPP_2020.pdf

[65] COSPAR. (2011, March 24). COSPAR Planetary Protection Policy. https://science.nasa.gov/science-red/s3fs-public/atoms/files/COSPAR_Planetary_Protection_Policy_v3-24-11.pdf

[66] Satellite Applications Catapult (n.d.). In-Space Services – A Major Opportunity for the UK. Active Debris Removal. https://issuu.com/satappscatapult/docs/in-space_services-_a_major_opportunity_for_the_uk_/s/10491735

[67] Rocket Lab. (2023). Upcoming Missions. https://www.rocketlabusa.com/missions/upcoming-missions

[68] New Zealand Space Agency. (2023, May 10). Active Debris Removal and On-Orbit Servicing Missions: Operational Policy. https://www.mbie.govt.nz/dmsdocument/26611-active-debris-removal-and-on-orbit-servicing-operational-policy-pdf

[69] Ibid., 30.

Constellations, Night Skies, Space Entertainment and Very Small Satellites

The emergence of satellite constellations has posed new challenges because many of the rules, norms and standards are premised on a single satellite and may not be appropriate deal with large constellations. New Zealand launches have contributed to several small constellations,[70] but the concern is with much larger constellations such as Starlink which have a significant impact on the space environment.

Issues have also been raised about the consistency of very large constellations with the Outer Space Treaty. Can a constellation become so large that it amounts to an appropriation in breach of Article 2 of the Outer Space Treaty, or do very large constellations harmfully interfere with the interests of others in space, in breach of Article 9?

But a particular and more specific concern has recently been raised by the International Astronomical Union (IAU) that the number of new low Earth's orbit satellite constellations interferes with optical and radio astronomy and the need to keep dark and quiet skies for science and society.[71] Chile, Ethiopia, Jordan, Slovakia, Spain and the IAU recently submitted a conference paper to COPUOS containing many recommendations aimed at protecting dark skies.[72] The issue of protecting the skies is not new, although as larger and larger satellite constellations are launched it has become much starker.

In 2001, the IAU submitted a conference paper on obtrusive space advertising and astronomical research.[73] This resulted in a US Federal Aviation Administration rule preventing US licensees from launching a payload containing material to be used for obtrusive space advertising. This was defined as 'advertising in outer space that is capable of being recognized by a human being on the surface of the Earth without the aid of a telescope or other technological device'.[74] More recently, the NZ

[70] New Zealand Ministry of Business, Innovation & Employment. (2023). Approved payloads and other licences. https://www.mbie.govt.nz/science-and-technology/space/permits-and-licences-for-space-activities/payloads-approved-for-launch/approved-payloads-and-other-licences

[71] UN Committee on the Peaceful Uses of Outer Space. (2017, June 8). The 'Dark and quiet skies' proposal as an initiative ... for protecting the environmental observing conditions for large astronomical observatories and world citizens. https://www.unoosa.org/res/oosadoc/data/documents/2017/aac_1052017crp/aac_1052017crp_24_0_html/AC105_2017CRP24E.pdf

[72] UN Committee on the Peaceful Uses of Outer Space. (2021, April 19). Recommendation to Keep Dark and Quiet Skies for Science and Society. https://www.unoosa.org/res/oosadoc/data/documents/2021/aac_105c_12021crp/aac_105c_12021crp_17_0_html/AC105_C1_2021_CRP17E.pdf

[73] UN Committee on the Peaceful Uses of Outer Space. (2001, December 18). Obtrusive space advertising and astronomical research. Background paper by the International Astronomical Union. https://www.unoosa.org/pdf/reports/ac105/AC105_777E.pdf

[74] Office of the Law Revision Counsel. United States Code. (n.d.). Chapter 509 – Commercial Space Launch Activities. https://uscode.house.gov/view.xhtml?path=/prelim@title51/subtitle5/chapter509&edition=prelim

Space Agency issued a permit to a Japanese company which would have allowed the launch of a satellite into space providing the temporary display of artificial 'shooting stars' into the night sky, amongst other purposes.

The display was short-lived and localised, therefore the Minister determined that this satellite did not constitute obtrusive space advertising. In the event the technology failed, and the display never took place.[75] But the issues raised by the IAU about the impact of satellite constellations are much more complex, and further debate on how to reconcile the interests of space actors and astronomers is inevitable. The review recommends the enactment of a regulation-making power covering constellations, as well as the protection of dark and quiet skies.[76]

At the opposite end of the spectrum is concern about very small satellites. For example, some of the satellites launched by Rocket Lab have been smaller than one Unit (or 'U', equivalent to a 10 cm cube).[77] These satellites are very hard to track, raising concerns about collision risks and the creation of orbital debris. However, there are also emerging new technologies aimed at improving the ability to track very small satellites. Submissions to the review, for example, mentioned beacon technology and propulsion as potentially useful technologies. Passive means of de-orbiting are also being considered.

The NZ Space Agency has adopted a policy for managing very small satellites,[78] but it is foreseeable that in the future regulations relating to the tracking of satellites and management of collision risks will be required, and accordingly the review recommended a regulation-making power so that regulations can be made requiring the use of these technologies.

Space Resource Utilisation

The term space resource utilisation refers to the extraction and use of mineral resources on the Moon and other celestial bodies. While the immediate interest in space resource utilisation relates to using those resources, such as water, that would

[75] Wall, Mike. (2020, May 16). Japanese satellite filled with 'shooting star' pellets won't spawn artificial meteor shower after all. Space.com. https://www.space.com/japan-shooting-star-satellite-artificial-meteor-shower-glitch.html

[76] UN Committee on the Peaceful Uses of Outer Space. (2021, April 19). Recommendation to Keep Dark and Quiet Skies for Science and Society. https://www.unoosa.org/res/oosadoc/data/documents/2021/aac_105c_12021crp/aac_105c_12021crp_17_0_html/AC105_C1_2021_CRP17E.pdf, 30.

[77] New Zealand Ministry of Business, Innovation & Employment. (2023, July 31). Payloads approved for launch. https://www.mbie.govt.nz/science-and-technology/space/permits-and-licences-for-space-activities/payloads-approved-for-launch

[78] New Zealand Space Agency. (n.d.). Payloads of a size less than 1 U: Operational Policy. https://www.mbie.govt.nz/dmsdocument/6985-payloads-of-a-size-less-than-1u-operational-policy

facilitate exploration beyond the Moon, there is also the potential for mining for commercial purposes.

While NASA is leading the Artemis missions, it regards international partnerships with both governments and private sector actors as playing a key role in achieving a sustainable return to the Moon and the first human mission to Mars.[79] Accordingly, it invited several countries, including New Zealand, to join the Artemis Accords. This required New Zealand to agree to a non-binding set of principles designed to guide the safe and sustainable exploration of outer space, including principles relating to the utilisation of space resources.[80]

The Outer Space Treaty 1967 sets out the principles regulating the exploration and use of outer space but, unsurprisingly given its age, does not explicitly regulate space resource utilisation. Given that, in international law resource utilisation is permitted, provided it is carried out consistently with the treaty requirements – for example, it is for the benefit of and in the interest of all countries and avoids harmful interference with the activities of other space actors.[81]

The Artemis Accords contain more detailed provisions, including those relating to the creation of safety zones, aimed at the deconfliction[82] of space activities, but these are not binding and at this stage there are only a small number of signatories to the Accords.[83]

Given the complexity of the issues, there is a need for additional rules, norms and standards to be developed at a multilateral level to ensure the conservation and long-term sustainability of space resources. The Legal Subcommittee of COPUOS has recently agreed to the establishment of a Working Group to look at the issue.[84] The New Zealand review team also recommended the enactment of regulation-making powers to regulate this activity so that the government can move reasonably quickly once space resource utilisation becomes a reality, and the international rules are clearer.[85]

---

[79] NASA. (n.d.). The Artemis Accords: Principles for a Safe, Peaceful, and Prosperous Future. https://www.nasa.gov/specials/artemis-accords/index.html

[80] Artemis Accords. (2020, October 13). https://www.nasa.gov/specials/artemis-accords/img/Artemis-Accords-signed-13Oct2020.pdf

[81] Ibid., Article I.

[82] Ibid.

[83] There were 13 signatories as of October 2021.

[84] UN Office for Outer Space Affairs. (2023, June). Working Group on Legal Aspects of Space Resource Activities. 66 COPUOS. https://www.unoosa.org/oosa/en/ourwork/copuos/lsc/space-resources/index.html

[85] Ibid., 30.

Conclusion

The statutory review of the Outer Space and High-altitude Activities Act 2017 highlights the complexity of the relationship between international and domestic law when regulating space activities. A particular challenge is how to provide for the regulation of new technologies, considering the difficulties of interpreting the 50-year-old treaties in the 'new space' environment. New Zealand has been, and continues to be, an active participant in the international debates on how to regulate 'new space activities' and the international efforts to develop new norms and standards for responsible space behaviour. Our positions are shaped by our values and domestic interests.

At the same time, international law struggles to keep pace with technology, and therefore State practice is also likely to play a significant role in its development.

Accordingly, the way we approach these issues in domestic law may also play some role in shaping what will ultimately become new norms and standards. It is difficult to predict how some of the technologies described in this paper will ultimately be regulated. What is easier to predict is that there will continue to be rapid technological advances that will pose ongoing challenges for both international and domestic law.

Bibliography

Artemis Accords. (2020, October 13). https://www.nasa.gov/specials/artemis-accords/img/Artemis-Accords-signed-13Oct2020.pdf.

Astromaterials Research & Exploration Science. NASA Orbital Debris Program Office. orbitaldebris.jsc.nasa.gov/mitigation.

COSPAR. (2011, March 24). *COSPAR planetary protection policy*. https://science.nasa.gov/science-red/s3fs-public/atoms/files/COSPAR_Planetary_Protection_Policy_v3-24-11.pdf

Dawn Aerospace. (2023). *Introducing the Dawn Mk-II Aurora*. https://www.dawnaerospace.com/spacelaunch.

European Space Agency. (n.d.). *Mitigating space debris generation*. https://www.esa.int/Space_Safety/Space_Debris/Mitigating_space_debris_generation.

Federal Register of Legislation, Australia. (2018). Space (Launches and Returns) Act 2018. https://www.legislation.gov.au/C2004A00391/2021-09-01/text.

Inter-Agency Space Debris Coordination Committee. (2020, March 1). IADC Space Debris Mitigation Guidelines. https://orbitaldebris.jsc.nasa.gov/library/iadc-space-debris-guidelines-revision-2.pdf.

International Civil Aviation Organization. (1944). Convention on International Civil Aviation. https://www.icao.int/publications/Documents/7300_cons.pdf.

International Organization for Standardization. (2023). ISO 24113:2019. *Space systems – Space debris mitigation requirements*. https://www.iso.org/standard/72383.html

Kea Aerospace. (2023). https://www.keaaerospace.com/.

Myers, Catherine. (2017, January 27). To Boldly go where no treaty had gone before. *Inside science*. https://www.insidescience.org/news/boldly-go-where-no-treaty-had-gone.

NASA. (n.d.). *The Artemis Accords: Principles for a safe, peaceful, and prosperous future*. https://www.nasa.gov/artemis-accords/.

New Zealand Ministry of Business, Innovation & Employment. (2022). Statutory Review of the Outer Space and High-altitude Activities Act 2017. https://www.parliament.nz/resource/en-NZ/PAP_122789/69be1c790012398b63ffa1fa354494434db50ca0

New Zealand Ministry of Business, Innovation & Employment. (2023a). *Approved payloads and other licences*. https://www.mbie.govt.nz/science-and-technology/space/permits-and-licences-for-space-activities/payloads-approved-for-launch/approved-payloads/.

New Zealand Ministry of Business, Innovation & Employment. (2023b, May). National Space Policy. https://www.mbie.govt.nz/science-and-technology/space/national-space-policy.

New Zealand Ministry of Business, Innovation & Employment. (2023c, May 18). *Permits and licences for space activities*. https://www.mbie.govt.nz/science-and-technology/space/permits-and-licences-for-space-activities.

New Zealand Ministry of Business, Innovation & Employment. (2023d, July 31). *Payloads approved for launch*. https://www.mbie.govt.nz/science-and-technology/space/permits-and-licences-for-space-activities/payloads-approved-for-launch.

New Zealand Ministry of Business, Innovation & Employment. New Zealand Ministry of Business, Innovation & Employment. (n.d.). *Modelling sustainable space and Earth environments*. https://www.mbie.govt.nz/science-and-technology/space/new-zealand-space-policy-review-consultation/modelling-sustainable-space-and-earth-environments.

New Zealand Ministry of Foreign Affairs & Trade. (2023). New Zealand Treaties Online. https://www.treaties.mfat.govt.nz/.

New Zealand Parliamentary Counsel Office. (2017a). New Zealand Legislation. Outer Space and High-altitude Activities (Definition of High-altitude Vehicle) Regulations 2017. https://www.legislation.govt.nz/act/public/2017/0029/latest/DLM6966275.html.

New Zealand Parliamentary Counsel Office. (2017b). New Zealand Legislation. Outer Space and High-altitude Activities (Licences and Permits) Regulations 2017. https://www.legislation.govt.nz/regulation/public/2017/0250/latest/DLM7364101.html

New Zealand Parliamentary Counsel Office. (2017c). New Zealand Legislation. Outer Space and High-altitude Activities Act 2017. https://www.legislation.govt.nz/act/public/2017/0029/latest/DLM6966275.html

New Zealand Space Agency. (2023, May 10). Active Debris Removal and On-Orbit Servicing Missions: Operational Policy. https://www.mbie.govt.nz/dmsdocument/26611-active-debris-removal-and-on-orbit-servicing-operational-policy-pdf

New Zealand Space Agency. (n.d.). Payloads of a size less than 1U: Operational Policy. https://www.mbie.govt.nz/dmsdocument/6985-payloads-of-a-size-less-than-1u-operational-policy

Office of the Law Revision Counsel. United States Code. (n.d.). Chapter 509 – Commercial Space Launch Activities. https://uscode.house.gov/view.xhtml?path=/prelim@title51/subtitle5/chapter509&edition=prelim.

Rocket Lab. (2023a). https://www.rocketlabusa.com/

Rocket Lab. (2023b). Upcoming Missions. www.rocketlabusa.com/missions/upcoming-missions.

Rocket Lab. (n.d.). Capstone Mission. https://www.rocketlabusa.com/missions/lunar

Santamaría, Germán. (2021, July 22). What is New Space? Solar MEMS Technologies. https://www.solar-mems.com/what-is-new-space

Satellite Applications Catapult. (n.d.). *In-space services – A major opportunity for the UK. Active debris removal*. https://issuu.com/satappscatapult/docs/in-space_services-_a_major_opportunity_for_the_uk_/s/10491735.

UN Committee on the Peaceful Uses of Outer Space. (2001, December 18). *Obtrusive space advertising and astronomical research*. Background paper by the International Astronomical Union. https://www.unoosa.org/pdf/reports/ac105/AC105_777E.pdf

UN Committee on the Peaceful Uses of Outer Space. (2010). *Terms of reference and methods of work of the working group on the long-term sustainability of outer space activities of the scientific and technical subcommittee*. Working paper submitted by the chair of the working group. https://digitallibrary.un.org/record/693562?ln=en

UN Committee on the Peaceful Uses of Outer Space. (2017, June 8). *The 'Dark and quiet skies' proposal as an initiative … for protecting the environmental observing conditions for large astronomical observatories and world citizens*. https://www.unoosa.org/res/oosadoc/data/documents/2017/aac_1052017crp/aac_1052017crp_24_0_html/AC105_2017CRP24E.pdf

UN Committee on the Peaceful Uses of Outer Space. (2018, June 27). *Guidelines for the long-term sustainability of outer space activities*. https://www.unoosa.org/res/oosadoc/data/documents/2018/aac_1052018crp/aac_1052018crp_20_0_html/AC105_2018_CRP20E.pdf

UN Committee on the Peaceful Uses of Outer Space. (2021, April 19). *Recommendation to keep dark and quiet skies for science and society*. https://www.unoosa.org/res/oosadoc/data/documents/2021/aac_105c_12021crp/aac_105c_12021crp_17_0_html/AC105_C1_2021_CRP17E.pdf

UN Office for Outer Space Affairs. (1962). *Declaration of legal principles governing the activities of states in the exploration and use of outer space*. https://www.unoosa.org/oosa/en/ourwork/spacelaw/principles/legal-principles.html

UN Office for Outer Space Affairs. (1966). *Treaty on principles governing the activities of states in the exploration and use of outer space, including the moon and other celestial bodies*. https://www.unoosa.org/oosa/en/ourwork/spacelaw/treaties/introouterspacetreaty.html

UN Office for Outer Space Affairs. (1967). *Agreement on the rescue of astronauts, the return of astronauts and the return of objects launched into outer space*. https://www.unoosa.org/pdf/gares/ARES_22_2345E.pdf

UN Office for Outer Space Affairs. (1972). *Convention on international liability for damage caused by space objects*. https://www.unoosa.org/pdf/gares/ARES_26_2777E.pdf

UN Office for Outer Space Affairs. (1976). *Convention on registration of objects launched into outer space*. https://www.unoosa.org/oosa/en/ourwork/spacelaw/treaties/introregistration-convention.html

UN Office for Outer Space Affairs. (1979). *Agreement governing the activities of states on the moon and other celestial bodies*. https://www.unoosa.org/pdf/gares/ARES_34_68E.pdf

UN Office for Outer Space Affairs. (2022). *UN committee on the peaceful uses of outer space: membership evolution*. https://www.unoosa.org/oosa/en/ourwork/copuos/members/evolution.html

UN Office for Outer Space Affairs. (2023a, June). *Working group on legal aspects of space resource activities*. 66 COPUOS. https://www.unoosa.org/oosa/en/ourwork/copuos/lsc/space-resources/index.html

UN Office for Outer Space Affairs. (2023b). *Long-term sustainability of outer space activities*. https://www.unoosa.org/oosa/en/ourwork/topics/long-term-sustainability-of-outer-space-activities.html

UN Office for Outer Space Affairs. (2023c). *Status of international agreements relating to activities in outer space*. https://www.unoosa.org/oosa/en/ourwork/spacelaw/treaties/status/index.html

UN Office for Outer Space Affairs. (n.d.). *Working group on the definition and delimitation of outer space of the legal subcommittee*. https://www.unoosa.org/oosa/en/ourwork/copuos/lsc/ddos/index.html

UN Office of Disarmament Affairs. (1967). *Treaty on principles governing the activities of states in the exploration and use of outer space, including the moon and other celestial bodies*. https://treaties.unoda.org/t/outer_space

UN Treaty Collection. (1967). *Treaty on principles governing the activities of states in the exploration and use of outer space, including the moon and other celestial bodies*. https://treaties.un.org/pages/showdetails.aspx?objid=0800000280128cbd

UN Treaty Collection. (1976). *Convention on registration of objects launched into outer space*. https://treaties.un.org/Pages/showDetails.aspx?objid=08000002800361b4

Wall, Mike. (2020, May 16). *Japanese satellite filled with 'shooting star' pellets won't spawn artificial meteor shower after all*. Space.com. https://www.space.com/japan-shooting-star-satellite-artificial-meteor-shower-glitch.html

Chapter 8
Transformational Trends in India's Space Programme

K. R. Sridhara Murthi and V. Gopalakrishnan

Indian Space: A Perspective of the Past Five Decades

India has completed 52 years since it sent into orbit its maiden satellite Aryabhata, an experimental scientific satellite, using a Soviet launch vehicle.[1] Since that modest step, the Indian Space Research Organisation (ISRO), the national space agency, has passed many eventful milestones. For most part of its journey, it has kept the ethos and inspiration given by Vikram Ambalal Sarabhai, who is considered as the founding father of India's space programme. He envisioned the national developmental context as a strong focus for developing and using space technology.[2] He also gave the mantra of a self-reliant approach. Within a decade of its formation, ISRO demonstrated its ability to develop its maiden launch vehicle, SLV-3, and its capability to launch objects into space.[3] By the next decade, taking some pioneering steps in the use of the emerging technology of solid-state detectors and through the innovative design of optics for sensors, it launched its first operational Earth observation satellite IRS-1A,[4] with a performance comparable to the globally leading observational spacecraft of the time. The indigenously developed second

[1] https://www.isro.gov.in/aryabhata_1.html DoA: June 10, 2023.

[2] https://www.isro.gov.in/sarabhaiformer.html DoA: June 10, 2023.

[3] https://www.isro.gov.in/mission_SLV_3E2.html DoA: June 10, 2023.

[4] Samudraiah, D. (2013, March). Indian Earth Observations Payloads for Earth Observation. NNRMS Bulletin (B) -37, pp. 19–26.

K. R. S. Murthi (✉)
Honorary Director, International Institute of Space Law and Professor, JAIN Deemed-to-be University, Bengaluru, Karnataka, India

V. Gopalakrishnan
Indian Space Research Organisation and Adjunct Faculty, National Institute of Advanced Studies, Bangalore, Karnataka, India

M. A. Pozza (ed.), *Ascending to Space*, Space Law and Policy,
https://doi.org/10.1007/978-981-97-0714-0_8

generation of the geostationary satellite, INSAT-2A, which was launched in 1992,[5] was a step ahead of the first-generation spacecraft. ISRO's journey over the past five decades has been studded with many such milestones, including the launch in 2008 of Chandrayaan-1,[6] the lunar orbiter that confirmed the presence of water on the Moon's surface.[7] The successful conduct of the Mars orbiter mission through insertion into a Martian orbit on 24 September 2014 was another notable milestone. ISRO's first successful launch of the geostationary satellite launch vehicle GSLV was accomplished in 2001.[8] Six key attributes characterise the outcomes of India's space programmes over these decades, namely the capability for autonomous space access, cost-effectiveness, applications competence, international cooperation, the ability to bring socio-economic impact, and strategic potency.[9]

As at the end of August 2022, ISRO has performed 115 satellite missions, 85 launch missions, 13 students' satellite launches and two re-entry missions, and has provided launch services for 345 foreign satellites from 34 countries.[10] The human resources strength within the space agency and its constituent units in the last decade, however, has been maintained at 17,000 despite the growing number of activities.[11] The Indian space industry, which comprises some 500 companies, supports the programmes implemented by the space agency, engaging an estimated 45,000-strong workforce.[12]

Over the past 45 years, the budgetary support has amounted to about ₹1200 billion.[13] The satellites developed and operated by ISRO are state-of-the-art. Currently 53 spacecraft are operated to serve diverse applications, such as satellite communications, earth observations, navigation services and scientific investigations.[14] The space communication satellites comprising 15 spacecraft provide more

---

[5] https://www.isro.gov.in/INSAT_2A.html DoA: June 10, 2023.

[6] https://www.isro.gov.in/Chandrayaan_1.html DoA: June 10, 2023.

[7] https://www.planetary.org/space-missions/chandrayaan-1 DoA: June 10, 2023.

[8] https://www.isro.gov.in/mission_GSLV_D1.htm, DoA: June 10, 2023.

[9] Kasturirangan, K. (2013). India in Space – A Conceptual Framework for the 21st Century. Dr. Satish C Seth Memorial Futurology Lecture series 5 organised by Indian Council of Management & Future and delivered at New Delhi on April 8, 2013.

[10] https://www.isro.gov.in/missions. DoA: June 10, 2023.

[11] Department Of Space. (2022). *Annual Report 2021–2022*. Bangalore: Government of India, Department of Space. Retrieved 06 30, 2023, from https://www.isro.gov.in/media_isro/pdf/AnnualReport/annual_report_english.pdf, DoA: June 10, 2023.

[12] Government of India. (2020, June 24). Unlocking India's Potential in Space Sector. Retrieved from ISRO: https://www.isro.gov.in/UNLOCKING.html, DoA: June 10, 2023.

[13] This pertains to expenditures of the Department of Space, Government of India during the fiscal years from 1976–77 to 2020–21. Data for the period up to 2004–2005 are sourced from Shankar, U. (2007), Economics of India's Space Programme. New Delhi, India: Oxford University Press. Data for the period from 2005–06 to 2008–09 are from the Annual reports published by Department of Space, Government of India. Data for the subsequent period up to FY 2020–21 are from Centre for Budget and Governance Accountability (2023, February, 25). Retrieved July 1, 2023, from OpenBudgetsIndia: https://openbudgetsindia.org/organisations/department-of-space

[14] https://www.isro.gov.in/Indian_Space_Situational_Assessment_2022.html, DoA: June10, 2023.

than 200 transponders[15] in different frequencies such as the C, extended C and Ku bands. The earth observation satellites are also diverse in terms of the spectral, spatial and temporal characteristics of their instruments and missions.[16] In addition to observations in the optical wavelengths, they also support radar imaging. The navigation satellite known as NavIC (Navigation with Indian Constellation) currently consists of eight satellites with coverage extending from latitude 30° South to 50° North, longitude 30° to 130° East, with a positional accuracy of better than 20 m in the primary service area.[17] These navigational satellites are also a component of the Worldwide Radio Navigation System. Three scientific spacecraft are operational, the Mars Orbiter Mission (MOM) spacecraft, the Astrosat and Chandrayaan-2.[18]

Transforming Programmes

The challenges and transformational trends in satellites are driven globally by the emergence of less expensive small satellite constellations in low earth orbits (LEO), coupled with the great expansion of the private sector's role in offering services in domestic markets and further exploring global market opportunities. There has also been a trend for large-sized high-power satellite platforms operating in geostationary orbit for certain applications. The global picture also indicates that there has been an asymmetric creation of capacity in relation to the demand, with varying levels of regulation in different markets. Therefore, the risk perceptions and entry barriers are significant in certain segments of the space industry. Their developments are also significantly influenced by domestic ecosystems and governmental interventions. Future demand for spacecraft capacity in India is robust, driven by the needs of national security as well as burgeoning civil and commercial requirements. Integration of satellites into much broader service architectures that span the digital economy, business intelligence, disaster management systems, resource management in agriculture, water resources, energy, health, infrastructure, logistics and transportation can be realistic.

Indian space launch vehicles have proven their capabilities for launching into any type of earth orbit and interplanetary mission.[19] Besides meeting domestic needs, the Indian launch vehicles have proved to be attractive and reliable for customers worldwide for small- and modest-sized launches.[20] This is evidenced by 424 successful launches of customer satellite payloads from 34 countries without any

[15] https://www.isro.gov.in/spacecraft/communication-satellites, DoA: June 10, 2023.

[16] https://www.isro.gov.in/EarthObservationSatellites.html DoA: June 10, 2023.

[17] Indian Space Research Organisation. (n.d.). Indian Regional Navigation Satellite System (IRNSS): NavIC. https://www.isro.gov.in/irnss-programme, DoA: June 10, 2023.

[18] https://www.isro.gov.in/spacesciexp.html DoA: June 10, 2023.

[19] https://www.isro.gov.in/Launchers.html DoA: June 10, 2023.

[20] https://www.isro.gov.in/launchservices.html DoA: June 10, 2023.

Table 8.1 Indian launch vehicle characteristics[a]

Launch vehicle	Total lift-off mass	Payload capacity	Number of launches
SLV	17 tonnes	40 kg LEO	4
ASLV	40 tonnes	150 kg LEO	4
PSLV-XL	320 tonnes	1750 kg SSO 1425 kg GTO	55
GSLV-Mk II	420 tonnes	2200 kg GTO	14
GSLV-Mk III	640 tonnes	4000 kg GTO	6

Additional note: Not included in the above are the three technology experiment missions, namely, Scramjet-TD, Reusable Launch Vehicle (RLV-TD) and a Crew Escape System. A newly developed small satellite launch vehicle (SSLV) with a payload capability of 500 kg had a successful developmental flight on February 10, 2023

[a]Data Source: Indian Launchers, https://www.isro.gov.in/Launchers.html. DoA: July 15, 2023

failure.[21] The capability of the current range of vehicles is summarised in Table 8.1. The major challenges triggering transformative trends in this area are the developments towards the reusability of space transportation systems and the lowering of the cost of access to space. This is being addressed in India through the development of a high-thrust semi-cryogenic engine and stage, which can replace the earth-storable core stage in the current GSLV Mk III launch vehicle (renamed as LVM 3, Launch Vehicle Mk III) to enhance its geostationary transfer orbit payload capability to 6 tonnes.[22] By further improving the performance of the solid boosters and cryogenic upper stage with additional fuel loading and clustering of the upper-stage engines, the capability of launching 10-tonne payloads into a geostationary transfer orbit or a 20-tonne payload into LEO can be envisaged.[23] This strategy can reduce both lead time and resource demands.

The existing Launch Vehicle Mark 3 (LVM3) has been chosen as the launch vehicle for the human space flight programme, and will be human-rated (HLVM3).[24] Human space flight will be implemented through developing additional systems essential for the safety and performance of human transportation into orbit, their activities in space and their return. The necessary infrastructure support for the mission is being built simultaneously.[25] The human space flight strategy in India does not support very large-scale diversion of resources from beneficial applications of space but it instead is aimed at providing foundational capabilities, technological diversity and new mission competencies.[26] The programme could enable mutually

[21] https://www.isro.gov.in/media_isro/pdf/ForeignSatellites/424_foreign_satellites.pdf DoA: July 4, 2023.

[22] Kasturirangan, K. (2021). Evolution of India's Space Transportation Systems. In: B. N. Suresh (Ed.), *Space and Beyond*. Singapore: Springer.

[23] https://thelogicalindian.com/trending/isros-next-generation-launch-vehicle-for-heavier-payloads-ready-by-2030-38365 DoA: July 04, 2023.

[24] https://www.isro.gov.in/Gaganyaan.html DoA: June 10, 2023.

[25] Ibid 25.

[26] https://www.isro.gov.in/Gaganyaan.html DoA: June 10, 2023.

rewarding future collaboration with international partners, while energising the downstream industries in India for further innovations. This is due to the proposed approach to involve industry in the realisation of flight systems on the one hand and also due to the potential for spin-offs in the fields of special materials, medicine, industrial safety and many others.

ISRO's ground facilities have been expanding in tandem with the need to advance space system capabilities.[27] These also include elements that contribute to Space Situational Awareness (SSA) and to the safe, secure and sustainable operation of Indian space assets.[28] The domestic SSA infrastructure includes a multi-object tracking radar, optical telescopes and a control centre known as NETRA (NEtwork for space objects TRacking and Analysis).[29] In addition to the reliance on domestic resources, in meeting its SSA needs, India is also actively engaged in international cooperation. Directorate of Space Situational Awareness and Management (DSSAM) engages in evolving improved operational mechanisms to protect Indian space assets through effective coordination amongst ISRO/DOS Centres, other space agencies and international bodies, and establishment of necessary supporting infrastructures, such as additional observation facilities for space object monitoring, and a control centre for centralised SSA activities.[30]

Transformative Trends for the Indian Space Economy

The recent past has witnessed favourable winds for transitioning the currently public investment-dominated space towards public–private partnerships and the eventual creation of a strong private sector role. The urgency for engaging and tapping the skills, knowledge and talents of young Indians forming part of the 1.4 billion population of India, whose median age is just below 29 years[31] needs no overemphasis. In addition, with an environment of significant economic performance in the post-Covid period,[32] indicative of sustainable future growth in the range of 6–8 per cent,[33] with the rising demands for democratisation of information, and above all, with the needs clearly manifesting for building a secure and equitable society, the potential for expanding space applications and space business can be

[27] https://www.isro.gov.in/GroundSegmentActivities.html DoA: July 05, 2023.

[28] ISRO SSA Control Centre Inaugurated by Dr. K. Sivan, Chairman, ISRO/ Secretary, DOS, December 14, 2020, https://www.isro.gov.in/ISRO%20SSAControl%20Centre.html (DoA: June 10, 2023).

[29] Ibid 29.

[30] Ibid 29.

[31] National Statistical Office. (2022). Youth in India. New Delhi: Ministry of Statistics and Programme Implementation, Government of India.

[32] https://www.indiabudget.gov.in/economicsurvey/doc/eschapter/echap01.pdf DoA: July 5, 2023.

[33] Ibid 33.

multifold. Space continues to be a powerful instrument for managing social divides and reducing vulnerability. The imperatives of international cooperation in the scientific exploration of space and for addressing issues of human development at a planetary level are gaining wider attention.

The Indian space economy is estimated to be worth US$7 billion.[34] This represents 1.57 per cent of the global space economy of US$447 billion in 2020.[35] In harmony with the global trend, the space economy of India is dominated by services, with the overall business impact constituting 80 per cent of its total size, while the share of public expenditure is 20 per cent.[36] Thus, there is a fourfold multiplier effect. Industry participation is leading to the realisation of the spin-off potential of space in terms of innovative products and processes. The services from space comprise direct-to-home television services, broadband internet, imaging services, and positioning and location-based services.[37] An industrial supply chain is well developed for providing components, equipment and subsystem assemblies for satellites and launch vehicles. In addition, industry also provides ground systems used for the manufacture, testing and assembly of space systems and for applications, which is indicative of the growing need for more space-based services as demands grow.

The budgetary allocations to space activities during the last 5 years ranged between 0.04 and 0.05 per cent of GDP.[38] A major part of the budget caters to the needs of operational services and human space flight, while support is also extended to scientific missions. Future plans for scientific missions include a solar observation spacecraft Aditya-L1,[39] an X-ray Observatory X-pose, a mission to Venus called Shukrayaan-1[40] and a twin satellite mission for aeronomy (upper atmosphere) studies, named Disha.[41] Advances in space technology now enable a capability to directly serve at the individual level from space. Personal navigation from

---

[34]Brunswick, Shelli. (2021, May 19). India at the Inflection Point: A New Era in the Space Ecosystem. *Space News*. https://spacenews.com/op-ed-india-at-the-inflection-point-a-new-era-in-the-space-ecosystem

[35]The Space Foundation. (2021). The Space Report 2021 – Q2:1, The Authoritative Guide to Global Space Activity, 1. https://www.thespacereport.org/

[36]Murthi and Gopalakrishnan (2022). Unlocking India's Space Sector: Legal and Policy Challenges. In Bhat and Guha, Fundamentals of National Space Laws (pp. 120–133). Gurgaon: Thomson Reuters.

[37]Murthi K R, Sridhara. (2017). A Review of India's Commercial Space Efforts. In book: Space India 2.0 – Commerce, Policy, Security and Governance Perspectives (pp. I.3) Publisher: Observer Research Foundation. Editors: Rajeswari Pillai Rajagopalan, Narayan Prasad.

[38]Indian Space Research Organisation. (2017–22). Annual Reports 2017–18 through 2021–22. https://www.isro.gov.in/annual-reports

[39]https://www.isro.gov.in/aditya-l1-first-indian-mission-to-study-sun, DoA: June 10, 2023.

[40]https://www.isro.gov.in/update/05-may-2022/isro-synergises-national-efforts-to-study-planet-venus

[41]'ISRO plans to build two satellites, DISHA-L&H, to study upper atmosphere', WION, https://www.wionews.com/india-news/isro-plans-to-build-disha-lh-two-satellites-meant-for-studying-upper-atmosphere-477883 (DoA: June 10, 2023).

smartphones with the use of satellite-delivered positioning signals is a common example for this. Such possibilities represent a potential to expand services in India where 350 million of its population are in the middle-income group, with a sizeable disposable income and appetite for consumption.[42] There are 750 million subscribers to smartphones,[43] and this is poised to grow further. An example is the potential for the growth of services by convergence of earth observation, positioning and other geospatial technologies for seamless integration into a broad range of IT-enabled services.[44] The advent of new data analytics tools and advances in Artificial Intelligence, machine learning, deep learning, blockchain and novel visualisation tools are aiding this transformation. Another trend that has begun in the field of space is the interest of the Indian private sector in global collaborations, as can be seen in the case of the OneWeb constellation, getting installed by UK-based OneWeb, which is backed by an Indian telecommunication service provider.[45] The collaboration between One Web and India takes shape with the largest investment coming from India through Bharti Global and the commitment expressed by One Web to enhance connectivity in India. Thirty-six satellites of the One Web's constellation have been launched by India's LVM3 on a commercial basis.[46] ISRO's earth observation satellites, being inherently capable of imaging globally, can achieve greater viability through global services and collaborative strategies. Further, since terrestrial imaging and electronics have witnessed revolutionary advances in recent decades, it is opportune to apply these to the space domain through innovations and 'spin-in' space developments. Low Earth Orbit (LEO) constellations will also change the connectivity paradigm in remote and rural geographies with low latency and better security, required for modern cloud-based applications and internet applications, as predicted by Telesat, one of the largest successful global satellite operators.[47] LEO constellations can thus be exploited for greater economies by a global marketing approach and use of less expensive but highly reliable technologies developed for consumer electronics.

Aspirations are aired in India to increase the present US$7 billion space economy to the US$50 billion level.[48] This dream calls for quantum leaps such as lowering the space launch cost tenfold for a given mass of payload, or a hundredfold increase in

---

[42] https://www.thehindubusinessline.com/opinion/does-anyone-miss-the-middle-class/article65237750.ece DoA: July 5, 2023.

[43] https://economictimes.indiatimes.com/industry/cons-products/electronics/india-to-have-1-billion-smartphone-users-by-2026-deloitte/articleshow/89750324.cms?from=mdr DoA: July 5, 2023.

[44] Sridhara Murthi, K. R., Kadursrinivas, Rao M. (2018). In emerging EO Newspace Global Markets – Challenges for Indian Remote sensing Systems. Presented at the 69th International Astronautical Congress, Bremen, Germany, 2018.

[45] https://economictimes.indiatimes.com/news/science/committed-to-provide-connectivity-across-india-by-2023-oneweb/articleshow/95045430.cms?from=mdr DoA: July 5, 2023.

[46] https://www.isro.gov.in/LVM3M2MissionLandingPage.html DoA: June 10, 2023.

[47] https://www.telesat.com/blog/why-leo-is-the-new-star-of-the-space-market/, DoA: June 10, 2023.

[48] Brunswick, India at the Inflection Point.

Table 8.2 Perspectives for multifold growth: India's space economy (created by the authors of this chapter)

Strategy	Impact	Challenge
Lowering launch cost ten-fold	Increase of demand multi-fold	Reusable systems development, Managing global competition, Creation of robust market through long-term exploration agenda
Increasing bandwidth hundred-fold and more	Transformative growth of downstream industry	Multi-beam satellites, New technologies, LEO/MEO constellations, Integration with terrestrial system
Information at consumer level, powered by space	Democratisation of info, knowledge economy	National system of innovations
Collaborations aiming at expanded markets	Transcending the lag	Balancing self-reliance
New applications – health and education	Greater access, quality	Using the power of academic sector

bandwidth handling capacity in a given size of spacecraft. it may also call for strategies that combine stronger roles for the domestic and global markets. The key developmental needs of India as it is emerging to be the third largest economy in the world provide the basis for the growth of the space economy to the aspired level. The strategy, impact and challenges associated with this aspiration are summarised in Table 8.2.

India has consistently endeavoured to expand international cooperation in the peaceful uses of outer space.[49] It is evidenced by its cooperative endeavours, which span 60 countries and five multinational organisations.[50] Diverse means of cooperation are pursued, including (i) the conduct of joint missions such as the Indo-French Megha Tropics mission[51] for studying water cycle in the tropical regions, (ii) hosting of payloads from other space agencies as seen in the case of Chandrayaan –1 that carried four instruments from Europe and an American instrument,[52] thereby contributing to the cooperation with ESA and NASA, and (iii) active participation in multilateral forums under the aegis of the United Nations, as well as many initiatives to strengthen regional cooperation as explained further here. India has also been providing capacity-building support to other developing nations through its Centre for Space Science and Technology Education in Asia and the Pacific[53] with a total number of beneficiaries of various training programmes including the online ones to more than 3700 officials from 124 countries. In fulfilment of India's commitment

[49] https://www.isro.gov.in/InternationalCoOperation.html, DoA: June 10, 2023.

[50] https://www.unoosa.org/documents/pdf/copuos/stsc/2022/statements/4_India.pdf, DoA: June 10, 2023.

[51] https://www.mosdac.gov.in/megha-tropiques, DoA: June 10, 2023.

[52] https://www.issdc.gov.in/docs/ch1/chandrayaan1_payload.pdf, DoA: June 10, 2023.

[53] https://www.isro.gov.in/international-cooperation, DoA: June 10, 2023.

made in UNISPACE+50, India successfully completed the third batch of UNNATI training on nanosatellite assembly and Training, from 15 October to 15 December 2022, benefitting 31 officials representing 19 countries.[54] Other noteworthy current cooperative initiatives include the South Asian Satellite, a joint Lunar Polar Mission which is being studied with JAXA of Japan, the concept of a BRICS remote sensing constellation, a small satellite for Bhutan and the development of NISAR (NASA-ISRO Synthetic Aperture Radar mission).[55] In the NISAR mission partnership, NASA is providing the mission's L-band synthetic aperture radar, a high-rate communication subsystem for science data, GPS receivers, a solid-state recorder and payload data subsystem. ISRO is providing the spacecraft bus, the S-band radar, the launch vehicle and associated launch services.[56]

Policy Reforms

Turning to the transformation in the policy and legal environment, major reforms were initiated by the central government, as announced by the Finance Minister in May 2020 as part of the *Aathma Nirbhar Bharat (Self-reliant India)* mission.[57] It was revealed that a new institution named the Indian National Space Promotion and Authorization Centre (IN-SPACe) had been created.[58] While inaugurating its headquarters, Prime Minister Narendra Modi set the tone for the reforms by terming them an opportunity to showcase the unprecedented talent of the youth of India and to bring about a revolution in the country's space industry.[59] He reiterated the role of IN-SPACe in facilitating the transfer of technologies between private sector start-ups and ISRO and also spoke about their access to facilities created by the government.[60] Thus, IN-SPACe would serve as a single window mechanism to support private sector expansion. Roles identified for IN-SPACe include (i) building of launch vehicles and satellites and providing space-based services; (ii) sharing of space infrastructure; (iii) establishment of temporary facilities within the premises and a reserve; (iv) establishment of new space infrastructure and facilities by

[54] Statement of Indian delegation on General Exchange of Views in the 66th Session of COPUOS, 2023, https://www.unoosa.org/documents/pdf/copuos/2023/Statements/31_AM/4_India_31May_AM.pdf (DoA: June 10, 2023).

[55] Ibid 55.

[56] https://nisar.jpl.nasa.gov/mission/isro-partnership/ (DoA: June 10, 2023).

[57] Ministry of Finance, India. (2020). Finance Minister announces new horizons of growth; structural reforms across Eight Sectors paving way for Aathma Nirbhar Bharat. New Delhi: Press Information Bureau.

[58] Government of India. (2021, October 2–8). Gazette of India, No CG-KA-W-04102021-230,126, 5.

[59] https://www.pmindia.gov.in/en/news_updates/pm-inaugurates-headquarters-of-in-space-at-bopal-ahmedabad/ DoA: June 10, 2023.

[60] Ibid.

non-government private entities; (v) initiation of launch campaign and launch; (vi) registration of Indian satellites; and (vii) usage of spacecraft data and rolling-out of space-based services. It is reported that about 60 start-ups have registered with IN-SPACe since the unlocking of the space sector was enabled by the government.[61] The areas of proposals for consideration include satellites, lunch vehicles, space applications, ground systems and debris management.[62] Start-up activities in India in the past few years have shown widely diverse business areas, ranging from the development of small satellite systems to that of launch vehicle systems. Some also dealt with advanced areas such as planetary spacecraft rovers, remote sensing applications based on analytics, laser space communications, and advanced electric propulsion thrusters and other components.[63]

The key needs and interests which have been driving policy changes in the field of space communications could be argued to be classified under three areas: (i) attracting private commercial industry towards space segment investments; (ii) a timely and responsive regulatory environment and user-friendly regulations for capacity lease from foreign systems; and (iii) a level playing field for public and private sector, ensured through regulation. In the field of earth observations, it is pertinent to consider that perhaps the key needs, which relate to the policies for access to high-resolution data in harmony with global practices and those relevant for the generation, include sharing, dissemination and value addition of geospatial data in a business-friendly environment.[64]

Through the enunciation of an overarching space policy,[65] the government is seen to be actively attempting to bridge the gaps in policy and regulatory space. These not only address areas such as the ease of doing business and facilitating the use of government facilities, but also promoting the establishment of space industry clusters and manufacturing hubs; ensuring necessary compliance with the obligations of international agreements to which India is a party; ensuring safety and the security aspects of space activities; and facilitating technology transfer.[66] This overarching policy is also expected to address diverse segments of space activities, including services in the field of space communications, remote sensing and space transportation systems.

[61] https://www.timesnownews.com/business-economy/industry/around-60-startups-registered-with-isro-since-unlocking-of-indian-space-sector-govt-article-92809322, DoA: June 10, 2023.

[62] https://www.IN-SPACe.gov.in/IN-SPACe?id=IN-SPACe_index DoA: June 10, 2023.

[63] https://www.startupindia.gov.in/nsa2021results/space.html DoA: June 10, 2023.

[64] Kaul, Ranjana (2017), *A Review of India's Geospatial Policy*. In book: Space India 2.0 – Commerce, Policy, Security and Governance Perspectives (pp.I.3) Publisher: Observer Research Foundation. Editors: Rajeswari Pillai Rajagopalan, Narayan Prasad.

[65] https://www.isro.gov.in/IndiaSpacePolicy.html DoA: June 10, 2023.

[66] Ibid.

Space Security Perspectives

The twin aspects of security from space and security in space are closely intertwined in the context of India's national security.[67] The prevailing national and international environment has been driving the need to consider security holistically in its multiple dimensions, ranging from the requirements to effectively deal with geopolitical challenges and the modern manifestations of terrorism, to the overcoming of impacts due to environmental disasters and disharmony in society.[68] In the particular domain of space, there is also the need to derive the maximum societal and economic contributions from space without compromising the priorities of national security. One could argue that this calls for reinforcing the mechanisms of coordination, backed by systems for sound predictive analysis of outcomes of different strategies in a dynamic environment.

The heritage of, and capabilities built into, the civilian space programme can act as a springboard for building further space capabilities for national security. With the beginnings made so far in the creation of dedicated capacity for secured communications, high-resolution imaging and PNT (Position, Navigation and Timing) services,[69] further strides are to be taken, addressing the diverse security challenges faced by India. Further, the needs and demands for SSA, and for safe, secure and reliable operations of India's space assets ought to be strengthened. Besides focused national efforts, this also implies an increased level of international cooperation.

India's position on space security appears to hinge upon three principal directions. The first direction is advancement of efforts for preventive and precautionary conduct at global level on matters of vitally common interest, to be achieved through binding multilateral regulatory regimes with the widest possible participation. The second direction is the development and application of necessary space technology tools to exercise its legitimate sovereign rights and secure its national security interests inter alia through appropriate deterrence and defence capabilities. The third direction relies on intensification of international cooperation in the peaceful uses of outer space and in strengthening the regional and international security.[70]

The above multi-pronged strategy constitutes a holistic approach which integrates the pursuit of India's legitimate national security interests with adherence to the principles of international space law. This is also consistent with the position taken

[67] Ajay Lele. (2016). India's Space Security Policy: A Proposal. IDSA Policy Brief, April 29. 2016, Institute for Defence Studies and Analyses, New Delhi.

[68] Ajay Lele. (2017). India's Strategic Space Programme: From Apprehensive Beginner to Ardent Operator. In book: Space India 2.0 – Commerce, Policy, Security and Governance Perspectives (pp. I.3) Publisher: Observer Research Foundation. Editors: Rajeswari Pillai Rajagopalan, Narayan Prasad.

[69] https://carnegieendowment.org/2022/09/01/india-s-space-priorities-are-shifting-toward-national-security-pub-87809

[70] Murthi, KR Sridhara and Rao, Mukund. (2014). ICoC: Perspective for India. In report: Awaiting Launch: Perspectives on the Draft ICoC for Outer Space Activities, Observer Research Foundation, New Delhi. Dr. Rajeswari Pillai Rajagopalan and Daniel A. Porras (Editors).

by India that threats of any form to damage the space assets or to disrupt the space-based services are to be prohibited through legally binding instruments.[71] Efforts are to be continued to evolve such instruments through relevant multilateral international fora including the Conference on Disarmament and UNCOPUOS. Space and ground assets serving the national security or even the commercial and civilian needs, have to be protected to ensure uninterrupted services to all users. These are considered as integral components of the critical national infrastructure to be safeguarded as part of the overall national space security measures.

Global environment is also seeing an increasing tendency towards the weaponisation of outer space and also advances in counter-space capabilities.[72] Demonstration of deterrence capability for ensuring the national security and protection of space assets to render unhindered services is a legitimate need. India's transparent conduct of the test known as Mission Shakti on May 27, 2019, is an example of the above context.[73] The test involved one of its microsatellites, which was subjected to an intentional destruction at low altitude by a ballistic missile defence interceptor.[74] Space technology use for Ballistic Missile Defence (BMD) has been an imperative aspect of the security environment around India and the BMD capabilities developed by the Defence Research and Development (DRDO) address both at the exo-atmospheric as well as endo-atmospheric altitudes.[75] The need for simultaneous tracking and stronger defence against multi-objects entry has also been addressed.

A related area is the application of space systems for early warning mechanisms where capabilities are progressively being strengthened. Effective use of the instrument of international cooperation is integral to the overall strategy. In the backdrop of the trend of establishing dedicated space command units by various spacefaring nations across the globe, India has established the Defence Space Research Agency (DSRA) in June 2019 to provide organisation focus and coordination for research and development of systems and technologies relevant to this field. Another domain of service is the Space Based Automatic Identification System (AIS-SB) which provides timely information about[76] seafaring vessels from space systems towards

[71] 'OEWG on Space 2022', https://meaindia.nic.in/cdgeneva/?14379?000 (DoA: June 10, 2023).

[72] 'Global Counter space Capabilities Report', Secure World Foundation, https://swfound.org/counterspace/ (DoA: June 10, 2023).

[73] https://www.mea.gov.in/Speeches-Statements.htm?dtl/31180/Speech+by+Prime

[74] Brian Weeden, 'Indian Direct Ascent Anti-Satellite Testing' Secure World Foundation, https://swfound.org/media/207370/swf-indian-da-asat-may-2022.pdf (DoA: June 10, 2023).

[75] Ministry of Defence, GOI, 'DRDO conducts successful maiden flight-test of Phase-II Ballistic Missile Defence interceptor off Odisha coast', https://pib.gov.in/PressReleasePage.aspx?PRID=1873179 (DoA: June 10, 2023).

[76] Pranav R. Stayanath, 'India's Space Security Policy, part 2: getting space security right', Space Review, Dt. February 20, 2023, https://www.thespacereview.com/article/4536/1 (DOA: June 10, 2023).

efficient monitoring of their movements. The AIS-SB provides data in the standard format to all the Indian Users especially for Maritime Domain Awareness (MDA).[77]

Uncontrolled growth of debris in outer space and its catastrophic effect on space objects of all nations has been a serious concern to international space community and can be assessed as a threat to national security whereby access to space could be compromised. India has been voluntarily implementing various measures to mitigate the problem of debris in outer space, in accordance with the space debris mitigation guidelines endorsed by the UN General Assembly.[78] India's implementation of debris guidelines covers diverse phases of its space activities including design, fabrication, launch, on-orbit operations and disposal of space objects. India has also displayed its commitment to implement the 21 guidelines on Long Term Sustainability (LTS) of outer space activities, evolved through a Working Group under UNCOPUOS and adopted by the UN General Assembly in June 2019.[79] It is also contributing further as the chair of the working group towards deliberations on LTS 2.0, towards evolving additional guidelines and sharing of experiences on the implementation of the earlier adopted guidelines.

Addressing the need for SSA, India established a Multiple Object Tracking Radar for monitoring space debris.[80] Further, efforts are under way for establishing optical tracking capabilities too.[81] With the existing capabilities in space debris monitoring, modelling and simulation, collision avoidance measures are practised diligently for protecting space assets from space debris.[82] A dedicated centre for SSA management was established in December 2020, for the observation and monitoring of space objects and the space environment.[83] The centre is engaged in processing observations and carries out various functions such as orbit determination, object characterisation and cataloguing, analysis of the evolution of the space environment, risk assessments and mitigation measures. The centre also promotes data exchanges and

---

[77] Indian Space Science Data Center. (2018–19). https://www.issdc.gov.in/others.html, DoA: June 10, 2023.

[78] India's Statement 61st LSC of UNCOPUOS on General Exchange of views on legal mechanisms relating to Space Debris Mitigation and Remediation measures, https://www.unoosa.org/documents/pdf/copuos/lsc/2022/Statements/4AprAM/11_India_4_April_AM.pdf (DoA: June 10, 2023).

[79] Brunswick, (2021). *India at the Inflection Point*. https://spacenews.com/op-ed-india-at-the-inflection-point-a-new-era-in-the-space-ecosystem/ed | India at the Inflection Point: A New Era in the Space Ecosystem – SpaceNews DoA: July 12, 2023.

[80] 'India's Efforts in Space Debris Management', Presentation by Indian Delegation in 59th Session of STSC, UNCOPUOS, 10th February, 2022 https://www.unoosa.org/documents/pdf/copuos/stsc/2022/19_INDIA_Item8_Indias_efforts_in_Space_Debris_Management.pdf (DoA: June 10, 2023).

[81] Ibid Note 30.

[82] Ibid Note 30.

[83] https://www.isro.gov.in/update/16-dec-2020/isro-ssacontrol-centre-inaugurated-dr-k-sivan-chairman-isro-secretary-dos DoA: June 10, 2023.

collaboration with international agencies such as IADC and other space agencies.[84] A recent instance of progress in this field is the signing of a memorandum of understanding (MoU) between India and the United States in 2022 for rendering mutual assistance and sharing data on the potential conjunction of space objects, collision avoidance measures and space weather.[85]

More recently, a holistic system named the ISRO System for Safe & Sustainable Operations Management (IS4OM) was formally dedicated to the nation in July 2022.[86] It is configured to ensure the safety of India's space assets to help the sustained utilisation of outer space for national development.[87] The system is aimed to safeguard all Indian space assets by preventing collision threats from space objects through specific orbit manoeuvres, and by complying with international guidelines on post-mission disposal and satellites' end-of-life operations. In order to comply with the international obligations of all space activities,[88] including that of private sectors of a State, it is contemplated to extend the scope of SSA activities to private sector space activities, which are engaged in all-round space activities, a move promoted through the space reforms initiatives introduced by the government in 2020.[89]

Cyber Security Protection Measures

The intersection of space and cyberspace is an integral component of broader security and foreign policy considerations in every space-dependent country.[90] With their progressive growth, the space and cyber sectors are interconnected and interdependent. Increasing reliance of satellites, ground stations and other space assets on the internet and other cyber networks for their functions creates vulnerability to cyber-attacks.[91]

---

[84] 'Indian Space Situational Awareness for the year 2022- Highlights', https://www.isro.gov.in/Indian_Space_Situational_Assessment_2022.html, DoA: June 10, 2023.

[85] Lele, Ajay. (2022, April 15). Indo–US SSA Agreement: Military Collaboration in Space. https://www.financialexpress.com/defence/indo-us-ssa-agreement-military-collaboration-in-space/2492962

[86] https://www.isro.gov.in/update/11-jul-2022/dedication-of-isro-system-safe-sustainable-operations-management-is4om-to-nation, DoA: June 10, 2023.

[87] Indian Space Policy, 2023, https://www.isro.gov.in/media_isro/pdf/IndianSpacePolicy2023.pdf, DoA: June 10, 2023.

[88] Article VI and IX of Outer Space Treaty (OST), 1967.

[89] Annual Report 20–21 – NewSpace India Limited (NSIL), pp. 09.

[90] Robinson, Jana. (2016, February 15). Governance challenges at the intersection of space and cyber security. *The Space Review*. https://www.thespacereview.com/article/2923/1, DoA: June 10, 2023.

[91] Baylon, Caroline. (2014, December). Challenges at the Intersection of Cyber Security and Space Security – Country and International Institution Perspectives. Chatham House Research Paper.

ISRO has implemented fortification measures such as[92] strong encryption of commands and authentication protocols in its older in-orbit remote sensing satellites to prevent unauthorised access to them. In order to control illegal access to information from the satellites (such as payload and satellite data), other measures such as directional transmissions, the use of dummy data and limiting of certain operations over areas invisible to Indian stations, have been utilised. More advanced measures such as strong encryption of both commands and information are planned for future satellites. Apart from encryption, techniques to protect satellites against jamming and spoofing are under development for implementation in future communication and navigation satellites.[93]

Working towards ensuring secured communication transmissions, the ISRO has made a major breakthrough in hack-proof communication technology. Free-space quantum key distribution (QKD) technology, which underpins quantum communication, was demonstrated over a distance of 300 m between two buildings in line of sight in March 2021.[94] The demonstration included live videoconferencing using quantum-key encrypted signals, replacing the conventional cryptosystems used for data encryption. ISRO is pursuing the technology further by demonstrating it between two Indian ground stations, as part of its goal of Satellite-Based Quantum Communication (SBQC).[95]

Concluding Notes

The 56th Otago Foreign Policy School, on the theme 'Ascending into Space: New Zealand's Role as a Space-Faring Nation' directed by Dr. Maria A. Pozza in 2022, was a unique opportunity for the international community to exchange notes on many current issues of space policy and also pursue dialogue on how a new space-faring nation such as New Zealand carves a role in strengthening the benefits of accessing space and seeking opportunities for international cooperation. India as a mature space-faring nation and New Zealand as a new space-faring country could find synergies to cooperate in the field of space. Cooperative ventures in launch

[92] India developing advanced security measures for its satellites, DT NEXT December 02, 2021 https://www.dtnext.in/technology/2021/12/02/india-developing-advanced-security-measures-for-its-satellites?infinitescroll=1; DoA: June 10, 2023.

[93] Government of India. Department of Space. (2021, December 1). Lok Sabha Unstarred Question No. 657 To be Answered on Wednesday, December 01, 2021. Space Debris. https://sansad.in/ls/questions/questions-and-answers DoA: July 12, 2023.

[94] https://www.isro.gov.in/Quantum%20Key%20Distribution%20(QKD).html DoA: June 10, 2023.

[95] Indian Space Research Organisation. (2021, March 22). Press Release: ISRO makes breakthrough demonstration of free-space Quantum Key Distribution (QKD) over 300 m. https://www.isro.gov.in/update/22-mar-2021/isro-makes-breakthrough-demonstration-of-free-space-quantum-key-distribution-qkd, DoA: June 10, 2023.

services could be explored. Joint scientific or technological missions in areas of mutual interest, such as those relevant to the fields of climatic and environment, can be pursued. Joint commercial ventures involving space industries in both countries can further be explored. Both sides can also benefit from the exchange of scientists and increased academic interaction among institutions in India and New Zealand for research in areas relevant to space science, applications and international policy or regulations, including cyber security situational awareness. Entering into a MoU that can lead to establishment of joint working groups in areas identified for further progress and evaluation could be pursued. The two countries could also examine cooperative possibilities for the pursuit of common interests in international fora.

India is at the cusp of an economic transformation and demographic transition at this juncture, which presents enormous opportunities for enterprise and the reinvention of its potency based on the yet-to-be-uncovered treasure house of its values for human development. It is also amidst a milieu of emerging consciousness of strong political and social leadership. A quantum leap in space enterprise can be realised with a metamorphosed role for the national space agency to seed new advances in technology, mission concepts and innovative models. Industry has to play its role in scaling up infrastructure and services, and meeting the burgeoning needs of security. Institutional reforms will be a continuing process, in tandem with the regulatory reforms necessary for enablement, sustainability and strategic initiatives. In the road map for the long-term development of space, national and international dimensions are to be developed in harmony, while investment from both the public and private sectors will be stepped up. Potential new areas would include developments in aerospace transportation systems, space tourism and lunar bases, and the exploration and use of resources from space or Near Earth Objects, planetary habitats and so on.[96] Pursuit of international cooperation needs to be strengthened to achieve this progress and to ensure the governance of space to promote the overall security and well-being of humanity as a whole.

Bibliography

Annual Reports of Department of Space, Government of India. (n.d.). https://www.isro.gov.in/.

Diwakar, P. G., Raghavaswamy, V., Saha, S. K., Kiran Kumar, A. S., Dadhwal, V. K., & Shivakumar, S. K. (2013). Indian remote sensing satellite series and applications: A saga of 25 years. In *Bulletin of the national natural resources management system, NNRMS (B)-37* (pp. 19–26). Department of Space, Government of India, Bangalore.

Kasturirangan, K. (2013). *India in space – A conceptual framework for the 21st century*. Dr Satish C Seth Memorial Futurology Lecture series 5 organised by Indian Council of Management & Future and delivered at New Delhi on April 8, 2013.

Lele, A. (2021). *Institutions that shaped modern India: ISRO*. Rupa Publications.

Lele, A. (2023). Indian space force: A strategic inevitability. *Space Policy, 65*, 101526. https://doi.org/10.1016/j.spacepol.2022.101526

[96] Kasturirangan, India in Space.

Manoranjan Rao, O. V., et al. (2012). *A brief history of rocketry in ISRO*. Universities Press (India) Private Limited.
Manoranjan Rao, P. V., et al. (2015). *From fishing hamlet to red planet: India's space journey*. Harper Collins Publishers.
Murthi, S., & Gopalakrishnan. (2022). Unlocking India's space sector: Legal and policy challenges. In S. B. Bhat & S. K. Guha (Eds.), *Fundamentals of national space laws* (pp. 120–133). Thomson Reuters.
Rajagopalan, R. P. (2022, September 1), *India's speace priorities are shifting toward national security*. Commentary, Carnegie Endowment for International Peace, Washington DC, USA.
Shankar, U. (2007). *Economics of India's space programme*. Oxford University Press.

Chapter 9
Knowing Me, Knowing You: A Critique of the UK Space Strategy

Fionagh Thomson

Introduction: The UK Space Strategy: What Is the Direction?

In 2021, the UK Space Agency (UKSA) published its first space strategy[1] with the vision:

> We will build one of the most innovative and attractive space economies in the world, and the UK will grow as a space nation. We will protect and defend the UK's interests in space, shape the space environment and use space to help solve challenges at home and overseas. Through cutting edge research, we will inspire the next generation and sustain the UK's competitive edge in space science and technology.

The provenance of the space strategy is unclear, and difficult to trace, but one previous policy document outlines the need for a space strategy: *Global Britain in a Competitive Age: the Integrated Review of Security, Defence, Development and Foreign Policy*.[2] This post-Brexit report frames space as part of cyberspace (the internet) and highlights the own–collaborate–access framework, asking which science and technologies (i.e., space capabilities) should the United Kingdom own, collaborate on, or only have access to?[3] The UKSA and the Ministry of Defence (MOD) both signed the final UK space strategy (UKSS), pressing home the focus on

[1] UK Space Agency, Department for Science, Innovation and Technology, Ministry of Defence, & Department for Business, Energy & Industrial Strategy. (2021, September 27). UK Space Strategy.

[2] Cabinet Office. (2021, March 16). *Global Britain in a Competitive Age: the Integrated Review of Security, Defence, Development and Foreign Policy.*

[3] von Busch, O., & Palmås, K. (2021). Global Britain in a Competitive Age: The Integrated Review of Security, Defence, Development and Foreign Policy, March 2021, Command Paper 403. Cabinet Office.

F. Thomson (✉)
Centre for Extragalactic Astronomy, Department of Physics, Durham University, Durham, UK
e-mail: fionagh.thomson@durham.ac.uk

M. A. Pozza (ed.), *Ascending to Space*, Space Law and Policy,
https://doi.org/10.1007/978-981-97-0714-0_9

dual use (shared military and civil use) in space capabilities.[4] Notably neither the UKSS nor the Integrated Review references the pre-Brexit national space policy published in 2015, which highlights similar issues to the UKSS including dual use.[5]

Outer space has always been a foreign policy tool for scientific, technological, and military reasons. Both governments and private organizations view space as a form of power, and government's space policies and programmes increasingly hold influence and prestige in international politics and diplomacy and are central to foreign policies.[6] Over time, space has appeared in different guises, each one waxing and waning in importance and leaving traces behind. Many underpin the UKSS's ten-point action plan that reads as a 'something for everyone' plan. One could argue that the document is welcome and ambitious in nature but lacks clear strategic direction and is more akin to a policy than a strategy.[7] The many promises given to different stakeholders consulted are unlikely to play out smoothly in the future. Trade-offs will have to be made. This chapter aims to shed light on the underlying assumptions and then highlight some anomalies through briefly exploring the following five questions: (1) which space topics can the United Kingdom lead on? (2) which space capabilities should the United Kingdom own, collaborate on, or only seek access to? (3) in seeking to become an innovation Nation, has the United Kingdom lost connection with the science and technology (S&T) research base? (4) is the government sufficiently joined up to support the future of the UK space industry? and (5) has space become fetishized[8] in an attempt to promote the benefits of space-based services?

This chapter will focus on space capabilities (from a downstream perspective) and draw on the author's background and research as a visual, space and medical ethnographer, human geographer, ecologist, environmental ethicist, and educational philosopher. This chapter presents a think piece and an overview of a fragmented

[4]The shift is towards a twin thread of defence/security and economic development, where funding and innovation will evolve from the commercial sector in order to improve security and defence where the world order is rapidly changing.

[5]UK Space Agency, *National Space Policy*. 13 December 2015.

[6]Nucera, G. G. (2019). International Geopolitics and Space Regulation. In *Oxford Research Encyclopedia of Planetary Science*.

[7]Andy German, states that "the strategy is welcome but adds little to the National Space Policy that it replaced, and its encyclopaedic nature identifying neither priorities nor actions renders it a policy rather than a strategy", personnel communications, 7 June 2023.

[8]This chapter uses the anthropological concept of 'fetish', as described by the eminent human geographer David Harvey: "By fetishism I mean the habit humans have of endowing real or imagined objects or entities with self-contained, mysterious, and even magical powers to move and shape the world in distinctive ways. The technological changes that we see all around us are, of course, very real. They are a constitutive feature of how we live our daily lives. We do not imagine them, so in this case, the fetish does not attach to some fantasy like "lady luck" or fate. The fetish arises because we endow technologies—mere things—with powers they do not have (e.g., the ability to solve social problems, to keep the economy vibrant, or to provide us with a superior life)" Harvey, D. (2003). The fetish of technology: Causes and consequences. *Macalester International, 13*(1), 7. (p3).

and complex topic (the UK space strategy) that to date has had few in-depth reviews, as most of the reviews are of the defence strategy.[9]

Setting the Scene

Before briefly discussing the ten-point plan in the UKSS, it is important to set the scene in three ways. Firstly, this chapter defines outer space with an overview of the three 'C's – congested, competitive, and contested. Secondly, a brief outline on the shifting nature of space power over the decades (both military and commercial) and the power of knowledge is considered. Thirdly, it is pertinent to unravel and challenge the latest incarnation of space: an extension of Earth's ecosystems, one that is democratic, open to all and increasingly cheap to access, often framed in evangelical rhetoric. In its place, this chapter will offer a view that space remains deeply colonial, still dominated by key nations, and led by (some) dual-use capabilities and free-trade objectives. Throughout this chapter, the reader is asked to keep watch for themes that do not always sit comfortably together. For example, the relatively short-term free-trade objectives, led by venture capitalists (VCs)[10] seeking high returns on their investments (ROI), and the longer-term environmental objectives, unlikely to generate high profits, if any, for shareholders – such as recovering biodiversity on intensively farmed agricultural lands,[11] preventing further loss of polar icecaps and reclaiming the endangered ecosystems of certain species' habitats.

What Is [Outer] Space?

Modern space is a dynamic, diverse, and evolving field that is a far cry from the world of astrophysics, or the complex role the night sky plays for different indigenous cultures.[12] To understand the political nature and power of space capabilities,

[9]cf. Bowen, B. E. (2022). *Original Sin: Power, Technology and War in Outer Space*. London: Hurst.

[10]The UKSS promotes Seraphim, a UK-based VC as a leading light – an indication of bias.

[11]There are many farmers, smallholders, who work tirelessly on improving and maintaining biodiversity.

[12]Thomson, F. (1996). *People, Trees & Portable Sawmills: Participatory environmental impact study of portable sawmills with forest communities in Papua New Guinea* (Unpublished MSc dissertation). University of Edinburgh; Thomson, F. (2023). Whiteboards, Dancing, Origami, Debate: The Importance of Practical Wisdom for Astrophysicists and Instrument Scientists. In J. F. Salazare & A. Gorman (Eds.), *The Routledge Handbook of Social Studies of Outer Space*. Abingdon: Routledge.

such as Earth Observations (EO), Positioning, Navigation and Timing (PNT)[13] and satellite communications (satcoms), there is a need to understand the different orbits. Put simply, there are four classes of orbital altitudes: Low-Earth orbit (LEO), medium-Earth orbit (MEO), geostationary orbit (GEO), and highly elliptical orbits (HEO).[14] Different orbits provide different views of Earth, loiter times,[15] and different types of services to users.[16] Satellites must be placed in specific orbits and altitudes, and assigned radio frequency spectrum slots. Space may seem big, but the orbits are similar to well-used traffic lanes, and LEO is becoming busiest of all. The geographical location of a Nation defines which orbits they can launch into. The United Kingdom offers access to sun-synchronous (for imaging, reconnaissance, and weather satellites), polar and high-inclination orbits.[17]

Outer space is often said to be increasingly *congested*, *contested* and led by *competition*.[18] But what is frequently missing from these discussions is a clear and unambiguous meaning of space, in part as space means many things to different actors.[19] We know space has become more *congested* as the number of satellites (living and dead) and the accumulation of space debris have increased significantly. Whether we have reached a tipping point is under discussion across the civil and

[13]PNT is a combination of three distinct, constituent capabilities: positioning, the ability to accurately and precisely determine one's location and orientation two or three-dimensionally (or three-dimensionally when required); navigation, the ability to determine a current and desired position and apply corrections to course, orientation and speed to attain a desired position anywhere around the world; and timing, the ability to acquire and maintain precise time from a standard, anywhere in the world, within user-defined timeliness parameters. When PNT is used in combination with map data and other information (e.g., weather or traffic data) the result is the modern navigation tool, the Global Positioning System (GPS).

[14]Qureshi, J., Butt, H., & Fayyaz, T. (2023). Design of Mega LEO Constellations for Continuous Coverage over Pakistan. *International Journal of Innovations in Science & Technology, 5*(1), 82–93.

[15]The time a satellite can maintain its position over a section of the Earth. In LEO, it's only minutes, while in GEO a satellite's position is constant as in this orbit, it is travelling at the same speed as the Earth's rotation. For this reason, satcoms satellites are placed in GEO.

[16]Bowen, B. E. (2020). *The Integrated Review and UK Spacepower: The Search for Strategy* (p. 4). Freeman Air & Space Institute, Kings College London. https://www.kcl.ac.uk/warstudies/assets/integrated-review-and-spacepower.pdf

[17]UK Space Agency, Department for Transport, Civil Aviation Authority, *a Guide to UK Spaceports*, UK Launch.

[18]Harrison, R. G. (2013). Unpacking the Three C's: Congested, Competitive, and Contested Space. *Astropolitics, 11*(3), 123–131.

[19]The term space is what sociologists call a boundary object (Leigh Star, S. (2010). This is not a boundary object: Reflections on the origin of a concept. *Science, Technology, & Human Values, 35*(5), 601–617) a term in everyday use that is interpreted in multiple ways by different communities. For example, non-space science communities often elide NewSpace with astrophysics. But space science and astrophysics are very different. Astrophysics is driven more by the accumulation of rigorous verifiable knowledge than ROI, and rarely informs policies (Thomson, Whiteboards, Dancing, Origami, Debate), despite the community's current attempts to influence the increasing launch of satellites negatively impacting optical/radio astrophysics (other fields of astrophysics are not affected).

defence space sector.[20] Venture capitalists tend to claim that current voluntary regulations work well, and space debris is not a problem.[21] Other commentators in the space sector cite inevitable imminent danger and the Keppler syndrome.[22] The focus on inexpensive launch is unlikely to reduce space debris as more satellites are put into desirable orbits by companies working to tight profit margins, where attention to tracking, station keeping, and end-of-life disposal may be an add-on rather than a necessity.

Previously due to the limited number of elite players, space debris was less of an issue, and there is an informal code of conduct.[23] But as the number of space actors increases, strain is placed on the limited resources of the radio frequency spectrum that is licensed by the International Telecommunication Union (ITU),[24] who have complained that universities and small companies are launching objects without completing official registration forms.[25] With increasing concerns about regulating space debris, there is a push towards developing criteria for good norms of practice, with the recent introduction of the Space Sustainability Rating (SSR) devised by the World Economic Forum (WEF). The WEF choose four Western organizations to develop the criteria,[26] with no representation from the global South or the Indo-Pacific region. One unanswered question is: why would current space operators, working to tight profit margins, pay[27] for the SSR's stamp of approval? Space has certainly become more *competitive* as more commercial actors are appearing, in part due to geopolitical shifts and the need to draw on commercial funding in times of austerity. According to Harrison, the United States has faltered due to technological

[20] Harrison, Unpacking the three Cs.

[21] The Seraphim Space Investment Trust made this claim at a presentation at the North East Space conference on 22 March 2023.

[22] In 1987 NASA scientist Donald J. Kessler proposed a theory, based on methods used in the study of asteroid belts, to predict collision patterns for active satellites in Earth's orbit. He calculated that, once past a certain critical mass, space debris will keep on increasing in a chain reaction; as collisions would create more debris and lead to more collisions.

[23] Beard, J. M. (2016). Soft law's failure on the horizon: The international code of conduct for outer space activities. *University of Pennsylvania's Journal of International Law*, 38, 335.

[24] ITU does not approve single satellites or constellations, but manages the international coordination, notification and recording of the specific radio frequencies transmitted and received by satellites.

[25] Harrison, Unpacking the Three C's.

[26] The SSR was launched in 2020 in London at the 4th Summit for Space Sustainability (organized by the UKSA and the US-based Secure World Foundation). The SSR is framed as an international initiative to promote voluntary action by satellite operators – to reduce the risk of space debris, in-orbit collisions, and 'unsustainable' space operations. This concept was conceived by the World Economic Forum (WEF). In 2018, the WEF through a competitive call chose four Western-based organizations to form a consortium to design the technical and programmatic aspects: ESA, the Massachusetts Institute of Technology, the University of Texas at Austin, and US-based BryceTech.

[27] At the launch the SSR omitted any mention of the cost of the licence. It is still difficult to locate on their website.

overreach, procurement problems and draconian export controls.[28] For some, the positive benefits of increased competitiveness are increased innovation and new players. Although as discussed in the next subsection below, the commercialization of space also brings unintended consequences. Competition in space is not only monetary but also about prestige, though this tends to be in space exploration, such as moon landings.

Space as *contested* is a more ephemeral definition and we ask: what is being contested, and who is contesting whom, that brings us to the slippery concept of power in space?

Changing Nature of Space Power and Foreign Policy: From Military to Trade and Political Ambition

Outer space has always held geopolitical power, for scientific, technological, and military reasons. The modern space era evolved as an extension of the Cold War that was the political and ideological power struggle between two dominant nations: the United States and the Soviet Union, lasting from 1947 to 1991.[29] This was an era of realpolitik, the concept of being pragmatic within the existing power and resources available rather than trying to achieve ideological goals and change the nature of the world. The overriding view was that whoever controlled space and its assets controlled the Earth.[30] But it was thought that as it was physically impossible to maintain dominance over every territory, the only strategy was to deny access to adversaries. Hence orbits, areas of space and launch points became geopolitical. The perceived power of launch remains today[31] and space power is defined more by a nation's access to satellites, launch systems and their related ground infrastructure, than crewed spaceflight or robotic probes – 'despite their ability to inspire people and have a propagandistic effect'.[32] Within the longer Cold War, there followed an era of liberal thinking, when collaboration was considered the most pragmatic way forward and collaborative organizations, such as the European Space Agency (ESA), were established. In 1967 the Outer Space Treaty was developed to create harmony, consensus and collaboration among the few, select spacefaring nations, although Bleddyn Bowen disagrees and argues that space has always been about competition and dominance.[33] More recently, with the increased number of commercial actors in

[28] Harrison, Unpacking the Three C's.

[29] Nucera, International Geopolitics and Space Regulation.

[30] Bowen, The Integrated Review and UK Spacepower.

[31] The UKSS uses a launch metaphor to structure the report (ignition, etc).

[32] Bowen, The Integrated Review and UK Spacepower, 5.

[33] Bowen, *Original Sin*.

space, there has been a shift and the potential dispersal of power as non-governmental actors join the stage, in an era labelled 'NewSpace'.[34]

'Spacepower' is not only military power but also the power to trade and develop a nation's economic status.[35] Since the beginning of the modern space era, spacefaring nations have followed two parallel, intertwined threads of power: political and economic (trade) objectives and military (defence and security) objectives. Notably, military objectives have been the fundamental drivers of the development of scientific research and technological innovation – such as the Global Positioning System (GPS) – the satellite radio navigation system owned by the United States and run by US Space Command[36] – though the civil world invested in satcoms early on. At times, space (and space science) is viewed as a diverse collection of technologies, devoid of political impact, although politics is inscribed into every mission and every material object through costs, procurement, export/import criteria, etc. With the increasing prominence of space-based capabilities in the modern world, space is often labelled as the fifth power, in addition to the traditional elements of terrestrial, maritime, aerial and, more recently, cyber.[37]

There is a sixth power, knowledge. Knowledge is more than information (raw data). It is about who has access to knowledge and who holds the skills to unpack, analyse and make sense of the original information, building on trustworthiness, not relying on blind trust. Knowledge as power is also how discussions about space are framed and the metaphors used. The most recent reinvention of space is as a natural ecosystem akin to the earth's ecosystems (forests, oceans, air), and arguably it has shifted the concept of space from military technologies and competitive trading to one that is benevolent, and designed to help all of humankind.[38] But for this author, this is arguably an illusion and space remains either military or dual-use, although the current concept of military (and by association dual-use) tends to imply war-mongering or defence and security tactics.[39]

[34]Boulton, F. (2021). Response to the UK government's Integrated Review of Security, Defence, Development and Foreign Policy. *Medicine, Conflict and Survival, 37*(2), 102–111.

[35]cf. *Global Britain in a Competitive Age.*

[36]Bogari, M. F. (2023). *Exploring the Relationship Between the Growing Number of Satellites and Space Debris in Low Earth Orbit, and People's Perception of Space Debris Environmental Impacts* [Doctoral dissertation, The University of Tennessee at Chattanooga]. https://scholar.utc.edu/theses/804/

[37]Svoboda, M. (2022). *The application of offensive realism in outer space as a fifth operational domain.* (Unpublished doctoral dissertation). Univerzita Karlova, Prague.

[38]This concept is also challenged from a defence perspective by Bowen, *Original Sin.*

[39]cf. Gray, C. S. (1996). The influence of space power upon history. *Comparative Strategy, 15*(4), 293–308.

Space Sustainability and Space as an Ecosystem: Misleading Rhetoric or for the Common Good?

Space sustainability is a new buzz phrase, although the exact definition remains ephemeral as to sustain simply means to maintain something. So, what is being sustained? The power of the most dominant spacefaring nations? Keeping the orbits (the traffic lanes) flowing free for their satellites? Using rhetoric taken from the environmental world, the United Nations Committee on the Peaceful Uses of Outer Space (UNCOPUOS) defines the long-term sustainability of outer space activities as 'the ability to maintain the conduct of space activities indefinitely into the future in a manner that realizes the objectives of equitable access to the benefits of the exploration and use of outer space for peaceful purposes, in order to meet the needs of the present generations while preserving the outer space environment for future generations.'[40]

This definition in environmental ethics is problematic as it offers up a Westernized approach towards the blue planet, one not based in ecology, where the term 'preserve' is rarely used, as ecosystems are dynamic and shift and change.[41] The use of natural resources is also contested, usually among the most dominant nations, although the concept of resource exploitation has a negative connotation in the environmental field. In contrast, the space industry and academic space sciences literally use the term 'exploiting resources' (e.g., mining of asteroids or the Moon) in talks, papers, and conferences, which attracts little public criticism.[42] There is also a tendency to equate exploring the solar system and inhabiting other planets as being a natural part of human evolution – our destiny. However, this view is based more on *Star Trek*, the US science fiction television programme – and the perceived right to explore is more akin to eighteenth-century colonial explorers' tales of the high seas and claiming land for their sovereigns. Space exploration is an option for a nation, although it is not supported by any mainstream contemporary theory of human evolution and migration. Often migration and dispersal occurred slowly over centuries – or more quickly through loss of habitat and/or natural disasters.[43] Exploration, setting sail to claim new lands, was/is for the rich and privileged, and

---

[40] UNCOPUOS. (2017, June 14). Guidelines for the long-term sustainability of outer space activities. Committee on the Peaceful Uses of Outer Space, sixtieth session. Fifty-fifth Scientific and Technical Subcommittee, Vienna, 29, 2. https://www.unoosa.org/documents/pdf/PromotingSpaceSustainability/Publication_Final_English_June2021.pdf

[41] Thomson, F. (2000). *Are ecological imperatives and democracy compatible for Environmental Ethics?* (Unpublished M.Phil. dissertation). Cambridge University.

[42] An exception is the Native American space engineer Dan Hawk, who campaigns tirelessly on this topic.

[43] Crate, S. A., & Nuttall, M. (2016). The concepts of adaptation, vulnerability, and resilience in the anthropology of climate change: Considering the case of displacement and migration. In S. A. Crate & M. Nuttall (Eds.), *Anthropology and Climate Change: From Encounters to Actions* (pp. 58–85). New York: Routledge.

thinking ahead for future generations while trying to survive the current, modern world, living hand to mouth, is a luxury for resource-poor nations.[44]

For me, one problematic theme in space sustainability is comparing the blue planet and its ecosystems (oceans, forest systems) to outer space and satellite orbits, and claims that protecting NewSpace (through commercialization) will democratize and open up the former closed, elite world of 'OldSpace'.

Space as a Natural Ecosystem: And Clearing of Debris Through Commercialization

The presence of an increasing amount of space debris, particularly in LEO, is often compared to the Great Pacific Garbage Patch (GPGP), a swirling vortex of debris floating in the Pacific Ocean, that increases daily.[45] Similarities certainly exist. The GPGP is human-made and – like space debris – has formed from non-biodegradable debris for over 50 years. Increased global concern has led a shift from knee-jerk tactics to thinking ahead, looking down the supply chain to the source, to prevent debris from being swept into the ocean.[46] Locating and tracking the ocean-borne debris is difficult.[47] Due to its low density, and the presence of millions of microscopic plastic particles, the patch is near-invisible in satellite imagery. Similarly, accurately tracking small pieces of space debris (smaller than 10 cm) remains challenging, despite endless media pieces claiming the successful development of new cutting-edge technologies. Both the oceans (the high seas) and outer space are framed as global commons, owned by no nation, and are often framed by 'the tragedy of the commons'.[48] This is a Westernized, arguably outdated,[49] economic principle that open, 'free-for-all' access to scarce resources leads inevitably to

[44] Notably, space organizations often cite the aim of supporting the United Nations Sustainable Development Goals (UNSDGs) with no further explanation on why, although the SDGs have few concrete outcomes.

[45] Aniss, M., Barnett, J. T., Brunner, E., Bruns, C. J., Christiansen, J., Falc, E., & Roundtree, A. K. (2020). *Water, rhetoric, and social justice: A critical confluence*. Lexington Books.

[46] Park, Y. J., Garaba, S. P., & Sainte-Rose, B. (2021). Detecting the Great Pacific Garbage Patch floating plastic litter using WorldView-3 satellite imagery. *Optics Express, 29*(22), 35,288–35,298.

[47] Yin, H., & Cheng, C. (2010, August). Monitoring methods study on the great pacific ocean garbage patch. In *2010 International Conference on Management and Service Science* (pp. 1–4). [Piscataway, N.J.]: IEEE.

[48] Hardin, G. (1968). The tragedy of the commons: The population problem has no technical solution; it requires a fundamental extension in morality. *Science, 162*(3859), 1243–1248.

[49] A discussion of this topic is beyond the scope of this chapter, but it is worth noting that there are many examples of community land/water management, where communal shared use has not depleted resources.

exploitation and denigration. And the sole solution is to develop laws and norms of responsible behaviour, defined and agreed upon by all parties involved.[50]

There are also key differences between the two phenomena. Space as a place is anthropocentric, human-made, and inherently designed for human beings living in a modern, Westernized world. Space is an artificial habitat for human beings, one with no living creatures. Space was designed as and remains a colonial entity, where 'colonial' is defined as the political control of one or more powerful nations, including their languages, ways of thinking and social and political structures.[51] Space as a working place and concept was initially devised, built, and managed by the military. As such, unlike the GPGP, space debris management benefits from an established United Stated Space Surveillance Network (SSN), the responsibility of US space command and operated by US space force.[52] However, the SSN system was never designed to effectively monitor increasing commercial space traffic – in LEO – or the ensuing decommissioned debris.[53] Another notable difference is the absence of unpaid environmental volunteers climbing aboard space-bound vessels – similar to Greta Thunberg's personal campaign against the climate change agenda – nor any self-funded innovators testing out novel ways of clearing debris. Entry to outer space is through access to designated launch sites by nations and organizations with sufficient financial resources and the ability to interpret and negotiate bureaucratic procedures laid out in international treaties. (This scenario paints less of a Wild West image than that presented by the media.)[54]

Instead, space debris, innovation and problem-solving are increasingly led by a global 'free market' philosophy – along a sliding scale from the dominant trade-led, light-touch regulatory approach in the United States, to the waning European Union's trade tariffs. In short, and over-simplified, identify markets and attract investors, and space debris will be cleared. This is a view highlighted by the redirection of SST responsibility from the US military to the Department of Commerce and the publication of the Atlantic Council report in April 2021, that states: 'The international law of space, centered on the 1967 Outer Space Treaty, is outdated and insufficient for a future of space in which economic activity is primary.'[55] In a

---

[50] To date the United States has rejected the definition of space as global commons as this would prevent the nation from claiming sole rights to any space asset.

[51] My point here is to highlight that space is not a democratic space, open to all.

[52] Giannopapa, C., & Antoni, N. (2023). Space traffic management and its dual use: Space security strategies and cooperation in Europe. *Acta Astronautica*, doi.org/10.1016/j.actaastro.2023.01.038

[53] The UK's primary military space sensor is at RAF Fylingdales (North Yorkshire). It provides a 24/7 missile warning and space surveillance capability for the UK and its allies.

[54] Wei Chen, K, Goswami, B., Jakhu, R.S, Freeland, S. (2022, August, 19) Outer space is not the "Wild West": There are clear rules for peace and war. *The Conversation*. https://theconversation.com/outer-space-is-not-the-wild-west-there-are-clear-rules-for-peace-and-war-188346

[55] Atlantic Council. (2021). *The Future of Security in Space: A Thirty-Year US Strategy*. https://www.atlanticcouncil.org/content-series/atlantic-council-strategy-paper-series/the-future-of-security-in-space;%20whether%20the%20Outer%20Space%20Treaty%20is%20fit%20for%20purpose%20in%202023%20is%20a%20hot%20topic%20of%20debate%20and%20beyond%20the%20scope%20of%20this%20chapter.

similar vein in the United Kingdom, the responsibility for space was transferred from the Department for International Development (DFID) to the Department for Business, Energy & Industrial Strategy (BEIS),[56] that worked with the UKSA.

As government funding dissolved in the shift towards NewSpace, companies began to look for viable markets to fund future SST developments.[57] Looking downstream to the end-of-life market are active debris removal systems (salvaging or de-orbiting), a necessary part of the space debris solution. Yet, this end-of-life market is currently considered unviable.[58] This is not only for lack of technical know-how but because of legal and regulatory barriers, in particular the current stance of 'whoever touches the debris is immediately liable'.[59] Looking upstream to extending the lifecycle of large satellites is In-Orbit Servicing and Manufacturing (IOSM) that on paper offers a more promising market. Through repairing, renewing, and rebuilding in LEO, IOSM aims to extend the lifecycle of satellites and reduce future space debris.[60] However, to operate and develop, IOSM needs the data, knowledge and technical expertise held by the SST community at every stage of a mission – from prelaunch planning, launch, collision avoidance, approach and contact to undocking, retreat and verification. In turn, IOSM offers the SST community a projected market value of US$4.5 billion by 2028, to fund future developments.[61] And so, it appears, the future of SST and IOSM are symbiotically linked, and a viable financial solution is identified.

However, there is a sting in the tail to introducing free-market, trade-led innovation to space debris solutions. To advance in a free-market context, both fields need to attract the 'best' innovators in industry, often perceived to be start-ups and small companies (and a focus of the UK Government's funding). They in turn need sufficient finance to become viable, as space ventures remain expensive. Currently commercial financing is dominated by VCs and in return for equity, VCs create the resources to build going concerns and encourage new ideas and players to the field.[62] But they also transform data, knowledge, and expertise into valuable monetary commodities to be traded and have an aversion to sharing their commercial

[56] In February 2023, the newly appointed Prime Minister Rushi Sunak split up BEIS, to create a new energy department (as part of his campaign promises) and merged the business-related work of BEIS into (1) the existing Department for Business and Trade and (2) the new Department for Science, Innovation and Technology.

[57] Euroconsult. (2020, March 17). *Commercial Space Surveillance & Tracking*. Final Report for the UK Space Agency.

[58] Know.Space. (2020, March 18). *In-Orbit Servicing: Dependencies with Space Surveillance and Tracking*. UK Space Agency. https://assets.publishing.service.gov.uk/government/uploads/system/uploads/attachment_data/file/917910/know.space_-_UKSA_-_SST-IoS_-_FINAL_REPORT_PUB.pdf

[59] But without sufficient funding, any bespoke instrumentation remains in low-technology readiness.

[60] Although the small, single-use CubeSats being hurled into space pose another problem.

[61] Know.Space. In-orbiting Servicing.

[62] Gray, The influence of space power upon history.

competitive advantage. Notably, the most valuable commodity is analysed data (insight) rather than raw data. Intellectual property rights are applied and sold to the highest bidder – yet often with no access to how the data was analysed. Products are sold as high-value black boxes – creating a shift in the ethos from open (non-military) to closed data sharing.

Therefore, we return to similarities between space debris and the GPGP: the ongoing conflict between free market forces and the common good – that in the worlds of IOSM and SST is the global sharing of trustworthy, timely data and the ability to interpret and apply this knowledge cooperatively at short notice.[63] So while this section questions the usefulness of comparing space to one of Earth's natural ecosystems, the next section considers a more helpful and honest representation of space.

Space as Dual Use: The Good, the Bad, the Unexpected

As outlined earlier, the concept of space as a place, was initially devised and built for military, scientific and political reasons. Military and dual use of space capabilities are often framed as only defence and security tactics. Bleddyn Bowen labels the development of space technologies as an *original sin*, since nuclear arms development drove early space technologies.[64] Yet key modern medical technologies in the West also have evolved from the battlefield, including e-medicine, blood donation and emergency procedures in hospitals. Many contemporary EO (earth observation) applications for climate science, disaster relief, etc. were originally technologies developed for Intelligence, Surveillance and Reconnaissance (ISR) in the military domain. Frequently, a component has been funded and/or developed by the military, and the key difference between EO and ISR is not the technology, but the intended use. SST is used to locate, track and, if possible, identify objects for both civil (space debris) and military purposes.[65] GPS evolved from PNT, a long-established, although lesser-known field of study. PNT is pivotal to maintaining both civil and military systems, including intelligence on the position of adversaries, timings for

---

[63] With the United Kingdom's withdrawal from the European Union, loss of access to valuable knowledge is a pressing issue and the bilateral EU–UK Trade and Cooperation Agreement (TCA) negotiated continued access to the European SST systems for UK-based space companies. But the document also frames sustainability as a free-market, trade-led endeavour that, for some legal commentators, takes us back fifty years to the 1970s (cf. Hart, D. (2021, January 18). The environmental implications of the Brexit deal. UK Human Rights Blog. https://ukhumanrightsblog.com/2021/01/18/the-environmental-implications-of-the-brexit-deal. Here there is only one bottom line: the invisible hand of the free-market economy, with the unsubstantiated belief that a trickle-down economy inherently leads to social and environmental benefits.

[64] cf. Bowen, *Original Sin.*

[65] Giannopapa, C., & Antoni, N. (2023). Space traffic management and its dual use.

international financial trading systems and the safety monitoring of modern transport systems.

The military also play a key role in forecasting shifts in environmental situations, using geospatial intelligence (GEOINT), originally developed by the US military but now used by climate scientists. As part of long-term strategic planning, the military carry out extensive detailed forecasting on changes in climate, loss of biodiversity that may lead to the movement of humans, unstable geopolitical situations, and areas of conflict. The military will also invest in and absorb the high risk of low TRL[66] technologies, developed by the civil space sector, long before a VC considers an investment a safe bet. As budgets decrease, the military are increasingly buying commercial-off-the-shelf (COTS) from civil organizations rather than building and testing their own equipment, a practice that brings its own quality control issues. However, the military still hold frameworks of knowledge, skills, practical wisdom, and ethics developed from lessons hard-learnt on the battlefield that are transferable to civil space. For example, the military focus on the quality and trustworthiness of communications for split-second decision-making, rather than only speed, which can be the difference between life and death.

Industry and the commercial sector will always be responsible for scaling up different technologies and systems. But the military have a great deal to offer the civil space sector. As Robert Weber and Kevin O'Connell write:

> creative thinking is needed in these challenging times. We need to change a 50-year mindset about how and why we use space for vital civil and national security missions, as well as the ways that we do it. It would be unfortunate for the national debate about the future of remote sensing to devolve into a feckless 'commercial versus NTM' debate ... We will need to draw upon the comparative advantages of each sector in order to maintain and advance the exquisite[67] contributions that remote sensing and satellite imagery bring to our science, safety, and security, every single day.[68]

In short, to resolve these issues, we need to be honest about the nature and status of space, as it is now, not as we want it to be. Rhetoric, hype, fear-mongering and wishful thinking will not solve our problems.[69]

---

[66] NASA designed a system for technology readiness which refers to a TRL, ranging from 1–4 (low) to 5–7 (mid-) and 8–9 (near application).

[67] The term exquisite is common in technological development, especially for the military. It means technology that is ingeniously designed, carefully thought through. It usually implies bespoke expensive trusted kit rather than cheap mass-made products.

[68] Weber, R. A., & O'Connell, K. M. (2011, November). Alternative futures: United States Commercial Satellite Imagery in 2020 (p. 24). Department of Commercial, Commercial Remote Sensing Regulatory Affairs; National technical means of verification (NTM) are monitoring techniques, e.g., satellite photography, used to verify adherence to international treaties. The phrase first appeared in the 1972 Strategic Arms Limitation Treaty (SALT I) between the United States and the Soviet Union.

[69] The environmental field learnt these lessons in the 1980s when a campaign of fear-mongering and exaggerated claims designed to garner attention about the environmental crisis helped create a counterculture of climate sceptics, who held up poor-quality research and unrealized claims. Many of the imminent predictions did not come to pass at the time, although many now have decades later.

Discussion: Space Through the Lens of the UK Space Strategy's Ten-Point Plan

Five key questions arose during the author's analysis of the foundational assumptions underpinning the UKSS:

- Which space activities should the UK lead on?
- Which space capabilities should the UK own, collaborate in or only seek access to?
- In attempting to be an 'innovation nation' have we dropped the ball on being a science superpower?
- Is government sufficiently joined up to support the cross-disciplinary nature of space and support the future UK space sector?
- Are we fetishizing the term 'space-based capabilities' in an attempt to draw more attention to the benefits of space?

Reframing the nature of space, each question is explored below using the relevant points from the UKSS action plan[70] as a lens for discussion,

The United Kingdom as a Space Leader: Running Before We Can Walk?

The United Kingdom has been involved in space since the 1950s but not as a major player such as the United States, China, India, or the former Soviet Union (now the Russian Federation), each of which has more sovereign launch capabilities.[71] Now the United Kingdom wants to lead in its own area, of which the most viable and pragmatic building on its current capabilities are: satcoms (focusing on Skynet, the sovereign system developed for the military); EO/ISR; command and control (organizational structures/processes to manage space activities); launch (only civil, as the military use different locations and systems), IOSM and PNT.

Point 6. Leading the global effort to make space more sustainable.

The United Kingdom plans to build an early advantage in robotics, in-orbit servicing, and manufacturing to establish global leadership in space sustainability (i.e., keeping orbits clear of space debris and focusing on SST). Many of these technologies remain in the early development stages (TRL 1-4). In the 1980s, during the Thatcher era, the UK Government moved away from a manufacturing economy and focused predominantly on building a knowledge economy that has left a legacy

---

[70] UKSA, UK Space Strategy (pps 43–46).

[71] Abhijeet, K. (2016). Development of national space law for India. *Astropolitics, 14*(2–3), 185–202.

of underfunded manufacturing industries. While the United Kingdom has begun to invest in space and space infrastructure, this will not address the legacy of years of lack of investment in national capabilities, coupled with minimal geo-return investment in ESA. Investment is increasing, both by government and private organizations, and the question is where this strategic targeted funding will be, and should be, directed. The space economist Pierre Lionnet has expressed caution and scepticism about overselling the future of the space industry, stating that consolidation rather than growth is needed. He states too many companies are being created, and many are pursuing similar projects and solutions, leading to market saturation. Before companies start scaling up, Lionnet suggests focusing on viable solutions, gaining higher revenues, and attracting more customers. He recommends that companies should work together, pooling skills and resources, rather than competing with one another. Lionnet's views mirror the five key outcomes of the space sector consultation on the 2020 UK roadmap on S&T.[72,73]

Theoretically one area the United Kingdom could lead in is space regulations, and in 2022 it led the UN policy and law group. A United Kingdom-based space kite mark[74] for responsible behaviour is currently in development[75] that will either complement or compete with the SSR. The kite mark (in progress) will be based around investors' needs, mirroring the United Kingdom's strength in global financial markets, and highlighting the commercial nature of space. It also raises the question: should the investors be leading the design of the criteria for the kite mark? In Scotland, there is talk of an alternative space sustainability mark; the country launched its own space strategy in October 2021,[76] independently of the wider UKSS. But will these 'fair-trade' criteria become a form of space greenwashing, or can the SSR, the UK kite mark and the (yet unnamed) Scottish criteria offer realistic and pragmatic pathways towards more responsible and democratic use of LEO and GEO (for all spacefaring nations)?

The Own–Collaborate–Access Conundrum

Previously, the UK Government has played the twin roles of relying on the United States for access to capabilities (i.e., launch and GEOINT) and collaborating with the European Commission through ESA to build costly, cutting-edge, large space

[72] Department for Science, Innovation and Technology and Department for Business, Energy & Industrial Strategy. (2021, July 1). *UK Research and Development Roadmap.*

[73] Kriening, T. (Host). (2023, 28 February). Space Café 33 minutes with Pierre Lionnet, [Video podcast]. Spacewatchglobal. Also P. Lionnet, personal communication, April 17, 2023.

[74] A mark that indicates that something meets the specifications of the British Standards Institution.

[75] Freeman, G. (2022, June 22–23). Future of the UK Space Industry. [Keynote address]. 4th Summit for Space Sustainability, London.

[76] Vidmar, M. (2020). New Space and Innovation Policy: Scotland's Emerging "Space Glen". *New Space, 8*(1), 31–51.

missions.[77] However, the 2021 Integrated Review asked the question: should the United Kingdom also own key space capabilities, to become a significant space actor and, in theory, change the world order? Notably, the own–collaborate–access framework has different implications for commercial use and for military use in terms of resilience and operational independence.[78] For example, currently, the United Kingdom has no sovereign military ISR, which means that it is reliant on the Five Eyes agreement with the United States, Canada, Australia, and New Zealand. This also means the United Kingdom cannot share any classified information from a military mission with another European country without permission from the country that holds prime ownership over that mission.[79] Regarding the commercial world, two points in the ten-point plan highlight the need to think carefully about the real-world impact of moving space assets along the own–collaborate–access spectrum.

Point 1. Capturing the European launch market – from access to ownership.

The United Kingdom decided to develop its own launch capabilities for small satellites, and six spaceport locations[80] were identified across the country. Five have government funding and one is privately funded (in Shetland, the most northerly group of islands in the United Kingdom and a market for polar orbits). Questions have been raised about the United Kingdom's ability to develop a launch market, including the environmental impact of post-launch marine debris.[81] On closer inspection, there seems no clear business case for any of the launch sites, beyond the fact that Scotland builds most of the small satellites in Europe, and the United Kingdom want to develop an end-to-end supply chain.[82] However markets cannot be created, they must be researched in advance, not wished into existence. If a market for launch appears without a viable business plan, then it is a result of good luck rather than good planning. Moreover, the main competitor for SaxaVord in Shetland is Andøya in northern Norway, an established spaceport for sounding rockets, supported by superior transport infrastructure and the world's eighth-richest

[77] Bowen, B. E. (2020). The Integrated Review and UK Spacepower.

[78] The United Kingdom/Boris Johnson bought a part share in a civil GPS system, OneWeb, for £5 million. But the government is currently planning a pilot with unconnected rural communities in England and has given the contract to the US-based Starlink, as they were operational.

[79] Wells, A. R. (2020). *Between Five Eyes: 50 Years of Intelligence Sharing*. Casemate Publishers. Note: each decision on sharing information is made on a case-by-case basis.

[80] Shetlands, Uist, Sutherland and Prestwick in Scotland, Gwynedd in Wales, and Cornwall in England. See UK Space Agency, Department for Transport, Civil Aviation Authority, *a Guide to UK Spaceports*, UK Launch.

[81] Lonsdale, J. A., & Phillips, C. (2021). Space launches and the UK marine environment. *Marine Policy, 129*, 104,479.

[82] cf. Frost & Sullivan. (2018). UK Spaceport Business Case Evaluation. https://assets.publishing.service.gov.uk/government/uploads/system/uploads/attachment_data/file/747540/FS_WP_UK_Spaceport_Business_100418_CAM-v6-Digital.pdf

nation.[83] One reason to launch from the United Kingdom may be the ability to gain launch and orbit licences easily through the Civil Aviation Authority (CAA). But while the CAA have developed a new system of licences, based on experience in the world of aviation not space, there are grumblings from the first wave of operators who were the unwilling guinea pigs for the licensing process. Unfortunately, the need to iron out many creases in the new regulations, not originally designed for the space environment, is an unwelcome though key feature of any disruptive technology that changes an existing system and inevitably sends out ripples of discontent.

Point 2. Fighting climate change with space technology – from collaboration to access.

For the United Kingdom to reach its net-zero goals, it must understand climate change to guide its decision-making and investments. The planned focus was to maintain and strengthen the United Kingdom's world-class earth observation research, which is recognized internationally, through ongoing collaboration in the European Union (EU) programme Copernicus, the Earth observation component of the EU's Space Programme, managed by ESA. Global data from LEO satellites and in-situ (non-space) ground-based, airborne, and seaborne measurement systems is offered free to all users..[84] One key source used by many Earth observation companies and research academics is Copernicus' Sentinel-2 optical mission (S2) that systematically collects multispectral land surface imagery with two satellites with a revisit cycle of 5 days at 10, 20, and 60 m spatial resolutions.[85] When the United Kingdom left the EU, their membership of the Copernicus consortium was expected to continue, although Policy Exchange,[86] an influential British conservative think tank, advised against the partnership.[87] Two years later, this European relationship has not continued.[88] The United Kingdom had allocated £750 million for Copernicus, and so it must look for other areas to invest in.[89]

The current government appeared unperturbed by the lost collaboration with Copernicus, and the science minister, George Freeman, stated: 'You only have to look at the increasing appetite for EO data . . . There are a number of applications . . .

[83]Ventura, L. (2023, June 15) Richest Countries in the World. *Global Financial Magazine*. https://www.gfmag.com/global-data/economic-data/richest-countries-in-the-world

[84]The European Commission manages the programme. It is implemented in partnership with the member states, ESA, the European Organisation for the Exploitation of Meteorological Satellites (EUMETSAT), the European Centre for Medium-Range Weather Forecasts (ECMWF), EU agencies and Mercator Océan.

[85]Szantoi, Z., & Strobl, P. (2019). Copernicus Sentinel-2 calibration and validation. *European Journal of Remote Sensing*, *52*(1), 253–255.

[86]https://policyexchange.org.uk

[87]See Elefteriu, G. (2022). *Copernican Revolution: A space policy reform agenda for transforming the UK space enterprise outside the EU's Copernicus programme*. London: Policy Exchange.

[88]In addition, the United Kingdom has designed instrumentation for Sentinel-2.

[89]Cookson, C. & Hollinger, P. (2022, June 11). European Space Agency offers UK alternative to EU's Copernicus project. *Financial Times*.

so there's no shortage of customers. We've got the funding . . . and there are a lot of countries that want to work with us.'[90] This may prove true, but in this situation, the United Kingdom has no operational independence, nor can they collaborate as they no longer have a seat at the table making top-level decisions on funding. The research community can only access the free data from the satellites, which may seem an acceptable outcome. However, when research scientists are no longer actively involved in programmes, they cannot set the science goals or have input into the design of instruments. International collaboration and good relationships are key to successful space science programmes – as is the relationship between cutting-edge innovation and a rigorous science research base, that includes the symbiotic roles of industrial research and development (R&D) and academic research.

Innovation Nation and Science Superpower: Shifting Models of Knowledge and Innovation

In July 2020 the UK Government published its Research and Development Roadmap, setting out a long-term vision to 'unlock' the power of science, research, and innovation.[91] The roadmap highlighted the importance of the United Kingdom becoming a science superpower – and the need for government, industry, NGOs, and academia to work together. In the report, science was defined as *scientia*, meaning knowledge beyond only the sciences,[92] and it highlighted the skills gap across industry. Key to the implementation of the roadmap was a sector-wide consultation that produced five key findings: more strategic inclusive funding; more strategic thinking, less competitiveness; more collaboration; and closing the skills gap across the UK industry. These issues are reflected in three of the ten points in the UKSS action plan[93]:

Point 3. Unleashing innovation across the space sector.
Point 4. Expand our horizons with space science and exploration (becoming a science superpower).
Point 9. Upskill and inspire future space workforce.

In July 2021, the United Kingdom published an innovation strategy, the first in 15 years, with the strapline 'leading the future by creating it'. The main goal of the strategy is for the United Kingdom to become a global hub for innovation by 2035, placing innovation at the centre of everything the nation does. The strategy identified the strengths and weaknesses of UK innovation, and the recommendations focus on:

---

[90] See, 77.

[91] Department for Science, Innovation and Technology and Department for Business, Energy & Industrial Strategy. (2021, July 1). *UK Research and Development Roadmap.*

[92] UK Research and Development Roadmap, p10.

[93] UK Space Strategy (pps 41–43).

business activities (including developing a joint finance and innovation hub linking the government's innovation agency and the British Business Bank), improving the neglected areas of innovation adoption, skills development, and encouraging long-term co-investment in these areas. Connecting digital and physical infrastructure was also identified as critical to the UK's future innovation capability and competitiveness, a concept well understood within the space sector across government, industry, and academia.

The strategy is ambitious but has no significant spending commitments as it appeared between fiscal events, and like the UKSS was heavily criticized for its lack of strategic detail. Hayaatun Sillem, the chair of the advisory Innovation Expert Group and CEO of the Royal Academy of Engineering, defended the strategy, stating: 'it's the first time [in twenty years] I have seen our government take a systemic view of innovation in this way'. She continued: 'the strategy has been crafted with a business audience in mind. The private sector carries out the lion's share of innovation activity, yet while our academic research base is the envy of the world, business investment in R&D in the UK continues to lag behind our peers.'[94] In this statement, the nature of innovation becomes clearer. Innovation does not mean academic research, although it does include industrial R&D. Notably, the Innovation Expert Group is dominated by representatives from industry and the investment community, with a few academics from 'relevant disciplines', economics and business.[95] A more recent report (August 2022) by the government think tank, UKOnward was published on the UK being a science superpower – it reiterated the need to focus on the impact and translation of R&D into applications to compete in international markets. It also questioned the predominant focus on academic research in developing a science superpower. There is a noticeable omission of academic research voices at the plethora of space conferences and key speakers are often exclusively from industry or government, although there are inevitably exceptions. However, there is also an understanding that the UK space industry is under-resourced,[96] and the skills needed will not be developed by higher education alone. The UK Government, led by UKSA staff and supported by the UK Space

[94] Sillem, H. (2021, July 23). Innovation strategy is a turning point for UK policy. *Research Professional News*. https://researchprofessionalnews.com/rr-news-uk-views-of-the-uk-2021-7-innovation-strategy-is-a-turning-point-for-uk-policy

[95] Government funding focuses on short-term projects rather than long-term programmes. Project-based funding is difficult for academia as some focus on low TLRs (blue-sky research) with long timescales. Start-ups also struggle with short-termist funding structures that are not designed either to build knowledge over time or to allow new players into the field. Currently, challenge prizes that set a problem for innovators to solve are in vogue. The benefits are marketed as being in the taking part, rather than in the winning. But this concept has unintended consequences for SMEs working to tight profit margins with limited resources, and that cannot invest time and energy in unpaid ventures that may lead nowhere. As a result, many SMEs will only invest effort in a challenge that is unambiguous, clearly worded, complex rather than complicated, has fair judging criteria and does not rely on insider knowledge and/or years of experience in the field.

[96] https://spaceskills.org/problem#the-state-of-the-space-sector

Skills Alliance, has carried out extensive work on how to close the space skills gap.[97]

In this current age of austerity, there is a need to rethink the sharing of scarce resources but without disconnecting the rigorous S&T research base from the complex process of innovation. Focusing on innovation and improving the process of transforming university-based research into viable industrial R&D and exchanging knowledge between the two sectors is sorely needed, and is the rationale behind a current funding stream for UK academia. "To be a science superpower we need to be an innovation nation" is a frequent mantra of the current Minister of Science, George Freeman.[98] To which one could add, to become an innovation nation, the UK needs both knowledge transfer (between academia and industry) and continual development of its research base.[99] One that is built on trustworthy, transparent, rigorous academic research,[100] interwoven into quality-controlled industrial R&D – and supported by an informed and joined-up policymaking process in government.

Space as an Informed/Uninformed Political Tool: Breakdown in Communication?

Any democratic government relies on a team of civil servants working together to create a valid base of knowledge for policymaking, drawing on knowledge across different departments to inform and guide ministers in decision-making. In 2020, the United Kingdom set up a National Space Council[101] (NSC) to provide ministerial leadership on developing its space sector. In November 2021, the NSC was dissolved under Liz Truss's new leadership and no new body has been fully established (although a Space Partnership[102] is currently in progress, which aims to bring academia, government, and industry together to advise on implementing the UKSS). Currently, there is also no dedicated minister for space, though the current

---

[97] The focus of the action point is on the younger and future generation rather than the current ageing, skilled members of society, who have extensive knowledge, skills, and experience. There is also the untapped market in the oil and gas industry where significant losses will occur; there is a need for a just transition from this sector, to avoid unethical and catastrophic treatment like that of the UK miners in the 1980s who were given no support as the coal mines were shut down. Notably, there is an absence of professional academic educational researchers in the UK space skills alliance and in ongoing work between UKSA and SP on addressing the skills gap.

[98] See Freeman, G. (2022, June 22–23). Future of the UK Space Industry. [Keynote address].

[99] Burnett, M., & Priestley, M. (2022). *Rocket Science: How can the UK become a science superpower?* https://www.ukonward.com/reports/rocket-science

[100] Academic S&T research institutes that win and lead contracts are often subcontractors to industry.

[101] The council was a cabinet committee, a group ministers whose collective decisions are binding across government.

[102] https://www.spacepartnership.org.uk

science minister has embraced the topic wholeheartedly,[103] joining United Kingdom-based space companies at international meetings.

In 2021, a House of Commons Science and Technology Committee[104] was set up to critically review the status of the UK space industry. The committee concluded that the £16 billion space and satellite industry in the United Kingdom is flourishing (a questionable statement according to some economists) but the approach to space policy across government has been criticized as 'disjointed and unclear' and lacks coherence.[105] The committee also expressed concern in four areas: the difficulty of accessing launch licences for operators; the unclear benefits for UK citizens of the £500 million purchase[106] of a share in the global navigation satellite system (GNSS) OneWeb; the lack of a Plan B if the United Kingdom could not participate in Copernicus; and the perceived over-reliance of the United Kingdom on foreign services for critical PNT that would put its national security at risk. This last point leads to an anomaly in point ten.

Point 10. Modernizing the transport system across the United Kingdom.[107]

The final point singles out a specific topic: improving and upgrading the United Kingdom's transport system. What is unusual is: why focus on the transport system from the many applications that space capabilities have to offer? Further, why is the sovereign PNT pilot programme still under consideration, as PNT not only holds dual use for defence purposes it also plays a pivotal role in the safety of modern transport systems. It is unclear if the government is seeking a collaboration with other nations to develop a PNT system or whether there was a lack of understanding by government advisors regarding the important role and nature of PNT. What is known is that the lead for the pilot PNT programme submitted evidence[108] to the select committee questioning the government's decision to pause the sovereign PNT programme. Space as a geopolitical policy tool has changed over the years from a predominantly military tool to a commercial one (with focus on dual use). Notably,

[103]The government's enthusiasm for space led to a press release by the minster the day before the failed horizontal launch by Virgin Orbit in Cornwall announcing that United Kingdom would be the first European launch site. The event was held as a premature celebration, with a silent disco, something highly unusual for a launch event, where tensions are high as so many things can go wrong.

[104]The House of Commons' select committees check and report on areas ranging from the work of government departments to economic affairs. Their results are public, and many require a response from the government.

[105]Science & Technology committee (2022). UKSS and UK satellite infrastructure Inquiry (second report, Nov, 22). UK House of Commons. https://committees.parliament.uk/work/1194/uk-space-strategy-and-uk-satellite-infrastructure/publications/. See also House of Commons Defence Committee, House. (2023). Defence Space: through adversity to the stars? (Third Report of Session 2022–23). https://committees.parliament.uk/publications/33442/documents/181807/default

[106]Boris Johnson bought the bankrupt OneWeb without ministerial support. The select committee found its procurement to be unorthodox and ordered such an action was not to be repeated.

[107]UKSA, UK Space Strategy, p43

[108]Andy Proctor, personal communication, March 15 2023

this policy tool has become increasingly important to UK politicians who work to a five-year political cycle, and are under pressure to make an impact before the next election date. This timescale is the antithesis of S&T in space, which works on 20-year cycles. One might question if rhetoric and increasing political interest led to a disconnect between the S&T knowledge base and the political desire for the United Kingdom to be an innovation nation and a science superpower?

Unintended Consequences and Fetishizing Space as a Panacea for All Humankind's Ills

Space is frequently lauded as providing solutions for many of the planet's problems: climate change, monitoring illegal fishing and human trafficking, among others. Satellites and their payloads have an important role to play in modern society, although the space industry may contend that their benefits (particularly in regard to EO, satcoms and PNT) are not always appreciated by the wider public. This is in part because many outside the space industry may equate space with looking up through telescopes to our solar system and far beyond into the extragalactic. Others equate space with being in and travelling through space such as Moon landings, astronauts, space exploration and, more recently, space exploitation. Some are aware of the life science research experiments carried out in the International Space Station, regarding health and well-being (e.g., studying bone density loss in astronauts and how this knowledge can improve our understanding of an ageing earth-born population and osteoarthritis).[109] This vision of outer space is perhaps unsurprising, given the way it is represented in the media and in educational outreach. Concerns over skills gaps in the space industry have led to space scientists giving inspirational speeches of being astronauts and the joy and wonder of working in space. But the space industry, like many other fields of work, offers a vast assortment of jobs, not all of them exciting and media-worthy, but each important to keeping the sector working.

The call to love space has intensified and the role of satellites in modern society has been placed on a pedestal. Yet satellites are only the vehicles that transport the payloads (such as the sensors and cameras) into space. Both are only tools to be employed for good (such as monitoring the polar icecaps) or bad (such as identifying targets for a bombing campaign), depending on one's ethical viewpoint.

This love for all things 'spacey' has becoming deafening, particularly in the space debris discussion fuelled (potentially) by 'the idea that we increasingly depend on vast, complex, interconnected webs of essential systems that may be unexpectedly

[109] See Robson-Brown, K., Hodkinson, P., Smith, N., Hawkey, A., Velho, R., & Carvil, P. (2021). *Why Space? The opportunity for Health and Life Science Innovation*. UK Space Life and Biomedical Sciences (LABS) Association.

vulnerable, placing economic and political stability at risk'.[110] With space debris a growing global issue, there is a striking increase in global insecurity, and anxiety which arguably has led to an excessive importance being placed on space-based capabilities that are in many instances only an extension of geostationary data, provided by organizations such as the Ordnance Survey. At times, using satellites is not the best option, launch is expensive and once in orbit, satellites are difficult to repair and change. Observing through cloud and our turbulent atmosphere can be difficult and using remotely piloted vehicles (RPVs) or humans on the ground may be a more reliable and/or cost-effective option. But many of these issues remain undiscussed, and instead there is a tendency to fetishize the benefits of space-based services, which brings us to our last point.

Point 7. Public services with space technology – improving or fetishizing.

Looking at direct benefits for UK citizens, the strategy highlights key public services that will benefit from space technology – healthcare, the environment, transportation, and infrastructure – by identifying where space-enabled applications available on the market could improve lives and reduce costs for the taxpayer. Examples include space-enabled sensors and tracking that detect problems in critical energy infrastructure before they cause outages; using satellite-enabled National Health Service[111] RPVs[112]; and turning around patients' test results in remote areas faster. The promises to improve healthcare research on the ground by providing faster internet to under-served and unserved communities do not match up with healthcare research findings on the ground.[113] Quicker test results do not automatically lead to better quality or faster access to healthcare – and providing internet access does not solve the many problems that exist within the United Kingdom's overburdened healthcare system.

Satellites and their payloads do not work in isolation for their intended purposes[114] – and they are only a cog in a network of information sources (from space to ground) including aeroplane or high-altitude balloon-borne sensors, lower-altitude RPVs and ground-based sensors. For example, studying the cryosphere and melting polar icecaps involves a variety of information sources from remote sensing using satellites (i.e., Copernicus' Sentinel-2) to research scientists on sledges/skis/

[110] Henke, C. R. & Sims, B. (2020.) Repairing Infrastructures: The Maintenance of Materiality and Power (p. 9). Cambridge, Mass., and London: MIT Press.

[111] The NHS is the free public healthcare service for England and Wales. Scotland has its own devolved healthcare system, NHS Scotland.

[112] Often referred to as drones or uncrewed aerial vehicles (UAVs); RPV is the term preferred by the academic research community to indicate the vehicles is piloted, albeit from a distance.

[113] Thomson, F. (2019). Telescopes, Microscopes, And Simulations: The Everyday Scientific Practice Of Deciding "What Is Real?" In C. Deane-Drummond, T. A. Stapleford, & D. Narvaez (eds.), *Virtue and the Practice of Science: Multidisciplinary Perspectives* (p. 56). Notre Dame, Ind.: Center for Theology, Science, and Human Flourishing, University of Notre Dame.

[114] Durrieu, S., & Nelson, R. F. (2013). Earth observation from space – The issue of environmental sustainability. *Space Policy, 29*(4), 238–250.

foot, spending weeks gathering data from the frozen ground. Using only satellite-based data always offers only partial knowledge on understanding any phenomena in-depth, a well-established fact within the civil EO and the military ISR communities.[115] Moreover, satellite-based data can be misleading if it does not link up with or build upon existing validated knowledge on the ground (whether formalized research or local community nous). As this book has an international audience, it is important to highlight the fetishizing of terms such as 'space-based capabilities' that extend beyond the United Kingdom (that includes the commercialization and control of space data, as discussed earlier).[116] For example, the concept of connecting under-served and unserved[117] communities to the internet to improve their healthcare raises a long-standing development studies dilemma: does parachuting in outside expertise (whether in person or via satellite) solve the problem if the expert does not understand the language or the local culture? Would this short-term fix discourage the training of, in this example, local health professionals? Other examples of unintended consequences are the satellite mapping of indigenous lands, using Westernized concepts of land ownership that contradict local systems of land use and stewardship. In my fieldwork in Papua New Guinea, the mapping of land by the World Bank created feuds between local clans.[118] Another use of satellite-based sensors is the real-time monitoring of miners' health statistics to avoid tiredness-related accidents,[119] for example in Chile. The data taken via bespoke glasses is sent in real time to supervisors as a form of surveillance, and this neither considers nor addresses the underlying social problem of why miners are working at danger levels of tiredness.

[115] cf Kumpula, T., Forbes, B. C., & Stammler, F. (2010). Remote sensing and local knowledge of hydrocarbon exploitation: the case of Bovanenkovo, Yamal Peninsula, West Siberia, Russia. Arctic, 165–178. See Thomson, Telescopes and Microscopes.

[116] It is important to note that the 2020 International Charter 'Space and Major Disasters' provides free satellite data to support disaster response worldwide (Le Cozannet, G., Kervyn, M., Russo, S., Ifejika Speranza, C., Ferrier, P., Foumelis, M., & Modaressi, H. (2020). Space-based earth observations for disaster risk management. *Surveys in Geophysics, 41*, 1209–1235), although there is no equivalent charter to support disaster management for non-human habitats.

[117] This term is taken from the United States-based satcom project Amazon Kuiper. (Andrew Woodcock, personal communication, March 21).

[118] Thomson, *People, Trees & Portable Sawmills*.

[119] Aidman, E., Chadunow, C., Johnson, K., & Reece, J. (2015). Real-time driver drowsiness feedback improves driver alertness and self-reported driving performance. *Accident Analysis & Prevention*, *81*, 8–13. See also https://www.prnewswire.com/news-releases/optalert-announces-chile-is-world-number-1-for-mining-driver-alertness-107022838.html

Potential Lessons Learnt by any Spacefaring Nation: Concluding Remarks

Space activities are far too complex and diverse to be covered comprehensively by one policy or one strategy.[120] However, one question for any nation is: which space assets and space-based capabilities should be owned, collaborated on or only hold access to?

Adopting a viable 'own–collaborate–access' framework will involve a variety of trade-offs. One key decision is: how much government intervention is desired, required, or possible in the development of space-based capabilities – and how much responsibility will be placed on industry? The role of academia also needs to be considered. Spacepower as trade has become of interest to politicians as a political tool, and if decision-making becomes disengaged from a rigorous research base of S&T it could lead to uninformed policy decision-making. For this reason, any nation would do well to build on a trustworthy research base and include academia as an equal and independent partner to government and industry.[121]

Developing sovereign capabilities may seem appealing and is perhaps key for military and information security. Creating dual-use applications may enhance the viability of a space-based capability (due to scarce resources in times of austerity) and the geographical location of a nation is also a key asset. However, building sovereign capabilities is extraordinarily expensive and is the preserve for only the richest space-faring nations. Collaboration may be a more viable way forward for space-based nations like the United Kingdom, which have traditionally relied upon collaboration or access only.

From a geopolitical perspective, space is a global place involving international collaborations across nations, sharing information as satellites orbit over different nations, above their airspace. Many environmental projects, that are unlikely to be profitable either nationally or internationally, require shared knowledge to monitor, for example, migrating birds and animals that do not stay within carefully drawn national political borders. In this vein, equity holders in companies that utilize space hold an important position of power in deciding which direction a satellite business' products or services will develop. Viable venture capitalists require profit generation although the concept of 'what is enough profit and in what timescale' will influence the direction of the investment. Highest return on investment in a short timescale

[120] On March 13, the UK government published an update to the 2021 Integrated Review: Cabinet Office. (2023, March 13). *Integrated Review Refresh: Responding to a more contested and volatile world.* Notable points: there is less reference to space than in the original document, no mention of sovereign space ports, the concept of space is still tied to cyberspace (satcoms and PNT), civil capabilities are mentioned, but the main focus is on the role of space in military defence, security, and dual use.

[121] Being a key actor in space also requires a nation to adopt an ethical and robust framework to support links to existing relevant knowledge in other fields of studies, across multiple disciplines beyond S&T – and to expand the current focus on technical, engineering, legal and commercial knowledge.

may lead to high-monetary value activities funded by large corporations, such as monitoring of mine tailings. Longer-term, less profitable investment also holds great value to humanity if redirection could be made to global concerns, such as reducing human trafficking and restoring endangered peatlands.

History has shown us that free-market trade objectives and environmental objectives are often incompatible. Yet there are options and opportunities for new forms of business models in space, not led by the quickest or highest return on investment. One option is to develop a portfolio of products on a 'pay-as-you-can' basis, where the high-paying products will support the supply of free or cheaper products (or knowledge) to support a cause for the common good (however this is defined).

Finally, responding to calls for the global space community to consider *how* space can promote peace, security, shared knowledge, and benefits to all nations. One way is to step back and focus on the nature of space as it is – not only as we wish it to be.[122] From this vantage point, humanity can make changes, building on solid foundations, with agreeable disagreements and healthy debates, to develop viable and ethical solutions for some of the pressing issues outlined in this chapter.

Bibliography

Abhijeet, K. (2016). Development of national space law for India. *Astropolitics, 14*(2–3), 185–202.

Aniss, M., Barnett, J. T., Brunner, E., Bruns, C. J., Christiansen, J., Falc, E., et al. (2020). *Water, rhetoric, and social justice: A critical confluence*. Lexington Books.

Atlantic Council. (2021). *The future of security in space: A thirty-year US strategy*. Atlantic Council. https://www.atlanticcouncil.org/content-series/atlantic-council-strategy-paper-series/the-futu re-of-security-in-space/. Accessed 1 Feb 2023.

Beard, J. M. (2016). Soft law's failure on the horizon: The international code of conduct for outer space activities. *University of Pennsylvania's Journal of International Law, 38*, 335.

Bogari, M. F. (2023). *Exploring the relationship between the growing number of satellites and space debris in low earth orbit, and people's perception of space debris environmental impacts* (Unpublished Doctoral dissertation). The University of Tennessee at Chattanooga. https://scholar.utc.edu/theses/804/

Boulton, F. (2021). Response to the UK government's integrated review of security, defence, development and foreign policy. *Medicine, Conflict and Survival, 37*(2), 102–111.

Bowen, B. E. (2019). From the sea to outer space: The command of space as the foundation of spacepower theory. *Journal of Strategic Studies, 42*(3–4), 532–556.

Bowen, B. E. (2020). *The integrated review and UK spacepower: the search for strategy*. Kings College, 4, https://www.kcl.ac.uk/security-studies/assets/kcl-fasi-british-spacepower-and-the-integrated-review-web4.pdf.

Bowen, B. E. (2022). *Original sin: Power, technology and war in outer space*. Hurst Publishers.

Burnett, M., & Priestley, M. (2022). *Rocket science: How can the UK become a science superpower*? https://www.ukonward.com/reports/rocket-science/

Cabinet Office. (2021, March 16). *Global Britain in a competitive age: The integrated review of security, defence, development and foreign policy, HMG*. https://www.gov.uk/government/

[122] For this author, space is not a natural environment that is necessarily open to all, only to those that can afford access.

publications/global-britain-in-a-competitive-age-the-integrated-review-of-security-defence-development-and-foreign-policy

Cabinet Office. (2023, March 13). *Integrated review refresh: Responding to a more contested and volatile world.*

Cookson, C. & Hollinger, P. (2022, June 11). European Space Agency offers UK alternative to EU's Copernicus project. *Financial Times.*

Crate, S. A., & Nuttall, M. (2016). The concepts of adaptation, vulnerability, and resilience in the anthropology of climate change: Considering the case of displacement and migration. In *Anthropology and climate change* (pp. 58–85). Routledge.

Defence Committee. (2023) *Defence space: Through adversity to the stars?* (Third Report of Session 2022–23). House of Commons, UK. https://committees.parliament.uk/publications/33442/documents/181807/default/

Department for Science, Innovation and Technology and Department for Business, Energy & Industrial Strategy. (2021, July 1). *UK Research and Development Roadmap.*

Durrieu, S., & Nelson, R. F. (2013). Earth observation from space–the issue of environmental sustainability. *Space Policy, 29*(4), 238–250.

Elefteriu, G. (2022). *Copernican revolution: A space policy reform agenda for transforming the UK space enterprise outside the EU's Copernicus programme.* Policy Exchange.

Euroconsult. (2020, March 17). *Commercial space surveillance & tracking.* UK Space Agency, Report.

Freeman, G. (2022, June 22–23). Future of the UK space industry. [Keynote address]. *4th summit for space sustainability,* London, UK.

Frost and Sullivan. (2018). *UK spaceport business case evaluation.* UK Space Agency https://assets.publishing.service.gov.uk/government/uploads/system/uploads/attachment_data/file/747540/FS_WP_UK_Spaceport_Business_100418_CAM-v6-Digital.pdf

Giannopapa, C., & Antoni, N. (2023). Space traffic management and its dual use: Space security strategies and cooperation in Europe. *Acta Astronautica, 212,* 41. https://doi.org/10.1016/j.actaastro.2023.01.038

Gray, C. S. (1996). The influence of space power upon history. *Comparative Strategy, 15*(4), 293–308.

Hardin, G. (1968). The tragedy of the commons: The population problem has no technical solution; it requires a fundamental extension in morality. *Science, 162*(3859), 1243–1248.

Harrison, R. G. (2013). Unpacking the three C's: Congested, competitive, and contested space. *Astropolitics, 11*(3), 123–131.

Hart, D. (2021, January 18). *The environmental implications of the Brexit deal.* UK Human Rights Blog. ukhumanrightsblog.com/2021/01/18/the-environmental-implications-of-the-brexit-deal

Harvey, D. (2003). The fetish of technology: Causes and consequences. *Macalester International, 13*(1), 7.

Henke, C. R., & Sims, B. (2020.) *Repairing infrastructures: The maintenance of materiality and power* (p. 9). MIT Press.

Know.Space. (2020). *In-orbit servicing: Dependencies with space surveillance and tracking* [Report: 18 March]. UK Space Agency. https://assets.publishing.service.gov.uk/government/uploads/system/uploads/attachment_data/file/917910/know.space_-_UKSA_-_SST-IoS_-_FINAL_REPORT_PUB.pdf

Kriening, T. (Host). (2023, 28 February). *Space Café 33 minutes with Pierre Lionnet,* [Video podcast]. Spacewatchglobal. https://spacewatch.global/2023/03/space-cafe-33-minutes-with-pierre-lionnet-the-space-economist-that-challenges-the-new-space-narrative/

Kumpula, T., Forbes, B. C., & Stammler, F. (2010). Remote sensing and local knowledge of hydrocarbon exploitation: The case of Bovanenkovo, Yamal Peninsula, West Siberia, Russia. *Arctic, 63,* 165–178.

Le Cozannet, G., Kervyn, M., Russo, S., Ifejika Speranza, C., Ferrier, P., Foumelis, M., & Modaressi, H. (2020). Space-based earth observations for disaster risk management. *Surveys in Geophysics, 41,* 1209–1235.

Leigh Star, S. (2010). This is not a boundary object: Reflections on the origin of a concept. *Science, Technology, & Human Values, 35*(5), 601–617.

Lonsdale, J. A., & Phillips, C. (2021). Space launches and the UK marine environment. *Marine Policy, 129*, 104479.

Nucera, G. G. (2019). International geopolitics and space regulation. In *Oxford research encyclopedia of planetary science*.

Park, Y. J., Garaba, S. P., & Sainte-Rose, B. (2021). Detecting the great Pacific garbage patch floating plastic litter using WorldView-3 satellite imagery. *Optics Express, 29*(22), 35288–35298.

Qureshi, J., Butt, H., & Fayyaz, T. (2023). Design of mega LEO constellations for continuous coverage over Pakistan. *International Journal of Innovations in Science & Technology, 5*(1), 82–93.

Robson-Brown, K., Hodkinson, P., Smith, N., Hawkey, A., Velho, R., & Carvil, P. (2021). *Why space? The opportunity for health and life science innovation.* UK Space Life and Biomedical Sciences (LABS) Association.

Science & Technology Committee. (2022). UK space strategy and UK satellite infrastructure Inquiry (second report, Nov, 22). UK House of Commons. https://committees.parliament.uk/work/1194/uk-space-strategy-and-uk-satellite-infrastructure/publications/

Sillem, H. (2021, Jul 23). Innovation strategy is a turning point for UK policy. *Research Professional News*. https://researchprofessionalnews.com/rr-news-uk-views-of-the-uk-2021-7-innovation-strategy-is-a-turning-point-for-uk-policy/

Strachan, H. (2021). Global Britain in a competitive age: Strategy of the integrated review. *Journal of the British Academy, 9*, 161.

Svoboda, M. (2022). *The application of offensive realism in outer space as a fifth operational domain.* (Unpublished doctoral thesis). Univerzita Karlova, Czech Republic.

Szantoi, Z., & Strobl, P. (2019). Copernicus Sentinel-2 calibration and validation. *European Journal of Remote Sensing, 52*(1), 253–255.

Thomson, F. (1996) *People, Trees & Portable Sawmills: participatory environmental impact study of portable sawmills with forest communities in, Papua New Guinea.* (Unpublished master of science thesis). University of Edinburgh.

Thomson, F. (2000) *Are ecological imperatives and democracy compatible for environmental ethics?* (Unpublished Master of Philosophy thesis). Cambridge University.

Thomson, F. (2018). The mirror and the lake: The good medical consultation. *Philosophy, Theology and the Sciences, 5*, 239–264.

Thomson, F. (2019). Telescopes, microscopes, and simulations: The everyday scientific practice of deciding "what is real?". *Virtue and the Practice of Science: Multidisciplinary Perspectives*, 56.

Thomson, F. (2023a). Whiteboards, dancing, origami, debate: The importance of practical wisdom for astrophysicists and instrument scientists. In J. F. Salazare & A. Gorman (Eds.), *The handbook of social studies of outer space* (1st ed.). Routledge.

Thomson, F. (2023b). Colonising Outer Space: comparing space debris with the Great Pacific Garbage Patch. *The Conversation*.

UK Space Agency. (2015, 13 December). *National space policy*. https://www.gov.uk/government/publications/national-space-policy

UK Space Agency. (2021, September 27). Department for Science, Innovation and Technology, Ministry of Defence, and Department for Business, Energy & Industrial Strategy. *UK Space Strategy*.

UK Space Agency. (2023). Department for Transport, Civil Aviation Authority, *a Guide to UK Spaceports*, UK Launch. https://assets.publishing.service.gov.uk/government/uploads/system/uploads/attachment_data/file/1151003/Spaceport_brochure_17.4.23.pdf

UNCOPUOS. (2017). Guidelines for the long-term sustainability of outer space activities. *Fifty-fifth Scientific and Technical Subcommittee, Vienna, 29*. https://www.unoosa.org/res/oosadoc/data/documents/2017/aac_1052017crp/aac_1052017crp_26_0_html/AC105_2017CRP26E.pdf

United States Geospatial Intelligence Foundation (USGIF). (2015). *GEOINT essential body of knowledge*. http://usgif.org/system/uploads/3858/original/EBK.pdf.

Ventura, L. (2023, June 15). Richest countries in the world. *Global Financial Magazine*. https://www.gfmag.com/global-data/economic-data/richest-countries-in-the-world.

Vidmar, M. (2020). New space and innovation policy: Scotland's emerging "space Glen". *New Space, 8*(1), 31–51.

von Busch, O., & Palmås, K. (2021). Global Britain in a Competitive Age: The Integrated Review of Security, Defence, Development and Foreign Policy, March 2021, Command Paper 403. by UK Cabinet Office. House of Commons Science and Technology Committee, UK space strategy and UK satellite infrastructure, Second Report of Session 2022–23.

Weber, R. A., & O'Connell, K. M. (2011). *Alternative futures: United States commercial satellite imagery in 2020*. Department of Commercial, Commercial Remote Sensing Regulatory Affairs.

Wei Chen, K, Goswami, B., Jakhu, R.S, & Freeland, S. (2022, August 19). Outer space is not the "Wild West": There are clear rules for peace and war. *The Conversation*. https://theconversation.com/outer-space-is-not-the-wild-west-there-are-clear-rules-for-peace-and-war-188346

Wells, A. R. (2020). *Between five eyes: 50 years of intelligence sharing*. Casemate Publishers.

Yin, H., & Cheng, C. (2010, August). Monitoring methods study on the great pacific ocean garbage patch. In *2010 international conference on management and service science* (pp. 1–4). IEEE.

Chapter 10
LISA: Global Space Science and New Zealand's Contribution

Jörg Frauendiener and Salvatore Vultaggio

Introduction

Most topics that were discussed at the Foreign Policy School were concerned with issues arising in the realm of our planet: satellites on terrestrial orbits, rockets leaving Earth and debris falling back down onto it. They are all bound by the pull exerted by the Earth's gravitational field. In contrast, the LISA mission transcends this limitation by sending satellites into orbits around the Sun.

In this chapter, we present the scientific goals of LISA, its technological development from the early 1990s until now and hint at the opportunities that it can offer to the academic, educational and industrial sectors of New Zealand. However, before discussing the numerous possibilities of involvement, it is necessary to dive into the scientific background of the mission. The acronym LISA stands for Laser Interferometric Space Antenna (LISA), and this immediately raises questions: what is laser interferometry? Why space? Antenna for what? It is, therefore, necessary to clarify these questions before we get to the technological and organizational aspects of the mission, which, in turn, will allow us to consider the possible avenues to get involved with it.

In short, LISA is an antenna for gravitational waves, using a detector mechanism based on laser interferometric principles located in space. In the first section of this chapter, we will briefly explain these terms and allude to the scientific benefits expected from LISA. In the next section, we give a short overview of the technological efforts that have gone – and still must go – into LISA to realize the mission. Finally, we describe how New Zealand has started contributing to the mission and why we believe it is beneficial on an even larger scale and for a longer time frame.

J. Frauendiener (✉) · S. Vultaggio
Department of Mathematics and Statistics, University of Otago, Dunedin, New Zealand
e-mail: joerg.frauendiener@otago.ac.nz

M. A. Pozza (ed.), *Ascending to Space*, Space Law and Policy,
https://doi.org/10.1007/978-981-97-0714-0_10

The Science of Gravitational Waves

Einstein's Theory of Space–Time

LISA is designed to detect gravitational waves. This is a phenomenon of physics based on Albert Einstein's theory of gravitation (Einstein, 1989). He predicted their existence in 1916 (Einstein, 1996). In almost a century of experimental tests, this theory has been verified repeatedly by many tests of different kinds (see Fig. 10.1 for an example), and gravitational waves are but the last confirmation that General Relativity is a *good* theory of gravity. In popular accounts, the idea of gravitational waves is quite colourfully described as 'ripples in the fabric of space–time'. However, this is not very helpful unless the notion of space–time is explained. It goes far beyond the scope of this contribution to present a mathematically precise definition, so we must content ourselves with a simple analogy. Everything in our Universe occurs in some place and at some time. Each *event* can be characterized by giving the location in the form of three spatial coordinates (e.g., longitude, latitude and height above sea level) and a time coordinate (e.g., the time of day in the Gregorian calendar). Space–time is simply the collection of all possible events, together with a prescription of how to measure their separation in time and space.

Before Einstein, it was generally believed that space–time was a fixed entity, analogous to a theatre stage on which the play of physics unfolds. However, after Einstein had formulated his General Theory of Relativity (GR) in 1915, it became

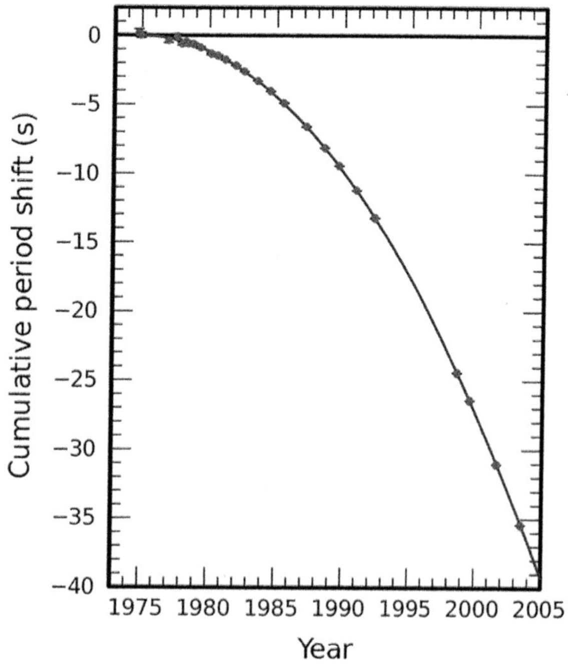

Fig. 10.1 One of the longest-run observations of a purely General Relativistic effect: the orbital decay of a binary pulsar caused by the loss of energy due to gravitational radiation (Weisberg et al., 2010). As the system loses energy, the stars composing it come closer and closer, rotating faster and faster. (Credits: Inductiveload, 2010)

clear that space–time is also an actor in that play; it can influence the course of the play, but it can also be affected by other actors. Thus, a more accurate analogy is that of a very sturdy but not completely rigid (four-dimensional) material, somewhat akin to a sheet or block of metal on which the locations (and times) of events are marked. But, when struck with a hammer, the material makes a sound and vibrates, and the effect of the blow propagates through the material as small perturbations or *ripples*. The stiffer the material, the faster the speed of the ripples through it, and the harder it is to excite it. The ripples of space–time travel with the speed of light (the fastest possible speed), which makes space–time orders of magnitude stiffer than Tungsten, for which the speed is just about 4 km/s. The tremendous stiffness means that it takes much effort to make a ripple. Indeed, sizeable ripples are created only when large massive bodies are accelerated quickly. The primary example is that of a *binary system*, two masses circling each other, such as Earth and the Moon, the Sun and Saturn, or, even more impressively, two black holes, and even for these, the ripple size will be tiny.

In summary, gravitational waves are created by violent processes in the Universe; they are generally minute in size and difficult to detect. So how can we 'see' them?

Gravitational Wave Detectors

To understand how the detectors for gravitational waves work, we need to discuss some of the effects that these waves have. Since they are perturbances of space–time which, as we recall, give us the means to determine durations and distances, they affect the distances between bodies, or even within bodies. They do this in a very characteristic way: they can change lengths only in directions which are transverse to their propagation direction and in such a way that, if in one of these directions the distance is increased, then in the perpendicular direction, it is compressed. This can occur in two independent ways (see Fig. 10.2), referred to as 'plus' or 'cross' polarization. Precisely this effect of changing distances is used for their detection.

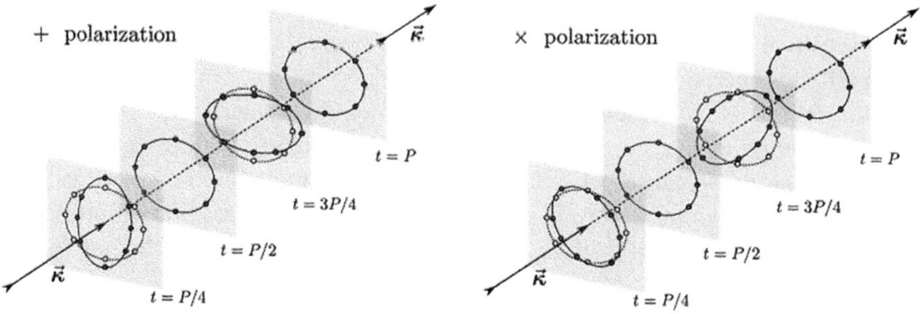

Fig. 10.2 The two possible polarizations of gravitational waves, plus (+) and cross (×), referring to the two ways in which they compress or stretch space–time. (Credits: Bishop & Rezzolla, 2016)

Fig. 10.3 J. Weber and the first bar detector, at the University of Maryland in 1969. (Credits: AIP Emilio Segrè Visual Archives, 1969)

There are two kinds of detectors: bar detectors and laser interferometric detectors. The first kind uses the effect of changing distances between the atoms of a single massive block of metal, usually in the shape of a sphere or a cylinder (Fig. 10.3). The impact of a gravitational wave on such a body displaces atoms inside and causes characteristic vibrations, which can be picked up electronically. Bar detectors were the first in use, from the 1960s onwards. However, up to the present, they have not been sensitive enough to detect any gravitational waves, so there are only a few of them left still operational (Di Mauro et al., 2021).

This brings us to the second class of detectors, laser interferometric detectors. These make use of the fact that distances change differently in different directions. They monitor the distance between a fixed central point and two bodies located at large distances from the centre in directions at 90° with respect to each other. The entire set-up resembles an 'L' (Fig. 10.4). The distances between the bodies and the centre are continuously monitored and compared using laser beams which are reflected back and forth between the centre and the bodies, which are, in fact, highly polished mirrors. Any change due to the stretching of one distance and the simultaneous compression of the other causes a shift in the interference pattern of the light,

Fig. 10.4 Above: The Laser Interferometer Gravitational-Wave Observatory's detectors in the United States. Below: Virgo and the European Gravitational Observatory's detectors in Italy. (Credits: LIGO Scientific Collaboration, 2020b; Virgo Collaboration, 2015)

that is, a change in the intensity of the light that is seen in a camera at the centre (LIGO Scientific Collaboration, 2020a). The effect on the relative distance of the bodies from the centre is minute: the gravitational waves expected from the most violent events, the merger of two black holes, change the length by a factor of 10^{-22}. This corresponds to the ratio of the diameter of an atom to the distance between the Sun and Saturn.

This tiny number explains the long time it took between the prediction of the existence of gravitational waves in 1916 and their detection in 2015. To measure such minute changes to a distance, many technological breakthroughs were necessary, not the least one being, of course, the invention of the laser, which – incidentally – is itself also due to the insights of Einstein.

The detection of gravitational waves is perhaps one of the most breathtaking technological achievements in the history of humanity. The first detection of a gravitational wave occurred on 14 September 2015. The Laser Interferometer Gravitational-Wave Observatory (LIGO) Scientific Community (LSC) refers to this event as

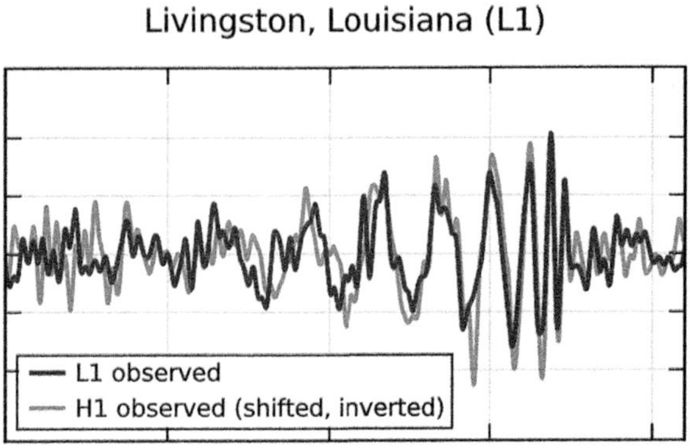

Fig. 10.5 This diagram shows the gravitational wave signals generated by this event over time as detected by the two LIGO detectors. Since the detectors are at different locations on Earth, they do not see exactly the same signal at the same time, but slightly different signals. Correcting for these differences, the two signals show a remarkable resemblance in many features, for instance their duration are both a quarter of a second. (Credits: LIGO Scientific Collaboration and Virgo Collaboration, 2016)

GW150914. It took the LSC several months to verify that the signal seen in both detectors – one in Livingstone (Louisiana) and Hanford (Washington State), 3000 km apart – was not a fluke but referred to a bona fide gravitational wave (Fig. 10.5). After running many consistency checks and comparing with computer simulations which determine the expected signals by solving Einstein's equations – a complicated problem which can take several days, even weeks to finish – the reality of the event became clear (LIGO Scientific Collaboration & Virgo Collaboration, 2016).

Simply outlining the chronology of the process which generated this gravitational wave signal shows the extraordinary character of the event: two black holes of approximately 30 solar masses finally merged after spiralling into each other at a third of the speed of light for an exceptionally long time; the final merger event lasted less than 20 ms, and in that instant, the system released the energetic equivalent of three suns in the form of gravitational waves, which rippled through space–time for 1.3 billion years until they were finally detected in LIGO's laboratories, as a deformation of one-thousandth the diameter of the nucleus of an atom. This was measured using a combination of the most stable lasers ever generated, the smoothest mirrors ever produced, and the second most-intense vacuum chamber on Earth.

In one swoop, this single event confirmed many theoretical and experimental expectations. It triggered the award of several Nobel Prizes to six scientists: the prize in Physics in 2017 was awarded for decisive contributions to the LIGO detector and the observation of gravitational waves to Rainer Weiss, Barry Barish and Kip Thorne. The Nobel Prize in Physics in 2020 was awarded for the discovery of a supermassive black hole in the centre of our galaxy to Reinhard Genzel and Andrea Ghez, and for the theory of black hole formation by gravitational collapse to Roger Penrose (Royal Swedish Academy of Sciences, 2017, 2020).

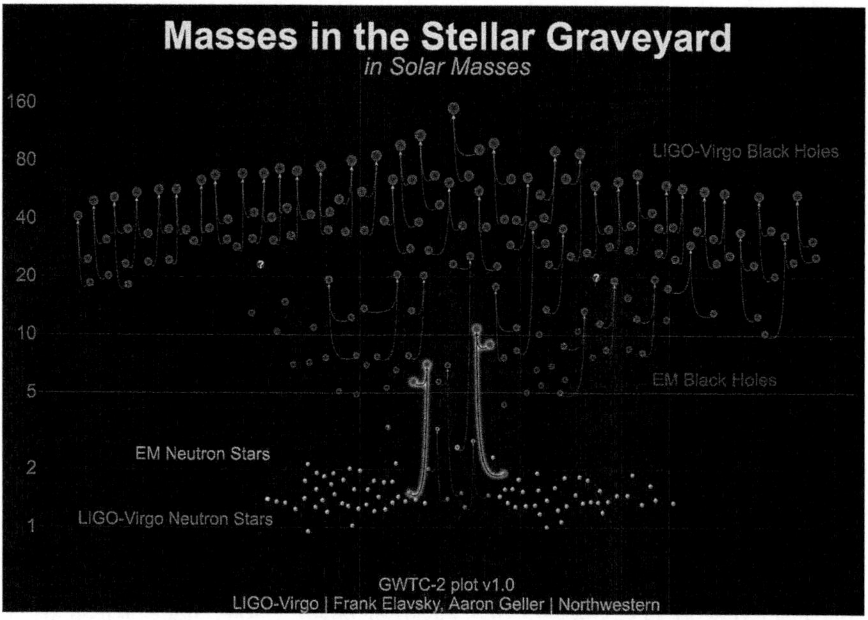

Fig. 10.6 All the detected binary mergers and their results. (Credits: LIGO Scientific Collaboration, 2021)

Since 2015 the LSC, with the additional detectors VIRGO in Italy and KAGRA in Japan, which have since become operational, has detected many more merger events. Most of those events are two black holes colliding and merging, but there are also events where a neutron star and a black hole, or even two neutron stars, have formed a new compact object (see Fig. 10.6). These events are exciting for several reasons, which we will discuss next.

What Can We Expect to See?

As we have seen, one of the crucial factors for detecting gravitational waves is the 'arm-length', the distance between the centre and the mirrors which reflect the laser light back and forth. For the earth-based detectors, the arm-length is around 4 km (there are plans for advanced detectors underground with an arm-length of up to 10 km). But LISA will have an arm-length of 2.5 million km. This is an entirely different ball game!

This means that the sensitivity of the apparatus will be high enough to see many violent events that have happened in the entire visible part of the Universe all the way back to the Big Bang. As with 'detectors' for electromagnetic radiation (such as telescopes, radio antennas, infrared cameras or X-ray detectors), there is a specific band of frequencies outside of which a gravitational wave detector is 'blind'. This is also the case for LISA, but its visibility band is broad enough to allow for many events to be seen.

An exciting aspect of this new way to observe the Universe with gravitational waves is multi-messenger astronomy, which allows us to observe the same event through many different windows. The detection of GW150914 was, clearly, a community effort. Considering the smallness of the signal, the only possibility of isolating it is to compare (at least) two measurements to distinguish it in both instruments from the local, random noise. Suppose VIRGO (at the time, the only other completed detector) had been operational. In that case, the position of the event could have been triangulated, and it could have been studied in more detail using other kinds of detectors and observatories.

This was exemplified just short of 2 years after the first detection event. GW170817 was first detected by VIRGO, and shortly after by LIGO's detectors, allowing (not without difficulties) (Castelvecchi, 2017) the identification of a small enough region in the sky for astronomers to point their telescopes at. Just seconds after the event, a gamma-ray burst was observed. Other observations – at different wavelengths – followed for days, making this the first multi-messenger detection of a neutron star collision ever (Fig. 10.7). By using the gravitational wave signal alone, it would have been impossible to reach this conclusion: the many different views of the event due to the corresponding electromagnetic observations helped us to understand it, and also provided valuable insights into the many other aspects of the structure of neutron stars.

Another fascinating aspect of LISA's coming online is the possibility of exploring many open questions in fundamental physics (Arun et al., 2022; Barausse et al., 2020). The advantage of having pushed open the gravitational wave window is that it extends our view back to the Big Bang, in stark contrast to electromagnetic waves, which can provide us with information only from about 300,000 years after the Big Bang (Fig. 10.8).

This is due to the decoupling, a process during the history of the Universe where the hot plasma that existed shortly after the Big Bang had cooled down sufficiently to let the individual charged particles, overwhelmingly electrons and protons, combine into neutral hydrogen atoms. With electromagnetic waves, we can see the structure of the Universe at that time encoded into the Cosmic Microwave Background.

Everything that happened before this recombination phase is shielded from electromagnetic waves, but completely transparent to gravitational waves. This will allow us to probe not only the predictions of high energy physics and particle physics but also the details of the Big Bang, which is one of the most mysterious events that modern cosmology grapples with.

Here are some of the scientific questions that LISA will explore:

- LISA records the inspirals (shrinking orbits) and mergers of binary black holes, the most powerful transformations of energy in the Universe, allowing precision measurements of systems composed only of pure dynamical space–time.
- LISA will map isolated black holes with high precision, verifying whether they agree with the stationary space–time configurations, discovered by the

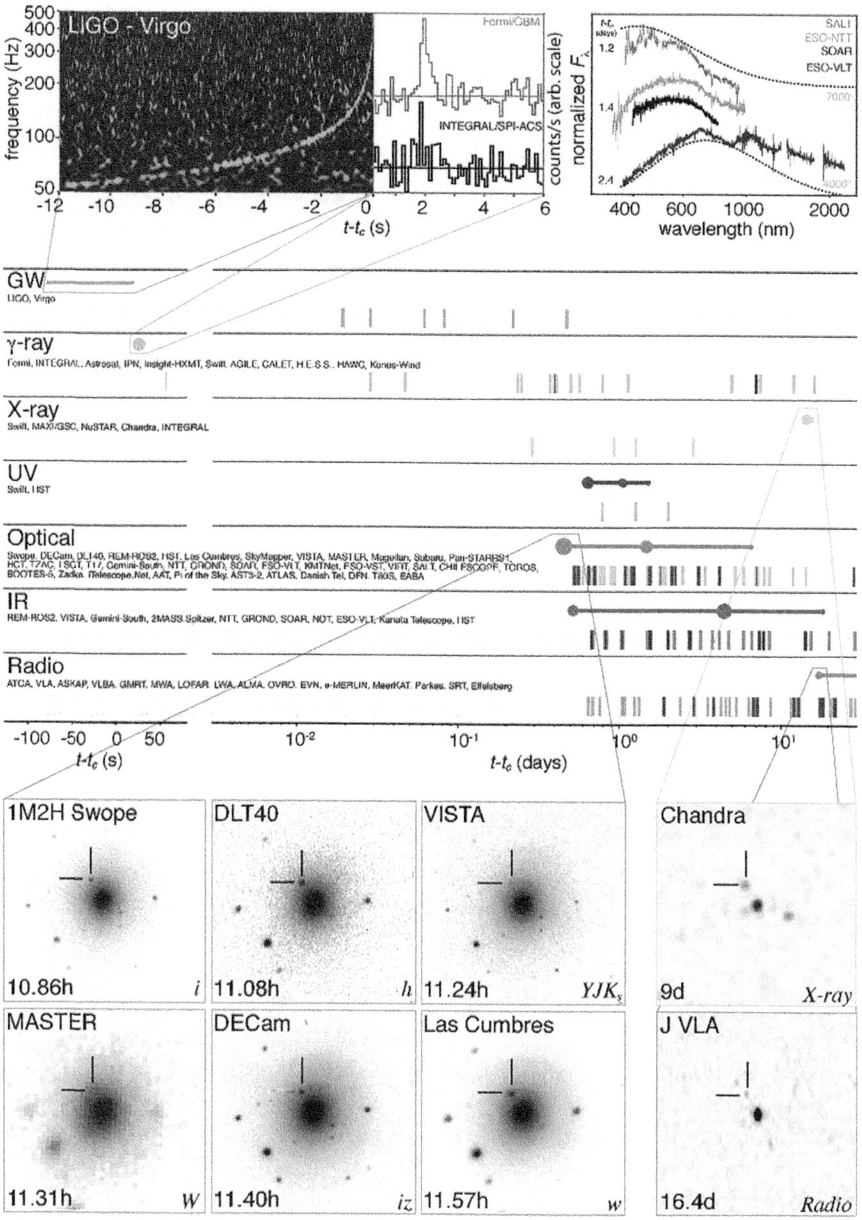

Fig. 10.7 Chronology of the multi-messenger detection of GW170817 in all the detectors that contributed to its determination (from gravitational waves to gamma waves, down to radio waves). Different ticks correspond to different signals, all correlating to different processes during the collision of the neutron stars. (Credits: Abbott et al., 2017)

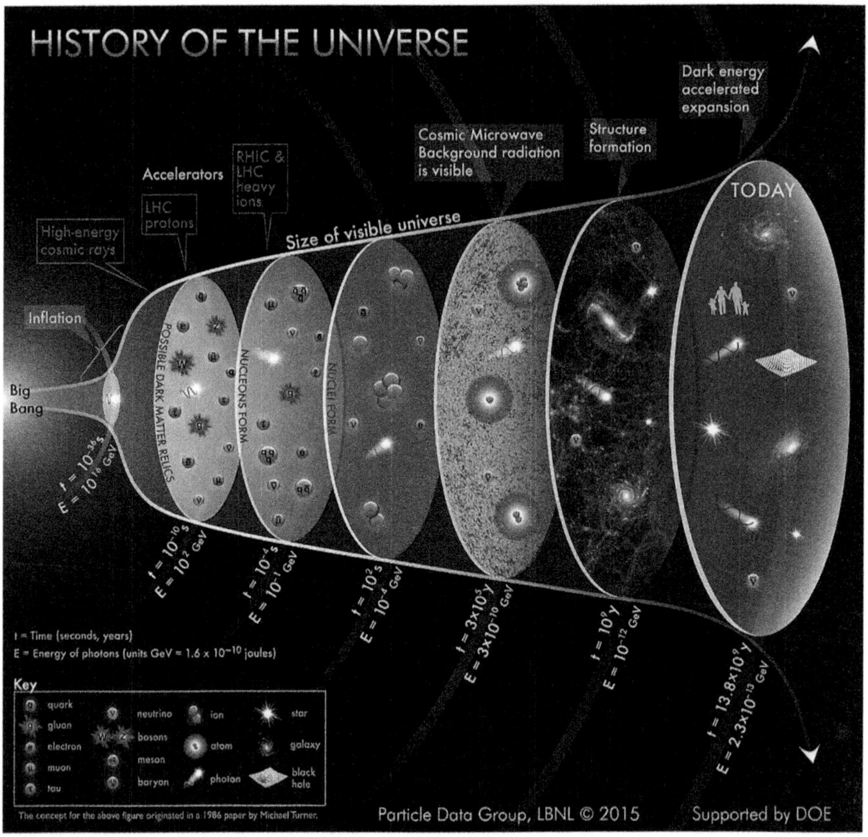

Fig. 10.8 The current picture of the history of the Universe. Everything earlier than 300,000 years is invisible to electromagnetic waves, but transparent to gravitational waves. (Credits: Particle Data Group, 2015)

New Zealander Roy Kerr in 1963. According to the 'no-hair' theorem these 'Kerr–Newman black holes' can be completely characterized using only three numbers: the mass of the black hole, its spin around its axis of rotation, and its electric charge.

- LISA directly observes how massive black holes form, grow and interact over the entire history of galaxy formation.
- LISA measures precise, gravitationally calibrated absolute luminosity distances to high redshift, with the potential to contribute uniquely to the measurement of the Hubble constant and dark energy.
- LISA studies in detail thousands of compact binary stars in our galaxy, providing new insights into the properties of matter at the extreme endpoints of stellar evolution.
- LISA may find entirely new phenomena of nature not detected using light or other particles (Amaro-Seoane et al., 2017).

In summary, LISA will open a further window to the Universe based on gravitational waves, which complements the existing electromagnetic and gravitational wave windows. This will allow us to probe many fundamental physics questions that have been puzzling scientists for some time now. This advance is only possible due to cutting-edge technology, which we will discuss next.

LISA Technology

LISA is a visionary project right at the edge of our current technology. Yet, it already has a long history of development. The first formulation of what will be LISA was very much a big LIGO in space (Faller et al., 1989): three (initially four) spacecraft would have carried more or less the same experimental setup as the ground detector, with most of it in a central spacecraft, and the reflective test masses in the other two, in a 90° (initially 120°) configuration. Over the course of a decade, many other designs were proposed – such as the six double triangles of the SAGITTARIUS mission – but they were all later merged into a single mission: LISAG (later LISA) was born in May 1993, at the conclusion of the call for mission proposal by the European Space Agency (ESA) of the same year (Danzmann et al., 1993). From 1997 to 2011, ESA and NASA (intermittently) tightly collaborated to develop the vision of the space detector further, going back to the original three-spacecraft configuration and laying the foundation for a preliminary mission aimed at testing the necessary technology (in November 2000, this mission would be named LISA Pathfinder) (European Space Agency, 2019b).

In 2005, ESA created the decennial plan COSMIC VISION 2015–2025 (approved in 2007), as a logical continuation of the effort culminating in the landing of the Huygens Probe on Titan, one of the 83 known moons of Saturn. The mission cycle includes many different themes, and LISA was selected as a candidate for 'The Gravitational Universe' as an L3 mission in October 2013 (the L missions are long-term missions within the active research cycle, together with JUICE (European Space Agency, 2014) – the L1 multi-band observer for the ice configuration of Jupiter's moons – and ATHENA (Piro et al., 2021) – the L2 X-ray telescope designed to study the large-scale structure of the Universe and the merging of black holes). LISA's launch was planned to be in 2034, but the complexity of the mission necessitated many adjustments 'in progress': the definitive launch date (if all goes to plan) is now set to be in 2037, after the spectacular result of the LISA Pathfinder mission (see below) concluded the Proposal Phase. By the end of 2017, Phase 0 of the mission was completed, highlighting the first necessary requirements for the preliminary development. The first draft of the design was finalized during Phase A in December 2021, and the project is now in Phase B1, in which its final design will be confirmed, and the Red Book (how ESA has historically named final reports on its projects) will be published (European Space Agency, 2022).

For now, LISA is designed to consist of three satellites in an equilateral triangle configuration, with an arm-length of 2.5 million km. They will move in heliocentric

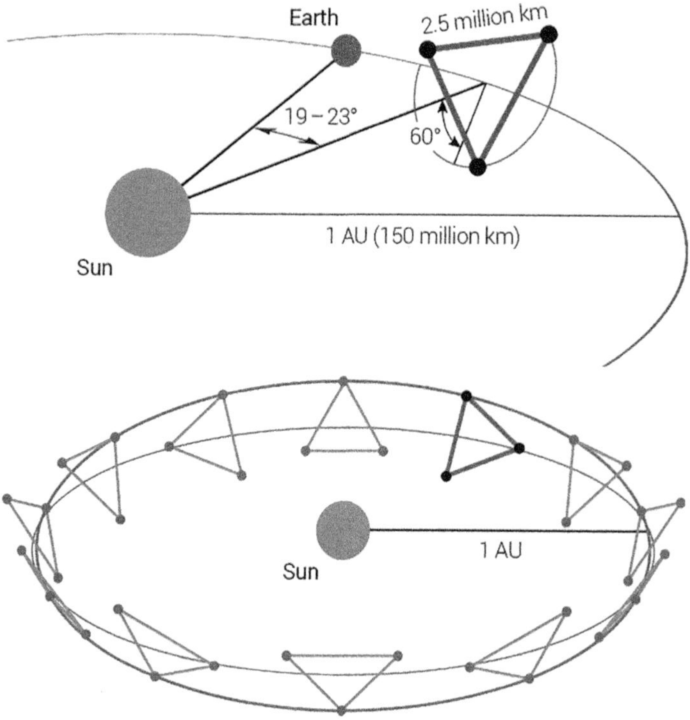

Fig. 10.9 The orbit of LISA in relation to Earth (above) and the Sun (below). Notice how the triangle rotates around its centre during 1 year, while the centre is always at the same distance from our planet. (Credits: Amaro-Seoane et al., 2017)

orbits at a distance of approximately 60 million km from Earth (see Fig. 10.9). Each satellite will act as a central body with the other two probes as 'mirrors', sending laser beams back and forth. Unlike the Earth-based detectors, which are 'L'-shaped, these detectors will have an angle of 60° between their arms. Thus, the whole set-up will operate as three laser interferometers.

However, the large distance between the spacecraft requires the optical system to be much more complex. The laser beam sent out by a probe has an initial power of about 4 watts. When it reaches the other probes, its power has decreased to some 100 picowatts; this is a decrease by a factor of about 10^{-10}. Therefore, it is impossible to just passively reflect the beam as is done in ground-based systems. Instead, each probe creates its own laser beam entirely in synch, phase-locked, with the arriving one, and sends this newly created intense laser beam onwards to the next probe, creating, in essence, two rings of coherent light between the three spacecraft. Consequently, each spacecraft must carry, among other systems, an optical bench, a laser, a telescope to receive the incoming light, a camera and a solar array for power supply.

The high complexity of the optical system makes it very sensitive to any noise caused by a 'bumpy flight' of the spacecraft; it can only be achieved in a particularly isolated environment: 'the quietest place in space' (Paul McNamara et al., 2018), as ESA calls it, is consistently created by the spaceships themselves as a 'bubble' around the test masses, allowing them to proceed undisturbed by solar wind, drag or tidal forces. We will describe the essence of this technique next.

LISA Pathfinder

As described above, a major challenge to the success of the mission comes from the drag that influences the trajectory of each probe. Recall that each probe follows its own path around the Sun, maintaining the equilateral triangle configuration 'automagically' due to the laws of physics. At least, this is the ideal situation. In reality, however, numerous external influences may have an impact on the path, such as the solar wind emitted from the Sun, micrometeorites or other small particles scattered along the course of the probes, since outer space is not perfectly empty. These will create a drag on the probes, causing them to veer off their intended paths and destroying the triangular configuration. They will also cause the flight of each spacecraft to be less smooth than is necessary for the laser light to stay in synch. Therefore, it is essential that the path of each satellite is followed as closely to the ideal (geodesic) path and as smoothly as possible.

The proposed solution is ingenious: each probe is hollow, containing a small metal cube made out of a gold–platinum alloy with a mass of 2 kg inside its cavity. Both the probe and the body inside it fall around the Sun, but the surrounding probe shields the cube from external influences. Therefore, the cube follows an ideal trajectory. The satellite around it follows almost the same path, but because it is subject to external drag, it must correct its motion. This is achieved by mini-thrusters, small rockets, which manoeuvre the probe so that the pathfinder, i.e., the small body inside, is kept still at a fixed location inside the cavity without touching the walls.

In this way, it can be arranged that the entire spacecraft follows an ideal path. While almost all other systems can be developed and tested in labs on Earth, the drag-free orbital motion can only be tested in space. Therefore, on 3 December 2015, the LISA Pathfinder mission was launched from Kourou in French Guiana and stayed operational for 576 days. It consisted of a miniature version of one of the three LISA spacecraft, containing two test masses and the whole preliminary system of thrusters aimed at allowing the masses to proceed in an almost perfect geodesic trajectory. Incidentally, the thrusters themselves are a new technology developed for this specific purpose.

The results were a pleasant surprise: LISA Pathfinder performed much better than expected, keeping the probe on track much better than necessary for the LISA mission (Fig. 10.10). The remaining noise level was five times smaller than the requirement. This proved that the drag-free motion technology is ready for the

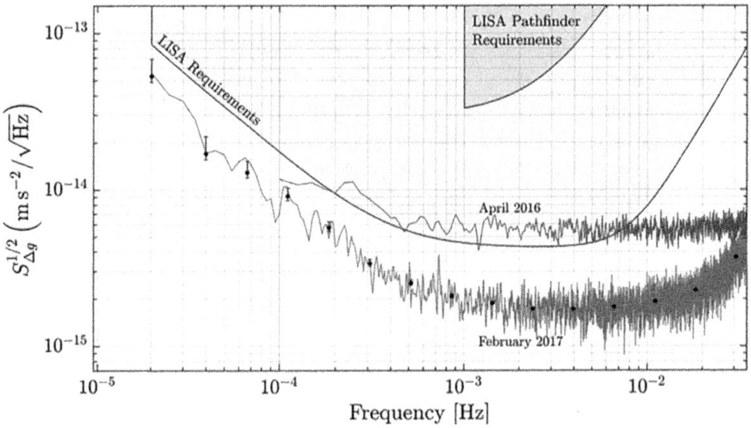

Fig. 10.10 The results of the LISA Pathfinder mission. The diagram shows the noise levels necessary for the smooth operation of the LISA spacecraft. The curves show the measured noise levels at different stages of the mission (Credits: Armano et al., 2016)

further development of the LISA detector. It was also reassuring that the entire structure could withstand the impact of the rocket launch. The success of the LISA pathfinder mission green-lighted the beginning of Phase B1, as mentioned above, perfectly in line with the mission's plan and estimated launch date.

LISA Collaboration: An International Collaborative Effort

It is probably evident from what we said above that the LISA mission is a highly ambitious and complex enterprise. A single entity cannot realize all the different aspects of the project. ESA and NASA coordinate the overall technological organization, but there are also many scientific aspects which have to be researched and newly developed. The entire organization of the effort is shown in Fig. 10.11.

The organization of the project is shared by three entities: ESA, NASA and the LISA Consortium. The figure shows that ESA and NASA mainly contribute the technology necessary to put the three satellites into orbit. The LISA Consortium is a union of academic institutions and individual scientists worldwide. It consists of several working groups in science, instrument development and data analysis. The consortium is responsible for the development of the scientific equipment on board the spacecraft, for the collection and storage of the data accumulated during the active phase of the experiment and for the scientific evaluation and interpretation of the data.

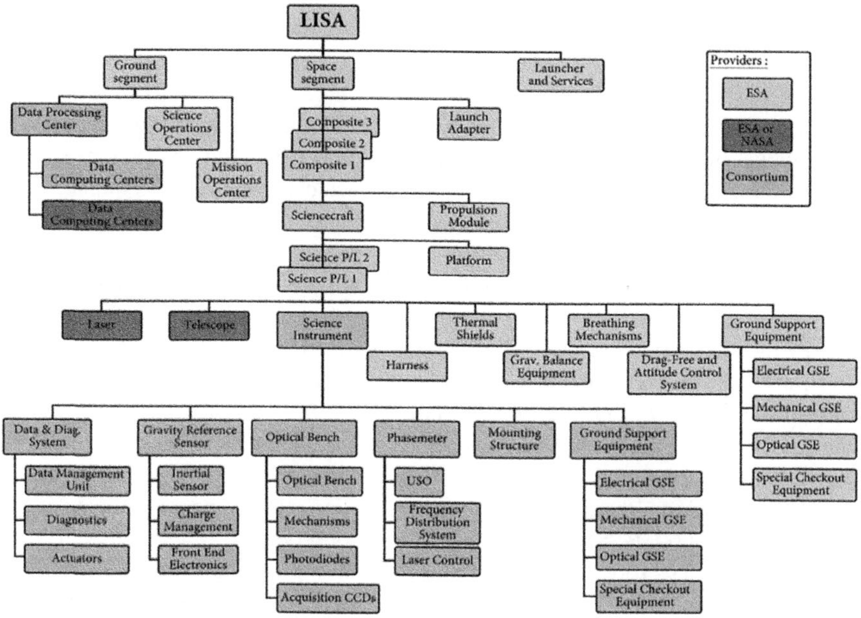

Fig. 10.11 The structure of the LISA Collaboration. This organigram refers to the operational aspects of the project. (Credits: Amaro-Seoane et al., 2017)

Industry Involvement

The LISA Pathfinder mission is a prime example of how public space agencies, the scientific community and industrial partners can be coordinated to realize the common goal of a successful mission. Many aspects of the subsystems on board the spacecraft had to be newly developed, tested and built. In many cases, this created new know-how, which is valuable to the industrial partners in many different technological sectors, such as, of course, the space industry, but also in laser technology and high-precision measurement.

There is a long list of industrial partners across Europe who contributed to the LISA Pathfinder mission. A (very short) partial list consists of (European Space Agency, 2019a):

- Austrian Aerospace (thermal hardware)
- Siemens (radio equipment)
- Airbus (Drag Free and Attitude Control System, or DFACS)
- Thales (solar arrays)
- EADS (power systems)
- RUAG Space (spacecraft structure)
- EUROCKOT (launch vehicle)
- GMV (software)
- NTE-SENER (data management)

A similar model is operational in the case of the LISA mission.

Data

The operation of the mission will be handled similarly to the LISA Pathfinder mission, which proved quite efficient. Once operational, the instrument will send a continuous stream of data to the ground stations and then on to the Science Operations Centre, which is run by shared ESA and Consortium personnel. From there, pre-processed and calibrated data are transferred to the data processing centres, several of which will exist across Europe and the United States. These are special data centres to extract scientifically meaningful information from the data. The processing of the data will be handled by the Consortium Science Community. The extracted information will be a catalogue of identified waveforms (Level 2 data) and further processed and interpreted (Level 3) data, consisting of catalogues of identified sources with faithful representations of posterior parameter distributions. These ‘science products’ will be transferred back to the Science Operations Centre, where they will be stored in a public archive.

It is expected that the daily amount of data which must be handled this way will amount to about 6 GB. Since LISA is an all-sky observatory, it will detect multiple overlapping signals (possibly in the thousands) during its operational period. Identifying and extracting these signals from the data stream is a challenging data analysis task. In anticipation of these challenges, several highly successful Mock LISA Data Challenges have engaged the scientific community for several years. It is anticipated that similar challenges will continue in the future to make the data analysis as efficient as possible.

Scientific Evaluation

The signal extraction is the part where the models of the physical processes which cause these signals come into play. The sophisticated statistical algorithms which are used to process the data streams are based on actual clean waveform signals which have been obtained based on different models about the structure of the various possible sources for gravitational waves. Depending on the kind of source, the waveforms have been computed from the exact equations of General Relativity or from appropriate approximations of those, such as the post-Newtonian approximation. Other models are based on the classical Newtonian theory of mechanics and use only the so-called quadrupole formula to derive an approximate waveform.

The waveforms of various sources depend very much on the intrinsic processes. Prime examples are neutron stars and supernova explosions, where very detailed information about the nuclear structure inside the stars is relevant and necessary because small changes in the intrinsic structure can have sizeable effects on the gravitational waveform signal.

These models and the waveforms they predict flow into the extraction algorithms and are used to verify the existence of events, together with an estimate of the parameters of the processes that caused that event.

Many groups in the LISA Consortium are working on the simulation of these processes. Others try to estimate the abundance of particular sources and their distribution across the Universe. This brings us now to the part that New Zealand plays in this enterprise.

New Zealand's Contribution to LISA

Marsden Council Grant

The Marsden Fund, in 2021, awarded its Council from Government grant to the project 'Gravitational Waves: Sources and Signals' (Royal Society Te Apārangi, 2021). This is a collaborative project between eight academic institutions (five in New Zealand and three in Europe). It is highly interdisciplinary, covering research areas from astrophysics, gravitational physics, mathematics and statistics. It is led by the University of Auckland. The team will look at both the statistical challenges faced when attempting to extract the gravitational wave signals from the raw data and the properties of crucial sources of gravitational waves. All the team members are part of the LISA Consortium, and the entire project is closely coordinated with the consortium.

Four specific goals will be aimed at during the three-year funding period. The first aim is to answer the question of how many compact sources are expected to be found in the Milky Way. Here, it is envisaged that there are not only binary systems consisting of two black holes contributing to the gravitational wave signals but also binary systems made up of neutron stars or even white dwarfs. Also, there could be binaries, triples or even quadruples. Their gravitational wave signals will look very different from those of the binaries.

The second aim is to obtain information about fundamental physics. Giant, supermassive black holes are ubiquitously found at the hearts of large galaxies. It is believed that the merger of two galaxies is followed by the merger of their central black holes; LISA can detect these events to the edge of the visible universe. It is also widely believed that dark matter (about the nature of which there exist various proposals) can influence the details of these mergers. Using particular models for dark matter, this project will explore its influence on the merger dynamics, using numerical simulations. Then, comparing these with actual measured LISA data will provide valuable insights into the nature of the dark matter, which is a total mystery at present.

The next aim has a more statistical flavour. Extreme mass-ratio inspirals (EMRIs) are processes in which a giant black hole captures a small compact object. EMRIs are among the most fascinating LISA sources, but the signal templates are challenging to compute with the necessary accuracy. This project will pursue two statistical strategies to reliably extract possible waveforms: one makes use of Markov chain Monte

Carlo (MCMC) algorithms with Bayesian calibration with approximate waveforms, and the other uses artificial intelligence with accurate numerical waveforms.

The final aim of the project is to extract signals from the stochastic gravitational wave background (SGWB). Roughly speaking, this is the combination of all the gravitational wave signals that cannot be individually resolved. But there is also a variety of mechanisms, including the inflationary phase immediately after the Big Bang, cosmological phase transitions, and the dynamics of hypothetical cosmic string networks, which can cause stochastic backgrounds, offering insight into the early Universe and ultra-high energy particle physics. Several statistical methods will be developed to extract, map and separate these SGWB sources, allowing LISA to detect or constrain these important cosmological backgrounds.

In addition, the overarching, non-scientific goal is to build momentum for a decades-long collaboration with international teams in one of the world's most exciting scientific endeavours by building up sufficient know-how at New Zealand universities. This will help realize the potential of gravitational wave observatories to advance stellar astronomy, galactic astrophysics and fundamental particle physics.

Opportunities

It is obvious from the descriptions given above that the role that the New Zealand team plays in the overall LISA mission is very minimal, even when, on the national scale, a Marsden Council grant is one of the most significant awarded to a scientific team. But it is just as evident that the LISA mission is not only a scientifically challenging project but necessarily also a project that must go to the limits of current technology – and beyond. It is only possible as a joint enterprise that crosses boundaries; national boundaries as well as the boundaries between the academic and industrial sectors. The latter 'transgression' is most attractive because here is where the know-how is created and technology transfer happens. This is to the benefit of both the scientific and the industrial partners. The industry in Europe and the United States put their own funds into developing the new technology because they expect the transfer of the know-how into other more commercial sectors of their business.

It would make sense for the New Zealand Government to give more support to the LISA mission. There are several reasons for this. Of course, there is the purely idealistic aspect of being part of a large enterprise that challenges the boundaries of modern science and technology and aims to demonstrate the capabilities of humankind as long as enough of us are dedicated. However, as we have seen, the LISA project is clearly not purely scientific. It is motivated by one of the most exciting and challenging aspects of modern science, but the pathway to its realization leads through equally difficult technological advances. More intense participation in the LISA project could help improve New Zealand's severe shortcomings in funding for research and development, as well as for education, that has been affecting the sector for such a long time. In particular, a formal, dedicated commitment to the mission could have several effects:

- It could boost the just-emerging space industry of New Zealand. More generally, it could create incentives for local companies in the relevant technological areas which want to contribute to the mission to put their own funds into research because it might become advantageous for other applications. New Zealand has a distinctive culture, in that industrial research is supposed to be funded mainly through governmental sources.
- This, in turn, could help establish career pathways for young scientists between industrial and academic partners, where industry-funded research is carried out at universities and other academic institutions. This model is realized all over Europe and the United States and seems to be very successful because it gives perspectives to emerging scientists. This might also help prevent the outflow of talented young scientists from New Zealand to other countries. They are mostly lost to the nation and must be replaced by importing overseas academics to the higher ranks of the universities. This seems to be counter-intuitive.
- It might foster even more international scientific relationships. A case in point here is the possibly emerging participation of New Zealand in the Horizon Europe framework. If realized, this would be an ideal vehicle to increase scientific collaborations with the EU, particularly concerning the LISA mission.
- As outlined above, there is a high demand in LISA for advanced data science and artificial intelligence methods. New Zealand is in a good position here since there are already many ambitious start-ups in this sector. Participation in the LISA mission, if made possible by governmental actions, could help expand this industry further and make New Zealand one of the leading countries in data science.
- The general problem in New Zealand, which affects many industries and may, incidentally, also be one of the reasons for the country's relative lack of industrial research and development, is the low standard of education in the STEM areas compared to other countries. The problem originates in secondary schools and propagates into universities, where it cannot be completely corrected. The consequence is that, on average, New Zealand graduates are not on the same level as their overseas counterparts. It would be an outstanding achievement if a commitment to the LISA project, or any scientific project with similar exposure, could help to motivate the young and make them see that there is an intrinsic value in pursuing a career in a STEM area. It would be even greater if the government could see this value also and would further strengthen education in STEM subjects (in particular in Mathematics), as is done in other OECD countries.

Conclusion

In this chapter, we have presented an overview of the LISA mission. This is a global initiative in space science that aims to put three satellites into orbits around the Sun. The mission aims to bring the spacecraft into a triangular configuration where they can operate as three laser interferometric detectors for gravitational waves. These will provide scientists with detailed information about some of the most violent and complex processes in the Universe, such as the collision and merger of galaxies and the supermassive black holes in their centres, or the merger of neutron stars. It is also expected that the mission will provide new insights into the beginning and the origin of the Universe, since gravitational waves have been travelling uninhibited through it since the Big Bang.

The size of the mission necessitates the global cooperation of states, institutions and individuals across academia and industry, thereby creating numerous possibilities for synergies, cross-fertilizations, new know-how and possible commercial applications. On 25th of January 2024, ESA's (https://www.esa.int/Science_Exploration/Space_Science/Capturing_the_ripples_of_spacetime_LISA_gets_go-ahead) Science Programme Committee approved the LISA Mission. This important step gives the go-ahead to build the instruments and spacecraft.

Acknowledgements The authors wish to acknowledge support for their research by the Marsden Fund Council from Government funding, managed by Royal Society Te Apārangi.

Bibliography

Abbott, B. P., Abbott, R., Abbott, T. D., Acernese, F., Ackley, K., Adams, C., Adams, T., Addesso, P., Adhikari, R. X., Adya, V. B., Affeldt, C., Afrough, M., Agarwal, B., Agathos, M., Agatsuma, K., Aggarwal, N., Aguiar, O. D., Aiello, L., Ain, A., et al. (2017). Multi-messenger observations of a binary neutron star merger. *The Astrophysical Journal, 848*(2), L12. https://doi.org/10.3847/2041-8213/aa91c9

AIP Emilio Segrè Visual Archives. (1969). *Joseph Weber checking the wires that connect the crystals on the 38 inch bar.* [Still Image]. Emilio Segrè Visual Archives General Collection. https://repository.aip.org/islandora/object/nbla%3A314209

Amaro-Seoane, P., Audley, H., Babak, S., Baker, J., Barausse, E., Bender, P., Berti, E., Binetruy, P., Born, M., Bortoluzzi, D., Camp, J., Caprini, C., Cardoso, V., Colpi, M., Conklin, J., Cornish, N., Cutler, C., Danzmann, K., Dolesi, R., ... Zweifel, P. (2017). *Laser interferometer space antenna.* https://doi.org/10.48550/ARXIV.1702.00786

Armano, M., Audley, H., Auger, G., Baird, J. T., Bassan, M., Binetruy, P., Born, M., Bortoluzzi, D., Brandt, N., Caleno, M., Carbone, L., Cavalleri, A., Cesarini, A., Ciani, G., Congedo, G., Cruise, A. M., Danzmann, K., de Deus Silva, M., De Rosa, R., et al. (2016). Sub-Femto-g free fall for space-based gravitational wave observatories: LISA pathfinder results. *Physical Review Letters, 116*(23), 231101. https://doi.org/10.1103/PhysRevLett.116.231101

Arun, K. G., Belgacem, E., Benkel, R., Bernard, L., Berti, E., Bertone, G., Besancon, M., Blas, D., Böhmer, C. G., Brito, R., Calcagni, G., Cardenas-Avendaño, A., Clough, K., Crisostomi, M., De Luca, V., Doneva, D., Escoffier, S., Ezquiaga, J. M., Ferreira, P. G., et al. (2022). New horizons for fundamental physics with LISA. *Living Reviews in Relativity, 25*(1), 4. https://doi.org/10.1007/s41114-022-00036-9

Barausse, E., Berti, E., Hertog, T., Huhes, S., Jetzer, P., Pani, P., Sotiriou, T., Tamanini, N., Witek, H., Yagi, K., Yunes, N., Abdelsalhin, T., Achucarro, A., Aelst, K. V., Afshordi, N., Akcay, S., Annulli, L., Arun, K. G., Avendano, A. C., ... Zumalacarregui, M. (2020). *Prospects for fundamental physics with LISA.* ArXiv:2001.09793 [Gr-Qc]. http://arxiv.org/abs/2001.09793

Bishop, N. T., & Rezzolla, L. (2016). Extraction of gravitational waves in numerical relativity. *Living Reviews in Relativity, 19*(1), 2. https://doi.org/10.1007/s41114-016-0001-9

Castelvecchi, D. (2017). Colliding stars spark rush to solve cosmic mysteries. *Nature, 550*(7676), 309–310. https://doi.org/10.1038/550309a

Danzmann K., Rüdiger A., Schilling R., Winkler W., & Winkler W. (1993). *LISA (Laser Interferometer Space Antenna). Proposal for a laser-interferometric gravitational wave detector in space* (MPQ-177; MPQ-Reports). https://www.mpq.mpg.de/4929192/mpq_reports#1993

Di Mauro, M., Esposito, S., & Naddeo, A. (2021). *Towards detecting gravitational waves: A contribution by Richard Feynman*. https://doi.org/10.48550/ARXIV.2111.00330

Einstein, A. (1989). Über das Relativitätsprinzip und die aus demselben gezogenen Folgerungen. In *The Swiss years: writings, 1900–1909* (Vol. 2, pp. 245–281). https://einsteinpapers.press.princeton.edu/vol2-doc/469

Einstein, A. (1996). Naherungsweise Integration der Feldgleichungen der Gravitation. In *The Berlin years: writings, 1914–1917* (Vol. 6, pp. 347–357). https://einsteinpapers.press.princeton.edu/vol6-doc/375

European Space Agency. (2014). *JUICE Red Book*. https://sci.esa.int/documents/33960/35865/1567260128466-JUICE_Red_Book_i1.0.pdf

European Space Agency. (2019a, 01). *Industrial contributions to LISA pathfinder*. https://sci.esa.int/s/8o2XDgW

European Space Agency. (2019b). *LISA Phase 0 CDF study*. https://sci.esa.int/web/lisa/-/59336-lisa-internal-phase-0-cdf-study-final-presentation

European Space Agency. (2022, May 4). *LISA mission moves to final design phase*. https://www.esa.int/Science_Exploration/Space_Science/LISA_mission_moves_to_final_design_phase

Faller, J. E., Bender, P. L., Hall, J. L., Hils, D., Stebbins, R. T., & Vincent, M. A. (1989). An antenna for laser gravitational-wave observations in space. *Advances in Space Research, 9*(9), 107–111. https://doi.org/10.1016/0273-1177(89)90014-8

https://www.esa.int/Science_Exploration/Space_Science/Capturing_the_ripples_of_spacetime_LISA_gets_go-ahead

Inductiveload. (2010). *Orbital decay of PSR B1913+16*. Wikipedia Commons. https://commons.wikimedia.org/wiki/File:PSR_B1913%2B16_period_shift_graph.svg

LIGO Scientific Collaboration. (2020a). *Instrument science white paper 2020*. https://dcc.ligo.org/LIGO-T2000407/public

LIGO Scientific Collaboration. (2020b, 19). *LIGO laboratory's response to COVID-19*. LIGO News. https://www.ligo.caltech.edu/news/ligo20200317

LIGO Scientific Collaboration. (2021). *Masses in the Stellar Graveyard: GWTC-2 + NSBHs (GW200105/GW200115)*. LIGO Lab. https://www.ligo.caltech.edu/image/ligo20210629b

LIGO Scientific Collaboration & Virgo Collaboration. (2016). GW150914: First results from the search for binary black hole coalescence with advanced LIGO. *Physical Review, 93*(12), 122003. https://doi.org/10.1103/PhysRevD.93.122003ss

LIGO Scientific Collaboration and Virgo Collaboration. (2016). *Data release for event GW150914 [Data set]*. Gravitational Wave Open Science Center. https://doi.org/10.7935/K5MW2F23

Paul McNamara, Stefano Vitale, Karsten Danzmann, & Markus Bauer. (2018, 05). *ESA creates quietest place in space*. ESA – LISA Pathfinder. https://sci.esa.int/s/8aNdq6A

Particle Data Group. (2015). *Particle Data Group at Lawrence Berkeley National Lab*. https://particleadventure.org/history-universe.html

Piro, L., Ahlers, M., Coleiro, A., Colpi, M., Oña Wilhelmi, E. de, Guainazzi, M., Jonker, P. G., Namara, P. M., Nichols, D. A., O'Brien, P., Troja, E., Vink, J., Aird, J., Amati, L., Anand, S., Bozzo, E., Carrera, F. J., Fabian, A. C., Fryer, C., ... van Eerten, H. (2021). *Multi-messenger-Athena Synergy White Paper (arXiv:2110.15677)*. arXiv. http://arxiv.org/abs/2110.15677

Royal Society Te Apārangi. (2021, 03). *Deciphering gravitational waves and decoding signals from the Universe*. https://www.royalsociety.org.nz/what-we-do/funds-and-opportunities/marsden/awarded-grants/marsden-fund-highlights/2021-marsden-fund-highlights/deciphering-gravitational-waves-and-decoding-signals-from-the-universe

Royal Swedish Academy of Sciences. (2017, October). *Press release: The Nobel Prize in Physics 2017*. https://www.nobelprize.org/prizes/physics/2017/press-release/

Royal Swedish Academy of Sciences. (2020, October). *Press release: The Nobel Prize in Physics 2020*. https://www.nobelprize.org/prizes/physics/2020/press-release/

Virgo Collaboration. (2015). *Virgo aerial view*. Wikipedia Commons. https://commons.wikimedia.org/wiki/File:Virgo_aerial_view_01.jpg

Weisberg, J. M., Nice, D. J., & Taylor, J. H. (2010). Timing measurements of the relativistic binary pulsar PSR B1913+16. *The Astrophysical Journal, 722*(2), 1030–1034. https://doi.org/10.1088/0004-637X/722/2/1030

Chapter 11
Space Weather: A Global Hazard from Space to New Zealand's Technological Infrastructure

Craig J. Rodger, Mark A. Clilverd, Anna Tarr, Daniel H. Mac Manus, Harriet George, Tanja Petersen, and Andrew Renton

Introduction

From a distance, we perceive the Sun as an unchanging source of light. While this is functionally true on a day-to-day human level, at a scientific level, the Sun has many complexities. It interacts with and 'forces' the Earth's system in multiple ways, including through:

- Gravity – an example of this is the tides.
- Electromagnetic radiation – for example, light and heat.
- Solar wind – the stream of charged particles leaving the Sun.

The Sun produces each of these constantly, though there can be complex and dynamic changes.

We term the Sun's influence on our world through the mechanisms mentioned above as 'space weather', primarily where these changes pose a hazard to electrical and technological systems, with examples being satellites, communications, pipelines and electrical power grids. We have only recently begun to realise the threat space weather could pose to our technologically reliant society. Humanity faces

C. J. Rodger (✉) · A. Tarr · D. H. Mac Manus
Department of Physics, University of Otago, Dunedin, New Zealand
e-mail: craig.rodger@otago.ac.nz

M. A. Clilverd
British Antarctic Survey (NERC UKRI), Cambridge, UK

H. George
Department of Physics, University of Helsinki, Helsinki, Finland

T. Petersen
GNS Science, Lower Hutt, New Zealand

A. Renton
Transpower New Zealand Limited, Wellington, New Zealand

M. A. Pozza (ed.), *Ascending to Space*, Space Law and Policy,
https://doi.org/10.1007/978-981-97-0714-0_11

multiple threats from space weather; space-based items of infrastructure, for example, satellites are very vulnerable to space weather as they are largely outside the atmosphere, which provides some shelter to ground-based technologies. As space weather covers multiple physical processes, it can affect various systems in different ways and to different magnitudes.

Space weather phenomena are triggered by changes in the Sun and in interplanetary space and produce impacts on the local Earth environment, ranging from regional hazards to global. Fundamentally, space weather is driven by changes in the Sun's magnetic field, which in turn produces changes in and around the Earth.[1] The aurora is the best-known effect of space weather on our Earth; it has delighted and fascinated humanity for millennia. The effects of space weather have been felt on Earth for billions of years but have only become hazardous since the development of complex technological systems and infrastructure (roughly after the creation of the electric telegraph in the 1830s).[2] Figure 11.1 shows an overview of space weather impacts, both on Earth and in space infrastructure.

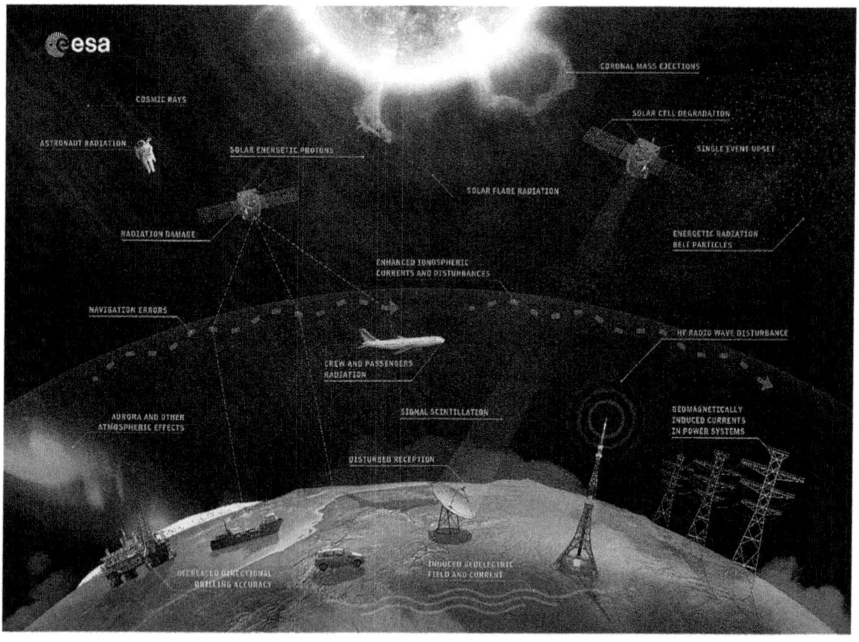

Fig. 11.1 Summary image of space weather effects and impacts on numerous economic and societal sectors (Reprinted from European Space Agency, Space Situational Awareness (SSA), ESA/Science Office, CC BY-SA 3.0 IGO, ESOC Brussels, 25 January 2018 www.esa.int/ESA_Multimedia/Images/2018/01/Space_weather_effects)

[1]Moldwin, M. (2022). *An Introduction to Space Weather*, 2nd edition. Cambridge: Cambridge University Press.

[2]Ibid.

In this chapter, we provide examples of space weather drivers and impacts and present examples of space weather research occurring in New Zealand. We also discuss the potential for space weather warnings to be provided to the New Zealand government and wider society.

The Geophysical Environment

The region of space of most concern when discussing space weather is referred to as geospace. This includes the terrestrial atmosphere and geomagnetic field of Earth, as well as solar emissions from our Sun (Fig. 11.2).

The Sun

The Sun drives almost every physical process on and near Earth as it is our dominant energy source.[3] Studies of the solar–terrestrial environment, especially the charged part of the atmosphere (the ionosphere) and the space around the Earth (the magnetosphere), tend to concentrate on the stream of particles from the Sun (the solar wind), as well as electromagnetic radiation.[4] The Sun undergoes changes in activity

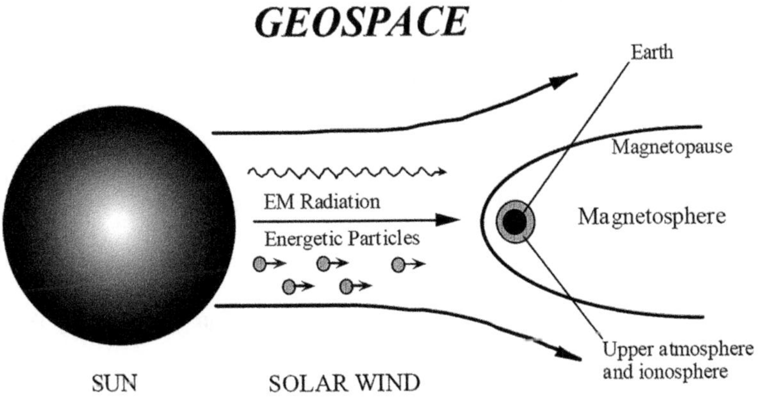

Fig. 11.2 Schematic diagram of the solar–terrestrial environment (Created by the authors of this chapter)

---

[3]Zohuri, M, & McDaniel, P. (2021), Introduction to Energy Essentials: Insight Into Nuclear, Renewable, and Non-Renewable Energies. London: Academic Press.

[4]Hargreaves, J. K. (1992). *The solar–terrestrial environment: An introduction to geospace – the science of the terrestrial upper atmosphere, ionosphere and magnetosphere*. Cambridge: Cambridge University Press.

over an approximately 11-year solar cycle, defined by the differences in the number of dark spots on the solar surface ('sunspots') from a near-zero incidence of sunspots at 'solar minimum', with an increase in sunspots up to the maximum at 'solar maximum'.[5] Solar explosions are associated with sunspot numbers and hence solar activity, such that more solar explosions happen at solar maximum when there are more sunspots.[6]

The Solar Wind

The Sun is constantly losing matter as high-speed electrons and protons escape from its outer layers.[7] Its outer atmosphere is so hot that it 'boils' off into space, escaping the large gravitational attraction of the Sun, in the form of a fully ionised gas, termed a plasma.[8] This stream of outward travelling matter is called the solar wind and forms due to open solar magnetic field lines from which the coronal plasma expands into the interplanetary space.[9] The stream of solar wind is not constant, with fluctuations ranging from roughly 250 to 750 km/s at Earth's orbit.[10]

The Geomagnetic Field and Magnetosphere

The Earth's magnetic field is easy to detect, which has allowed observations of the geomagnetic field to be made for well over 350 years, leading to good quality understanding of its properties, variation and relationships.[11]

The charged plasma that makes up the solar wind – carrying with it the Sun's magnetic field – interacts with Earth's geomagnetic field and determines the structure of the magnetosphere.[12] The total geomagnetic field is made up of an internal field and an external field. The external magnetic field is generated by extraterrestrial

[5] Moldwin, M. (2022). *An Introduction to Space Weather*, 2nd edition. Cambridge: Cambridge University Press.

[6] Ibid.

[7] Jursa, A. S. (1985). Handbook of Geophysics and the Space Environment. Springfield: Air Force Geophys. Lab.

[8] Ibid.

[9] Ibid.

[10] Hargreaves, J. K. (1992). *The solar–terrestrial environment: An introduction to geospace – the science of the terrestrial upper atmosphere, ionosphere and magnetosphere*. Cambridge: Cambridge University Press.

[11] Chapman, S. (1951). *The Earth's Magnetism*, 2nd ed. New York: John Wiley and Sons.

[12] Jursa, A. S. (1985). Handbook of Geophysics and the Space Environment. Springfield: Air Force Geophys. Lab.

sources (such as the solar wind) which tend to vary over quite short time scales,[13] whereas the internal field is generated by the Earth itself through the motion of molten iron and nickel rock in the outer mantle.[14] The internal field is approximately dipolar, with magnetic field lines emerging from near the centre of Antarctica and curving around to re-enter in the Arctic. A useful mental image is the common children's magnetic field experiment using a bar magnet and iron filings, but obviously on a much bigger scale.

The solar wind is deflected by Earth's magnetic field, producing a geomagnetic cavity around Earth's magnetosphere and the Earth itself (see, for example, Fig. 11.2[15] or an appropriate space physics textbook). The supersonic velocity of the solar wind produces a bow-wave like shock which forms far from the Earth's centre, compressing the magnetic field on the side of Earth facing the Sun, known as the dayside. The solar magnetic field and the plasma from the Sun act as one, and thus both are deflected around the Earth by the geomagnetic field. The region inside the cavity created by the Sun's magnetic field meeting Earth's geomagnetic field is known as the magnetosphere.[16] On the nightside, the side of Earth facing away from the Sun, the magnetic field lines are swept out until they are almost parallel, to the magnetospheric tail.

Van Allen Radiation Belts

The intensity of Earth's geomagnetic field decreases radially outwards and is represented by field lines that are curved and become closer together as they approach the poles.[17] Under the influence of the geomagnetic field, the trapped charged particles gyrate in a helical motion around the field lines, bounce between hemispheres and drift around the Earth.[18] In 1958, the first US satellites, Explorer 1 and Explorer 3, were launched into orbit and carried Geiger counters into near-Earth space for the first time.[19] The Explorers found there were locations around the Earth where the onboard Geiger counter recorded zero counts; one of the graduate students in the team, Carl McIlwain, realised this was due to saturation, i.e. the

---

[13] Chapman, S. (1951). *The Earth's Magnetism*, 2nd ed. New York: John Wiley and Sons.

[14] Kono, M., & Roberts, P. H., (2002). Recent geodynamo simulations and observations of the geomagnetic field. *Reviews of Geophysics, 40* (4).

[15] Davies, K. (1990). *Ionospheric radio*. DOI: IET Digital Library, https://digital-library.theiet.org/content/books/ew/pbew031e, Figure 2.12.

[16] Jursa, A. S. (1985). Handbook of Geophysics and the Space Environment. Springfield: Air Force Geophys. Lab.

[17] Ibid.

[18] Ibid.

[19] Baker, D. N., and Panasyuk, M. I. (2017). Discovering Earth's radiation belts. *Physics Today, 70*(12).

counters reported zero counts because they were saturated by very high fluxes.[20] This showed that the magnetic field of the Earth traps high-energy particles with electron energies spanning tens of keV to at least 10 MeV.[21] These particles form the radiation belts, sometimes known as the Van Allen belts after the project leader, J. Van Allen, of the University of Iowa.[22] The radiation belts are located from immediately above the atmosphere out to roughly ten Earth radii away.[23] Most satellites orbit inside or through the belts, hence they are an important space weather impact region.

The Ionosphere

The Earth's ionosphere is a region of the upper atmosphere that lies at an altitude of 60–1000 km above the Earth's surface, where the particles in the atmosphere become charged due to solar radiation – this process is called 'ionisation'.[24] The first direct evidence for the existence of the ionosphere came in mid-December 1901 when Guglielmo Marconi received radio signals in Newfoundland, now part of Canada, sent across the Atlantic from a station he had built in Cornwall, England.[25] This achievement was difficult to explain, for it was correctly understood that radio signals were a form of electromagnetic radiation like light, differing only in their longer wavelengths. As such it was correctly identified that these waves would travel in more or less straight lines and that diffractive effects would not be sufficient to cause transmissions far around the Earth.

Within a few months, Marconi had provided additional, and for many, conclusive evidence that radio waves could propagate round the Earth.[26] In 1902, Arthur Kennelly and Oliver Heaviside independently suggested that radio waves might

---

[20] Gilmor, C. S., & Spreiter, J. R., Discovery of the Magnetosphere. New York: John Wiley and Sons.

[21] Jursa, A. S. (1985). Handbook of Geophysics and the Space Environment. Springfield: Air Force Geophys. Lab.

[22] Gilmor, C. S., & Spreiter, J. R., Discovery of the Magnetosphere. New York: John Wiley and Sons.

[23] Jursa, A. S. (1985). Handbook of Geophysics and the Space Environment. Springfield: Air Force Geophys. Lab.

[24] Hargreaves, J. K. (1992). *The solar–terrestrial environment: An introduction to geospace – the science of the terrestrial upper atmosphere, ionosphere and magnetosphere*. Cambridge: Cambridge University Press.

[25] Davies, K. (1990). *Ionospheric radio*. IET Digital Library, https://digital-library.theiet.org/content/books/ew/pbew031e

[26] Kraus, J. D. (1988). *Antennas*, 2nd ed. New York: McGraw–Hill.

propagate in this manner by reflection from an electrified layer,[27] now recognised as the ionosphere.

The ionosphere is defined as the part of the upper atmosphere where ions and electrons are present in quantities sufficient to affect the propagation of radio waves. The lower altitude bound of the ionosphere tends to be quoted as somewhere between 50 and 60 km.[28] The upper altitude bound is not well defined, hence an arbitrary value of 1000 km is assumed (above which is the inner magnetosphere and plasmasphere).[29] Energy inputs into the ionosphere, such as solar radiation and galactic cosmic rays, maintain a supply of free electrons which interact with electromagnetic waves (i.e. radio waves).[30]

The ionosphere plays a vital role in many radio wave–based communications, navigation and surveillance systems. For the case of long-range radio communication, or over-the-horizon backscatter (i.e. reflection) radar surveillance, the changing electrical conductivity of the ionosphere causes radio waves to reflect. This is useful for applications such as medium- and long-range communications and radar.[31] Obviously, not all systems rely on reflection from the ionosphere, some making use of direct communication with satellites (for example, GPS[32] and Starlink[33]). This will typically involve high radio frequencies that can penetrate the ionosphere without significant reflection or bending, with the later known as refraction.[34] However, even during normal conditions, the radio waves are still influenced by the ionosphere as they propagate through it. This is likely to involve some bending in the path, a slowing of the propagation speed, and/or some level of amplitude decrease. All these factors can contribute to degradation in system operation.[35] A

[27] Ratcliffe, J. A. (1972). *An introduction to the ionosphere and magnetosphere*. Cambridge: Cambridge University Press.

[28] Davies, K. (1990). *Ionospheric radio*. IET Digital Library, https://digital-library.theiet.org/content/books/ew/pbew031e

[29] Hargreaves, J. K. (1992). *The solar–terrestrial environment: An introduction to geospace – the science of the terrestrial upper atmosphere, ionosphere and magnetosphere*. Cambridge: Cambridge University Press.

[30] Ibid.

[31] Davies, K. (1990). *Ionospheric radio*. IET Digital Library, https://digital-library.theiet.org/content/books/ew/pbew031e

[32] El-Rabbany, A. (2006). *Introduction to GPS: the Global Positioning System*. 2nd ed. Boston: Artech House.

[33] Kan, M. (2022). *What Is Starlink? SpaceX's Much-Hyped Satellite Internet Service Explained*. PC Magazine Australia. https://au.pcmag.com/networking/86102/what-is-starlink-spacexs-much-hyped-satellite-internet-service-explained.

[34] Katz, D. M. (2016). *Physics for Scientists and Engineers: Foundations and Connections*, Boston: Cengage Learning.

[35] Davies, K. (1990). *Ionospheric radio*. IET Digital Library, https://digital-library.theiet.org/content/books/ew/pbew031e

schematic of the ionosphere altering the propagation of radio waves can be found in Fig. 11.5 of George and Rodger (2019).[36]

Primary Space Weather Drivers

The Sun loses plasma from its outer layers as a matter of course, but sunspot activity on its surface increases the likelihood of explosions of magnetic field–carrying plasma and electromagnetic radiation from its surface.[37] These explosions, when they are directed towards Earth, have effects on its environment and can impact human activity and technology. The impacts on Earth differ depending on the type and intensity of the solar explosion.

Solar Flares

A solar flare is an explosion in the Sun's atmosphere releasing a total energy of up to 6×10^{25} Joules.[38] To give context, this is equivalent to approximately 14 billion one-megaton H-bombs – more than a million times bigger than the size of *all* the nuclear weapons currently stockpiled on Earth.[39] Solar flares take place in the solar atmosphere – the solar corona – heating the local plasma to tens of millions of degrees. As the corona is heated to such high temperatures, it can radiate into X-ray wavelengths and optical frequencies, and into radio frequency spectrum as well.[40]

Most flares occur in active regions around sunspots. They are powered by the sudden release of magnetic energy stored in the corona over a timescale of minutes to tens of minutes.[41] Recent reviews on solar flares can be found in Shibata (2015)[42] and Green et al. (2018).[43] Solar flares are linked to the following physical processes

---

[36] George, H., and Rodger, C. J. (2019). Space Weather and Aviation: Impacts of Solar Flares. *Journal of the Royal New Zealand Air Force – Part B, 5*(1), 102–121.

[37] Moldwin, M. (2022). *An Introduction to Space Weather*, 2nd edition. Cambridge: Cambridge University Press.

[38] Ibid.

[39] Rough calculation undertaken by the lead author.

[40] Katz, D. M. (2016). *Physics for Scientists and Engineers: Foundations and Connections*, Boston: Cengage Learning.

[41] Moldwin, M. (2022). *An Introduction to Space Weather*, 2nd edition. Cambridge: Cambridge University Press.

[42] Shibata, K. (2015). Solar and stellar flares and their impact on planets. *Proceedings of the International Astronomical Union, 11*(S320), 3–24.

[43] Green, L. M., Török, T., Vršnak, B., Manchester, W., and Veronig, A. (2018). The Origin, Early Evolution and Predictability of Solar Eruptions. *Space Science Reviews, 214*, 46.

that have space weather impacts: solar X-ray flares, solar radio noise bursts and solar proton events.

Coronal Mass Ejections: 'Solar Tsunamis'

Coronal mass ejections (CMEs) are the explosion of plasma and magnetic field into space from on or near the Sun's surface. A large CME can have a mass of 10^{12} kg.[44] CMEs travel radially away from the Sun's surface, so only some CMEs are Earth directed. Colloquially, CMEs are known as solar tsunamis, as they are effectively a wave of solar matter travelling through space. The speed at which a CME travels relates to the force of the eruption; a fast CME could reach Earth in as little as 12 h, while the average travel time is 1–2 days, and more recent reviews on CME can be found in Vourlidas et al. (2019), Georgoulis et al. (2019), and Nitta et al. (2021).[45]

An Earth-directed CME will hit the Earth's magnetosphere. This impact will squash and deform the magnetosphere, changing the field shape.[46] These changes induce electrical currents in space and on the ground, triggering what is known as a geomagnetic storm. Geomagnetic storms produce enhanced auroras as well as move the auroral regions closer to the equator.[47] Geomagnetic storms kicked off by a CME can have two important space weather effects:

1. Increasing the hot electron content in the Van Allen belts. The increase in radiation can damage both satellites and any person outside the atmosphere (e.g. in space stations or travelling to the Moon or Mars)
2. The changing magnetic field in space drives currents in the Earth's upper surface layers which can damage components of the electrical power grid

[44] Moldwin, M. (2022). *An Introduction to Space Weather*, 2nd edition. Cambridge: Cambridge University Press.

[45] Vourlidas A., Patsourakos, S., and Savani, N. P. (2019). Predicting the geoeffective properties of coronal mass ejections: current status, open issues and path forward. *Philosophical Transactions of the Royal Society A*, 37720180096 20180096; Georgoulis, M. K., Nindos, A., and Zhang, H. (2019). The source and engine of coronal mass ejections. *Philosophical Transactions of the Royal Society A, 377*(2148); Nitta, N. V., Mulligan, T., Kilpua, E. K. J., et al. (2021) Understanding the Origins of Problem Geomagnetic Storms Associated with "Stealth" Coronal Mass Ejections. *Space Science Reviews, 217*, 82.

[46] Moldwin, M. (2022). *An Introduction to Space Weather*, 2nd edition. Cambridge: Cambridge University Press.

[47] Ibid.

Why Do We Care About Space Weather?

Space weather has a huge potential to disrupt and damage the technological and electrical infrastructure that we rely on day to day. Space weather is a wide field – as our technology changes, so does our susceptibility to the impacts of space weather. Once aurora was only a marvellous display in the skies; however, today it might be a sign that our communications and navigation systems will be degraded. In the last decades, there have been examples of damage occurring to technological systems during 'big', and sometimes 'very big' space weather events.[48] Scientists, and increasingly policymakers, worry about what might happen during an extreme space weather event. We think these events have roughly a return period of once every 100–200 years,[49] although there is significant uncertainty around these return periods. This worry is starting to be reflected in the actions of some national governments and UN agencies.[50]

The discipline of space weather study is only a few decades old, and given this, there are many knowledge gaps. Our ability to forecast and model space weather events is not fully developed. It is also very difficult to predict how a given technology system will respond to the changing space weather environment; different designs and internal algorithms will have different strengths and weaknesses. However, arguably only in the last 5–10 years has space weather been in the consciousness of global decision-makers. Space weather is a challenging, if very scientifically interesting (due to its complexity), intersection between science, engineering and societal need.

Solar Flare Space Weather Impacts

One of the most extreme space weather potential impacts from solar flares to date occurred in late May 1967. For most of the scientific community, the importance of this event was not recognised until 2016 due to the work of Delores Knipp.[51]

---

[48] Béland, J., and Small, K. (2004). Space weather effects on power transmission systems: The cases of Hydro-Québec and Transpower New Zealand Ltd. In Daglis, I. A. (Ed.), *Effects of Space Weather on Technological Infrastructure* (pp. 287–299). Dordrecht: Kluwer Academic; Hapgood, M., Liu, H., & Lugaz, N. (2022). SpaceX—Sailing close to the space weather? *Space Weather*, 20, e2022SW003074; Allen, J. (2010), The Galaxy 15 Anomaly: Another Satellite in the Wrong Place at a Critical Time. Space Weather, 8.

[49] Hapgood, M., Angling, M. J., Attrill, G., Bisi, M., Cannon, P. S., Dyer, C., et al. (2021). Development of space weather reasonable worst-case scenarios for the UK National Risk Assessment. *Space Weather*, 19, e2020SW002593.

[50] Examples being International Civil Aviation Organization, the World Meteorological Organization, and United Nations Committee on the Peaceful Uses of Outer Space.

[51] Outlined in Knipp, D. J., et al. (2016). The May 1967 great storm and radio disruption event: Extreme space weather and extraordinary responses. *Space Weather, 14*, 614–633.

Formerly, a US Air Force officer, she is now an academic at the University of Colorado, Boulder.

May 1967 fell during a high stakes period in the Cold War. It was a time of heavy military activity in the demilitarized zone in Vietnam, and the lead-up to the Six-Day War in the Middle East early the following month. During this tense period, the Sun delivered a space weather event that almost pushed us into nuclear war. A year before the solar maximum, a number of large and complex sunspots had developed by late May 1967. Over a few days, multiple sunspot groups merged, leading to more tangled magnetic fields in the groups. This produced strong solar flare activity, with 76 significant solar flares occurring over 2 weeks. The primary impact came from a white-light solar flare which occurred at 1840 UT (effectively the successor to GMT) on 23 May 1967, approximately at sunset for European time zones and near local noon in the central states and provinces of North America. In the Arctic, there were near 24-h sunlit conditions, with the Sun at low elevations.[52]

The May 1967 solar flare is notable for producing the largest known solar radio noise burst of the past century. The burst, combined with the ionospheric disturbances driven by the X-ray flares, solar particle events and CMEs, together caused critical levels of disruption to important technology systems, including military control and communication systems.[53] One example was the high-latitude Ballistic Missile Early Warning System (BMEWS) radar sites (see Fig. 11.3). These operated at 440 MHz, and had been deployed in the early 1960s to provide 15 min warning of intercontinental ballistic missile attacks on the United States, Canada and the United Kingdom.[54] The solar radio burst overwhelmed the BMEWS observations. At the same time, radio links in the central United States and Canada, both military and civilian, were subject to significant interference and signal loss.[55]

The interference was immediately interpreted as radio jamming.[56] At that time, jamming of surveillance sensors was likely to be interpreted as a potential act of war and expected at the beginning of a major nuclear attack. Very little information has been released to date regarding the seriousness of this event and what happened in the US strategic command centres. However, there is some instructive context available. The May 1967 space weather event occurred not long after the start of a solar forecasting service, which began operating inside the North American Air Defence (NORAD) Command Cheyenne Mountain Complex in Colorado in late 1965.[57]

NORAD solar forecasters were able to explain that the radio interference was likely to be coming from the Sun, as this could be determined by the BMEWS radars. This is important, as bombers were positioned to take to the skies and, given they

[52] Ibid.

[53] Ibid.

[54] Ibid.

[55] Ibid.

[56] Ibid.

[57] Ibid.

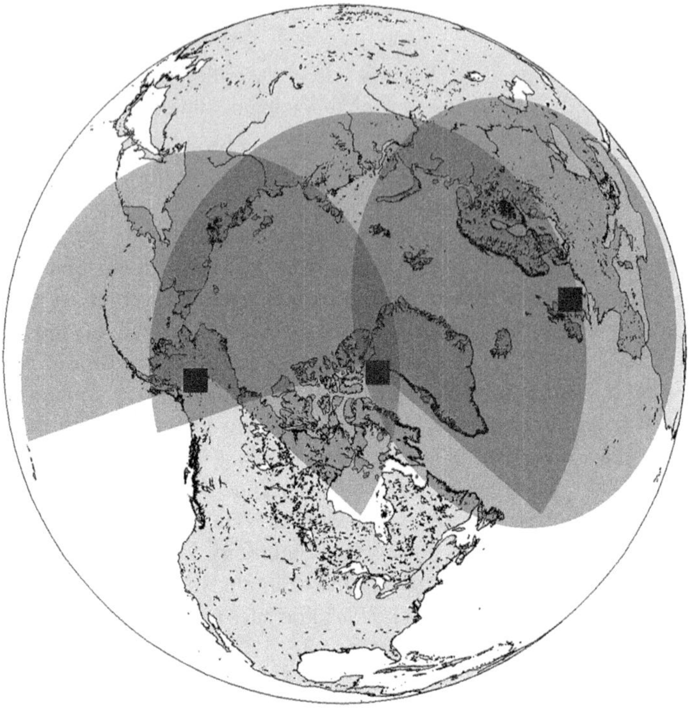

Fig. 11.3 The three BMEWS sites located from Alaska to Yorkshire which were 'jammed' by the Sun in late May 1967. The United States believed this was caused by the Soviet Union and prepared for nuclear attack (Created by the authors of this chapter)

would have been difficult to recall with limited radio signals, and this was a route to nuclear devastation.[58]

The May 1967 event has been used as an example of the importance of space weather and space environment information to decision-makers. This event highlights the importance of space weather situation awareness to inform and contextualise a highly unusual solar event for governmental decision-makers. Several other historic examples of significant space weather events can be found in George and Rodger (2019).[59]

---

[58] Ibid.

[59] George, H., and Rodger, C. J. (2019) Space Weather and Aviation: Impacts of Solar Flares. *Journal of the Royal New Zealand Air Force – Part B*, 5(1), 102–121.

CME Space Weather Impacts on Spacecraft

The impact of a CME on the Earth's magnetosphere can include a strong geomagnetic storm; these storms are commonly linked to large or very large increases in the population of energetic electrons trapped in the radiation belts of the magnetosphere.[60] A CME-triggered geomagnetic storm sets off multiple processes by which cold electrons located near the Earth are accelerated to much higher energies, from tens of keV through to MeV.[61] The very large increases in trapped energetic electrons lead to a highly enhanced radiation environment across the radiation belts, producing an enhanced radiation hazard to Earth-orbiting satellites. The hazard is most pronounced for spacecraft in medium or geostationary Earth orbits as a result of the significant amount of time they spend inside the heart of the radiation belts due to their orbit. Low Earth orbit spacecraft are much closer to the Earth, so they tend not to be as exposed unless they pass through the polar regions or over the South Atlantic, where the magnetic field is relatively weaker.

Solar proton events during solar flares can also lead to radiation enhancements in the polar cap, which also produces much higher radiation doses for spacecraft.[62] The International Space Station orbits at a relatively low 408 km, so it is usually safe from space radiation but has on board the heavily shielded Zvezda module for astronauts to shelter inside.[63] There are also plans for astronauts to use the on-orbit 'lifeboat' to return to Earth if the radiation risk is judged to be too high.[64]

There are several effects on spacecraft from the enhanced radiation caused by a CME: electronics and solar panels can degrade, spacecraft components can become radioactive, single event upsets can take place in the onboard microelectronics (i.e. changing binary ones to zeroes in the onboard systems, or vice versa), false stars can be seen in star tracker systems (used for location and attitude) and surface charging followed by electrical arcing can take place inside the satellite. Depending on the impact, one can think of them as being akin to human health impacts: cancer (long-term progressive degradation of systems), strokes and Alzheimer's disease (relative sudden loss of function of some systems), which together can be serious enough to make the spacecraft non-operational. As such, major space weather events can degrade, disrupt and even kill satellites.

---

[60]Moldwin, M. (2022). *An Introduction to Space Weather*, 2nd edition. Cambridge: Cambridge University Press.

[61]Balasis, G., Daglis, I. A., & Mann, I. R. (2016). Waves, Particles, and Storms in Geospace: A Complex Interplay, Oxford: Oxford University Press.

[62]Moldwin, M. (2022). *An Introduction to Space Weather*, 2nd edition. Cambridge: Cambridge University Press.

[63]Ross, J. F. (2006). The Invisible Killers. *Smithsonian Magazine*, Washington: Smithsonian Institution.

[64]New Space Economy (28 March 2023). *NASA's ISS Procedures: Responding to Space Weather*. https://newspaceeconomy.ca/2023/03/28/nasas-iss-procedures-responding-to-space-weather

CME Space Weather Impacts on GNSS

In the last few decades, global navigation satellite systems (GNSS) have moved from being military tools to fundamental parts of economic and societal operation.[65] GNSS entail constellations of Earth-orbiting satellites transmitting position and time information, allowing location determination and precise timing. Many people rely on GNSS-derived information to navigate in their normal daily lives, and the timing information provided by GNSS is vital to the operation of high-speed computer networks worldwide. For most people, GNSS is synonymous with the US global positioning system (GPS); however, several nations have GNSS constellations at various levels of development and coverage. Examples are GLONASS (Russia), Galileo (European Union) and BeiDou (People's Republic of China).

GNSS spacecraft are typically in mid- and geostationary Earth orbits and hence live inside the radiation belts; while the US GPS satellites are known to be highly radiation shielded,[66] it is not clear that this is true for all existing GNSS constellations. In addition to the radiation risk, an operational GNSS needs to be able to communicate with its users, who are most likely on or near the Earth's surface; therefore, the radio signals need to propagate through near-Earth space – which is not empty – through the ionosphere and atmosphere to reach the users. While GNSS receivers include average ionospheric and atmospheric models to try to remove the impact of these regions, space weather leads to additional impacts that the models cannot include.

One example is ionospheric scintillation,[67] the rapid modification of radio waves caused by small-scale structures in the ionosphere, between tens of metres and tens of kilometres. Scintillation events are linked to space weather, but the relationship is complex. Severe scintillation conditions can completely prevent a GNSS receiver from locking on (i.e. position and timing information are lost). In contrast, less severe scintillation conditions reduce the position and timing accuracy. In practice, all satellite communications that pass through the ionosphere will be impacted at some level. An example of this took place in March 2002 when ionospheric scintillation is thought to have resulted in a loss of communications during military operations in Afghanistan,[68] resulting in the deaths of US military personnel.

---

[65] Filjar, R., Damas, M. C., Iliev, T. B. (2021). Resilient satellite navigation empowers modern science, economy, and society. *IOP Conference Series: Materials Science and Engineering*, 1032, 012001.

[66] Cannon, P., et al. (2013). Extreme space weather: Impact on engineered systems and infrastructure. Summary Report, Royal Academy of Engineering, London.

[67] For example Linty, N., Farasin, A., Favenza, A., and Dovis, F. (2019). Detection of GNSS Ionospheric Scintillations Based on Machine Learning Decision Tree. *IEEE Transactions on Aerospace and Electronic Systems, 55*(1), 303–317.

[68] Kelly, M. A., Comberiate, J. M., Miller, E. S., and Paxton, L. J. (2014), Progress toward forecasting of space weather effects on UHF SATCOM after Operation Anaconda, *Space Weather, 12*, 601–611.

Geomagnetic storms not only influence the ionosphere, they can also heat the rest of the atmosphere through electrical currents induced at high altitudes, along with auroral energy flows, known as joule heating.[69] Such heating causes the atmosphere to swell, increasing its density at high altitudes, hence increasing drag for satellites in low Earth orbit. Such drag can cause satellites to go missing (due to orbital changes) or even to be entirely lost into the atmosphere. An impressive example of this was seen in early 2022: SpaceX launched 49 Starlink satellites on 3 February, but the next day, a geomagnetic storm hit Earth.[70] By 8 February, SpaceX announced that 'Preliminary analysis show[s] the increased drag at the low altitudes prevented the satellites from leaving safe mode to begin orbit-raising manoeuvres, and up to 40 of the satellites will re-enter or already have re-entered the Earth's atmosphere'.[71] The loss of these spacecraft was widely reported in the media.[72]

Space Weather Impacts on Aviation

Global space weather forecasting has recently started to support global civil aviation. Examples of aviation-specific space weather impacts can be seen in Fig. 11.4. In July 2014, the International Civil Aviation Organization (ICAO) formally requested the World Meteorological Organization (WMO) to develop space weather forecasting to support global aviation.[73] While the process leading to the creation of global aviation space weather forecasts took more than a decade, this service started at 1200 UT on 7 November 2019,[74] demonstrating a global response to this global hazard. Obviously, the focus of the new service is on the aviation operations perspective,[75] where space weather events can produce degradation or disruption of communications, navigation and surveillance systems, as well as leading to an elevation in radiation dose levels to crew and passengers at various flight altitudes. As such, space weather

[69] Palmroth, M., et al. (2021). Lower-thermosphere–ionosphere (LTI) quantities: Current status of measuring techniques and models. *Annals of Geophysics, 39*, 189–237.

[70] SpaceX—Sailing close to the space weather? *Space Weather*, 20, e2022SW003074;

[71] Wetzel, C. (2022), Solar Storm Knocks 40 SpaceX Satellites Out of Orbit, *Smithsonian Magazine*, Washington: Smithsonian Institution.

[72] BBC. (2022, February 9). SpaceX loses 40 satellites to geomagnetic storm a day after launch. https://www.bbc.com/news/world-60317806

[73] World Meterological Organization (2020), Space Weather. https://community.wmo.int/en/activity-areas/wmo-space-programme-wsp/space-weather-introduction

[74] International Civil Aviation Organization (19 November 2019). *New global aviation space weather network launched*, https://www.icao.int/Newsroom/Pages/New-global-aviation-space-weather-network-launched.aspx

[75] International Civil Aviation Organization. (2018). *Manual on Space Weather Information in Support of International Air Navigation* (Doc 10,100), 2018. https://www.icao.int/airnavigation/METP/Panel%20Documents/Doc.10100.Space%20Weather%20Manual%20FINAL%20DRAFT%20Version.pdf

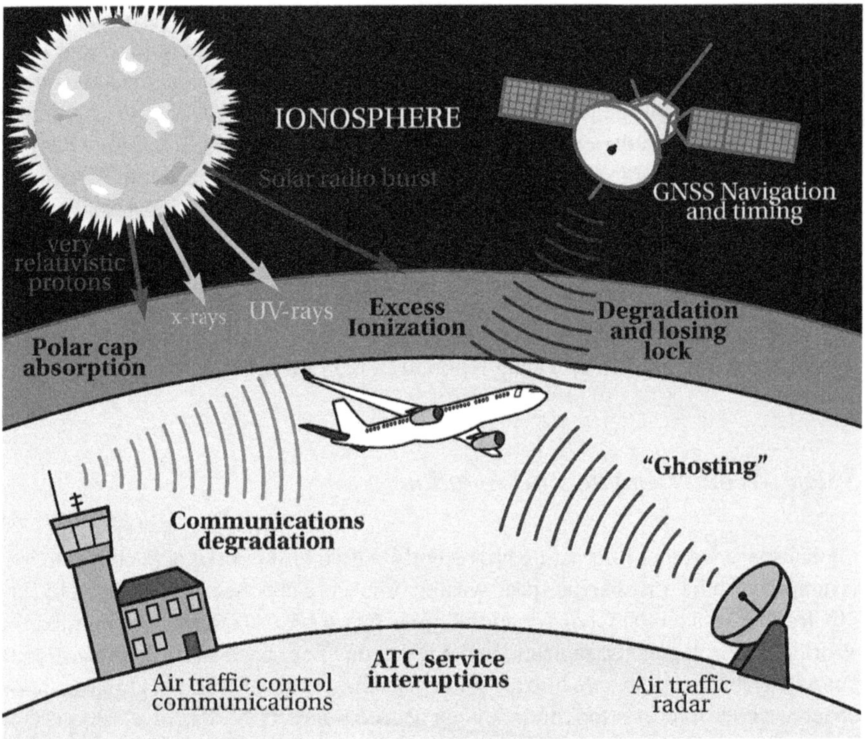

Fig. 11.4 Examples of the effects of space weather on the ionosphere and aviation traffic control services, with a particular focus on flare-linked impacts to aviation (Created by the authors of this chapter)

impacts on the aviation industry are important, given the impacts and disruption it can cause to aviation activities. However, more work needs to be done in this field by ICAO in conjunction with Nation States (and the local aviation industry) with a view towards better understanding of these impacts in order to better safeguard these activities.

CME Space Weather Impacts on Ground Systems

The UN Committee on the Peaceful Uses of Outer Space (COPUOS) includes an Expert Group on Space Weather that released a thematic report in 2017, which recognised space weather as a global challenge with potentially catastrophic impacts, noting that:

> The largest potential socioeconomic impacts arise from space weather driven geomagnetically induced currents in electrical power networks . . . The direct impacts from a collapse of the electrical power grid are damage to the infrastructure and loss of service. More

> significant are flow-down impacts, which include the loss of any services that rely on the availability of electricity, which, in the interconnected economy of the twenty-first century[,] could quickly lead to extreme impacts. Such loss of power can also result in extensive damage to property and infrastructure, as well as loss of life.[76]

Reliable electricity supply is the lifeblood of any modern Nation. The cost of damage to network components is small compared to the knock-on consequences of electrical outages to essential lifeline services such as water, gas, telecommunications and traffic and railway signalling, as well as the associated business and household impacts that rely on these interconnected services.

To date, relatively modest geomagnetic disturbances have caused damage to transformers, and in some cases blackouts. This has occurred in Norway,[77] South Africa,[78] Sweden,[79] Canada,[80] the United States,[81] and New Zealand.[82] These CME-triggered geomagnetic storms are termed 'large' or 'very large', but are much smaller than expected during an extreme event. The best-known impact on a power grid is the blackout of March 1989 when Hydro-Québec's (Transénergie et Équipement) electric transmission system collapsed in 92 s whereby protective relays were tripped, the grid collapsed and about nine million people were left without electricity for a minimum of 9 h and a maximum of up to a few days.[83]

---

[76] United Nations Committee on the Peaceful Uses of Outer Space Expert Group on Space Weather. (2017). *Report on Thematic Priority 4: International Framework for Space Weather Services for UNISPACE+50*. https://www.unoosa.org/oosa/oosadoc/data/documents/2018/aac.105/aac.1051171_0.html.

[77] Transformer tripped on 8 September 2017 in Tromsö, Norway. Daniel, B., Boehme, K., Kereit, M., & Rebizant, W. (2020). HV Transformer Protection and Stabilization under Geomagnetically Induced Currents. *Energies*, 13, 4693.

[78] Transformer damaged in 13–14 March 1989. Thomson, A. (2010), Space weather and power grids, Earthwise, 26.

[79] Power outage in Malmö, Sweden in 29–31 October 2003. Pulkkinen, A., Lindahl, S., Viljanen, A., and Pirjola, R. (2005), Geomagnetic storm of 29–31 October 2003. Geomagnetically induced currents and their relation to problems in the Swedish high-voltage power transmission system, *Space Weather*, 3, S08C03, doi:https://doi.org/10.1029/2004SW000123

[80] Blackout in Quebec, Canada in 13–14 March 1989. Guillon, S., Toner, P., Gibson, L., and Boteler, D. (2016). A Colorful Blackout: The Havoc Caused by Auroral Electrojet Generated Magnetic Field Variations in 1989. *IEEE Power & Energy Magazine, 14*(6).

[81] Transformer damaged in New Jersey, USA during 13–14 March 1989. Kappenman, J., (2010). *Geomagnetic Storms and Their Impacts on the U.S. Power Grid* (Meta-R-319), Goleta: Metatech Corporation.

[82] Transformer damaged in Dunedin on 6 November 2001, at the same time systems tripped out in Christchurch. Béland, J., and Small, K. (2004). Space weather effects on power transmission systems: The cases of Hydro-Québec and Transpower New Zealand Ltd. In Daglis, I. A. (Ed.), *Effects of Space Weather on Technological Infrastructure* (pp. 287–299).

[83] Béland, J., and Small, K. (2004). Space weather effects on power transmission systems: The cases of Hydro-Québec and Transpower New Zealand Ltd. In Daglis, I. A. (Ed.), *Effects of Space Weather on Technological Infrastructure* (pp. 287–299). Dordrecht: Kluwer Academic; Bolduc, L. (2002). GIC observations and studies in the Hydro-Québec power system. *Journal of Atmospheric and Solar-Terrestrial Physics, 64*(16), 1793–1802; Guillon, S., Toner, P., Gibson, L., and

New Zealand is one of the few countries which has already experienced direct damage from a large geomagnetic storm. On 6 November 2001, alarms were triggered simultaneously at Transpower's (the owner and operator of the country's high-voltage electricity transmission system) control centres, voltage control equipment for Christchurch city tripped out, as did a transformer at the Halfway Bush substation in Dunedin after a transformer failed within a minute of the storm starting.[84] It was beyond repair, and roughly NZ$2 million worth of equipment had to be replaced.[85] This event caused Transpower to develop procedures to respond during a future geomagnetic disturbance,[86] and in the subsequent 20 years, no significant power network disruption has occurred. However, as we will note below, to date, New Zealand has not been tested to the same level since November 2001, and an extreme space weather event is expected to be significantly larger.

Extreme Space Weather Events

Through August and September 1859, a space weather activity occurred that was the strongest yet identified (for which there are scientific observations).[87] This storm is particularly famous due to Richard Carrington's having visually observed a white-light solar flare for the first time,[88] leading to this two-month-long period of space weather activity being known as the Carrington Event.[89] A series of solar flares

---

Boteler, D. (2016). A Colorful Blackout: The Havoc Caused by Auroral Electrojet Generated Magnetic Field Variations in 1989. *IEEE Power & Energy Magazine, 14*(6).

[84] Béland, J., and Small, K. (2004). Space weather effects on power transmission systems: The cases of Hydro-Québec and Transpower New Zealand Ltd. In Daglis, I. A. (Ed.), Effects of Space Weather on Technological Infrastructure (pp. 287–299). Dordrecht: Kluwer Academic; Marshall, R. A., Dalzell, M., Waters, C. L., Goldthorpe, P., and Smith, E. A. (2012). Geomagnetically induced currents in the New Zealand power network. *Space Weather, 10*, S08003; Mac Manus, D. H., Rodger, C. J., Dalzell, M., Thomson, A. W. P., Clilverd, M. A., Petersen, T., Wolf, M., Thomson, N. R., and Divett, T. (2017). Long-term Geomagnetically Induced Current Observations in New Zealand: Earth Return Corrections and Geomagnetic Field Driver, *Space Weather, 15*, 1020–1038.

[85] Personal communication to the author by Transpower New Zealand engineers.

[86] Béland, J., and Small, K. (2004). Space weather effects on power transmission systems: The cases of Hydro-Québec and Transpower New Zealand Ltd. In Daglis, I. A. (Ed.), *Effects of Space Weather on Technological Infrastructure* (pp. 287–299).

[87] Hapgood, M., Angling, M. J., Attrill, G., Bisi, M., Cannon, P. S., Dyer, C., et al. (2021). Development of space weather reasonable worst-case scenarios for the UK National Risk Assessment. *Space Weather*, 19, e2020SW002593.

[88] Carrington, R. C. (1860). Description of a singular appearance seen in the Sun on September 1, 1859. *Monthly Notices of the Royal Astronomical Society, 20*, 13–15.

[89] Cliver E. W. & Dietrich, W.F. (2013). The 1859 space weather event revisited: limits of extreme activity. *J. Space Weather Space Clim.*, 3, A31.

resulted in powerful CMEs impacting the Earth, producing aurora as near to the Equator as Tahiti. These CMEs triggered the 1–2 September 1859 geomagnetic storm, the most intense in recorded history.[90] This activity was widely recognised at the time as being a special event, the resulting magnetic disturbances producing widespread auroral displays and disruption to telegraph transmissions, attracting much public attention and generating widespread reports in newspapers and scientific articles.[91] The US Geological Survey has estimated that there is a 6–7 per cent chance of an 1859-type solar storm in the next 10 years, a 150-year return period.[92]

An extreme space weather event is likely to produce multiple extreme impacts. The UK Royal Academy of Engineering's report on extreme space weather provides a summary of possible impacts and a timescale for these impacts[93] An extreme event would most likely start with one or more extreme solar flares; it is worth noting that when the Sun is very active, a series of rapid, very large solar flares is likely to occur. The Sun is 150 million km from Earth, or 8 min at the speed of light.[94] So, 8 min after the flares have occurred, the electromagnetic radiation will arrive in the form of X-rays and solar radio noise bursts.

As a result of the X-ray 'thickening' within the ionosphere, it will produce communication problems on the dayside, particularly for high-frequency radio systems. The solar radio noise bursts would be likely to overwhelm the weak GNSS signals, as well as interfere with air traffic control and radar systems. This period should only last hours and would likely be limited to the Earth's dayside. The solar flare would also accelerate protons into space, leading to a solar proton event. Due to their high energies, these particles will travel very fast, arriving within hours of the solar flare. As the protons are charged, they will be funnelled by the Earth's magnetic field into the atmosphere of the polar regions,[95] producing a communications blackout and enhanced radiation doses for aircraft passengers. Large solar proton events tend to last a few days, leading to the assumption that an extreme event will not be shorter in duration than this.

Extreme space weather events are linked to unusually fast-moving CMEs, arriving at the Earth only 12–24 h after the flares start (as was the case for the Carrington

[90] Tsurutani, B. T., Gonzalez, W. D., Lakhina, G. S., and Alex, S. (2003), The extreme magnetic storm of 1–2 September 1859, *Journal of Geophysical Research, 108*(A7), 1268.

[91] See the review Boteler, D. H. (2006). The super storms of August/September 1859 and their effects on the telegraph system. *Advances in Space Research, 38*(2), 159–172.

[92] Love, J. J. (2012). Credible occurrence probabilities for extreme geophysical events: Earthquakes, volcanic eruptions, magnetic storms. *Geophysics Research Letters, 39*, L10301.

[93] Cannon, P., et al. (2013). Extreme space weather: Impact on engineered systems and infrastructure. Summary Report, Royal Academy of Engineering, London. https://www.raeng.org.uk/publications/reports/space-weather-summary-report.

[94] Moldwin, M. (2022). *An Introduction to Space Weather*, 2nd edition. Cambridge: Cambridge University Press.

[95] Rodger, C. J., Clilverd, M. A., Verronen, P. T., Ulich, T., Jarvis, M. J., and Turunen, E. (2006), Dynamic geomagnetic rigidity cutoff variations during a solar proton event, *Journal of Geophysical Research*, 111, A04222, doi:10.1029/2005JA011395.

Event). The arrival of the CME will cause an extreme geomagnetic disturbance that triggers the processes leading to increased radiation in the radiation belts, which may cause satellite damage or death. The arrival will also produce small-scale ionospheric structures across mid- and high latitudes, certainly extending from New Zealand latitudes and likely reaching Scott Base in Antarctica, disrupting communications and navigation systems which rely upon the ionosphere. It is likely that GNSS signals will be highly unreliable, or absent, for up to a few days. The geomagnetic storm will induce currents in electrical power networks, causing disruption and damage. It is possible that power networks will collapse either directly due to primary equipment damage from the large geomagnetically induced currents produced or due to the significant reactive power flows caused by transformers saturating (i.e. their cores becoming fully magnetised) and control systems becoming overloaded. Depending on the levels of damage, these networks may take days at least to restart if they have collapsed, and months, if not to years, to rebuild if primary equipment such as power transformers has been damaged or destroyed.

As an example, it has been estimated that if a storm as extreme as the Carrington Event occurred today, it would destroy more than 300 of the 2100 high-voltage transformers in the United States, disabling the entire network.[96] Replacement transformers, each costing multi-millions, would be unlikely to be available for a year or more. The economic impact in the first year was initially estimated at US$2 trillion.[97] Follow-up studies suggest that 20–40 million people would be affected for between 16 days and 2 years, and the total financial impact would be US$0.5–2.7 trillion in the United States alone.[98] If the damage were limited to the United States, there would still be global economic disruption. However, the geomagnetic disturbance would disrupt and damage power grids on a global scale. This would be more likely at high than low latitudes, except for locations within a few degrees of the magnetic equator, where larger impacts are also expected.[99]

It is instructive to look at the geomagnetic disturbances seen in the recent past and compare them with what might be expected for an extreme geomagnetic event like

[96] Baker, D. N., et al. (2008). *Severe Space Weather Events: Understanding Societal and Economic Impacts*. Washington, D.C.: National Academies Press.

[97] Ibid.; JASON. (2011). *Impacts of Severe Space Weather on the Electric Grid* (JSR-11-320). McLean, Va.: MITRE Corporation.

[98] Lloyd's. (2013). Solar Storm Risk to the North American Electric Grid: A Lloyds Space Weather Study. https://assets.lloyds.com/assets/pdf-solar-storm-risk-to-the-north-american-electric-grid/1/pdf-Solar-Storm-Risk-to-the-North-American-Electric-Grid.pdf; Oughton, E.; Copic, J.; Skelton, A.; Kesaite, V.; Yeo, Z. Y.; Ruffle, S. J.; Tuveson, M.; Coburn, A. W.; and Ralph, D. (2016). *Helios Solar Storm Scenario*. Cambridge Risk Framework series; Centre for Risk Studies, University of Cambridge.

[99] For example, Carter, B. A., Yizengaw, E., Pradipta, R., Weygand, J. M., Piersanti, M., Pulkkinen, A., Moldwin, M. B., Norman, R., and Zhang, K. (2016). Geomagnetically induced currents around the world during the 17 March 2015 storm. *Journal of Geophysical Research: Space Physics, 121*, 10,496– 10,507.

the Carrington Event. According to Faraday's law of induction,[100] the magnitude of electrical currents induced in a power grid depends on the speed of the changing magnetic field; this expectation has been observationally confirmed for New Zealand, where a high-quality correlation has been shown between the size of currents and the rate of change of the horizontal component of the geomagnetic field.[101]

Figure 11.5 (below) presents the daily maximum absolute value of the one-minute resolution observed rate of change of the horizontal component (labelled $|\Delta H|$) from 1 January 2001 to 31 December 2020, observed at New Zealand's official geomagnetic field observatory at Eyrewell, near Christchurch. As noted earlier, the largest magnetic disturbance in New Zealand in recent history occurred on 6 November 2001, which is the 191 nT/min spike on the left-hand side of the upper plot in Fig. 11.5. The next largest event, which peaked at 171 nT/min, occurred on 31 October 2003 during the 'Halloween Storms'. Figure 11.5 also shows that there have been several short, well-defined geomagnetic disturbances, but that generally the daily maximum variability is only a few nT/min. One might think of the range of values shown in blue as from small to large disturbances.

As can be seen in Fig. 11.5, the upper panel shows the daily maximum value observed at New Zealand's official geomagnetic observatory. This ranges from small to large disturbances. The lower panel shows very large and extreme disturbances. The magenta symbols are from Canada during the March 1989 blackout. The red stars are the extreme storm changes expected for UK latitudes, based on extreme value statistics applied to 30 years of European magnetometer data (the range is shown by the stars 1 and 2). The black square labelled 'Near Miss' is the expected maximum magnetic field change for New Zealand latitudes, based on the July 2012 'CME that missed', thought to be a modern Carrington Event the Earth narrowly avoided.

In contrast, very large, or extreme, geomagnetic disturbances are included in the lower panel of Fig. 11.5. The blue line which starts in the lower left-hand side of the panel are the same daily maximum $|\Delta H|$ changes plotted in the upper panel. The magenta symbols indicate the magnetic field changes observed at Ottawa during the March 1989 storm which led to the Hydro-Québec blackout.[102] The blackout was triggered by a magnetic field change of 390 nT/min; later in the same storm, there was another, larger disturbance (while the network was blacked out and hence

[100] Katz, D. M. (2016). *Physics for Scientists and Engineers: Foundations and Connections*, Boston: Cengage Learning.

[101] Mac Manus, D. H., Rodger, C. J., Dalzell, M., Thomson, A. W. P., Clilverd, M. A., Petersen, T., Wolf, M. M., Thomson, N. R., and Divett, T. (2017), Long-term geomagnetically induced current observations in New Zealand: Earth return corrections and geomagnetic field driver, *Space Weather*, 15, 1020–1038.

[102] Guillon, S., Toner, P., Gibson, L., and Boteler, D. (2016). A Colorful Blackout: The Havoc Caused by Auroral Electrojet Generated Magnetic Field Variations in 1989. *IEEE Power & Energy Magazine, 14*(6).

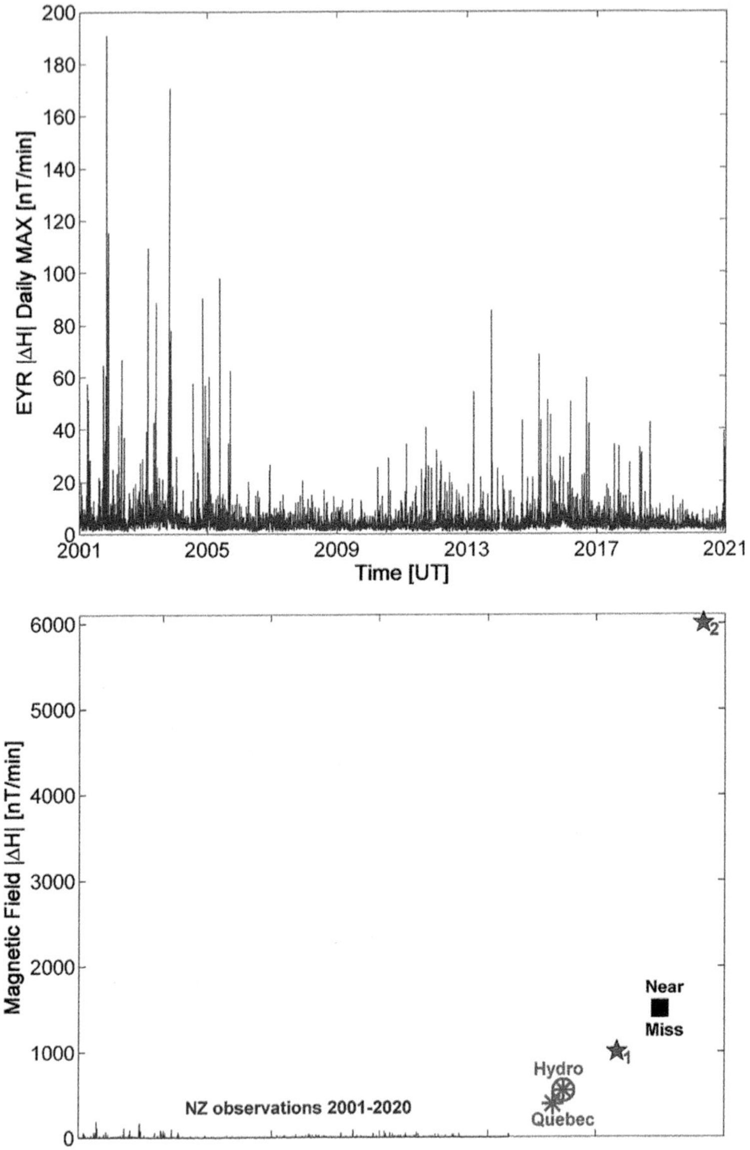

Fig. 11.5 Contrasting the absolute value of the rate of change of horizontal component of the geomagnetic field (|ΔH|) (Created by the authors of this chapter)

effectively safe), which had a value of 550 nT/min.[103] These two values are shown by the magenta stars and correspond to a very large disturbance. Finally, we show the extreme disturbance values in red. The two stars correspond to the 200-year

[103] Ibid.

return period geomagnetic field change estimates made for the United Kingdom, based on the application of extreme value statistical analysis to 30 years of European magnetometer data.[104] UK-determined extreme values are very appropriate for the New Zealand context as we are located at similar geomagnetic coordinates, with Dunedin mapping to Edinburgh, and London to Wellington. The lower extreme range is 1000 nT/min (red star labelled 1 in Fig. 11.5), and the upper range is 6000 nT/min (red star labelled 2).

While these extreme storm values may appear very large to people familiar with geomagnetic field changes, there is additional support for such extreme numbers. On 23 July 2012, an extremely fast and large CME was launched from the Sun and observed in situ by NASA's STEREO-A spacecraft.[105] This event missed the Earth, but this could have been equivalent to the 1859 Carrington Event. Later, modelling of the expected impact of the 2012 CME found magnetic rates of change at New Zealand latitudes peaking at around 1200 nT/min,[106] shown by the black square in the lower panel of Fig. 11.5.

A New Zealand Response to Space Weather

Internationally, there are very large efforts in space weather research, spanning basic research through to engineering hazard mitigation, as well as developing policy and response frameworks. In New Zealand, there is also activity, principally in scientific research and data collection. The Space Physics group of the University of Otago is probably the most active set of researchers working on space weather problems in New Zealand.[107] In addition, New Zealand has magnetic observatories at Eyrewell and Scott Base, operated by GNS Science and contributing to the international INTERMAGNET network.[108]

Some parts of the New Zealand scientific community are very active in the space weather sphere. The risk to the power grid is recognised by Transpower

[104] Thomson, A. W. P., Dawson, E. B., and Reay, S. J. (2011). Quantifying extreme behaviour in geomagnetic activity. *Space Weather, 9*, S10001; Cannon et al., Extreme space weather.

[105] Baker, D. N., X. Li, Pulkkinen, A., Ngwira, C. M., Mays, M. L., Galvin, A. B., and Simunac, K. D. C. (2013). A major solar eruptive event in July 2012: Defining extreme space weather scenarios. *Space Weather, 11*(10).

[106] Ngwira, C. M., Pulkkinen, A., Mays, M. Leila, Kuznetsova, M. M., Galvin, A. B., Simunac, K., Baker, D. N., Li, X., Zheng, Y., and Glocer, A. (2013). Simulation of the 23 July 2012 extreme space weather event: What if this extremely rare CME was Earth directed? *Space Weather, 11*, 671–679.

[107] This is based on the publication outputs of this research group, as seen at: https://space.physics.otago.ac.nz/publications/. Further evidence comes from this research group leading what we believe are the only space weather focused externally funded research projects in New Zealand (contracts: UOOX1502 and UOOX2002).

[108] https://www.intermagnet.org/

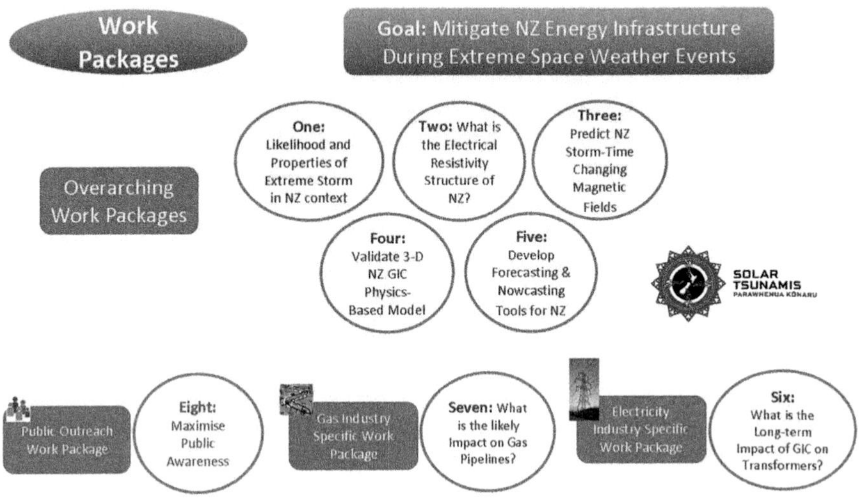

Fig. 11.6 Summary of the work packages inside the MBIE-funded Solar Tsunami's research programme (2020–2025) (created by the authors of this chapter). This research project will help prepare New Zealand for an extreme space weather event, with a particular focus on energy infrastructure (electrical power transmission and gas pipelines)

New Zealand (the body responsible for power transmission). In 2015–2018, some of this chapter's authors undertook an initial investigation, funded by the Ministry of Business, Innovation and Employment (MBIE), of the risks to the Transpower network from space weather.[109] This work established that extreme geomagnetic storms were a significant hazard to the New Zealand electrical transmission network.[110] In turn, this research stimulated a new MBIE-funded project to mitigate the risk to New Zealand's energy infrastructure during extreme space weather events, the Solar Tsunamis MBIE Endeavour Fund programme.[111] Figure 11.6 shows the work packages for this $15 million, five-year research programme, which began in 2020.[112] Involved in this work are New Zealand and internationally funded partners that include the University of Otago, the University of Canterbury, Victoria University of Wellington, GNS Science, the British Geological Survey, the British

[109]This was New Zealand Ministry of Business, Innovation and Employment Hazards and Infrastructure Research Fund contract UOOX1502.

[110]See, for example, Rodger, C. J., Mac Manus, D. H., Dalzell, M., Thomson, A. W. P., Clarke, E., Petersen, T., Divett, T. (2017). Long-term geomagnetically induced current observations from New Zealand: Peak current estimates for extreme geomagnetic storms. *Space Weather, 15*, 1447–1460; Ingham, M., Rodger, C. J., Divett, T., Dalzell, M., and Petersen, T. (2017). Assessment of GIC based on transfer function analysis. *Space Weather, 15*, 1615–1627.

[111]This is New Zealand Ministry of Business, Innovation and Employment Endeavour Fund Research Programme contract UOOX2002.

[112]Ibid.

Antarctic Survey, the University of Texas at Arlington and Otago Museum.[113] We are currently using the UK extreme geomagnetic change parameters, shown in Fig. 11.5, to identify risks to the Transpower network down to individual transformer level across all of New Zealand. This research work is already allowing Transpower to consider the risk to their assets, review and enhance their existing system-switching response plan, identify the individual units most exposed, and develop possible mitigation routes – with the associated long-term business plans needed to bring mitigation priorities into operation.[114]

Space weather is a global hazard, but the risks are local; they depend on the region, national technological systems and the local ground conditions. Much scientific research is underway to better understand the physical changes that will occur on and near the Earth during an extreme space weather event. Solar storms all differ, yet we understand their basic chronology and their consequences. In most countries, the first step undertaken is to identify the local space weather risks, which typically requires a lot of discussion between government and industry. In New Zealand, those in industry and government whose areas of responsibility are at risk of space weather impacts are aware of the risks, for example, Transpower, the Civil Aviation Authority and the Defence Force. Space weather appears on New Zealand's national risk register,[115] as it does in other countries. 'Severe Space Weather' was added to the UK risk register in 2011, which stimulated the development of space weather forecasting through the UK Meteorological Office, as well as a preparedness strategy.[116] At the time of writing, the Space Weather risk does not yet have a risk-coordinating agency identified in the New Zealand risk register. The UK preparedness strategy could provide a useful framework for our policymakers, even if only as a starting point. The UK space weather community has developed severe space weather scenarios,[117] which enables officials to discuss infrastructure resilience against space weather with relevant experts in government and industry. This has included UK space weather planning exercises based on the scenarios to prepare for various future extreme events.[118]

---

[113] For further information see: http://auroraalert.otago.ac.nz/solartsunami/

[114] Mac Manus, D. H., Rodger, C. J., Dalzell, M., Renton, A., Richardson, G. S., Petersen, T., & Clilverd, M. A. (2022). Geomagnetically induced current modeling in New Zealand: Extreme storm analysis using multiple disturbance scenarios and industry provided hazard magnitudes. *Space Weather*, 20, e2022SW003320; Transpower. (2022). Manage Geomagnetic Induced Currents. Transpower Report PR-DP-252/V05, System Operator Division.

[115] The register is described on the Department of the Prime Minister and Cabinet website: https://www.dpmc.govt.nz/our-programmes/national-security/national-risk-approach/new-zealands-nationally-significant-risks

[116] Department for Business, Energy and Industrial Strategy. (2021). UK Severe Space Weather Preparedness Strategy. https://assets.publishing.service.gov.uk/government/uploads/system/uploads/attachment_data/file/1020551/uk-severe-space-weather-preparedness-strategy.pdf

[117] Hapgood, M., Angling, M. J., Attrill, G., Bisi, M., Cannon, P. S., Dyer, C., et al. (2021). Development of space weather reasonable worst-case scenarios for the UK National Risk Assessment. *Space Weather, 19*, e2020SW002593.

[118] Ibid.

Space weather prediction and forecasting centres have been established in many other countries to advise the government, industry and wider society. Large countries with strong space and technology bases, such as the United States[119] and Russia,[120] invested in such centres early on. This also happened in countries with smaller populations who had specific needs, for example, Australia,[121] Finland,[122] and Canada.[123] Some countries have only developed active space weather forecasting relatively recently, such as the United Kingdom.[124] Forecasting provides a form of situation awareness of what might happen soon or helps identifying which technological disruptions are due to space weather.

Clearly planning and developing a national space weather forecasting system would take some time. It seems sensible to start any such process by examining the level of space weather risk in New Zealand and also thinking about how one might provide forecasting information in a local context. Risk identification might well need to happen first, as this would help identify the level of hazard and hence what a reasonable level of investment might be.

It is our opinion that there are four possible routes to follow:

1. Task a New Zealand body to provide local space weather forecasting. We suggest that the logical choice of organisations to undertake this work would be those already active in hazard identification and warning, and having strong relationships with government, society and the appropriate New Zealand scientific community. Examples are the Meteorological Service or GNS Science (noting this is clearly not an exclusive list).
2. Cede sovereignty and ask a 'friendly nation' to produce space weather forecasting and advice for New Zealand. One could imagine, perhaps, asking the Space Weather Services of the Australian Bureau of Meteorology to extend their regional forecasting to include the other side of the Tasman.
3. Encourage the development of global space weather prediction services through an international framework (e.g. the WMO). This could flow on from the existing International Civil Aviation Organization and WMO space weather services, but not aimed solely at aviation hazards.
4. Monitor the outputs from other countries' space weather prediction centres, many of which are publicly available on the Internet, and look for solar storms which

[119] Starting with the U.S. Department of Commerce National Bureau of Standards Radio Section. Caldwell, B., McCarron, E., and Jonas, S. (2017), An abridged history of federal involvement in space weather forecasting, *Space Weather*, 15, 1222–1237.

[120] One early example being work undertaken by Skobeltsyn Institute of Nuclear Physics Moscow State University, triggered by the development of space flight. Panasyuk, M. (2001). Space Weather: Russian Perspectives. In *Space Weather* (eds P. Song, H.J. Singer and G.L. Siscoe).

[121] Australian Bureau of Meteorology, Space Weather Services. https://www.sws.bom.gov.au/

[122] Finnish Meteorological Institute. https://space.fmi.fi/main/space-weather/

[123] Canadian Space Weather Forecasts Centre. https://www.spaceweather.gc.ca/

[124] Met Office Space Weather Operations Centre. https://www.metoffice.gov.uk/weather/specialist-forecasts/space-weather

might be about to happen or are actually occurring. This would certainly be a simple solution, and potentially better than nothing. This role might be filled by staff from the Monitoring, Alerting, and Reporting Centre of the National Emergency Management Agency (NEMA).

We suggest that for options 2, 3 and 4, just having a source of activity predictions is not enough; there would need to be some local route to interpret the predictions and issue local warnings. In all cases from 1 to 4, planning beforehand what to do following the warnings is clearly vital.

Concluding Remarks

We do not know when extreme space weather will occur – it could be in the next few centuries, or it could be tomorrow. If such an event happened very soon, we may see how today's technology and systems cope without any possible intervention. We hope that the growing international attention to the space weather hazard will also transfer more widely to New Zealand.

However, there is a growing body of knowledge and active work on mitigation processes. Local research, with very strong industry links, is occurring in New Zealand, allowing our energy industry partners to develop new mitigation approaches. Regarding earthquakes, volcanoes and tsunamis, it is important to recognise and plan for these hazards. However, unlike some other hazards, for space weather, we can develop the capability to have high-quality warnings and predication through space weather forecasting. Finally, we can always look forward to the fact that an extreme space weather event should also give us wonderful aurora!

Bibliography

Allen, J. (2010). The galaxy 15 anomaly: Another satellite in the wrong place at a critical time. *Space Weather, 8*.

Baker, D. N., & Panasyuk, M. I. (2017). Discovering Earth's radiation belts. *Physics Today, 70*(12), 46.

Baker, D. N., et al. (2008). *Severe space weather events: Understanding societal and economic impacts*. National Academies Press.

Baker, D. N., Li, X., Pulkkinen, A., Ngwira, C. M., Mays, M. L., Galvin, A. B., & Simunac, K. D. C. (2013). A major solar eruptive event in July 2012: Defining extreme space weather scenarios. *Space Weather, 11*(10), 585.

Balasis, G., Daglis, I. A., & Mann, I. R. (2016). *Waves, particles, and storms in Geospace: A complex interplay*. Oxford University Press.

BBC. (2022, February 9). *SpaceX loses 40 satellites to geomagnetic storm a day after launch*. https://www.bbc.com/news/world-60317806.

Béland, J., & Small, K. (2004). Space weather effects on power transmission systems: The cases of Hydro-Québec and Transpower New Zealand Ltd. In I. A. Daglis (Ed.), *Effects of space weather on technological infrastructure* (pp. 287–299). Kluwer Academic.

Bolduc, L. (2002). GIC observations and studies in the Hydro-Québec power system. *Journal of Atmospheric and Solar-Terrestrial Physics, 64*(16), 1793–1802.

Boteler, D. H. (2006). The super storms of August/September 1859 and their effects on the telegraph system. *Advances in Space Research, 38*(2), 159–172.

Caldwell, B., McCarron, E., & Jonas, S. (2017). An abridged history of federal involvement in space weather forecasting. *Space Weather, 15*, 1222–1237.

Cannon, P., et al. (2013). *Extreme space weather*: Impact on engineered systems and infrastructure. Summary Report, Royal Academy of Engineering, London.

Carrington, R. C. (1860). Description of a singular appearance seen in the sun on September 1, 1859. *Monthly Notices of the Royal Astronomical Society, 20*, 13–15.

Carter, B. A., Yizengaw, E., Pradipta, R., Weygand, J. M., Piersanti, M., Pulkkinen, A., Moldwin, M. B., Norman, R., & Zhang, K. (2016). Geomagnetically induced currents around the world during the 17 March 2015 storm. *Journal of Geophysical Research: Space Physics, 121*, 10,496–10,507.

Chapman, S. (1951). *The Earth's magnetism* (2nd ed.). Wiley.

Cliver, E. W., & Dietrich, W. F. (2013). The 1859 space weather event revisited: Limits of extreme activity. *Journal of Space Weather and Space Climate, 3*, A31.

Daniel, B., Boehme, K., Kereit, M., & Rebizant, W. (2020). HV transformer protection and stabilization under geomagnetically induced currents. *Energies, 13*, 4693.

Davies, K. (1990). *Ionospheric radio*. IET Digital Library, https://digital-library.theiet.org/content/books/ew/pbew031e.

Department for Business, Energy and Industrial Strategy. (2021). *UK Severe Space Weather Preparedness Strategy*. https://assets.publishing.service.gov.uk/government/uploads/system/uploads/attachment_data/file/1020551/uk-severe-space-weather-preparedness-strategy.pdf.

El-Rabbany, A. (2006). *Introduction to GPS: The global positioning system* (2nd ed.). Artech House.

Filjar, R., Damas, M. C., & Iliev, T. B. (2021). Resilient satellite navigation empowers modern science, economy, and society. *IOP Conference Series: Materials Science and Engineering, 1032*, 012001.

George, H., & Rodger, C. J. (2019). Space weather and aviation: Impacts of solar flares. *Journal of the Royal New Zealand Air Force – Part B, 5*(1), 102–121.

Georgoulis, M. K., Nindos, A., & Zhang, H. (2019). The source and engine of coronal mass ejections. *Philosophical Transactions of the Royal Society A, 377*(2148), 20180094.

Gilmor, C. S., & Spreiter, J. R. *Discovery of the magnetosphere*. Wiley.

Green, L. M., Török, T., Vršnak, B., Manchester, W., & Veronig, A. (2018). The origin, early evolution and predictability of solar eruptions. *Space Science Reviews, 214*, 46.

Guillon, S., Toner, P., Gibson, L., & Boteler, D. (2016). A colorful blackout: The havoc caused by Auroral Electrojet generated magnetic field variations in 1989. *IEEE Power & Energy Magazine, 14*(6), 59.

Hapgood, M., Angling, M. J., Attrill, G., Bisi, M., Cannon, P. S., Dyer, C., et al. (2021). Development of space weather reasonable worst-case scenarios for the UK National Risk Assessment. *Space Weather, 19*, e2020SW002593.

Hapgood, M., Liu, H., & Lugaz, N. (2022). SpaceX – Sailing close to the space weather? *Space Weather, 20*, e2022SW003074.

Hargreaves, J. K. (1992). *The solar–terrestrial environment: An introduction to geospace – The science of the terrestrial upper atmosphere, ionosphere and magnetosphere*. Cambridge University Press.

Ingham, M., Rodger, C. J., Divett, T., Dalzell, M., & Petersen, T. (2017). Assessment of GIC based on transfer function analysis. *Space Weather, 15*, 1615–1627.

International Civil Aviation Organization. (2018). *Manual on space weather information in support of international air navigation* (Doc 10100), 2018. www.icao.int/airnavigation/METP/Panel%20Documents/Doc.10100.Space%20Weather%20Manual%20FINAL%20DRAFT%20Version.pdf.

International Civil Aviation Organization. (2019, November 19). *New global aviation space weather network launched*, https://www.icao.int/Newsroom/Pages/New-global-aviation-space-weather-network-launched.aspx

JASON. (2011). *Impacts of severe space weather on the electric grid (JSR-11-320)*. MITRE Corporation.

Jursa, A. S. (1985). *Handbook of geophysics and the space environment*. Air Force Geophys. Lab.

Kan, M. (2022). What Is Starlink? SpaceX's Much-Hyped Satellite Internet Service Explained. *PC Magazine Australia*. https://au.pcmag.com/networking/86102/what-is-starlink-spacexs-much-hyped-satellite-internet-service-explained.

Kappenman, J. (2010). *Geomagnetic storms and their impacts on the U.S. Power Grid* (Meta-R-319). Metatech Corporation.

Katz, D. M. (2016). *Physics for scientists and engineers: Foundations and connections*. Cengage Learning.

Kelly, M. A., Comberiate, J. M., Miller, E. S., & Paxton, L. J. (2014). Progress toward forecasting of space weather effects on UHF SATCOM after operation Anaconda. *Space Weather, 12*, 601–611.

Knipp, D. J., et al. (2016). The May 1967 great storm and radio disruption event: Extreme space weather and extraordinary responses. *Space Weather, 14*, 614–633.

Kono, M., & Roberts, P. H. (2002). Recent geodynamo simulations and observations of the geomagnetic field. *Reviews of Geophysics, 40*(4).

Kraus, J. D. (1988). *Antennas* (2nd ed.). McGraw–Hill.

Linty, N., Farasin, A., Favenza, A., & Dovis, F. (2019). Detection of GNSS ionospheric scintillations based on machine learning decision tree. *IEEE Transactions on Aerospace and Electronic Systems, 55*(1), 303–317.

Lloyd's. (2013). *Solar storm risk to the North American electric grid: A Lloyds space weather study*. https://assets.lloyds.com/assets/pdf-solar-storm-risk-to-the-north-american-electric-grid/1/pdf-Solar-Storm-Risk-to-the-North-American-Electric-Grid.pdf

Love, J. J. (2012). Credible occurrence probabilities for extreme geophysical events: Earthquakes, volcanic eruptions, magnetic storms. *Geophysical Research Letters, 39*, L10301.

Mac Manus, D. H., Rodger, C. J., Dalzell, M., Thomson, A. W. P., Clilverd, M. A., Petersen, T., Wolf, M., Thomson, N. R., & Divett, T. (2017). Long-term geomagnetically induced current observations in New Zealand: Earth return corrections and geomagnetic field driver. *Space Weather, 15*, 1020–1038.

Mac Manus, D. H., Rodger, C. J., Dalzell, M., Renton, A., Richardson, G. S., Petersen, T., & Clilverd, M. A. (2022). Geomagnetically induced current modeling in New Zealand: Extreme storm analysis using multiple disturbance scenarios and industry provided hazard magnitudes. *Space Weather, 20*, e2022SW003320.

Moldwin, M. (2022). *An introduction to space weather* (2nd ed.). Cambridge University Press.

New Space Economy. (2023, March 28). *NASA's ISS Procedures*: Responding to Space Weather. https://newspaceeconomy.ca/2023/03/28/nasas-iss-procedures-responding-to-space-weather

Ngwira, C. M., Pulkkinen, A., Mays, M. L., Kuznetsova, M. M., Galvin, A. B., Simunac, K., Baker, D. N., Li, X., Zheng, Y., & Glocer, A. (2013). Simulation of the 23 July 2012 extreme space weather event: What if this extremely rare CME was earth directed? *SpaceWeather, 11*, 671–679.

Nitta, N. V., Mulligan, T., Kilpua, E. K. J., et al. (2021). Understanding the origins of problem geomagnetic storms associated with "stealth" coronal mass ejections. *Space Science Reviews, 217*, 82.

Oughton, E., Copic, J., Skelton, A., Kesaite, V., Yeo, Z. Y., Ruffle, S. J., Tuveson, M., Coburn, A. W., & Ralph, D. (2016). *Helios Solar Storm Scenario*. Cambridge Risk Framework series; Centre for Risk Studies, University of Cambridge.

Palmroth, M., et al. (2021). Lower-thermosphere–ionosphere (LTI) quantities: Current status of measuring techniques and models. *Annals of Geophysics, 39*, 189–237.

Panasyuk, M. (2001). Space weather: Russian perspectives. In P. Song, H. J. Singer, & G. L. Siscoe (Eds.), *Space weather.*

Pulkkinen, A., Lindahl, S., Viljanen, A., & Pirjola, R. (2005). Geomagnetic storm of 29–31 October 2003. Geomagnetically induced currents and their relation to problems in the Swedish high-voltage power transmission system. *Space Weather, 3,* S08C03. https://doi.org/10.1029/2004SW000123

Ratcliffe, J. A. (1972). *An introduction to the ionosphere and magnetosphere*. Cambridge University Press.

Rodger, C. J., Clilverd, M. A., Verronen, P. T., Ulich, T., Jarvis, M. J., & Turunen, E. (2006). Dynamic geomagnetic rigidity cutoff variations during a solar proton event. *Journal of Geophysical Research, 111,* A04222. https://doi.org/10.1029/2005JA011395

Rodger, C. J., Mac Manus, D. H., Dalzell, M., Thomson, A. W. P., Clarke, E., Petersen, T., & Divett, T. (2017). Long-term geomagnetically induced current observations from New Zealand: Peak current estimates for extreme geomagnetic storms. *Space Weather, 15*, 1447–1460.

Ross, J. F. (2006). The invisible killers. *Smithsonian Magazine*. Smithsonian Institution.

Shibata, K. (2015). Solar and stellar flares and their impact on planets. *Proceedings of the International Astronomical Union, 11*(S320), 3–24.

Thomson, A. (2010). Space weather and power grids. *Earth, 26.*

Thomson, A. W. P., Dawson, E. B., & Reay, S. J. (2011). Quantifying extreme behaviour in geomagnetic activity. *Space Weather, 9*, S10001.

Transpower. (2022). Manage geomagnetic induced currents. *Transpower report PR-DP-252/V05*, system operator division.

Tsurutani, B. T., Gonzalez, W. D., Lakhina, G. S., & Alex, S. (2003). The extreme magnetic storm of 1–2 September 1859. *Journal of Geophysical Research, 108*(A7), 1268.

United Nations Committee on the Peaceful Uses of Outer Space Expert Group on Space Weather. (2017). *Report on thematic priority 4*: International Framework for Space Weather Services for UNISPACE+50. www.unoosa.org/oosa/oosadoc/data/documents/2018/aac.105/aac.1051171_0.html.

Vourlidas, A., Patsourakos, S., & Savani, N. P. (2019). Predicting the geoeffective properties of coronal mass ejections: Current status, open issues and path forward. *Philosophical Transactions of the Royal Society A, 377*(2148), 20180096.

Wetzel, C. (2022). Solar storm knocks 40 SpaceX satellites out of orbit. *Smithsonian Magazine*, Washington: Smithsonian Institution.

World Meterological Organization. (2020). *Space weather.* https://community.wmo.int/en/activity-areas/wmo-space-programme-wsp/space-weather-introduction

Zohuri, M., & McDaniel, P. (2021). *Introduction to energy essentials: Insight into nuclear, renewable, and non-renewable energies*. Academic Press.

Chapter 12
Light Pollution and the Future of Space Science and Astronomy

John Hearnshaw

Introduction

This chapter focuses on two topical issues which threaten the future of ground-based astronomy and space science. They are the plans to launch tens of thousands of low Earth orbit (LEO) satellites by a number of companies, including SpaceX and OneWeb, for global internet communications. These satellites result in trails that degrade wide-field imaging by astronomical telescopes.

The second issue is the ever-increasing problem of light pollution from artificial light at night (ALAN) that brightens the night sky, causing a serious deterioration of the conditions needed for astronomical research. ALAN has impacted vast areas of the globe and astronomers have fewer and fewer of the darkest sites left where observatories can still operate.

The International Astronomical Union (IAU), in collaboration with the UN Office for Outer Space Affairs (UNOOSA), has produced two ground-breaking reports and virtual conferences, in 2020 and 2021, highlighting the satellite-constellation issue and seeking measures to mitigate the problem. A submission to the Scientific and Technical Subcommittee of COPUOS, the Committee for the Peaceful Uses of Outer Space, was made in April 2022. In the United States, the SATcon1 (June 2020) and SATcon2 (July 2021) workshops also addressed the issue of satellite constellations as a threat to astronomy.

The impact of ALAN on astronomy means that there are now very few good dark sites left in the world for astronomical research. Major efforts are being made by the IAU and the International Dark-Sky Association (IDA) to mitigate the problem. In general, local governments control outdoor lighting in communities, such as towns and districts in most countries, but only national governments have the resources to

J. Hearnshaw (✉)
University of Canterbury, Christchurch, New Zealand
e-mail: john.hearnshaw@canterbury.ac.nz

M. A. Pozza (ed.), *Ascending to Space*, Space Law and Policy,
https://doi.org/10.1007/978-981-97-0714-0_12

apply and enforce a uniform set of lighting ordinances. Good lighting practices should determine the content of these ordinances, and that in turn requires international collaboration and consultation to combat one of the most serious environmental threats of the modern era.

An Overview of Ground-Based Astronomy and Artificial Light

The threat to ground-based astronomy posed by large satellite constellations in low Earth orbit (LEO) for the purposes of global internet communications is increasing. Further, the problem of artificial light at night producing a brightening of the night sky known as skyglow, which impedes the observation of faint astronomical objects by ground-based telescopes, is a challenge that needs urgent attention from the international community.

Galileo was the first person to use a telescope for astronomical observations, in 1609. But as a result of man-made light pollution in the sky, from satellites or street lights, ground-based astronomy may be impossible by about 2030.

At present, astronomers are spending billions of dollars on facilities for research using telescopes on the ground. Space astronomy is still only economical for certain specialised types of observation which are impossible from the ground – including very high angular resolution optical astronomy or observations at certain wavelengths, such as in the ultraviolet or infrared which are not transmitted through the terrestrial atmosphere.

Meanwhile, space communications companies such as SpaceX and OneWeb are claiming that LEO satellites in large numbers are more effective for providing global internet communications than any ground-based solution, such as optical fibres or microwave links, and especially so for developing countries in remote locations. This provides a conundrum for astronomy, given that LEO satellites can leave trails on astronomical images, thereby ruining many observations, especially for wide-field telescopes.

It is ironic that satellites are seen as more economical for internet communications but not for many branches of astronomy, and at the same time that the launching of satellites into space is mainly unregulated, and the existing outer space treaties are largely ineffective in preventing unlimited satellite launches.

As for artificial light at night (known as ALAN), this grew enormously throughout the twentieth century, mainly from electric street lighting, with the result that there are fewer and fewer truly dark locations remaining on Earth where astronomers can work under an unpolluted sky. Skyglow from ALAN has continued to increase into the twenty-first century, in spite of the astronomical, environmental and human health hazards that ALAN poses, and this is now threatening even some of the most remote mountain observatories being used for large new telescope projects.

Satellite Constellations and Their Impact on Astronomy

What Are Satellite Constellations?

A satellite constellation comprises thousands or tens of thousands of LEO satellites to provide global internet communications. LEO means the height above the Earth's surface is in the range 160–2000 km.

As of 1 April 2020, there were a total of 2666 active satellites, of which 1918 were in LEO. By 1 January 2021, 3372 satellites were active and 3170 were inactive. By June 2022, there were 5328 active LEO satellites. In the next decade, more than 100,000 satellites are planned in LEO. Clearly the number of satellites in LEO is doubling roughly every 2 years, mainly as a result of companies racing to take advantage of the opportunities for global internet coverage.

However, the LEO space is now becoming dangerously overcrowded. This is the space occupied by the International Space Station and other well-known satellites such as the Hubble Space Telescope. It is especially of concern that there are already at least 128 million pieces of debris in LEO. Of these, around 34,000 are over 10 cm in size, and they pose a significant hazard for all LEO satellites.

Nevertheless, LEO offers many advantages for the internet. Being close to the Earth, latency (the time for radio signals to travel up and down) is short, at about 40 milliseconds (ms) or less. In LEO orbit, the maximum time during which a satellite is above the local horizon for an observer on Earth is about 20 minutes. This time is long enough for the transfer of data to or from a ground station.

In LEO the typical satellite's orbital velocity is about 27,000 km/h. Orbits can be in any plane, equatorial, polar or intermediate between these. This compares to geostationary orbits (GEO) where satellites orbit eastwards above the equator at an altitude of 35,786 km with a velocity of about 11,300 km/h. Latency for GEO satellites is at least 250 ms.

Why Do Satellite Constellations Pose a Threat to Astronomy?

Satellite constellations can leave trails on astronomical images. Starlink satellites from SpaceX are typically launched in clusters of 60 on a single Falcon 9 rocket. Since May 2019, there have been more than a hundred such launches. After release, they enter a parking orbit at 440 km before being redirected to their final operational orbit at 550 km.

The problem for astronomy arises because satellites can be in sunlight and visible from a telescope on the ground which is in darkness. That is especially so for a few hours around dusk or dawn and for elevations close to the observer's horizon. In the parking orbit, solar panels are deployed, and these contribute greatly to reflected sunlight.

Fig. 12.1 An image of the NGC 5353/4 galaxy group made at Lowell Observatory in Arizona on 25 May 2019. The trails on the image are from the Starlink satellites of SpaceX. (Courtesy of Victoria Girgis, Lowell Observatory)

Figure 12.1 shows Starlink satellite trails recorded at the Lowell Observatory in Arizona in May 2019. The image is severely affected by parallel trails of satellites in their parking orbit.

The operational lifetime of LEO orbits at 550 km is about 5–10 years, and the problem of trails persists throughout this time.

A number of companies have launched, or plan to launch, satellite constellations for global internet coverage. Apart from the Starlink satellites of Elon Musk's SpaceX, which has plans for at least 42,000 satellites, the British company OneWeb has also launched hundreds of satellites and has plans for some 7000 in total. OneWeb satellites orbit at 1200 km above the Earth's surface, where the adverse impact on astronomy is much worse, as some satellites can be in sunlight even at midnight at this higher altitude. Telesat in Canada has plans for 1671 Lightspeed satellites from 2023, while Amazon in the United States has plans for 3236 satellites in its Kuiper programme from 2026. Russian, Chinese and South Korean companies also plan to launch satellite constellations, with some predictions estimating over 100,000 LEO satellites in orbit within a decade. If that eventuates, satellite launches are unchecked and satellite companies do not strive to mitigate the concerns of astronomers, then the future of ground-based wide-field astronomy is in jeopardy within the next 10 years.

Modelling the Impact of Satellite Constellations

The impact of satellite constellations on astronomy depends on a number of factors. These are the time of night, season, latitude of observer, altitude of the satellites above the Earth, elevation of the telescope above the horizon and the albedo of the satellites (the fraction of light they reflect). All these factors can be modelled for a particular location on Earth, and this has been done by Hainaut and Williams (2020) and Hainaut (2020) at the European Southern Observatory. Results are also presented in the report *Dark and Quiet Skies for Science and Society* (2020).[1]

Results of the modelling are shown in Fig. 12.2 for 1000 Starlink satellites and 4500 OneWeb satellites for a telescope at the Cerro Tololo Inter-American Observatory in Chile, at latitude 30° S. In winter with 12 hours of darkness, satellite trails

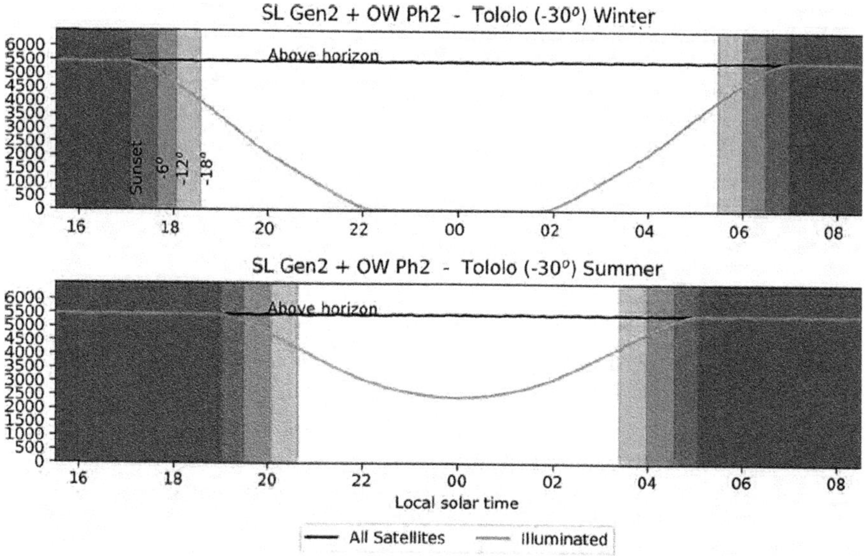

Fig. 12.2 Evolution over the night of the number of satellites above the horizon at latitude 30° S at Cerro Tololo Observatory, Chile at the summer and winter solstices. The black line is for 5500 Starlink and OneWeb satellites, while the cyan curve shows those detectable by being in sunlight. The white area corresponds to astronomical night, and shading indicates twilight at dawn and dusk. In winter no satellites are visible for 4 hours around midnight, but in summer about half the satellites remain visible even at midnight. (Courtesy Olivier Hainaut, European Southern Observatory)

[1]Hainaut, O. R., & Williams, A. P. (2020). Impact of satellite constellations on astronomical observations with ESO telescopes in the visible and infrared domains. *Astronomy & Astrophysics, 636*, A121; Hainaut, O. R. (2020). *Large satellite constellations and their impact on astronomy*. www.eso.org/~ohainaut/satellites; Walker, C. et al. (2020). *Dark and Quiet Skies for Science and Society: Report and recommendations*. [n.p.]: IAU, UNOOSA and IAC. www.iau.org/static/publications/dqskies-book-29-12-20.pdf.

would be visible for all but 2 hours of the night, an hour each side of midnight. The situation is worse in summer, with about 3000 satellites still being illuminated even at midnight.

The overall impact on ground-based optical astronomy can be summarised as follows:

- For narrow-field imaging, less than 1 square degree, about 10 per cent of all frames will be affected for observations in 2020 (with 5500 satellites in LEO) near dawn and dusk. By 2030, with 100,000 satellites, all frames will be adversely affected at twilight.
- For wide-field imaging (4 square degrees) half of all frames are adversely affected in 2020, rising to all frames having multiple trails by 2030.
- Very wide-field imaging, such as from the Vera Rubin telescope in Chile (10 square degree field), 50 per cent of all frames are expected to have ten or more satellite trails when observing begins in 2023. By 2030, all frames will be adversely affected, some with hundreds of trails.

The adverse impact of satellite constellations will not be limited to optical astronomy. The news is also bad for radio astronomy, as radio downlinks from satellites will impact radio telescopes. Eleven countries with major radio telescopes have radio quiet zones, but radio signals from satellites are not covered by this legislation. Side lobes from satellite antennae may still have an impact on telescopes even if the downlink is not directed towards radio observatories.

Mitigating the Effect of Satellite Constellations on Astronomy

A number of proposals have been made to mitigate the harmful effects of satellite constellations on astronomy. Mitigation proposals include the following:

1. Launch fewer or no satellite constellations in LEO.
2. Orbits to be no higher than 600 km.
3. Darken satellites to lower their albedo, or use visors to shield reflected sunlight.
4. Control each satellite's attitude in orbit so it reflects less sunlight towards Earth.
5. Use image processing to remove trails from images.
6. Avoid satellite trails by using accurate ephemerides (tables of trajectories) for all satellites, and exposing images at times when satellites in the field of view are at a minimum. However, this would greatly complicate telescope observing logistics.

Only option 1 is really effective. The other measures may ameliorate the problem slightly, but at the present time they do not appear to be an adequate solution.

Dark and Quiet Skies Conferences, Satcon Workshops and the New IAU Centre

The International Astronomical Union (IAU), with the UN Office for Outer Space Affairs (UNOOSA) and the Canary Islands Institute of Astrophysics (IAC) held online virtual conferences in October 2020 (Walker et al. 2020a) and October 2021 (Walker et al. 2021a). Each conference was followed by the publication of detailed reports, prepared by associated working groups in the months preceding the conference. The reports were published in December 2020 and January 2022.[2]

In addition, in the United States workshops sponsored by the Association of Universities for Research in Astronomy (AURA) and by the American Astronomical Society (AAS) were also held in 2020 and 2021. These workshops were known as SATcon1 and SATcon2, and associated reports organised by AURA and AAS were published in June 2020 (Walker et al. 2020b) and July 2021 (Walker et al. 2021b) respectively to discuss the impact of satellite constellations on astronomy.[3]

Meanwhile, the new Centre for the Protection of the Dark and Quiet Sky from Satellite Constellation Interference was announced by the IAU on 3 February 2022, as a joint project with NOIRLab (the National Optical–Infrared Laboratory of the National Science Foundation) and the Square Kilometre Array Observatory (SKAO).

The inaugural director of the IAU Centre is Piero Benvenuti (Italy) and co-directors are Connie Walker (United States) and Federico Di Vruno (United Kingdom and Argentina). The centre began operations on 1 April 2022.

The work of the new centre will include the following:

- Collecting data on LEO satellite orbits
- Liaising with the satellite industry on mitigation of the satellite problem for astronomy
- Assessing the impact of satellite constellations on astronomical observations
- Providing software tools for removing trails from images

[2] *Dark and Quiet Skies for Science and Society*; Walker, C. et al. (2021). *Dark and Quiet Skies II for Science and Society* [SATCON2]: *Working Group Reports*. [n.p.]: NOIRLab, AURA and American Astronomical Society. www.iau.org/static/science/scientific_bodies/working_groups/286/dark-quiet-skies-2-working-groups-reports.pdf.

[3] Walker, C. et al. (2020). *Impact of Satellite Constellations on Optical Astronomy and Recommendations Toward Mitigations* (SATCON1 report). NOIRLab, AURA and American Astronomical Society. aas.org/sites/default/files/2020-08/SATCON1-Report.pdf; Walker et al. *Dark and Quiet Skies II for Science and Society*.

The Need for International Regulation and Agreement

At present, there are just five outer space treaties adopted by the UN General Assembly. The Outer Space Treaty of October 1967 reads: 'The exploration and use of outer space . . . shall be carried out for the benefit and in the interests of all . . . mankind . . . Outer space . . . and celestial bodies shall be free for exploration and use by all States . . . on a basis of equality and in accordance with international law'.[4] There is no treaty or law governing the impact of space activities on ground-based astronomy.

As for the future, international action is needed from the IAU Centre, especially in establishing a dialogue with the satellite constellation companies. A new treaty governing LEO satellite constellations is needed, and this should be addressed by further lobbying of the UN Committee on the Peaceful Uses of Outer Space (COPUOS), and a new treaty needs to be drafted by UNOOSA. The problems posed by satellite constellations should be brought to the attention of the International Science Council (formerly ICSU) and through the ISC to national academies, space agencies and governments.

Light Pollution: Fewer and Fewer Truly Dark Sites Are Left on Earth Suitable for Astronomical Research

New Astronomical Observatories in the Nineteenth Century

Some of the early astronomical observatories, such as the Paris Observatory (founded in 1667) and the Royal Observatory, Greenwich (1675) were established for maritime astro-navigation and timekeeping. However, the rise of astrophysics from 1860 led to a new type of observatory. Examples are the Potsdam Astrophysical Observatory (1874), the Lick Observatory (1888), the Yerkes Observatory (1897) and the Mount Wilson Observatory (1904). The last three are in the United States.

In fact, in the nineteenth century, 43 observatories were established, mainly in cities of Europe and North America. Nearly all these were established in the second half of the century and were spurred by the rapid advances in astrophysics, especially using stellar spectroscopy.

None of those founded in cities before 1900 are still used for astronomical observations. Why is this? Because light pollution has brightened the night sky and made astronomical observations impossible. That is the rather shocking history

[4] United Nations Office for Outer Space Affairs. (1966, December 19). *Resolution Adopted by the General Assembly 2222(XI). Treaty on Principles Governing the Activities of States in the Exploration and Use of Outer Space, including the Moon and Other Celestial Bodies*. www.unoosa.org/oosa/en/ourwork/spacelaw/treaties/outerspacetreaty.html.

of ground-based optical astronomy and the fate of many observatories during the twentieth century.

The Installation of Electric City Street Lighting

The rapid growth of electric street lighting in the twentieth century was almost entirely responsible for the demise of most of the observatories established before 1900 as sites for observational astronomy. The first gas street lights were installed in London in 1807, in Baltimore in 1816 and in Paris in 1820. These had very low lumen outputs of yellow to red light, and a negligible impact on skyglow.

Some key developments in electric street lighting are given in Table 12.1 (Figs. 12.3 and 12.4).

LEDs have low power consumption, require low maintenance, and have good shielding (they shine mainly downwards), but have strong blue light

Table 12.1 Key developments in street lighting technology

Type of lighting	First use
First electric street lights in Paris (carbon arcs)	1878
Edison and Swan incandescent filament street lights	1880
Tungsten filament lights	1904
Low-pressure sodium	1930s
Fluorescent lights	1931
High-pressure sodium	1965
Light emitting diodes (LED)	2006

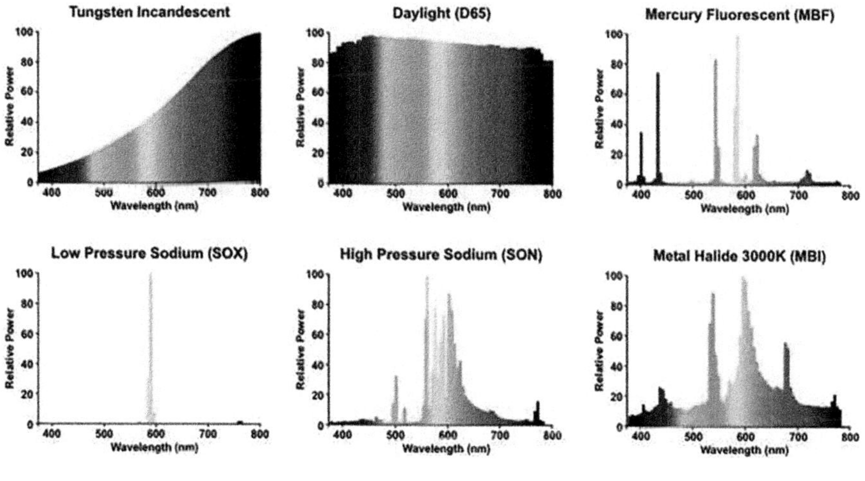

Fig. 12.3 Spectral power distributions of some lamps used for street lighting. (Courtesy of James Hooker, Lamptech, United Kingdom)

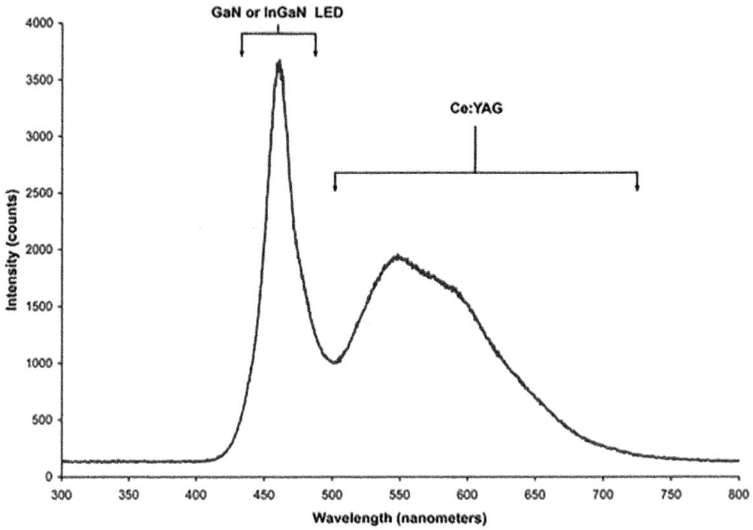

Fig. 12.4 Spectral power distribution of a typical white LED showing a strong peak of blue emission at about 465 nanometres (nm) from GaN (gallium nitride)

emission (Fig. 12.4), which scatters about four times more than yellow to red light, so the skyglow is much greater. The problem with the first LEDs is a strong blue peak in the spectral power distribution. Some 30 per cent of the luminous energy is emitted in the blue wavelengths below 500 nm. Not only does blue light contribute excessively to skyglow, but it also has an adverse impact on the environment and on human health.

Today our megacities are awash with light 24/7. There has been about a 2 per cent per annum increase in sky brightness in recent years. The result is that 80 per cent of the world's population and over 99 per cent of the population of the United States and Europe live under light-polluted skies. Sixty percent of Europeans and 80 per cent of North Americans cannot see the Milky Way. In general, stars are no longer visible in the megacities of the United States, Europe and Asia. Today the eastern United States, western Europe, India, eastern China, South Korea and Japan are all heavily light polluted, with the result that astronomical observations are not possible in any of these places.

Only a Few Locations Left on Earth for Astronomy!

The best astronomical sites left in the world are high-altitude mountain tops in places with very low light pollution and low cloud cover. Since the 1960s, all major new observatories have been constructed on such sites. These include:

- Northern Chilean Andes (Cerro Paranal 2635 m; Cerro Tololo 2200 m; La Silla 2400 m).
- Mauna Kea, Hawaii (4207 m).
- La Palma, Canary Islands (Roque de los Muchachos Observatory 2423 m).
- Mount Maidanak, Uzbekistan (2600 m).
- Hanle, Ladakh, northern Kashmir, India (4500 m).
- Ali, western Tibet, China (5100 m).

These are some of the very best sites remaining on Earth, all with low or zero light pollution and excellent weather patterns for astronomy.

There are few other sites on Earth that can compare favourably to these. Certainly there are sites with major observatories and excellent weather, but compromised to some extent by light pollution (such as the Kitt Peak National Observatory in Arizona). Alternatively, there are sites with very little light pollution but where the weather patterns are not of the first grade (such as Siding Spring Observatory in New South Wales).

Principles of Good Lighting to Save Astronomy

The basic principles of good lighting in the vicinity of astronomical observatories are well established. Near observatories, skyglow should not exceed natural airglow (atmospheric light emission) by more than 10%. This limit has been advocated by the IAU since 1980 (Cayrel et al. 1980). Natural airglow is typically about 0.25 microcandela (mcd)/m^2, so skyglow from ALAN should not exceed 0.025 mcd/m^2.

All exterior lights must be shielded so that they shine only downwards (full cut-off luminaires). Blue light (with a wavelength less than 500 nm), which scatters in the atmosphere much more readily than do longer wavelengths, should be eliminated or greatly reduced, by means of filters or the use of light types deficient in blue emission. In the case of LED lights, the correlated colour temperature (CCT, measured in kelvins) indicates the approximate amount of blue light present. LED street lights should have a CCT less than 2700 K, and ideally amber LEDs with a CCT of about 2200 K should be used.

Motion sensors, especially for security lights or lights in low-density pedestrian areas, should have motion sensors so they are off when no motion is detected. LED street lights should be controlled by a central management system. This is a computerised control system that dims or extinguishes lights in the early hours, say between midnight and dawn.

Any lighting ordinance should adopt all these principles. In addition, skylights in residential and commercial buildings should be discouraged, windows should be covered by opaque curtains or blinds after some curfew hour, such as 10 pm. Light trespass (light shining into premises where illumination is not intended) needs to be strictly controlled. Also, sports and recreational facilities should have no floodlighting after 10 pm.

The Need for National Action to Combat ALAN

Light pollution by the end of the twentieth century was out of control, with essentially all large cities awash with light 24/7. Although many communities have implemented light pollution controls, these are mainly in rural areas to protect dark skies, either in the vicinity of astronomical observatories, or to promote dark sky places for astrotourism. By 2020, there were 223 dark sky places worldwide recognised with accreditation from the International Dark-Sky Association (IDA) in Tucson, Arizona, by the Starlight Foundation in Tenerife or by the Royal Astronomical Society of Canada. These protected areas cover just over 20 million hectares, or only 0.14 per cent of the Earth's total land area (excluding oceans).

Lighting ordinances in towns and cities have helped control urban skyglow, but not sufficiently to protect astronomical research near cities. The benefits of darkness at night are mainly for the environment and for human health. Tucson, a major centre for observational astronomy, was one of the first in the world to have a city-wide lighting ordinance to control ALAN, in 1972. In New Zealand, the Mackenzie District Council adopted a lighting ordinance in 1981 to limit light pollution near the Mount John Observatory at Lake Tekapo. This was one of the first lighting ordinances in the southern hemisphere, if not the very first.

Traditionally, exterior lighting has been the domain of local government (such as councils in cities, counties or districts). However, local government agencies are not well equipped to tackle a global environmental crisis, especially as the lighting technology using LEDs is evolving rapidly, and the requirements of lighting ordinances are complex and quite technical, and thus call for expertise that is generally lacking at local government level.

The conclusion is that national governments need to impose national legislation on local bodies. Only then will the necessary technical issues be taken into account and the burden on local councils to introduce lighting controls be lifted. It is notable that both France and Croatia have introduced national legislation for nationwide lighting controls. Many other countries now need to follow suit.

The Need for International Action to Combat Light Pollution

International action is needed to save astronomy as a science and to combat ALAN, one of the major global environmental threats of the twenty-first century. The UN Environment Programme (UNEP) should provide guidelines for states parties (member states) so that national legislation follows globally accepted protocols. It now seems clear that this global top-down approach is needed to save the planet from the ill effects of light pollution, as the problems are now too widespread and deep-rooted to leave to local government authorities.

To promote this top-down approach, we should lobby various international agencies for support and advice, both on the light pollution problem as well as on the threat to astronomy from satellite constellations. These agencies include:

- UNOOSA – UN Office for Outer Space Affairs
- COPUOS – Committee on the Peaceful Uses of Outer Space
- IDA – International Dark-Sky Association
- IUCN – International Union for Conservation of Nature
- WHO – World Health Organization
- OECD Environment Directorate
- ISC – International Science Council
- UNESCO – UN Educational, Scientific and Cultural Organization
- UNEP – UN Environment Programme

The first four in this list are already involved in mitigating the effects of satellite constellations or light pollution, or both. However, the issues need to come to the attention of all these agencies if effective international lobbying is to take place and progress to be made.

References

Cayrel, R., Graham-Smith, F., Fisher, A. J., & de Boer, J. B. (1980). *Guide lines for minimizing urban sky glow near astronomical observatories* (IAU/CIE publication no. 1). International Astronomical Union.

Hainaut, O. R. (2020). *Large satellite constellations and their impact on astronomy*. www.eso.org/~ohainaut/satellites

Hainaut, O. R., & Williams, A. P. (2020). Impact of satellite constellations on astronomical observations with ESO telescopes in the visible and infrared domains. *Astronomy & Astrophysics, 636*, A121.

Walker, C. et al. (2020a). *Dark and Quiet Skies for Science and Society: Report and recommendations*. [n.p.]: IAU, UNOOSA and IAC. www.iau.org/static/publications/dqskies-book-29-12-20.pdf

Walker, C. et al. (2020b). *Impact of satellite constellations on optical astronomy and recommendations toward mitigations* (SATCON1 report). [n.p.]: NOIRLab, AURA and American Astronomical Society. aas.org/sites/default/files/2020-08/SATCON1-Report.pdf

Walker, C. et al. (2021a). *Dark and Quiet Skies II for Science and Society: Working Group Reports*. [n.p.]: IAU, UNOOSA and IAC. www.iau.org/static/science/scientific_bodies/working_groups/286/dark-quiet-skies-2-working-groups-reports.pdf.

Walker, C. et al. (2021b, July 12–16). *SATCON2 working groups report*. [n.p.]: NOIRLab, AURA and American Astronomical Society. www.noirlab.edu/public/products/techdocs/techdoc033/

Chapter 13
New Zealand's Growing Space Sector: A Technological and Science Perspective

Nicholas James Rattenbury

Introduction

New Zealand's space sector is in a phase of rapid growth, catalysed by the success of Rocket Lab. The increasing activity in space science, engineering and related topics suggests that interest and appetite in these fields has been long latent or under-supported. It is generally held that increased investment in the local space sector is likely to generate rewards in the form of valuable intellectual property, increased high dollar-to-weight export products, high-value services and an increased standing in international academic and educational forums. The opportunities and benefits to New Zealand as a space-active nation, however, must be balanced against the risks and cost. This balancing act is itself an opportunity: one in which New Zealand demonstrates its commitment to both the international community as a responsible actor in space based on the extant norms in that community, while also ensuring that the particular values of New Zealand society are reflected in our activities.

This chapter highlights some of the activities in the New Zealand space sector, illustrates some of the major tensions listed above, and considers options for the future of the sector. A view from the tertiary education sector is presented, including a selected summary of space-related university research, educational offerings and capacity development initiatives. Commercial activity is also broadly described and some of the elements of the New Zealand Government responsible for regulating New Zealand space activity are outlined. A number of challenges facing the New Zealand space sector are also considered.

N. J. Rattenbury (✉)
Department of Physics, University of Auckland, Auckland, New Zealand
e-mail: n.rattenbury@auckland.ac.nz

M. A. Pozza (ed.), *Ascending to Space*, Space Law and Policy,
https://doi.org/10.1007/978-981-97-0714-0_13

Academia

Interest in space research and education has increased, again partly owing to the increased profile brought by the operations of Rocket Lab. In this section, a very brief summary of some of the more recent activities being undertaken at New Zealand universities is considered. For the present purposes of this chapter, only a high-level overview is presented. The activities are characterised broadly as either research or education, and so a summary of any advisory services that universities may have provided to, for example, Government or other third parties, is not considered.

The following broad overview of university activity in space research is intended to impress upon the reader the breadth of interest across the New Zealand research community in space. This overview is not intended to be a census of activity.

The motivations for engaging in space research are diverse. A researcher might be interested in the development of technology to go into space, such as payloads and the spacecraft that carry them. Other researchers might be interested in benefiting from space-originated data, irrespective of the platform that provided these data. Still, other researchers seek to develop or find innovation in the development of service provision to a local and international space economy. Here is a brief account of some of the space-related research being undertaken in New Zealand. This summary is brief and not exhaustive.

Propulsion Systems

University research activity in propulsion can be divided according to their use case. Activity can be broadly characterised as either "in-space" or "to-space" systems, drawing a distinction between the theory and practice of moving space assets from Earth-orbit to further afield, and that relating to lofting craft from the Earth's surface.

Electric propulsion systems convert electrical potential energy into kinetic energy, which is used to change the momentum of a spacecraft (see e.g., Goebel & Katz, 2008). This is distinct from earlier systems which usually use the reaction forces arising from chemical processes. Electric propulsion systems are becoming an increasingly popular means of propelling spacecraft already in space (see e.g., Henry, 2017). This is because such systems are more efficient in terms of fuel usage. As fuel must take up at least some of a spacecraft's mass budget, minimising the amount of fuel needed for a mission has substantial benefits.

University research projects in New Zealand encompass several "in-space" electric propulsion types. The first type of propulsion system under study uses plasma energised by radiofrequencies and manipulated by magnetic fields (Caldarelli et al., 2021, 2022; Charles et al., 2019; Filleul et al., 2019, 2021, 2022; Balkenhohl et al., 2022). Research is also underway into the use and optimisation of high-temperature superconducting magnet coils to impel plasma as part of an electric propulsion system (Olatunji et al., 2021a, b, 2022; Berry et al., 2021; Long, 2021). High-altitude aerospace propulsion systems and rocket attitude control systems are also current research areas (see e.g., Bryson et al., 2016; Hann et al., 2010, 2012).

Synthetic Aperture Radar

Space-based synthetic aperture radar (SAR) is a well-known technique for Earth observation (see e.g., Wiley, 1985). It advantageously utilises the movement of a radar system in its orbit around the Earth to provide imagery at high resolution. The use of SAR data was identified early as being of value to New Zealand for environment and security monitoring (Krecke et al., 2021a). New Zealand has a relatively large Exclusive Economic Zone (EEZ). Oversight of the EEZ would require a significant increase in the number of military or civilian aircraft capable of accessing this large region. While existing SAR satellites can provide data on demand, this comes at significant cost and not necessarily within the timeframes required to support security or emergency operations. However, developing a national SAR mission carries its own significant costs. Recent work abroad investigated the extent to which small – and therefore relatively inexpensive – satellites could provide SAR imagery (Engelen et al., 2012) and NZ research investigated what would be required for a small satellite SAR mission for ship detection in New Zealand's EEZ (Krecke et al., 2021a, b).

Novel Materials

Returning payloads safely from space to Earth is a significant technological challenge in commercialising space and orbital environments. An aspect that is usually considered is ensuring the safe return of material and personnel balances with the need to meet mass and volume budgets for a spacecraft mission, where costs rapidly increase with size and weight (Andrews et al., 2011; Carandente & Savino, 2014). New Zealand research is underway to evaluate low-density and low-cost metal foam or mesh (Blosser et al., 2002) as the basis of new heat-shielding materials (Nieke et al., 2023).

Astrodynamics

Modelling and predicting the path of a spacecraft is critically important. Ensuring that a payload is delivered to its correct orbit, that a vehicle is entering Earth's atmosphere at the correct angle, that two objects are not on a collision-course, that a space probe will arrive at its destination safely; these are all aspects of astrodynamics.[1] While Newton's laws account sufficiently for the observed motion demonstrated by most spacecraft, increased demand for accuracy and precision require a corresponding need for computational resource and therefore a corresponding need for new and rapid algorithms for spacecraft trajectory determination and optimisation.

The increasingly popular electric propulsion systems of the types outlined above have thrust characteristics very different to conventional chemical propulsion systems. These newer means of spacecraft propulsion and the increasing demand for higher accuracy trajectory predictions require the development of new trajectory design algorithms, and this is the subject of ongoing New Zealand research (Graham et al., 2019, 2022; Armellin, 2021).

An accurate and precise understanding of the location of all objects in Earth orbit is of paramount importance in protecting the safety of spacecraft and their payloads, and their crew, if any. Space situational awareness (SSA) is the study and process leading to the continual updating and real-time analysis of the orbits of spacecraft, space debris and other objects that could potentially cause harm (see e.g., Pirovano et al., 2020). Directly imaging spacecraft in orbit is another active area of New Zealand research (Weddell et al., 2019; Muruganandan et al., 2022). Images of a spacecraft can help determine its orientation and rates of rotation. This is important in the situations where communications have been lost with the spacecraft and its current state of health unknown. Direct imaging can help operators to diagnose problems and regain control in such cases. Such imaging requires adaptive optics to account for the disruptive effect of Earth's turbulent atmosphere (Hickman et al., 2019, 2020). An adaptive optics system measures the effect of the atmosphere on incoming light, and in real-time, corrects for any distortions. This results in images with reduced distortion, allowing finer details to be discerned.

Free Space Optical Communications

Free space optical communication (FSOC) via laser light offers a substantial increase in the rate of data that can be transmitted between space and Earth (see Rattenbury, 2021). FSOC also provides heightened security, higher efficiencies, and takes up less space and mass on a spacecraft compared to their RF counterparts. An optical ground terminal similarly takes up less space than a comparable RF antenna system. New Zealand research is underway to establish an optical communication ground station as part of an Australia-New Zealand network, in collaboration with researchers at the DLR (Bennet et al., 2020; MBIE, 2022). A conventional optical communication system can be secured using quantum cryptography, and joint research between New Zealand and Australian researchers on this topic is currently in progress.

[1] Synonymous with orbital mechanics.

Earth Observation and Space Weather

Atmospheric warming owing to the rise of methane emissions is a topic of research worldwide (see e.g., Fletcher & Schaefer, 2019). The MethaneSAT mission is designed to search for methane emissions over wide areas and is expected to launch late in early 2024 (Powell, 2023; Rohrschneider et al., 2021). According to Benmergui et al. (2020), "[i]ts goal is to characterize changes in anthropogenic methane emissions with an initial focus on the global oil and gas production sector", and is "being developed to make a major contribution to the goal of lowering CH_4 emissions from oil and gas systems by 45% by 2025" (Wofsy & Hamburg, 2019). MethaneSAT is billed as New Zealand's first Government-funded space mission (MBIE, 2021a). During the first 12 months in orbit, Rocket Lab will operate MethaneSAT using the Mission Operations Control Centre at The University of Auckland's Te Pūnaha Ātea Space Institute. After that initial period, control of MethaneSAT will be handed over to Auckland's Te Pūnaha Ātea Space Institute. The data received from MethaneSAT will be analysed by a team led by Dr. Sara Mikaloff-Fletcher (NIWA).

Global Navigation Satellite System (GNSS) signals are used by navigation, positioning and time-keeping systems. These signals are also reflected from the surface of the Earth, and these reflected signals can be detected and used to deduce the properties of the surface reflecting them. NASA's Cyclone Global Navigation Satellite System (CYGNSS) uses GNSS signals from the Global Positioning System (GPS) to conduct GNSS-R[eflectometry] remote sensing. *Rongowai*[2] is a New Zealand-based research project which uses sensors installed on Air New Zealand Q300 aircraft to collect GNSS-R signals (Laverick et al., 2020; Moller et al., 2021; Linnabary et al., 2020).

Changes in output from the Sun, especially rapid and energetic outbursts, can cause damage to spacecraft and, in extreme cases, to ground infrastructure (Speidel & Rattenbury, 2021). The study of space weather (see e.g., Bothmer & Daglis, 2007; Daglis et al., 2021) relates the status, changes and predictions relating to the space environment and has been the subject of New Zealand research for decades (see e.g., Seppälä et al., 2014, 2013; Kruglyakov et al., 2022; Smith et al., 2021, 2022).

One source of global atmospheric data is from satellites carrying radiometers to detect thermally excited microwave radiation emitted by greenhouse gases. New Zealand is leading research into a novel radiometer system which converts microwave radiation into optical wavelengths, where detection is more efficient (Rueda et al., 2016, 2019; Strekalov et al., 2016; Sayson et al., 2019).

[2] https://spoc.auckland.ac.nz/.

Life Processes in Space

New Zealand space research covers topics extending from extra-solar planet detection (see e.g., Bond et al., 2004), astrobiology (Westall et al., 2015; Djokic et al., 2017) and life processes in space (Chen, 2021). The technological challenge of crewed spaceflight remains one of the most exacting, high risk and high-profile human endeavours. Matching this achievement and impact would be the first confirmed detection of life outside our own Earth's biosphere. Life and life processes then often motivate technological innovation in national space research programmes.

Mars has long been a target of intense scrutiny as a possible past, current or future host of life (see e.g., Mumma, 2012). Mars landers, rovers and orbiters have carried numerous scientific payloads to detect evidence of life. Choosing where to search on the surface of Mars has been the topic of New Zealand research and reflects the developments in research into early life formation processes on Earth (Westall et al., 2015; Ruff et al., 2020) – particularly relating to extremophile life processes in hot spring environments (Campbell et al., 2015; Teece et al., 2020).

Human health in space is a priority research area, especially given the renewed interest in long-duration crewed space exploration missions. Lisa Brown (Faculty of Medical and Health Sciences, University of Auckland) leads efforts to promote aerospace medicine as a research area in New Zealand. Closely related to human health and the long-term human presence in space is the performance of microbial life in low, or micro-gravity environments (see e.g., Chen, 2021).

Crystallising proteins in microgravity produces protein crystals of high quality and suitable for detailed structural analyses (McPherson & DeLucas, 2015). A spacecraft payload for protein crystallisation in space has been developed at the University of Canterbury.[3]

Research into life processes in space is important for New Zealand as this area directly enhances worldwide research into two of the most high-profile and exciting areas of space research: the search for extra-solar life and how best to maintain the health of crews during extended off-world exploration. Research into microgravity protein crystallisation also offers significant opportunities for discovery in biomedicine.

Sustainability

New Zealand's space sector is set to continue to grow, offering an opportunity to diversify the nation's economy. When considering the technological focus in New Zealand as described in the above sections, it is pertinent to note that most space-related economic activities focus on high-technology, knowledge-intensive development of goods and services. Spacecraft hardware is, almost by definition,

[3] https://www.canterbury.ac.nz/news/2021/launching-a-space-lab-into-orbit.html.

necessarily lightweight and with a high dollar-to-cost ratio: logically, this means that such products are at the forefront of considerations for a nation geographically remote from its end-user markets. Furthermore, New Zealand's growing list of linkages in space research and development offers opportunities to leverage the local intellectual capacity and drive to generate skilled personnel and services. This economic development raises the challenge of ensuring that any degradation to our environment as a result is made with due consideration, and that such development can be made sustainable. Globally, there has been a shift towards non-governmental interests acting in space. Indeed, space activity in New Zealand is dominated by the private sector (Stocks, 2022). Government's role is to set and enforce regulatory structures and policies that necessarily correlate to its international legal obligations (Pozza & Dennerley, 2022).

Sustainability research is an active area in New Zealand, and this also extends to ensuring that our space-adjacent activities are placed on a sustainable footing (see e.g., Dhopade, 2021). Government has signalled its commitment to the sustainable development of the space sector with its joint venture Project Tāwhaki. This project seeks to "[d]evelop aerospace activities and R&D facilities" on a 1000 ha property on the Kaitorete Spit and "[p]rotect and rejuvenate the Kaitorete environment" (MBIE, 2021b). Some work has been done, or is under way, critically assessing the promises of satellite megaconstellations (Speidel, 2021) and their impact on the natural dark sky environment (Cirkovic et al., 2021). New Zealand legal innovation has been cited as having potential for the governance of space as a commons (Venkatesan et al., 2020; Tepper & Whitehead, 2018).

That the low Earth orbit volume is getting increasingly crowded is well known (see e.g., Feder, 2022). As additional spacecraft and space vehicles are lofted to orbit, and as in-orbit activity increases, there is a corresponding increase in the risk that spacecraft could collide with each other, or with a piece of debris. Uncontrolled exploitation of space will degrade the environment to a state in which the operation in, or traversal through, polluted orbits will carry a significant risk to spacecraft or human life. A responsible actor in space must enact processes that evaluate the risk that any given satellite might cause harm. Specifying an orbital debris mitigation plan is one requirement of obtaining a New Zealand payload licence.[4] More generally, research at the University of Canterbury considers the impact of New Zealand's launch activities over extended time scales (Watt, 2022).

Deployable Structures

Spacecrafts often comprise movable subsystems, such as actuators, deployable solar panels or antennas. In all cases, the performance and reliability of these subsystems is paramount: options are severely limited for spacecraft operators to free a jammed

[4]Outer Space and High-altitude Activities Act 2017, 16(2).

mechanism, for example. The research and design of mechanical structures is an active area of research in New Zealand (see e.g., Stabile et al., 2022; De Zanet et al., 2022; Honeth et al., 2022; Nath & Aglietti, 2022). Researching the precision engineering required by deployable structures opens up further opportunities for New Zealand to service an international supply chain for high dollar-to-weight space-ready components.

Tertiary Education

In this section we review the recent developments in the tertiary education sector, relating to space systems, engineering and science. Several New Zealand universities (University of Auckland, University of Canterbury, Victoria University of Wellington) have started to provide degrees or specialisations, and we briefly list these here. Universities also foster and support student clubs and engagement activities relating to space. While not part of a formal education curriculum, these engagement opportunities offer the chance for students to develop skills and identify areas of endeavour most aligned with their interests.

The University of Auckland offers a Master in Aerospace Engineering degree, as well as a postgraduate Diploma and Certificate. Space systems is also available as a sub-discipline within the Applied Physics specialisation of the Bachelor of Advanced Science (Hons) degree. The University of Canterbury offers a Minor in Aerospace Engineering as part of the BE(Hons) Mechanical Engineering degree and The Victoria University of Wellington offers a major in space science within its Bachelor of Science degree. These new courses of study reflect the growth of the New Zealand space sector and the need for suitably trained graduates. In addition, postgraduate research at all levels is pursued at various NZ universities, driven by the interests of individual researchers or research groups. We should note, however, that a formal degree in space science or engineering, structured and named as such, is not a prerequisite for a university or its students to engage in world-class teaching and research into space science, systems, engineering or related topics. Indeed, such research and research-led teaching has long been a part of the New Zealand tertiary landscape. The recent rise in specialist space science or engineering degrees or specialisations is reflective of this: conventional study in traditional STEM subjects underlies the bulk of intellectual and technical endeavour relating to space.

A great deal of education occurs outside of the lecture room, workshop or laboratory. Space-related university clubs and societies have long been attracting students who have similar interests. A complete list of such groups, active and past, would be too long to include here – but they must not be undervalued.[5] Multiple

[5] Some groups are part sponsored by a university department. UC Aerospace (formerly the University of Canterbury Rocketry Club), for example, is sponsored by the Department of Mechanical Engineering at the University of Canterbury.

international organisations exist to provide student enrichment activities relating to space. One such initiative is CanSat (see e.g., Shinichi, 2018; Walker et al., 2010). A CanSat comprises most of the subsystems that are found in a satellite, packaged into a 350 mL can. The CanSat is launched via balloon or sounding rocket. Payload data and satellite telemetry are collected and analysed. In this way, a CanSat-based programme replicates much of the process of building, testing, launching and operating a space satellite payload, without much of the regulatory restrictions. Another organisation which has long been active globally is AMSAT – for amateur radio in space enthusiasts (see e.g., Baker & Jansson, 1994). The AMSAT community has created several satellites for the purposes of education in radio and space communications. AMSAT-ZL is the New Zealand subsection of the international AMSAT community and has been developing a not-for-profit amateur radio satellite of its own, called KiwiSat[6] (see also Makarov, 2015).

Under an agreement between the MBIE and NASA, internships were made available for young New Zealand researchers to work at a NASA facility, with the first interns attending in 2019.[7] As of writing, internships are being offered[8] at NASA Jet Propulsion Laboratory (JPL) under the Visiting Student Research Programme. In previous years, internships were offered at NASA's Ames Research Center under the International Internship (I2) programme.

Auckland Programme for Space Systems

The Auckland Programme for Space Systems is a cross-institution enrichment programme for undergraduates at The University of Auckland (APSS, 2022). At the heart of the APSS Programme is a competition to design a CubeSat mission that will collect data from orbit that services a New Zealand societal need. The first satellite created by the APSS was APSS-I/Quaketec and was New Zealand's first satellite built by undergraduates with a scientific payload and delivered to orbit (Rocket Lab, 2020a, b; UoA, 2020a). It was launched on a Rocket Lab Electron on 20th November 2020 (Return To Sender). The APSS was created to provide undergraduate students from across all university faculties the opportunity to engage with the conceptualisation, design, construction and operation of a satellite. Some APSS student competition teams have found success thereafter, securing funding to develop a business surrounding their core ideas, for example, Zenno Astronautics[9] had their origins in the APSS (Radio New Zealand, 2018; UoA, 2020b; Uniservices, 2023). The APSS was originally supported by the University of Auckland Vice

[6] https://www.kiwisat.org.nz/.

[7] https://nz.usembassy.gov/nasa-internships/.

[8] https://www.mbie.govt.nz/science-and-technology/space/nasa-internships/.

[9] https://zenno.space/.

Chancellor's Strategic Development Fund and is supported by US-based engineering alumnus Neil Paton and his wife Louise (UoA, 2018).

University Research Centres

The interest generated by the Auckland Programme for Space Systems catalysed a wider discussion at The University of Auckland regarding the development of space science and engineering as part of the University's formal teaching and research offerings (Poland, 2019). In 2018 a Space Systems Institute at The University of Auckland was created. In parallel, advertising by The University of Auckland began for the Inaugural Director of the Space Systems Institute, a position to be funded under the Entrepreneurial Universities initiative of the Tertiary Education Commission.[10] Te Pūnaha Ātea Auckland Space Institute became the new name of the Space Systems Institute in January 2019 and the Inaugural Director took over leadership of the Institute in September 2019 (UoA, 2019).[11] The Institute operates the National Satellite Test Facility (NSTF) which provides facilities to subject spacecraft and their subsystems to simulated launch conditions and space environments.[12]

Commercial Activity

Commercial activity has accelerated in New Zealand's space sector, with established businesses being joined by a variety of start-up companies. We must restrict our inspection of the NZ space sector commercial activity to only a broad overview here to set the increasing amount of economic activity into context. MBIE commissioned Deloitte Access Economics to prepare a report on New Zealand's space sector and estimate the contemporary and projected contribution to New Zealand's economy (Deloitte, 2019). That report is based partly on 104 responses to a survey conducted by Deloitte. According to the report "Many space economies around the world were built on large institutional space programmes", and "New Zealand is a unique example of a space sector almost entirely driven by commercial activity. It was commercial operations – those of Rocket Lab – that spurred the development of the NZSA" (Pozza & Dennerley, 2022). New Zealand's national space agency was created in order to facilitate the activities of a commercial actor, and the agency is a unit wholly within our Ministry of Business, Entrepreneurship and Innovation

[10] https://www.tec.govt.nz/funding/funding-and-performance/funding/fund-finder/entrepreneurial-universities/.

[11] The name of the Institute was subsequently changed to Te Pūnaha Ātea Space Institute.

[12] https://space.auckland.ac.nz/home/facilities/national-satellite-test-facility-nstf/.

(MBIE). We briefly consider some potential effects of this arrangement further below.

Regional networking collaborations have been established, with the goal of developing relationships between stakeholders in the development of local space economies. Aerospace Christchurch is constituted of volunteers working to "promot [e] the interests of the Christchurch and Canterbury aerospace community".[13] Aerospace Auckland is a similar entity and was created from an earlier group from within Tātaki Auckland Unlimited, an Auckland Council-controlled organisation. Both organisations host events for representatives from the commercial and cultural sectors, local and national government and tertiary institutions.

Government and Regulation

This section introduces the principal domestic regulations governing space activities from New Zealand. It is not a complete analysis of the entirety of regulations that might control space activities, and we do not touch on the international agreements, treaties or conventions that jointly are often referred to as "International space law".[14] In 2021, New Zealand signed the Artemis Accords, a bilateral agreement between New Zealand and the United States of America to "establish a common vision via a practical set of principles, guidelines, and best practices to enhance the governance of the civil exploration and use of outer space with the intention of advancing the Artemis Program" (Artemis, 2020). As part of the Artemis Program, NASA seeks to return astronauts to the Moon, and to send the first astronauts to Mars.[15] The NZSA leads space policy, regulation and development of the New Zealand space sector. It was formed in April 2016 principally and initially to

[13] https://www.christchurch.space/.

[14] For an introduction to this topic, the reader can refer to the resources managed by the UN Office for Outer Space Affairs (United Nations Publications, 2018). Briefly, New Zealand has agreed to the Treaty on Principles Governing the Activities of States in the Exploration and Use of Outer Space, including the Moon and Other Celestial Bodies (also known as the Outer Space Treaty); the Agreement on the Rescue of Astronauts, the Return of Astronauts and the Return of Objects Launched into Outer Space (also known as the Rescue Agreement); and the Convention on International Liability for Damage Caused by Space Objects (also known as the Liability Convention). These agreements were made in 1967, 1969 and 1974, respectively. Most recently, New Zealand acceded to the Convention on the Registration of Objects Launched into Outer Space (the Registration Convention), in 2018.

[15] The principles of the Accords relate to civil space activities and regulate activities not just on the surfaces of the Moon or Mars: "[t]hese activities may take place on the Moon, Mars, comets, and asteroids, including their surfaces and subsurfaces, as well as in orbit of the Moon or Mars, in the Lagrangian points for the Earth-Moon system, and in transit between these celestial bodies and locations" (Artemis, 2020).

manage the intentions of Rocket Lab to launch spacecraft from New Zealand (Pozza & Dennerley, 2022). The NZSA regulates the use of space from New Zealand via the Outer Space and High-Altitude Activities Act (2017) (New Zealand Government, 2017a).[16] Rocket Lab launched its first test rocket in May 2017 (Rocket Lab, 2017) and its first commercial launch was in November 2018 (Rocket Lab, 2018). The regulations above came into force on 21 December 2017. It should be noted that "Prior to the legislation coming into force, the Government had an agreement with Rocket Lab USA Inc. and Rocket Lab NZ authorising their launch activity from New Zealand".[17]

Recently, the NZSA published a consultation document seeking feedback on a draft strategy for developing the New Zealand aerospace sector (New Zealand Government, 2022a). That consultation document sets out four "Areas" for development. The first Area focuses on the desiderata of the NZ aerospace sector, with reference to a draft and aspirational "2030 Future State". The second Area refers to the aspects of the aerospace sector that will be required to achieve and support the Future State. These supportive aspects are three in number and are referred to as "Pillars". The first of these relates to how the number of high-wage, high-skilled jobs might be increased, leading to growth in high-value exports and services (New Zealand Government, 2022a, page 11). The second Pillar relates to how Government can provide an enabling environment, with aligned policies and a suitable regulatory framework [ibid]. The final Pillar refers to the manner in which aerospace might become more embedded into the national psyche, seeking ways in which engagement in the aerospace industry might be promoted, and how more people can be made aware of the benefits of an aerospace industry and related space technologies (New Zealand Government, 2022a, page 12). The third Area sets several Goals for the aerospace sector, those goals being listed as (i) Build a sustainable air passenger journey [sic], (ii) Safely integrate all forms of autonomous aerial vehicles, (iii) At the forefront of global sustainable space activities, (iv) Actively support a permanent human presence in space and (v) Critical decision-making made easy through aerospace-enabled data, tools and applications (New Zealand Government, 2022a, pages 13–14). The fourth and final Area sets out the plan to achieve the ambitions of the strategy (New Zealand Government, 2022a, pages 15–16).

Running concurrently with the call for consultation on the New Zealand Aerospace Strategy is a call for consultation on New Zealand's space policies (New Zealand Government, 2022b). According to the policy consultation document, the portfolio of New Zealand space policies has the following objectives: (i) Growing an innovative and inclusive space sector, (ii) Protecting and advancing our national security and economic interests, (iii) Regulating space activities safely

---

[16]See also the related secondary legislation, the Outer Space and High-Altitude Activities (Licences and Permits) Regulations 2017 and the Outer Space and High-Altitude Activities (Definition of High-altitude Vehicle) Regulations 2017 (New Zealand Government, 2017b, c).

[17]https://www.mbie.govt.nz/science-and-technology/space/about-us/.

and securely, (iv) Promoting the responsible uses of space internationally, and (v) Modelling a sustainable space and Earth environment. New Zealand currently has three Government Ministers who have aerospace and space sector affairs as part of their respective portfolios including the Minister for Economic and Regional Development, the Minister for Research, Science and Innovation and the Minister for Transport. The fact that New Zealand has three Ministers with oversight of space activity might be considered a reflection of the importance of space across multiple sectors.

The remainder of this chapter summarises some of the key challenges that New Zealand currently faces. The nature of legislation and regulation means that it cannot rapidly keep pace with technological innovation and should allow the development of the space industry while ensuring safety. Regulators need to work more closely with industry to be best appraised of the risks, and to take care not to establish an overly rules-based approach, thereby risking being rapidly outdated. Good regulation manages risk associated with activity without putting unnecessary costs or delays and must avoid regulations which strangle innovation (Pozza & Dennerley, 2022).

The sector must be continually monitored and the regulation governing it assessed as the sector develops. A statutory review of the Outer Space and High-Altitude Activities Act (OSHAA Act) was returned to Parliament in May 2022 (New Zealand Government, 2022c). The review was set at 3 years following the act's introduction as it dealt with a new area of regulation.[18]

Challenges and Pathways

That the home of the NZSA is in MBIE sends a clear message that New Zealand's relationship with space is primarily a commercial one. Across the New Zealand research funding portfolio, the only sources of funding that can pay the high costs of space development and activity are those from MBIE. Some space research activities can be managed within a modest university department's means, particularly those that are computation-based or theoretical in nature. However, as soon as any research calls for the development of technologies that are expected to operate in the space environment, the costs of space-rated consumables alone demand significant budgets. Expertise is expensive also, especially when that expertise has to be attracted to the country from abroad. Other funding streams are available, such as from venture capitalists, private investors, or from other agencies, such as the US Air Force Office

[18] An interesting tension arising from the Act and discussed in the review is that there is currently no definition of "outer space" in the OSHAA Act. In contrast, a definition of "high-altitude" is given. This, in turn, raises some issues, including, for instance, whether or not there is clarity on the relationship between launch licences and high-altitude licences issued under the OSHAA Act.

Table 13.1 Proportion of GDP spent on R&D and the number of non-commercial or research-focused space satellite missions. GDP data are from (New Zealand Government, 2018) and satellite data are from (Krebs, 2022)

Nation	% GDP spent on R&D	Science satellites
New Zealand	1.23	1
Denmark	2.96	15
Finland	2.9	10
Ireland	1.54	1
Israel	4.25	24
Singapore	2.18	15
Australia	2.11	14
OECD	2.38	

of Scientific Research.[19] The highest-valued funding opportunities unsurprisingly require returns on investment, which are most often couched in terms of increased commercial activity or market share. Scientific discovery using space satellites with little to no direct application to a market for goods or services suffers as a result. Table 13.1 lists the proportion of GDP spent on research and development by New Zealand and some of its peer nations, alongside the number of satellites from those nations characterised as having non-commercial or research-focused missions. An unsurprising correlation is evident. Diversifying the nation's range of space mission activity to include purely research-driven inquiry will require raised levels of science funding to support this.

Within the current New Zealand research framework, funding is available at levels and on time frames which could only support modest home-grown spacecraft missions, payloads or research programmes. Building a "simple" or small spacecraft is still challenging and expensive. However small satellites can deliver excellent results, have a (relatively) short development cycle and are therefore well-suited for technology demonstration and establishing flight heritage. Going beyond the small and/or simple, New Zealand would need to invest heavily in a national spacecraft mission. In the context of funding, this would require more of a mission-led governance, rather than a principal-investigator-led contested allocation of funds. In any case, growing capacity is going to take many political cycles, sustained and targeted investment and a national approach.

A government makes decisions on the way it supports the economy it serves, and the policy underlying that decision-making process falls somewhere along a spectrum. At one end of the spectrum, the decision-making process follows a regulatory or market-rational policy (Johnson, 1982). In this mode, the government does not attempt to pick winners in the economic marketplace. Economic actors compete, and the best succeed. The engagement of government in this environment is limited largely to regulatory pathfinding, seeking to remove administrative or legal barriers from the economic actors. At the other end of the spectrum, decisions are made following a developmental or plan-rational policy. In this mode, government sets out an economic development plan based on a specific target industry. It could be argued

[19] https://www.afrl.af.mil/AFOSR/.

that New Zealand currently follows a more market-rational approach to economy development. In contrast, countries like Japan have a more plan-rational policy (Hsu, 2012). Given the high costs of research, development, and activity in the space sector, and the relatively low contribution from GDP to research and development, it could be argued that a more plan-rational policy for supporting space activity is to be favoured in New Zealand. The following excerpt from a review of the New Zealand space sector echoes these aspects.

> The overwhelming impression is that the New Zealand space sector is small enough to form Team NZ and work together in a cohesive way, too small to tackle everything without the dilution that would render each endeavour somewhat pointless, but not so small that it couldn't collectively, pragmatically choose one or two niche themes in the overlap between space and other disruptive areas, and go after the challenge of becoming the best in the world at them.
>
> Put another way, if New Zealand does not do this, then its space sector will be too diluted, and with a few exceptions its space industry will struggle to be competitive. (Boyce, 2022)

The New Zealand-DLR Joint Research Programme currently funds eight research projects in New Zealand via MBIE's Catalyst Fund.[20] Recently, a similar programme was announced for joint research with NASA.[21] These initiatives seek to develop research collaborations with specific overseas institutions. The NZ-DLR Joint Research Programme has a multi-phase structure, where an initial tranche of projects was funded with a view to exploring possible research opportunities between the two countries. Following the initial phase, specific projects were invited to apply for a second tranche of funding. It could be said that such institution-centric and phased collaborative funding arrangements are a step in the direction of directed allocation of scarce resources over multiple grant rounds. This structure is also seen in the UK Space Agency's International Bilateral Fund (UK Government, 2023).

A decadal plan is at the heart of many other nation's space activities. As an example, the Australian decadal plan for 2021–2030 was published by the Australian Academy of Science, overseen by an executive working group, 12 expert working groups and the Academy's National Committee for Space and Radio Science (National Committee for Space and Radio Science, 2022). The principal US agencies that provide primary federal funding for astronomy and astrophysics[22] commission a survey into the status and opportunities in that field (National Academies of Sciences, Engineering, and Medicine, 2021). The survey identifies important areas and goals for the field and makes recommendations for actions. A New Zealand space sector decadal plan is a possible evolution of the current work underway in defining the nation's aerospace strategy and space policy portfolio

[20] https://www.mbie.govt.nz/about/news/new-zealanddlr-frontier-joint-research-programme-funding-announced/.

[21] https://www.beehive.govt.nz/release/aerospace-sector-reach-new-heights-govt-strategy-and-funding.

[22] National Aeronautics and Space Administration, National Science Foundation, Department of Energy, Air Force Office of Scientific Research.

(New Zealand Government, 2022a, b). The decadal plan would set the agenda from a Team NZ perspective and would serve to avoid or at least mitigate the "dilution" risk referred to in the excerpt above. There are several organisations which could commission a decadal plan, including Te Apārangi Royal Society of New Zealand.

Summary

Space is hard, expensive, time-consuming, challenging and frustrating. It is also inspiring and rewarding. The space-active nation cachet projects globally, elevating that nation into a group whose members number relatively few. Engagement and investment in space-related activity has significant opportunities for the nation's academic, economic, political and environmental sectors. To what extent this activity continues and does so without the presence necessarily of Rocket Lab or any other individual commercial enterprise, will depend on a number of factors. These include (i) to what extent research funding is offered at sufficient levels, under appropriate conditions and at sufficient timescales; (ii) to what extent support is offered for current and future collaboration between institutions and Governments; (iii) to what extent continued dialogue is maintained between relevant stakeholders within the New Zealand space sector and political decision-makers.

The significant upsurge in New Zealand space activity has the curious history of being instigated by a commercial launch provider: Rocket Lab. Commonly elsewhere, space capability was enabled by military research and development spending, or by government fiat. Our national space agency was created in order to facilitate the activities of this commercial actor, and the agency is a unit wholly within our Ministry of Business, Entrepreneurship and Innovation.

The tertiary research and education sector has responded to the call for projects and activity which reflects our position as a space-faring nation. In a few short years, several space research and development projects have started. Significant space projects require significant financial, political and technical support. Currently, funding from the national research investment portfolio which have the required levels demand a strong case be made for their return on investment. Pure science or inquiry-driven space mission research projects would need these requirements relaxed.

Talent is spread across the country and New Zealand is too small a nation to achieve much with a parochial mindset particularly in the tertiary sector. Government funding of research and development as a fraction of GDP lags that of our peer nations and the OECD average. Space is expensive, funding is scarce and our talent pool – particularly in the universities – is geographically spread. Space missions or programmes have timescales that extend beyond a single political cycle. A 5- or 10-year plan would serve to mitigate these challenges.

Growth in the New Zealand space sector brings risks and responsibilities. As a recent entrant to the set of space-capable nations, we can learn from the experiences of more established space nations. We can establish law, policy and operating procedures that take the best practices from operations abroad while at the same time ensuring that the specific values of this society are respected.

Aspects of New Zealand space sector and its origin stand in stark contrast to those of other nations. The creation of the NZSA was a rapid reaction to the needs of a commercial entity seeking to engage on one of humankind's most technologically challenging pursuits: the access to and use of space. National legislation was created to regulate these activities while leaving sufficient headroom for additional activities. The increase in attention to aerospace and space in the nation has boosted interest and demand for tertiary research projects, and educational pathways into the sector. The nation's universities have risen to this challenge. Commercial activity – some of which predating the establishment of the NZSA – has accelerated and benefits from a current market-driven policy environment.

The future of New Zealand space sector will depend on to what extent the limitations we face as a nation are mitigated. With some long-term planning, coordination and commitment, New Zealand can achieve the goal of being a responsible actor in space, a permanent home for commercial and research activity, and a useful partner in international endeavours.

References

Andrews, J., Watry, K., & Brown, K. (2011). *Nanosat deorbit and recovery system to enable new missions*. https://api.semanticscholar.org/CorpusID:86518846

APSS. (2022). *Auckland Programme for Space Systems*. https://apss.space.auckland.ac.nz/. [Online; accessed 19 Sept 2022].

Armellin, R. (2021). Collision avoidance maneuver optimization with a multiple-impulse convex formulation. *Acta Astronautica, 186*, 347–362.

Artemis. (2020). *The Artemis Accords: Principles for cooperation in the civil exploration and use of the moon, mars, comets, and asteroids for peaceful purposes*. https://www.nasa.gov/specials/artemis-accords/img/Artemis-Accords-signed-13Oct2020.pdf. [Online; accessed: 13 Sept 2022].

Baker, K., & Jansson, D. (1994). Space satellites from the world's garage—The story of AMSAT. In *Proceedings of National Aerospace and Electronics Conference (NAECON'94)*, (vol. 2, pp 1174–1181).

Balkenhohl, J., Glowacki, J., Rattenbury, N., & Cater, J. (2022). A review of low-power applied-field magnetoplasmadynamic thruster research and formulation of an improved semi-empirical performance model. In *37th international electric propulsion conference*.

Benmergui, J. S., Rohrschneider, R., Omara, M., Gautam, R., Chan Miller, C., Sun, K., Franklin, J. E., Hamburg, S., Preetz, B., & Wofsy, S. C. (2020). Science planning for the MethaneSAT mission. *AGU Fall Meeting Abstracts, 2020*, A015–A011.

Bennet, F., Ferguson, K., Grant, K., Kruzins, E., Rattenbury, N., & Schediwy, S. (2020). An Australia/New Zealand optical communications ground station network for next generation satellite communications. In *Free-space laser communications XXXII* (Vol. 11272, p. 1127202). SPIE.

Berry, T., Olatunji, J. R., & Acheson, C. (2021). Modelling the thermal effects of tumbling on CubeSats equipped with HTS coils. In *TENCON 2021–2021 IEEE Region 10 Conference (TENCON)*, pp. 157–162.

Blosser, M., Chen, R., Schmidt, I., Dorsey, J., Poteet, C., & Bird, R. (2002). Advanced metallic thermal protection system development. In *40th AIAA aerospace sciences meeting & exhibit*, pp. 504.

Bond, I. A., Udalski, A., Jaroszyński, M., Rattenbury, N. J., Paczyński, B., Soszyński, I., et al. (2004). OGLE 2003-BLG-235/MOA 2003-BLG-53: A planetary microlensing event. *The Astrophysical Journal, 606*(2), L155.

Bothmer, V., & Daglis, I. A. (2007). *Space weather: Physics and effects*. Springer Science & Business Media.

Boyce, R. (2022). *Observations from across the Tasman*. Available upon request.

Bryson, H., Sültrop, H. P., Buchanan, G., Hann, C., Snowdon, M., Rao, A., Slee, A., Fanning, K., Wright, D., McVicar, J., Clark, B., Harris, G., & Chen, X. Q. (2016). Vertical wind tunnel for prediction of rocket flight dynamics. *Aerospace, 3*(2), 10.

Caldarelli, A., Filleul, F., Charles, C., Rattenbury, N., & Cater, J. (2021). Pre- liminary measurements of a magnetic steering system for RF plasma thruster applications. In *AIAA Propulsion and Energy 2021 Forum*, pp 3401.

Caldarelli, A., Filleul, F., Charles, C., Boswell, R., Rattenbury, N., & Cater, J. (2022). Radial characterization of an ion beam in a deflected magnetic nozzle. In *37th international electric propulsion conference*.

Campbell, K. A., Lynne, B. Y., Handley, K. M., Jordan, S., Farmer, J. D., Guido, D. M., Foucher, F., Turner, S., & Perry, R. S. (2015). Tracing biosignature preservation of geothermally silicified microbial textures into the geological record. *Astrobiology, 15*(10), 858–882.

Carandente, V., & Savino, R. (2014). New concepts of deployable de-orbit and re-entry systems for CubeSat miniaturized satellites. *Recent Patents on Engineering, 8*(1), 2–12.

Charles, C., Tsifakis, D., Bennet, A., Boswell, R., Braun, W., Rivas-Davila, J., Takahashi, K., Ando, A., Dudas, E., Benidar, A., et al. (2019). Lab to launch. In *Proceedings of the International Astronautical Congress, IAC*, vol. 2019, pp IAC–19 C4 4 1 x55179. International Astronautical Federation, IAF.

Chen, Y.-K. (2021). *Ad Meliora: Space microbial research for the benefit of humanity* (Master's thesis). The University of Auckland, Auckland, New Zealand.

Cirkovic, E., Committee, S. O., et al. (2021). *IAU dark and quiet skies*. UNOOSA, NoirLabs, SATCON2, International Law Working Group Report.

Daglis, I. A., Chang, L. C., Dasso, S., Gopalswamy, N., Khabarova, O. V., Kilpua, E., Lopez, R., Marsh, D., Matthes, K., Nandy, D., et al. (2021). Predictability of variable solar–terrestrial coupling. In *Annales Geophysicae* (Vol. 39, pp. 1013–1035). Copernicus GmbH.

De Zanet, G., Viquerat, A., & Aglietti, G. (2022). Dynamic interferometric measurements of thermally induced deformations on telescope based on high-strain composite tape-springs. *Thin-Walled Structures, 179*, 109657.

Deloitte. (2019). *New Zealand space sector: Its value, scope and structure*. https://www.mbie.govt.nz/assets/new-zealand-space-sector-its-value-scope-and-structure.pdf. [Online, accessed 17 May 2023].

Dhopade, P. (2021). *Bringing eco-design to space missions*. https://www.rnz.co.nz/national/programmes/ninetonoon/audio/2018823870/bringing-eco-design-to-space-missions. [Online; accessed 29 Aug 2022].

Djokic, T., Van Kranendonk, M., Campbell, K., et al. (2017). Earliest signs of life on land preserved in ca. 3.5 Ga hot spring deposits. *Nature Communications, 8*, 15263.

Engelen, S., Oever, M., Mahapatra, P., Sundaramoorthy, P., Gill, E., Meijer, R., & Verhoeven, C. (2012). *NanoSAR-case study of synthetic aperture radar for nano-satellites*.

Feder, T. (2022). Ballooning satellite populations in low Earth orbit portend changes for science and society. *Physics Today, 75*(4), 25–28.

Filleul, F., Charles, C., Boswell, R., Rattenbury, N., Cater, J., & Sutherland, O. (2019). Radio frequency microdischarge neutraliser. In *36th international electric propulsion conference*.

Filleul, F., Caldarelli, A., Charles, C., Boswell, R., Rattenbury, N., & Cater, J. (2021). Characterization of a new variable magnetic field linear plasma device. *Physics of Plasmas, 28*(12), 123514.

Filleul, F., Caldarelli, A., Boswell, R., Charles, C., Rattenbury, N., & Cater, J. (2022). Ion magnetization effects on plasma generation in a magnetic nozzle RF device. In *37th international electric propulsion conference*.

Fletcher, S. E. M., & Schaefer, H. (2019). Rising methane: A new climate challenge. *Science, 364*(6444), 932–933.

Goebel, D. M., & Katz, I. (2008). *Fundamentals of electric propulsion: Ion and hall thrusters*. Wiley.

Graham, D. R., Rattenbury, N. J., & Cater, J. E. (2019). Mission feasibility from trajectory optimization and the state of space systems research at The University of Auckland. In *AAS/AIAA Astrodynamics Specialist Conference*.

Graham, D., Englander, J., Rattenbury, N., & Cater, J. (2022). Low-thrust trajectory design from lunar rideshare to venus capture. *Journal of Spacecraft and Rockets, 59*(6). https://doi.org/10.2514/1.A35282

Hann, C. E., Snowdon, M., Rao, A., Tang, R., Korevaar, A., Skinner, G., Keall, A., Chen, X., & Chase, J. G. (2010). Rocket roll dynamics and disturbance – Minimal modelling and system identification. In *2010 11th International Conference on Control Automation Robotics & Vision* (pp. 1736–1741).

Hann, C., Snowdon, M., Rao, A., Winn, O., Wongvanich, N., & Chen, X. (2012). Minimal modelling approach to describe turbulent rocket roll dynamics in a vertical wind tunnel. *Proceedings of the Institution of Mechanical Engineers, Part G: Journal of Aerospace Engineering, 226*(9), 1042–1060.

Henry, C. (2017). *All-electric satellites halfway to becoming half of all satellites*. Space News, Pocket Ventures LLC.

Hickman, S., Weddell, S., & Clare, R. (2019). Image correction with curvature and geometric wavefront sensors in simulation and on-sky. In *2019 international conference on image and vision computing New Zealand (IVCNZ)*, pp. 1–6.

Hickman, S., Muruganandan, V. A., Weddell, S., & Clare, R. (2020). Image metrics for deconvolution of satellites in low earth orbit. In *2020 35th international conference on image and vision computing New Zealand (IVCNZ)*, pp. 1–6.

Honeth, M., Yalagach, A., & Aglietti, G. (2022). Wire driven mechanisms for deployable components for optical payloads. SSC22-WKVI, pp. 1–9.

Hsu, K.-L. (2012). Two paradigms of the developmental state approach, with special reference to South Korea and Taiwan. *American Journal of Chinese Studies, 19*(1), 13–28. American Association of Chinese Studies.

Johnson, C. (1982). *MITI and the Japanese miracle: The growth of industrial policy, 1925–1975*. Stanford University Press.

Krebs, G. (2022). *Gunter's space page*. https://space.skyrocket.de/index.html. Accessed: 15 June 2022.

Krecke, J., Villano, M., Ustalli, N., Austin, A. C. M., Cater, J. E., & Krieger, G. (2021a). Design of SmallSat SAR for dedicated New Zealand applications. In *EUSAR 2021; 13th European conference on synthetic aperture radar*, pp. 1–5.

Krecke, J., Villano, M., Ustalli, N., Austin, A. C. M., Cater, J. E., & Krieger, G. (2021b). Detecting ships in the New Zealand exclusive economic zone: Requirements for a dedicated SmallSat SAR mission. *IEEE Journal of Selected Topics in Applied Earth Observations and Remote Sensing, 14*, 3162–3169.

Kruglyakov, M., Kuvshinov, A., & Marshalko, E. (2022). Real-time 3-D modeling of the ground electric field due to space weather events. A concept and its validation. *Space Weather, 20*(4). https://doi.org/10.1029/2021SW002906

Laverick, M., Moller, D., Ruf, C., Musko, S., O'Brien, A., Linnabary, R., Thomas, W., Seal, C., & Wharton, Y. (2020). Integrating the OpenSky network into GNSS-R climate monitoring research. *Multidisciplinary Digital Publishing Institute Proceedings, 59*(1), 11.

Linnabary, R., O'Brien, A., Ruf, C., Musko, S., & Moller, D. (2020). Analysis of GNSS-R coverage by a regional aircraft fleet. In *IGARSS 2020–2020 IEEE International Geoscience and Remote Sensing Symposium*, pp. 6270–6273.

Long, N. (2021). High temperature superconductors in space-realising the value of an enabling technology. *43rd COSPAR Scientific Assembly. Held 28 January–4 February*, 43:72.

Makarov, K. (2015). *Design of attitude determination and control system for KIWISAT amateur satellite* (MEng thesis). Massey University.

MBIE. (2021a). *MethaneSAT space mission*. https://www.mbie.govt.nz/science-and-technology/space/space-related-opportunities-in-new-zealand/methanesat-mission/. [Online; accessed 29 Aug 2022].

MBIE. (2021b). *Project Tāwhaki – A unique partnership for Kaitorete*. https://www.mbie.govt.nz/science-and-technology/science-and-innovation/international-opportunities/new-zealand-r-d/innovative-partnerships/project-tawhaki/. [Online; accessed 29 Aug 2022].

MBIE (2022). *International research projects*. https://www.mbie.govt.nz/science-and-technology/space/nzspacetalk/international-research-projects/. [Online; accessed: 29 Aug 2022].

McPherson, A., & DeLucas, L. J. (2015). Microgravity protein crystallization. *npj Microgravity, 1*, 15010.

Moller, D., Ruf, C., Linnabary, R., O'Brien, A., & Musko, S. (2021). Operational airborne GNSS-R aboard air New Zealand domestic aircraft. In *2021 IEEE International Geoscience and Remote Sensing Symposium IGARSS*, pp. 1284–1287.

Mumma, M. J. (2012). The search for life on Mars. Origin of life Gordon Research Conference. Galveston, TX. https://ntrs.nasa.gov/citations/20120003707

Muruganandan, V. A., Lambert, A., Clare, R., & Weddell, S. (2022). Improving the resolution of low earth orbit objects by multi-exposure imaging and deconvolution.

Nath, N., & Aglietti, G. S. (2022). Study the effect of tri-axis vibration testing over single-axis vibration testing on a satellite. In *2022 IEEE Aerospace Conference (AERO)*, pp. 1–10.

National Academies of Sciences, Engineering, and Medicine. (2021). *Pathways to discovery in astronomy and astrophysics for the 2020s*. https://doi.org/10.17226/26141

National Committee for Space and Radio Science. (2022). *Australia in space: A decadal plan for Australian space science 2021–2030*. Australian Academy of Science. https://www.science.org.au/files/userfiles/support/reports-and-plans/2022/australia-in-space-a-decadal-plan-for-australian-space-science-2021-2030.pdf. [Online; accessed 22 May 2023].

New Zealand Government. (2017a). *Outer Space and High-altitude Activities Act 2017*. https://www.legislation.govt.nz/act/public/2017/0029/latest/DLM6966461.html. [Online; accessed: 12 Sept 2022].

New Zealand Government. (2017b). *Outer Space and High-altitude Activities (Definition of High-altitude Vehicle) Regulations 2017*. https://www.legislation.govt.nz/regulation/public/2017/0251/latest/DLM7416501.html. [Online; accessed: 12 Sept 2022].

New Zealand Government. (2017c). *Outer Space and High-altitude Activities (Licences and Permits) Regulations 2017*. https://www.legislation.govt.nz/regulation/public/2017/0250/latest/DLM7364101.html. [Online; accessed: 12 Sept 2022].

New Zealand Government. (2018). *Research, science and innovation system performance report*. https://www.mbie.govt.nz/dmsdocument/1499-research-science-and-innovation-system-performance-report-2018. [Online; accessed: 12 Sept 2022].

New Zealand Government. (2022a). *Developing the New Zealand aerospace strategy*. https://www.mbie.govt.nz/dmsdocument/23715-developing-the-aotearoa-new-zealand-aerospace-strategy-pdf. [Online; accessed: 19 Sept 2022].

New Zealand Government. (2022b). *New Zealand space policy review consultation*. https://www.mbie.govt.nz/dmsdocument/23736-new-zealand-space-policy-review-consultation-document. [Online; accessed: 19 Sept 2022].

New Zealand Government. (2022c). *Statutory Review of the Outer Space and High-altitude Activities Act 2017*. https://www.mbie.govt.nz/assets/report-on-the-statutory-review-of-the-oshaa-2017.pdf. [Online; accessed: 12 Sept 2022].

Nieke, P., Chopovda, V., Schleutker, T., Gülhan, A., Rattenbury, N., & Cater, J. (2023). Additively manufactured titanium alloy sandwich structures for thermal protection. In *AIAA Scitech Forum*. Submitted.

Olatunji, J. R., Acheson, C., Szmigiel, M., Wimbush, S. C., & Long, N. J. (2021a). Heat load calculations on an HTS coil integrated into a small satellite during a sun-synchronous low earth orbit. *Journal of Physics: Conference Series, 1975*(1), 012029.

Olatunji, J. R., Strickland, N. M., Goddard Winchester, M. R., Kinefuchi, K., Ichihara, D., Long, N. J., & Wimbush, S. C. (2021b). Modelling of a 1 T high-temperature superconducting applied field module for a magnetoplasmadynamic thruster. In *TENCON 2021–2021 IEEE Region 10 Conference (TENCON)*, pp. 173–178.

Olatunji, J., Acheson, C., Szmigiel, M., Wimbush, S., & Long, N. (2022). Orbital and thermal modelling of a 3U CubeSat equipped with a high-temperature superconducting coil. *Acta Astronautica, 190*, 413–429.

Pirovano, L., Santeramo, D. A., Armellin, R., Di Lizia, P., & Wittig, A. (2020). Probabilistic data association: The orbit set. *Celestial Mechanics and Dynamical Astronomy, 132*(2), 1–27.

Poland, O. (2019). *University of Auckland space cadets taking their mission seriously*. https://www.auckland.ac.nz/en/news/2019/11/25/space-cadets.html. [Online; accessed 29 Aug 2022].

Powell, A. (2023). *Buying crucial time in climate change fight*. The Harvard Gazette. https://news.harvard.edu/gazette/story/2023/03/methane-tracking-satellite-may-be-fastest-way-to-slow-climate-change/. [Online; accessed 25 May 2023].

Pozza, M. A., & Dennerley, J. A. (2022). *Risk management in Outer Space Activities: An Australian and New Zealand perspective* (Space law and policy series). Springer.

Radio New Zealand. (2018). *NZ Students on mission to sort space junk*. https://www.rnz.co.nz/national/programmes/ninetonoon/audio/2018668448/nz-students-on-mission-to-sort-space-junk. [Online; accessed 22 May 2023].

Rattenbury, N. (2021). *New Zealand optical communications ground station feasibility study*. Technical report, The University of Auckland.

Rocket Lab. (2017). *Rocket Lab Electron 'Its a Test' flight successfully makes it to space*. https://www.rocketlabusa.com/updates/rocket-lab-successfully-makes-it-to-space-2/. [Online; accessed 27 May 2023].

Rocket Lab. (2018). *It's business time*. https://www.rocketlabusa.com/missions/completed-missions/its-business-time/. [Online; accessed 27 May 2023].

Rocket Lab. (2020a). *Return to sender*. https://www.rocketlabusa.com/missions/completed-missions/flight-16/. [Online; accessed 17 May 2023].

Rocket Lab. (2020b). *Rocket Lab to launch most diverse mission yet*. https://www.rocketlabusa.com/updates/rocket-lab-to-launch-most-diverse-mission-yet/. [Online; accessed 17 May 2023].

Rohrschneider, R. R., Wofsy, S., Franklin, J. E., Benmergui, J., Soto, J., & Davis, S. B. (2021). *The MethaneSAT mission*.

Rueda, A., Sedlmeir, F., Collodo, M. C., Vogl, U., Stiller, B., Schunk, G., Strekalov, D. V., Marquardt, C., Fink, J. M., Painter, O., et al. (2016). Efficient microwave to optical photon conversion: An electro-optical realization. *Optica, 3*(6), 597–604.

Rueda, A., Sedlmeir, F., Kumari, M., Leuchs, G., & Schwefel, H. G. (2019). Resonant electro-optic frequency comb. *Nature, 568*(7752), 378–381.

Ruff, S. W., Campbell, K. A., Van Kranendonk, M. J., Rice, M. S., & Farmer, J. D. (2020). The case for ancient hot springs in Gusev crater, Mars. *Astrobiology, 20*(4), 475–499.

Sayson, N. L. B., Bi, T., Ng, V., Pham, H., Trainor, L. S., Schwefel, H. G., Coen, S., Erkintalo, M., & Murdoch, S. G. (2019). Octave-spanning tunable parametric oscillation in crystalline Kerr microresonators. *Nature Photonics, 13*(10), 701–706.

Seppälä, A., Lu, H., Clilverd, M. A., & Rodger, C. J. (2013). Geomagnetic activity signatures in wintertime stratosphere wind, temperature, and wave response. *Journal of Geophysical Research: Atmospheres, 118*(5), 2169–2183.

Seppälä, A., Matthes, K., Randall, C. E., & Mironova, I. A. (2014). What is the solar influence on climate? Overview of activities during CAWSES-II. *Progress in Earth and Planetary Science, 1*(1), 1–12.

Shinichi, N. (2018). CanSat and CubeSat history in Japan – How they started and contributed to education and technologies. In *The Sixth UNISEC-Global Meeting*. UNISEC.

Smith, A. W., Forsyth, C., Rae, J., Rodger, C. J., & Freeman, M. P. (2021). The impact of sudden commencements on ground magnetic field variability: Immediate and delayed consequences. *Space Weather, 19*(7), e2021SW002764.

Smith, A., Rodger, C., Manus, D. M., Forsyth, C., Rae, I., Freeman, M., Clilverd, M., Petersen, T., & Dalzell, M. (2022). The correspondence between sudden commencements and geomagnetically induced currents; insights from New Zealand. *Space Weather*, e2021SW002983.

Speidel, U. (2021). What the tropical pacific wants from Starlink for Christmas: Will LEO networks finally bridge the digital divide to remote islands? In *Asian Internet Engineering Conference*, pp. 34–40.

Speidel, U., & Rattenbury, N. (2021). *Solar storms and the Internet*. https://blog.apnic.net/2021/07/22/are-solar-storms-a-threat-to-the-internet/. [Online; accessed 29 Aug 2022].

Stabile, A., Yotov, V. V., Aglietti, G. S., De Francesco, P., & Richardson, G. (2022). Effect of boundary conditions on a high-performance isolation hexapod platform. *Mechanism and Machine Theory, 177*, 105020.

Stocks, P. (2022). Economic transition through aerospace. *New Zealand International Review, 47*(1), 6–9.

Strekalov, D. V., Marquardt, C., Matsko, A. B., Schwefel, H. G., & Leuchs, G. (2016). Nonlinear and quantum optics with whispering gallery resonators. *Journal of Optics, 18*(12), 123002.

Teece, B. L., George, S. C., Djokic, T., Campbell, K. A., Ruff, S. W., & Van Kranendonk, M. J. (2020). Biomolecules from fossilized hot spring sinters: Implications for the search for life on Mars. *Astrobiology, 20*(4), 537–551.

Tepper, E., & Whitehead, C. (2018). Moon, Inc.: The New Zealand model of granting legal personality to natural resources applied to space. *New Space, 6*(4), 288–298.

UK Government. (2023). *Guidance: International Bilateral Fund (IBF)*. https://www.gov.uk/government/publications/international-bilateral-fund/guidance-international-bilateral-fund-ibf. [Online; accessed 27 May 2023].

Uniservices. (2023). *How Zenno Astronautics is making a difference in the world*. https://www.uniservices.co.nz/zenno-astronautics. [Online; accessed 22 May 2023].

United Nations Publications. (2018). *International Space Law: United Nations Instruments*. https://www.unoosa.org/res/oosadoc/data/documents/2017/stspace/stspace61rev_2_0_html/V1605998-ENGLISH.pdf. [Online; accessed 12 Sept 2022].

UoA. (2018). *Alumnus gift to help Kiwis explore space*. https://www.auckland.ac.nz/en/news/2018/11/06/alumnus-gift-to-help-kiwis-explore-space.html. [Online; accessed 17 May 2023].

UoA. (2019). *New professor at Auckland wins major award for cleaning up space junk*. https://www.auckland.ac.nz/en/news/2019/11/18/new-professor-at-auckland-wins-major-award-for-cleaning-up-space.html. [Online; accessed 17 May 2023].

UoA. (2020a). *New Zealand's first student-built satellite ready for lift off*. https://www.auckland.ac.nz/en/news/2020/11/03/new-zealand-s-first-student-built-satellite-ready-for-lift-off.html. [Online; accessed 17 May 2023].

UoA. (2020b). *About the APSS*. https://apss.space.auckland.ac.nz/about/. [Online; accessed 17 May 2023].

Venkatesan, A., Lowenthal, J., Prem, P., & Vidaurri, M. (2020). The impact of satellite constellations on space as an ancestral global commons. *Nature Astronomy, 4*(11), 1043–1048.

Walker, R., Galeone, P., Page, H., Castro, A., Emma, F., Callens, N., & Ventura-Traveset, J. (2010). ESA hands-on space education project activities for university students: Attracting and training the next generation of space engineers. In *IEEE EDUCON 2010 conference* (pp. 1699–1708). IEEE.

Watt, R. (2022). *Private communication*.

Weddell, S., Clare, R., & Lambert, A. (2019, January). Near earth object image restoration with multi-object adaptive optics. In *Proc. 1st NEO and Debris Detection Conference* (pp. 22–24).

Westall, F., Foucher, F., Bost, N., Bertrand, M., Loizeau, D., Vago, J. L., Kminek, G., Gaboyer, F., Campbell, K. A., et al. (2015). Biosignatures on Mars: What, where, and how? Implications for the search for Martian life. *Astrobiology, 15*(11), 998–1029.

Wiley, C. A. (1985). Synthetic aperture radars: A paradigm for technology evolution. *IEEE Transactions on Aerospace and Electronic Systems, AES-21*(3), 440–443.

Wofsy, S. C., & Hamburg, S. (2019). MethaneSAT – A new observing platform for high resolution measurements of methane and carbon dioxide. *AGU Fall Meeting Abstracts, 2019*, A53F–A502F.

Printed by Printforce, the Netherlands